Chris Magoc
7-91

Land, Water, and Culture

AQUA RAZA TIERRA
DESIGNED & PRINTED BY LC
TRES MUNDOS DE TAOS 11/78

Land, Water, and Culture

New Perspectives on Hispanic Land Grants

EDITED BY

Charles L. Briggs

& John R. Van Ness

New Mexico Land Grant Series

John R. Van Ness, Series Editor

University of New Mexico

Albuquerque

Se dedica este libro
a los herederos de las mercedes
y a su lucha por la tierra.

We dedicate this book
to the land grant heirs
and to their struggle for the land.

Library of Congress Cataloging-in-Publication Data

Land, water, and culture.

(New Mexico land grant series)
Includes bibliographies and index.
1. Land grants—New Mexico—History. 2. Land grants—Colorado—History. 3. Pueblo Indians—Land tenure—History. 4. Indians of North America—New Mexico—Land tenure—History. 5. Mexican Americans—New Mexico—History. 6. Mexican Americans—Colorado—History. I. Briggs, Charles L., 1953– . II. Van Ness, John R. III. Series.
HD243.N5L36 1987 333.1′6′09788 87–10957
ISBN 0–8263–0989–5

First edition.

Contents

Illustrations

Maps

Acknowledgments

A host of individuals and institutions have contributed to the project. The Center for Land Grant Studies is a New Mexico based, non-profit corporation that is dedicated to conducting research on land grants and disseminating the results to scholarly and lay audiences. This volume has grown out of discussions that were occasioned by conferences sponsored by the center and funded by the New Mexico Humanities Council. Much of the research was conducted in a host of archives and libraries in the region and beyond. Mr. Arthur Olivas of the Photo Archives, History Section, Museum of New Mexico and Stanley Hordes, Myra Ellen Jenkins, and Richard Salazar of the New Mexico Records Center and Archives deserve special mention for the hours they have spent in helping us locate sources. Andrew Smith and Kathryn Nelson assisted us with the photography. Clark Knowlton, Frances Swadesh Quintana and Marianne Stoller have heightened our awareness of land grant issues through the years. Much credit is due to the support and patience of our editors, Elizabeth Hadas and Barbara Guth. Financial support for this undertaking was provided by the editors' respective institutions, Ursinus and Vassar colleges. President Richard Richter and Dean William Akin at Ursinus were especially encouraging and supportive. The Pueblo and Hispano peoples of southern Colorado and northern New Mexico have shared with us their past and present and their hope that they will regain control over their own destiny. To them we owe whatever understanding of community life and human-land relationships that we may have attained.

Land, Water, and Culture

Introduction

Charles L. Briggs and John R. Van Ness

One of the most important institutions that Spain and Mexico left in the Southwest was the land grant. Beginning with the initial efforts to colonize Texas, New Mexico, Colorado, Arizona, and California, both individuals and groups of settlers were awarded parcels of land by the Crown. The grants were variously for grazing livestock, farming, and establishing villages and towns. Some grants were awarded in recognition of military service, while others responded to pressure to extend Spanish and Mexican dominion into areas controlled by Native Americans or those threatened by the expansion of other nations. A plethora of legal ritual and documentation surrounded the process of awarding and retaining rights to a land grant, and this provides strong evidence for the economic, political, social, and symbolic significance of these grants.

The reasons behind the contemporary importance of land grants are many, but several can be singled out. One is that the way in which land and water allocation and use was governed in the Southwest under American rule has important precedents, which reach back through centuries of Mexican and Spanish history and law; this trail even leads, as the reader will soon see, to Moorish and Roman precedents. A second explanation is to be found in the nature of the land itself. The Southwest is characterized by extreme environmental contrasts between high mountains, fertile valleys, and vast stretches of arid and relatively barren land. In New Mexico, for example, most of the river valleys form tiny fissures in the great expanse of mountains, deserts, and arid hills. As a region in which precipitation is scant and most of the land is not arable, a substantial area is needed to support even a small human population. The Hispanic land grant system was particularly well suited to these conditions, and the majority of the usable land was allocated in grants long before the United States gained control of the region.

A final reason for the importance of the grants pertains to the impact of the American conquest of this region during the Mexican American War. The Treaty of Guadalupe Hidalgo, which ended the war in 1848, contained an article stating that "property of every kind now belonging to Mexicans . . . shall be inviolably respected." Land grants clearly formed the most important property rights of the then Mexican citizens, both Hispanic and Native American. A large body of evidence suggests, however, that both the United States government and a host of individuals who came to the Southwest from the eastern states systematically violated the rights of individuals and communities to hold and use land and water that they had legally acquired through grants from Spain and Mexico. These violations left a legacy of bitterness that has not diminished in the ensuing decades. Recent events in New Mexico and Colorado, some of which are documented in the following essays, show that Hispanics and Native Americans alike have not given up the struggle to reclaim the land they believe is rightfully theirs. Thus, the land grant issue is crucial both from a historical perspective and in terms of contemporary politics and culture.

The Literature on Spanish and Mexican Land Grants

This volume constitutes the third number in the Land Grant Series. It follows *Mercedes Reales* by Victor Westphall, an up-to-date synthesis of the history of the Hispanic land grants in the northern Rio Grande Region, and *Four Leagues of Pecos* by G. Emlen Hall, a definitive treatment of the complex and unique history of the Pecos Pueblo grant, 1800–1933.

Land, Water, and Culture was planned to respond to a number of concerns. The authors share a belief in the importance of the scholarly study of Hispanic land grants and related issues in the Southwest. The problems that arise from land grant research have a bearing on broader substantive and methodological questions in law and legal scholarship, history, anthropology, ethnohistory, sociology, political science, geography, and other fields. Furthermore, land grant issues do not simply represent a case of historical water over the dam. Our personal experience in southwestern land grant communities has shown us that these

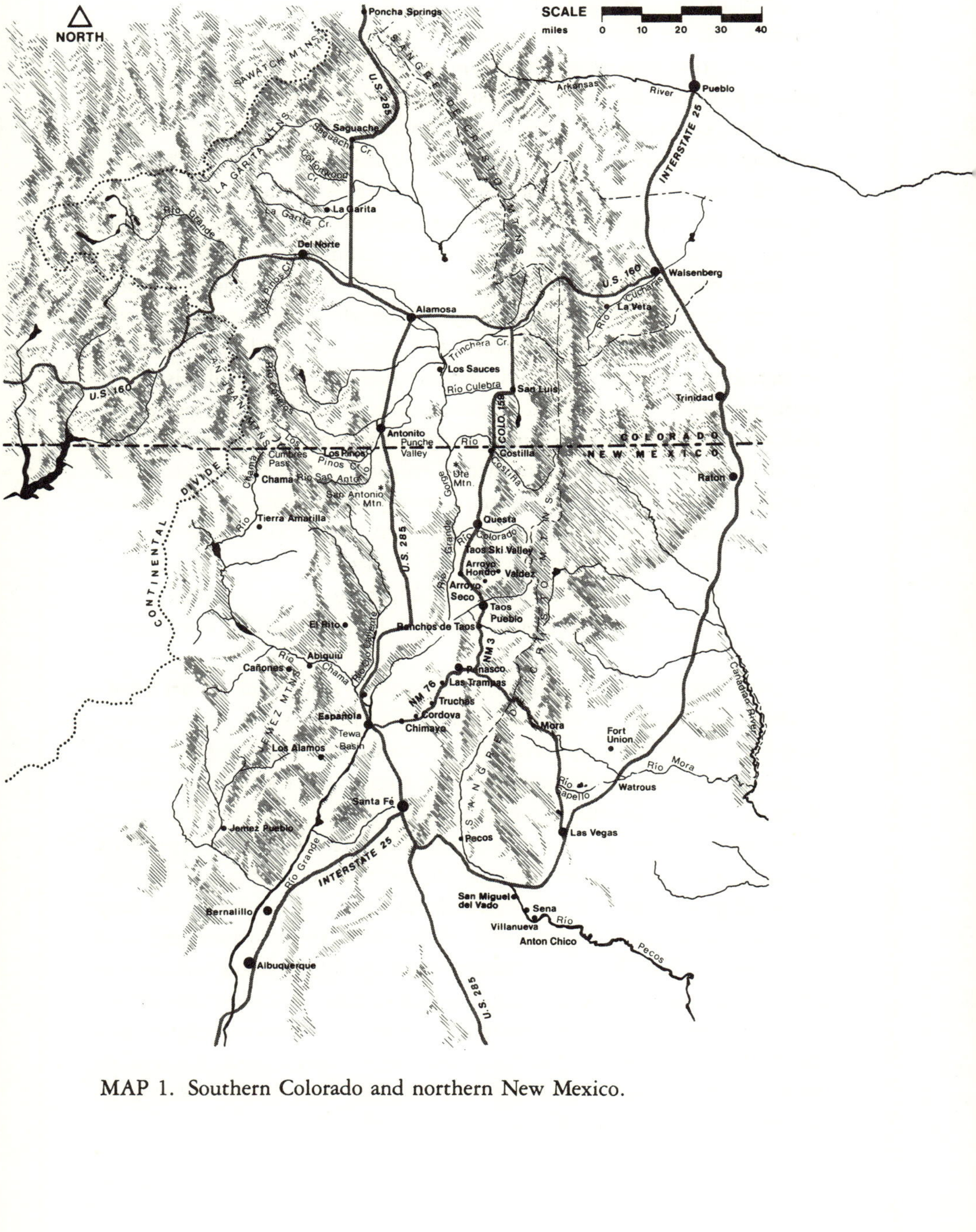

MAP 1. Southern Colorado and northern New Mexico.

issues will not simply fade away. Violence prompted by the illegal and extralegal expropriation of Hispanic grant lands and water rights has erupted in New Mexico and Colorado intermittently over the past century, and the potential for violent confrontations has not diminished. The need to redress past wrongs and to achieve a just solution to land tenure problems is, thus, a pressing social and political issue.[1]

A final concern which we share pertains to the inadequacy of the existing literature on land grants. The authors of many of the early publications were lawyers; their attempts to translate documents, codify Spanish and Mexican law, and relate the history of particular grants usually grew out of their work either as counsel for claimants or as attorneys representing the U.S. government.[2] Historians have also documented the histories of individual grants, the granting process, the political context in which grants were awarded, and the litigation initiated, as well as other issues.[3] Anthropologists and sociologists have explored the way in which land grants influenced the social organization and social life of Hispanic and Native American communities as well as the impact of land loss upon them.[4] Political scientists, and historians who focused on political questions, have explored the political processes that have affected the outcome of land grant litigation and the political forces generated by disputes related to land grants.[5] A few land grants, such as the Maxwell grant (see Map 2), have been the subject of a number of books and a host of articles by scholars of various disciplinary stripes.[6]

These extensive and varied contributions to land grant research notwithstanding, a number of crucial gaps remain. We know, for instance, very little about the ways events in New Mexico were affected by broader economic patterns. The study of Hispanic resistance to Anglo-American domination was virtually ignored until recently; very little information is available regarding who staged the periodic resistance movements and how land grant residents sought to preserve their way of life through day-to-day activities. A vast body of oral tradition preserves the way in which land grant communities think about their history and land and water rights, but few scholars have troubled to ask the people about such tradition.[7] Curiously, although grant research is devoted to the subject of landholding, few studies treat the physical characteristics of the land, the way it has been used by residents, and the way in which these factors have affected the settlement of grants. That is to say, the human ecology has been largely ignored.

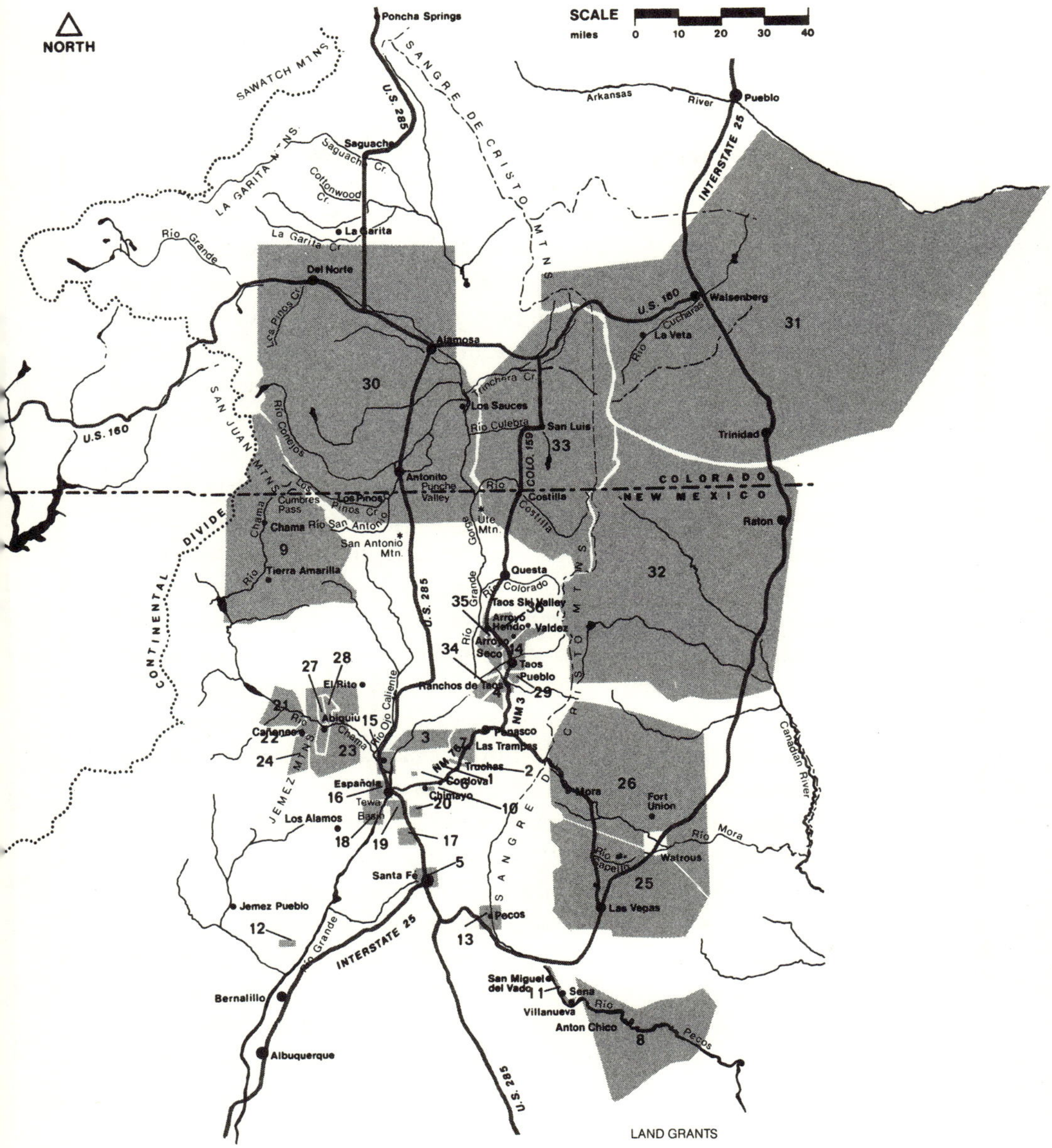

LAND GRANTS

1 Pueblo Quemado
2 Francisco Montes Vigil
3 Sebastian Martin
4 Cristobal de la Serna
5 Santa Fe
6 Santa Cruz
7 Las Trampas
8 Anton Chico
9 Tierra Amarilla
10 Santo Domingo de Cundiyo
11 San Miguel del Bado
12 Cubero
13 Pecos Pueblo
14 Taos Pueblo
15 San Juan Pueblo
16 Santa Clara Pueblo
17 Tesuque Pueblo
18 San Ildefonso Pueblo
19 Pojoaque Pueblo
20 Nambe Pueblo
21 Piedra Lumbre
22 Juan Bautista Valdez
23 Juan Jose Lobato
24 Polvadera
25 Las Vegas
26 Mora
27 Plaza Colorada
28 Plaza Blanca
29 Don Fernando
30 Conejos
31 Vigil y St. Vrain
32 Beaubien y Miranda
33 Sangre de Cristo
34 Gijosa
35 Lucero de Godoy-Martinez
36 Arroyo Hondo

MAP 2. Land grants in southern Colorado and northern New Mexico.

Other deficiencies in the literature take the shape of biases or distortions. Most scholars who have worked on land grant issues are neither Hispanic nor Native American. Emerging from Anglo-American historical, legal, and cultural backgrounds, they have not generally sought to understand how the basic assumptions behind Spanish and Mexican law and the way of life of Hispanic and Native American communities may differ from their own. One of the most striking misconceptions involves the projection of legal principles based on individual, fee-simple ownership and Anglo-American common law (i.e., as based on precedent) onto a legal system which emphasizes community ownership of commonlands and the importance of local custom in establishing legal precedents. The crux of the problem is that this kind of distortion not only underlies a great deal of scholarly writing but has effected hundreds of court decisions and government policies. As a consequence Hispanics and Native Americans have been deprived of the lands upon which they have depended for centuries.

Moreover, the available literature has failed to carry the land grant issues to a broad audience, especially to those whose interests are not confined to Southwestern scholarship or law and land tenure. The contributors to this volume believe that the history and current status of Hispanic land grants in the Southwest constitute an issue of national and international importance. It concerns judgments regarding the extent to which the United States government has lived up to its treaty obligations vis-à-vis its own citizens of Hispanic and Native American descent and its neighbor, Mexico. Few people in the United States realize that the many questions regarding the moral and legal justification for expropriating land in our Southwest are only slightly removed from the problems which have led to lengthy and bloody conflict in Guatemala, El Salvador, Nicaragua, and elsewhere in Latin America.[8] The literature has not even succeeded in bringing the topic before the eyes of the larger scholarly community. Land grants scholars need to demonstrate to others in their disciplines that their research can yield insights into problems of general theoretical and methodological concern. A closely related need is to overcome a narrow regional parochialism by incorporating theoretical and methodological advances in general scholarship into research on land grants.

It is equally important to extend our reach closer to home. Most works on land grants assume a considerable knowledge regarding both historical processes (such as the procedures for confirming a land grant) and of specific grant histories.[9] The literature is also shaped by the disciplinary background and theoretical bias of the authors. This places lay persons and scholars from other disciplines at a loss, since writers seldom give their readers any sense of their working assumptions and theoretical perspectives.

Plan of the Book

This volume is designed precisely to fill the gaps just described. The authors are variously trained in law and legal scholarship, history, anthropology, and folklore. They bring to the volume, we believe, both greater breadth and depth of scholarship, since it is our aim to reach a new and wider audience as well as to explore in greater detail facets of land grant history and its contemporary importance heretofore neglected. We have attempted to remedy the deficiencies in the literature outlined above through the inclusion of articles employing different disciplinary perspectives. The volume also endeavors to show what the various disciplinary perspectives offer land grant research and what, increasingly, we hope, land grant research can contribute to several academic disciplines.

The essays have been limited to the northern New Mexico and southern Colorado region (see Map 1) because so much has been written about it, there are so many grants, so many questions remain unanswered, and the land issue is still very much alive politically and socially. Loss of land has changed and is changing lives of land grant residents today. Thus, this discussion is far from esoteric.

Malcolm Ebright, author of the first chapter, was trained in law. He has devoted most of the past two decades to land grant research as well as to litigation on behalf of land grant claimants. His essay identifies two principal features of Spanish and Mexican land law: he traces the importance accorded to community ownership of land back to medieval Spain, and earlier to its Moorish and Roman precedents. He argues that custom—the local understandings and practices that have been maintained for generations—has a very real legal force in establishing rights to and uses of land. Ebright points out that the Anglo-American jurisprudents, who came to New Mexico following 1846, have misinterpreted or ignored, often intentionally, these features of Spanish and Mexican law.

Chapter 2 is contributed by G. Emlen Hall, whose credentials include legal training as well as formal training as a historian, coupled with long practical experience in land and water ajudication as a member of the staff of the New Mexico State Engineer's Office. Hall's essay focuses on the important issue of Pueblo Indian land and water rights. Indeed, there is a major Native American dimension to the Hispanic land grant problem, for such grants are the basis of the Pueblos' land rights under United States law. This essay has broad implications because Native American land rights have been, and remain, an issue of national importance.

Chapter 3 is devoted to the cultural ecology of the Hispanic land grants, an important perspective that has been largely ignored in land grant scholarship. The goal of this essay is to show that the Hispanic settlements in northern New Mexico and southern Colorado cannot be understood without examining the unique upland environment and the Hispanic adaptations to it.

A rich, but largely untapped, resource for land grant research is oral history. However, collecting and using oral historical data requires a different approach and a different set of analytical tools from those normally used by historians and social scientists. The fourth chapter is an introduction to methodology and the use of oral data in land grant research. In particular, the essay treats the ways in which oral historical testimony may be used in land litigation. Its strengths and limitations are highlighted through comparisons with archival data pertaining to the Cordova, New Mexico community land grant.

Resistance to expropriation or alienation of Hispanic grant lands has been neglected until recently. However, the Alianza Federal de Mercedes, led by Reies Tijerina, brought national attention to unrest in the region through the well-publicized incident in 1967 at the Rio Arriba County Courthouse at Tierra Amarilla, New Mexico. The authors of chapter 5, Robert Rosenbaum and Robert Larson, are historians who have devoted their research to the political history of territorial New Mexico. Their essay adds much to our understanding of the organized resistance movements that have periodically swept the region since the 1870s.

The final chapter, by Sylvia Rodríguez, an anthropologist and Taos native, describes the importance of land symbolism to Hispano and Indian identities in the Taos region. In particular, drawing on the theories of ethnic identity formulated by Fredrik Barth and Edward Spicer, Rodríguez gives us a framework for understanding the persistence of strong ethnic group identities in the region. Through a case study of a contemporary land and water dispute, we learn how this issue serves to focus political activism along the lines of ethnic divisions and reinforces ethnic group social boundaries. Thus, the timeliness of the entire volume is forcefully brought home to the reader.

In sum, this volume seeks to add new dimensions to the study of Spanish and Mexican land grants. It also attempts to encourage others to take up this stimulating and important field of research, for in addition to the substantive and theoretical discussions in each chapter, each author devotes some attention to questions of methodology and sources of research data, as well as what they deem to be the most pressing needs for further research. Finally, the authors hope that the volume will reach a wider audience, and that the study of Hispanic land grants will influence discourse in such areas as Chicano studies and ethnic politics in America.

Notes

1. The pressing need for broad and systematic study of land grants was pointed out by Clark Knowlton more than twenty years ago. His efforts led to the first interdisciplinary collection of papers on the subject, Clark S. Knowlton, ed., "Spanish and Mexican Land Grants in the Southwest: A Symposium," *The Social Science Journal* 13 (1976).

2. For example see: Samuel Ellison, *History of New Mexico* (Santa Fe, 1884) in J. Manuel Espinosa, "Memoir of a Kentuckian in New Mexico 1848–1884," *New Mexico Historical Review,* 13 (1938): 1–13; William W. Morrow, *Spanish and Mexican Private Land Grants* (San Francisco: Brancroft-Whitney, 1923); Alois B. Renehan, *The Pueblo Indians and Their Land Grants* (Albuquerque: Thos. Hughes Printer, 1923); Matthew G. Reynolds, *Spanish and Mexican Land Laws* (St. Louis: Buxton and Skinner Stationery Co., 1895); Ralph Emerson Twitchell, *The Leading Facts of New Mexico History* (Cedar Rapids, IA: Torch Press, 1912); W. F. Stone, "The United States Court of Private Land Claims," *Minutes of the New Mexico Bar Association* (Santa Fe, 1904).

3. See William A. Keleher, *Maxwell Land Grant, A New Mexico Item* (Santa Fe: Rydal Press, 1942; Reprint Albuquerque: University of New Mexico Press, 1984); Jim Berry Pearson, *The Maxwell Land Grant* (Norman: University of Oklahoma Press, 1961) for historical studies of a single grant. For examples of more specialized studies see: Harold H. Dunham, "New Mexico Land Grants with Special Reference to the Title Papers of the Maxwell Grant," *New Mexico Historical Review* 30 (1955); Richard Greenleaf, "Atrisco and Ciruelas, 1722–1769," *New Mexico Historical Review,* 42 (1967); Myra Ellen Jenkins, "The

Baltasar Baca 'Grant': History of an Encroachment," *El Palacio* 68 (1961); Howard R. Lamar, "Land Policy in the Spanish Southwest, 1846–1891: A Study in Contrasts," *Journal of Economic History* 22 (1962).

4. See Clark S. Knowlton, "Land Grant Problems Among the State's Spanish Americans," *New Mexico Business* 20 (1967); Olen Leonard, *The Role of the Land Grant in the Social Organization and Social Processes of a Spanish-American Village in New Mexico* (Albuquerque: Calvin Horn Publisher, Inc., 1970); Frances Leon Swadesh, *Los Primeros Pobladores* (Notre Dame, IN: University of Notre Dame Press, 1974).

5. Robert W. Larson, "The White Caps of New Mexico: A Study of Ethnic Militancy in the Southwest," *Pacific Historical Review* 44 (1975); Roxanne Dunbar Ortiz, *Roots of Resistance: Land Tenure in New Mexico, 1680–1980* (Los Angeles: University of California, 1980); Robert J. Rosenbaum, *Mexicano Resistance in the Southwest* (Austin: University of Texas Press, 1981); Andrew Bancroft Schlesinger, "Las Gorras Blancas, 1889–1891," *Journal of Spanish-American History* 1 (1971).

6. Dunham, "New Mexico Land Grants with Special Reference to the Title Papers of the Maxwell Grant"; Keleher, *Maxwell Land Grant, A New Mexico Item;* Lawrence R. Murphy, "The Beaubien and Miranda Land Grant 1841–1846," *New Mexico Historical Review* 42 (1967); Pearson, *The Maxwell Land Grant;* Morrison F. Taylor, *O. P. McMains and The Maxwell Land Grant Conflict* (Tucson: University of Arizona Press, 1979).

7. A notable exception is provided by the work of Mary Romero, "Transformation of Culture Through Appreciation" (Ph.D. diss., University of Colorado, 1980), which traces the resistance attributed to the Gorras Blancas of the Las Vegas, New Mexico area (see Map 1) through both documents and interviews with the participants' descendants. See Alfonso Ortiz, *The Tewa World: Time, Space, Being and Becoming in a Pueblo Society* (Chicago: University of Chicago Press, 1969) for an indepth study of the way the Pueblo Indians view the land and their relationship to it.

8. For a compelling account of such conflict in one Mexican village see Paul Friedrich, *Agrarian Revolt in a Mexican Village* (Chicago: University of Chicago Press, 1977).

9. Although publications such as White, et al., *Land Title Study* (Santa Fe: New Mexico State Planning Office, 1971) have attempted to make this body of knowledge more accessible to the general public.

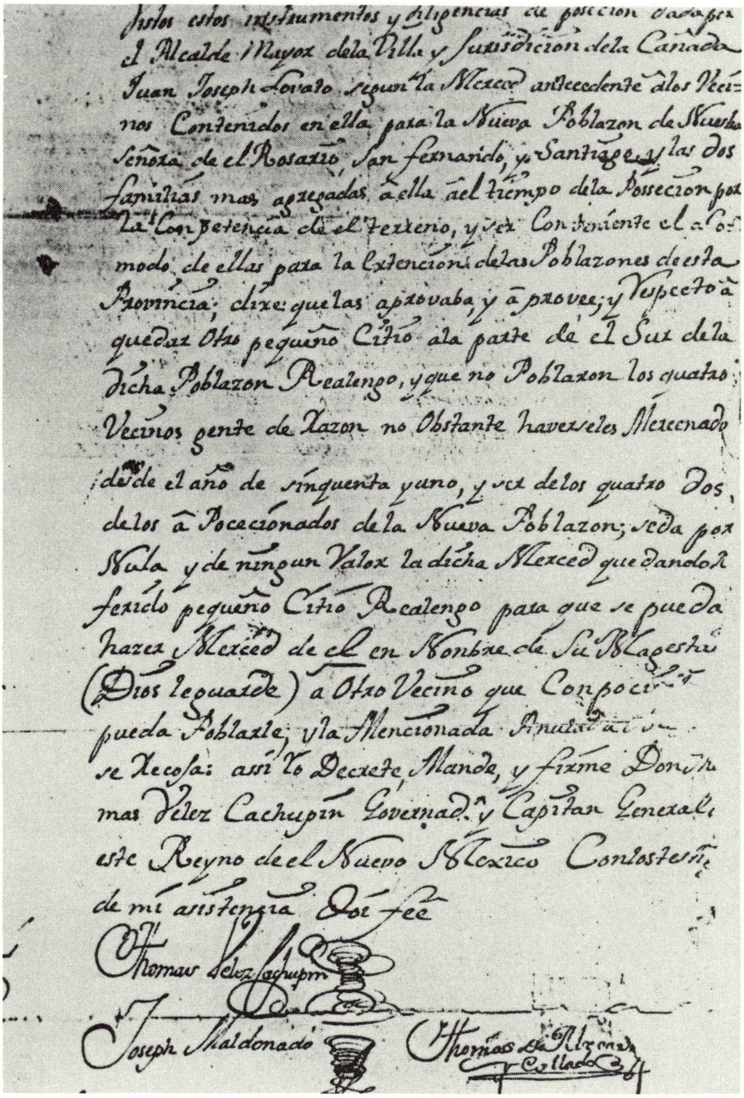

Approval by Governor Vélez Cachupin of the act of possession of the Nuestra Señora del Rosario, San Fernando y Santiago or Truchas grant. Courtesy of State Records Center and Archives, SANM I, #771.

ONE

New Mexican Land Grants

ONE

New Mexican Land Grants
The Legal Background

Malcolm Ebright

Spanish law was first shaped over the centuries when the Iberian peninsula was beset with successive waves of conquest. When the reconquest of the Moors was completed under Ferdinand and Isabella, Spanish law became the instrument of Spain's own conquests.[1] One of the main reasons for the successful establishment of the great Spanish empire was Spain's mastery of the practice of law and government and the Spanish love for the abstract field of jurisprudence. When Spanish sovereignty was projected into New Mexico by Juan de Oñate in 1598, the theory and practice of Spanish law played a major role in the settlement of that province.[2]

The *mercedes de tierra* or grants of land made by Oñate and succeeding governors were an important device for establishing control of New Mexico by a handful of Spaniards, and it was a device born out of and maintained by Spanish jurisprudence. But this jurisprudence had a grassroots, homespun character in New Mexico. The New Mexican land grant was above all the creature of custom—the time-honored way of doing things—and custom has always been a feature of Spanish law.[3]

The cycle of conquest brought a new legal system to New Mexico in 1846 with different legal concepts. The Anglo-American system of jurisprudence imposed on New Mexico by the U.S. occupation was the vehicle for wresting control of the land grants from many of their Hispano owners.

This is the story of a region whose unique landscape required a special relationship to the land, one sanctioned by law—the land grant. It is also the story of the decline of the land grant brought about by an alien legal system. The story is woven of the threads of conquest and accommodation, custom and justice, together with greed and injustice. And since the fabric is not yet complete, there is still the possibility and the hope that the end will be fashioned in fairness.

Land Grants in Spain and Mexico

When Columbus first set foot on the island of Hispaniola (today's Haiti and the Dominican Republic), he brought with him the baggage of Spain's institutions, including the legal system out of which the land grants were made. By 1492 Spain's legal institutions had been shaped by a series of invasions, each bringing a different legal influence into the crucible of Spanish jurisprudence.

First came the Romans, then the Visigoths, and finally the Moors. The Romans brought the first formal legal system to Spain, though it was not the one centered around the famous Justinian Code, which came later. The law of Rome at this time consisted of the writings of the great lawyers and several codes that were collections of decrees issued by the Roman rulers of the fourth and fifth centuries. Of major importance were the municipal codes of Rome which served as a model for other cities in the Roman Empire. These codes reinforced existing Spanish customary law relating to municipal ownership of lands and other property. Rent paid to the city for this property was used to help finance public works and the costs of government.[4] This concept of municipally owned property used as a partial substitute for taxes is also found in the Spanish *propio.*

The invasion of Spain by the Visigoths in 476 was the culmination of a series of attacks on Spain by various barbarian tribes beginning in the year 409. The Visigoths, tolerant of existing Spanish law and custom, did not attempt to impose their own Germanic laws in Spain. By the seventh century the Visigoths promulgated a code called the Fuero Juzgo which was an amalgam of Roman and Visigothic law. Germanic law placed a greater emphasis on custom than did Roman law, so this first major Spanish code gave formal sanction to the continuing power of customary law. The Fuero Juzgo was to remain Spain's principal code of laws until it was replaced in 1255 (by Las Siete Partidas); it met with less than universal acceptance, however, and customary law continued to have major importance.[5]

The third major wave of conquest of the Iberian peninsula took place in 711 with the coming of the Moors; they were not finally repelled from Spain until 1492. Formal Moorish law left little imprint on Spanish law, but the effect of Moorish custom is still being felt in places that inherited the Spanish legal system. Moorish irrigation practices had a particularly powerful influence on Spanish laws and customs,[6] so much so that many words connected with irrigation in New Mexico are of Moorish origin. Examples are *acequia* (irrigation ditch), *noria* (well), *atarque* (diversion dam), and *zanja* (feeder ditch).[7]

During the reconquest of Spain from the Moors, two practices developed which were to shape the future of the institution of land grants both in Mexico generally and in New Mexico in particular. The first was the practice of rewarding individual *conquistadores* by giving them land. This practice was the forerunner of what became the private land grant in New Mexico. The second practice reveals the origin of the New Mexican community land grant on the Iberian peninsula.

During the long period of the reconquest—from the eighth to the fifteenth centuries—the Spanish *pueblos* assumed a strategic importance, both as fortified centers holding the land against the Moors and as colonizing centers from which new settlements were planted. This importance made it possible for individual pueblos to gain control, usually by grant from the king, of the land surrounding the pueblo, which was administered according to local custom rather than by codified law. These outlying lands were generally used in common.[8] The Spanish pueblo with its common lands was the counterpart of today's community land grant.

The lands of the Spanish land-owning towns were divided into several classes according to their use. The *monte,* mountainous land generally covered with trees and brush, was used primarily for gathering wood and acorns. The *prado* was high quality pasture land, often irrigated. The *dehesa* was fenced pasture land. The *ejido* was a multipurpose piece of land just outside the town, used as a threshing floor, a garbage dump, and for keeping stray animals, among other uses. Collectively these lands of the pueblo were called *tierras concegiles* (lands of the council) and were usually used in common.[9] The tierras concegiles provided the means of maintaining a self-sufficient community; they were the keystone of its economic and social life.

The lessons learned from the experience of the Reconquest were applied when Spain was formulating her land policies for the New World, and when the Americas were colonized, the institution of common lands was transplanted in New Spain.[10] In New Mexico these lands were sometimes called *ejidos,*[11] while other land grant documents from New Mexico describe the common lands by the uses to which they were put: *pastos* (pastures), *abrevaderos* (watering places), and *leña* (firewood).[12]

Another Spanish institution of great importance to the settlement of the New World was the *encomienda.* The encomienda was a grant to a Spaniard of the fruits of Indian labor. Initially it was collectible either in material tribute or in personal service, but it soon became tantamount to slavery. By holding an Indian town in encomienda, a Spanish conquistador had the right to collect tribute from the town and sometimes to require personal service from the Indians. Although the encomienda by itself did not give the Spaniard a right to the land of the Indians, often encomenderos came to believe that they owned this land.[13]

The institution of the encomienda grew out of the Moorish conquest in Spain which entailed the same problems faced by Cortés in Mexico: rewarding conquerors, defending conquered lands, and protecting conquered peoples. Cortés made encomienda grants knowing that they had been misused in Cuba and realizing that he had no authority to make them. In 1522 Cortés told the king he had made such grants and requested their approval. The king replied that royal policy forbade them and ordered Cortés to revoke all encomienda grants. Cortés did not follow this order, but tried instead to persuade the king that encomiendas were necessary to induce colonists to settle in Mexico.[14] This same argument was used as a justification for the system of land grants that soon developed in Mexico.

Debate over the encomienda raged in the Spanish royal court for many decades until 1542, when the crown issued new laws forbidding the requirement of personal service as an incident of the encomienda. A storm of protest greeted this news when it reached the Indies, and King Carlos V backed down. Enslavement of Indians remained illegal, but actual practice often deviated from the letter of the law, especially on remote frontiers like New Mexico.[15] Although the encomienda was introduced in New Mexico with Oñate, it was abolished after the 1680 Pueblo Revolt.

In 1542 the need for a special body in Spain to govern the Spanish colonial empire resulted in the establishment of the Council of the Indies. Unique conditions in the Americas called for specific laws tailored to conditions there. For a century and a half the king and the Council of the Indies issued these laws without organizing them into any kind of comprehensive code. Finally in 1681, the monumental *Recopilación de las Leyes de los Reynos de las Indias* was published to fill this need. The *Recopilación* directed that its laws were to be the primary ones to apply to the Indies.[16] In cases where the *Recopilación* was silent, the laws of the Kingdom of Castile were to apply.[17] The general basis for the community land grant and for the use of common lands in the Americas was outlined in the *Recopilación.*

The Spanish land-holding towns established in New Spain were based upon the rules for establishing settlements found in the *Recopilación* and the Castilian agricultural villages with which the conquerors were familiar. The 1555 grant to the town of San Miguel in Central Mexico was typical; each head of a family (*vecino*), received a building lot (*solar de casa,* usually 50 square varas),[18] a garden plot (*suerte*) and one or two *caballerías* of land for field crops (a caballería contained approximately 105 acres). In addition, each vecino received a sheep pasture located within a six-mile square surrounding the town. Finally, most towns owned an *ejido* for common usage. The settlers were required to reside on the land for a minimum period (at San Miguel it was initially ten years, later reduced to six), and maintain a horse and weapons. These conditions were similar to those imposed on some New Mexico land grants.[19]

In addition to these grants made to communities, individual private land grants were made in Mexico. Often these were grazing lands varying in size depending on whether the grant was for cattle (a *sitio de gañado major* of 4,316 acres) or for sheep (a *sitio de gañado menor* of 1,918 acres).[20]

By 1535 large land grants were not in favor and instructions were issued not to distribute lands "to excess." Several methods were employed to circumvent this policy of encouraging small to moderate sized landholdings. One method was simply to purchase grants made to others, in spite of the standard provision that grants were to be settled or stocked with animals by the grantee himself and that the grant could not be sold for a certain minimum period of time (generally from four to ten years). Often those selling the grant were in fact mere "straw men" who were paid to apply for the grant with the understanding that they would transfer it as soon as they received it. Another common method of increasing the size of one's holdings was to simply appropriate unused land adjacent to land lawfully granted. Many times the land that was seized in this manner was Indian land.[21] Similar methods of land speculation and land grabbing later took place in New Mexico in the eighteenth and nineteenth centuries.

The Indian land-holding system that Cortés encountered was remarkably similar to that of the Spanish, but was changing at the time of Spanish arrival toward a greater emphasis on private property. For example, land whose harvest was used to support local *caciques* (chiefs), but which was owned by the Indian community, came to be considered as the property of the cacique. This arrangement made it easier for Spaniards to acquire Indian land, such as the land of a cacique who was in debt.[22]

A theme encountered in Central Mexico that was later repeated in New Mexico is that of Spanish stock overrunning and damaging Indian fields. This problem was not limited to the Indians, however, for Spanish farmers also filed numerous complaints with the Viceroy concerning damages to their crops by herds of sheep and cattle.[23] Indian crop-damage cases, heard by a General Indian Court, were probably more numerous than cases involving Spanish farmers because of the greater area covered by Indian farms and because of an attitude on the part of some Spanish ranchers that they had a right to graze their cattle on Indian fields. For example, in 1551 an *estanciero* (rancher) named Alonso de Villaseca complained to the Audiencia (a judicial body with advisory powers) that the Indians of Toluca had maliciously fenced off their cornfields to keep his cattle out! The rancher was ordered to remove his cattle from the Indians' land during the growing season, but from December to March, the Indians had to allow the Spaniard's cattle to graze on their land.[24]

This ruling was in accordance with the ancient Castilian custom of *derrota de mieses* or stubble grazing. According to this custom, which was followed in New Mexico as well as Central Mexico, every owner of private farmland had to open his fields to the livestock of the town where he lived from after harvest until spring planting.[25]

The themes found in the history of land grants in Spain and Central Mexico are repeated in New Mexico: the importance of custom in Spanish law, the varying emphasis on private and communal land, and the continual battles between the Spanish colonists and the Indians over choice land, and for a short time the encomienda. The encomienda disappeared in New Mexico, but the other themes continued, each with its own array of problems.

Land Grants in New Mexico

During the early years of the first permanent settlement of New Mexico, the faithful followers of Juan de Oñate were rewarded for their loyalty with encomiendas.[26] Although encomenderos were forbidden by law from living on the lands granted to them in encomienda (generally an Indian Pueblo or part of it), most ignored this law. There was a great deal of encroachment on Indian lands, and encomenderos often levied excessive tribute on the Indians.[27]

As in Central Mexico, this soldier-citizen upper class was not interested initially in farming, preferring to live off Indian labor and tribute instead. But eventually, the encomenderos asked for and received grants of land for farming and/or stock raising. As they had done in the Mexican heartland, the Spaniards grew wheat to supplement beans and corn, the staples of the diet of the Pueblo Indians. The Indians resisted foreign foods, and when they rebelled against the Spanish in 1680, forcing the Spanish to retreat to El Paso, some Indian leaders demanded that all seeds other than corn and beans be burned.[28]

Since one of the major reasons for the Pueblo Revolt was the abuses connected with the encomienda, this practice was not followed after the Revolt,[29] and a new era of relations between the Spanish and the Pueblos was ushered in. One aspect of this relationship was improved defense against raids by nomadic Indians, because the Pueblos now served as allies of the Spaniards on retaliatory expeditions.[30] Another facet of improved Hispano-Pueblo relations was a different pattern of land use and settlement than had developed in the first part of the seventeenth century. The prerevolt pattern was one of widely scattered large properties worked primarily by Indians—a pattern much like that of the North Mexican hacienda. But settlement of New Mexico proceeded along different lines with the end of the encomienda. Typical settlements were made up of smaller units, like the rancho, strung along the Rio Grande and its tributaries. Although the Spaniard was traditionally a town dweller, and although royal policy encouraged formation of compact plazas where settlers could gather for defense against Indian raids, it was typical of the independently minded New Mexican to build his house near his fields, where he could keep an eye out for wild animals or nomadic Indians who might take his crops.[31]

Since the archives of New Mexico were destroyed in the Pueblo Revolt, little information has survived concerning prerevolt land grants.

The power to make land grants was given to the governor, although lesser officials also granted land to individuals or to groups of settlers.[32] The first land grants that we know of in New Mexico were made by Governor Diego de Vargas after his reconquest of the province in 1692.[33] Many of these grants were made to loyal followers of de Vargas and to individuals who had possessed land grants prior to the revolt and who were willing to resettle them.[34]

Regulation of the granting of land in New Mexico was based as much on custom as on written law, particularly during the Spanish Period from 1598 to 1821. It was not until the Colonization Law of 1824 and the regulations of 1828, during the Mexican Period,[35] that any detailed land grant laws were enacted for New Mexico, and these generally validated the customary procedure that developed there over the previous 230 years.[36] Under these regulations, anyone seeking a land grant would address a petition to the governor describing the land sought and his qualifications for receiving a grant, and stating that there were no adverse claims. The governor would then, in most cases, refer the petition to the local alcalde for his recommendations as to whether the grant should be made. The primary considerations were whether the land was being used or claimed by others, the sufficiency of the petitioner's qualifications, and in the case of a community grant, the existence of resources like pasture, water, and firewood.[37]

If the governor happened to be personally familiar with the land and with the petitioner, he might himself report on the advisability of making the grant.[38] Frequently neighboring Pueblo Indians and Spaniards would be summoned at this stage to be given an opportunity to object to the grant if they thought it would be an encroachment on their land; in other cases this would not occur until the final step, or it would not occur at all.[39]

If the recommendation of the alcalde was favorable, then the governor would make the grant, directing the alcalde to perform the final step—the ceremony of delivery of possession. On an appointed day, the grantee would go to the land to meet the local alcalde. Also summoned to be present were the neighboring landowners. This was the last chance for anyone to object to the grant, and sometimes the alcalde was called upon to settle a protest on the spot. If the alcalde found that the grant would not be prejudicial to anyone, he proceeded with the ceremony of delivery of possession.[40]

If feasible, the grantee and the alcalde would walk the boundaries, together with the neighboring property owners, placing monuments—usually a mound of stones or a cross—on the boundary lines or corners. This practice was designed to prevent future boundary disputes, but it was not very successful. Generally, even the most basic kind of survey was lacking, and boundaries were usually described by natural landmarks, such as an arroyo, or a ridge, a river, or a neighbor's property. This practice was to cause myriad problems when the grants were later adjudicated by the United States. When a survey was performed, it was done by means of a *cordel*—a rope varying in length from 50 to 100 varas.[41] Since these ropes were subject to shrinkage or stretching, boundary measurements by means of the cordel sometimes provoked heated arguments.[42] To complete the act of possession, the alcalde took the grantee by the hand and walked him over the land, while the grantee plucked up grass, threw stones to signify his dominion over the land, and shouted "Long live the King!"[43]

The documents evidencing these steps—the petition, the alcalde's report, the grant by the governor, and the act of possession—were assembled into one document called the *expediente,* a copy of which was given to the grantee as his evidence of title. The copy was the *testimonio.* Many problems later faced by American courts dealt with the adequacy, by United States standards, of these documents. Often originals became worn with handling, and certified copies were made by alcaldes. But United States courts later held that these copies were invalid, even though there was no other method at the time of preserving these important documents.[44]

As in Spain and Central Mexico, land grants in New Mexico were divided into two main categories which again were determined more by custom than by written law. A private grant was made to an individual who would own the entire grant and could sell it after the possession requirement was met. In the eighteenth century, land grants in New Mexico tended to be private grants, probably an outgrowth of the seventeenth-century encomienda practice. Community grants became more prevalent in the nineteenth century.[45]

In the case of a community grant, individuals in a group of settlers would each receive an allotment of land for a house (*solar de casa*), an irrigable plot (*suerte*), and the right to use the remaining unallotted land on the grant in common with the other settlers for pastures, watering places, firewood, and logs for building, as well as for hunting, fishing, gathering herbs, and rock quarrying, among other uses.[46]

Depending on the lay of the land, these allotments were often combined into one plot—usually a strip of land running from the river to the foothills.[47] The settler would own his allotment free and clear after four years,[48] and could sell it as private property. But the common lands were owned by the community and could not be sold.[49]

Between the classic private grant and the classic community grant there were many hybrid grants containing aspects of each type. Often as settlement progressed on a private land grant, its character would become more like a community grant. Since grant documents did not define a grant as either private or community, the classification of land grants became another problem for U.S. courts.

Not only was there a wide variety of land grants in terms of their legal classification, but actual settlements on these grants also varied from a physical standpoint. Eighteenth-century governors like Tomás Vélez Cachupín and Pedro Fermín de Mendinuetta were legalists, trying to follow the laws relating to settlements, as well as practical men who saw the defensive value of settlements built around compact plazas.[50] Houses built wall-to-wall in a square, without windows on the outside, formed a protective fortress—sometimes with a circular watchtower (*torreón*) at one or more corners. Although villages like Truchas, Chimayó, Córdova, and Las Trampas were built on this pattern, the tendency of other New Mexican settlers was to build their houses along streams and rivers against the specific orders of the governors. Even the largest settlements in the province, designated as *villas,* were built on a random rather than the orderly plan called for in the *Recopilación.*[51] After Santa Fe's founding in 1610, the villa of Santa Cruz de la Cañada was founded in 1695 near persent-day Española, and in 1706 the villa of Albuquerque was reported by Governor Cuervo y Valdez to have been established. Both Santa Cruz and Albuquerque followed the helter-skelter make-up of Santa Fe, and Albuquerque did not even meet the minimum requirements set forth in the *Recopilación* for a villa.[52]

The primary means of subsistence on New Mexican settlements was agriculture and stock raising (in addition an artisan class grew up in Albuquerque and Santa Fe by the late 1700s).[53] The pattern of land use for settlements on community land grants reveals intense usage of the land near the watercourses for agriculture and homes, and less intense uses, such as grazing, as one progressed farther from the rivers on to the common lands. New Mexico documents reveal that grazing animals intruding on planted fields was as much of a concern there as it had been in Central Mexico.[54]

Although few records have survived concerning the use of common lands in New Mexico, for Santa Fe documentary evidence exists on the practice of stubble grazing. Under that system, every local citizen's animals were allowed to graze on harvested private fields before the next planting, giving these fields the character of common lands during this period. Also in Santa Fe, there are records of a plot of swampy land called the Ciénega that was used by Santa Fe residents as common lands in the 1700s when its lush grass could be mowed by any Santa Fe resident to feed his animals.[55]

Raids by the Comanche, Apache, Ute, and Navajo hampered the expansion of settlements beyond the Albuquerque, Santa Fe, and Santa Cruz population centers, but intrepid settlers continued to start new settlements in spite of the danger. Ojo Caliente was settled by 1735, Abiquiu by 1734, Las Trampas in 1751, Ranchos de Taos by 1744, Tomé in 1739, Valencia in 1740, and Belen in 1750.[56] Repeated Indian raids caused the Ojo Caliente settlers to withdraw to more secure settlements. Time after time the governor of New Mexico ordered these settlers to return to their village, but many preferred to forfeit their lands rather than risk their lives again, after they had already lost members of their families during Indian attacks. These forfeited lands would then be settled by new *pobladores* (settlers).[57]

The settlement that is now Ranchos de Taos on the Cristóbal de la Serna grant suffered so much from Indian attacks that by the 1770s the settlers moved in with the Indians of Taos Pueblo for mutual protection. But Ranchos de Taos was soon reestablished, and the population began to increase there and elsewhere in the Taos Valley after the Comanche Peace Treaty was achieved by Governor Anza in 1786 and maintained into the 1800s by his successor, Governor Fernando de la Concha.[58] After the turn of the century, land grants were made more frequently, not only in the Taos Valley, but also in the Mora Valley and along the Chama River, as settlements began to increase dramatically. A larger proportion of these grants were community grants than had previously been the case.[59]

Spanish policy before Mexican independence in 1821 prohibited trade with *extranjeros* (foreigners), who were not allowed to receive land grants. The Mexican regulations of 1828 changed this by authorizing grants to be made to both Mexicans and foreigners. With the inception of the Santa Fe trade in 1821, Anglo merchants and trappers began to settle in New Mexico, marry Hispanas, and even become naturalized Mexican citizens. Many of them sought and received land grants, either alone or in partnership with Hispanos.[60]

The most notorious land grants during this period were those made by Governor Manuel Armijo in the 1840s—mostly to partnerships of Anglos and Hispanos. Grants such as the Beaubien-Miranda (Maxwell) and Sangre de Cristo grants were in clear violation of the Mexican Colonization Law of 1824 which limited the amount of land that one person could receive. Since these grants were both made to two persons, they were limited by that law to 96,000 acres. Yet the Sangre de Cristo grant was patented at 998,780 acres and the Beaubien-Miranda grant at a whopping 1,714,764 acres. Ironically, these highly questionable grants were among the first to be confirmed by the United States; their combined acreage (2,713,545) exceeds the entire acreage of New Mexico grants confirmed by the Court of Private Land Claims, thus calling in question the entire process of land grant adjudication.[61]

During both the Spanish and the Mexican Periods, disputes over land and water were settled primarily according to the customs followed in the remote outpost that was New Mexico. Records of litigation reveal that local custom was more often the basis for decision than were the formal rules of Spanish law.[62] Local government and the administration of justice had acquired a great deal of autonomy in New Mexico during the Mexican Period, to the point where alcaldes and ayuntamientos would sometimes defy orders from the governor when they believed them to be unjust,[63] or local authorities would simply delay for years the execution of an unpopular directive.[64] The legal system was composed of the local alcaldes and ayuntamientos and the governor, with occasional appeals made to higher authorities in Central Mexico.[65] A body of decisions was produced by this legal system that often dealt with the same questions United States courts would soon face: land and water rights and the validity of land grants under Spanish and Mexican law. These decisions would have been extremely valuable as an aid and touchstone for U.S. land grant adjudication, but even today they remain a resource that is largely untapped. Instead of attempting to learn how New Mexican authorities dealt with land grants, the United States imposed its own view of Spanish and Mexican law on the adjudication process—a view that was colored by the bias of a completely different legal system.

The Treaty of Guadalupe Hidalgo

Changes in New Mexico brought about by the opening of the Santa Fe Trail paved the way for the invasion by United States forces led by General Stephen Watts Kearny in August 1846. Kearny promised the people of New Mexico that their property would be protected by the United States.[66] However, it became a matter of international negotiation to determine what form this guarantee would take.

The negotiations leading up to the Treaty of Guadalupe Hidalgo took place in the autumn of 1847 when General Winfield Scott's army had occupied Mexico City. Representing the United States in these negotiations was Nicolas Trist, a man caught in the middle. He attempted to hammer out a fair treaty in spite of the inflexible policy of his government on many issues. The exact terms of the property guarantee given by Kearny with regard to land grants were the result of protracted negotiations. In August 1847, when Scott's army was in position to advance on Mexico City, the Mexican government appointed four commissioners to meet with Trist. Both sides had draft treaties that their respective governments had given them as bases for negotiation.[67]

The first draft treaty suggested by the United States contained no mention of a land grant guarantee, although Trist was instructed not to object if the Mexican commissioners requested one. These commissioners did request a series of articles on land grants to the effect that all grants made by the Mexican authorities were valid and would be recognized as such by the United States. Trist objected to these articles because they validated all land grants. He said that those grants whose conditions had not been fulfilled should not be respected, nor should those made after the cut-off date of 13 May 1846, the day hostilities began between the United States and Mexico. Trist suggested wording to establish a test of the validity of land grants; only those found to be valid by this standard would be respected. This test was embodied in Article 10 which said that grants would be valid to the extent that they were valid under Mexican law.[68]

Article 10 would have provided a fair standard for adjudicating land grants; unfortunately it was deleted from the treaty by the U.S. Senate prior to ratification. This caused innumerable problems in the subsequent adjudication of land grants. Without a standard by which to test the validity of a land grant, Congress and the courts were free to make their own rules, which they did, and the results were not always just.

Recently, a Mexican historian labeled the Treaty of Guadalupe Hidalgo "one of the harshest in modern history."[69] It was imposed on Mexico—not fairly negotiated. The war began mainly because the United States wanted to fulfill its "manifest destiny" to expand its territory across the entire continent.[70] With the U.S. Army advancing on and finally occupying Mexico City, Secretary of State James Buchanan called the draft treaty "a carefully considered ultimatum."[71] Nicolas Trist negotiated the treaty after ignoring orders from his government to return to Washington. President Polk urged the deletion of Article 10 in his message to the Senate, claiming that Trist did not have the authority to include it. But when Secretary of State Buchanan explained the deletion of Article 10 to the Mexican government, his only specific objection was that portion providing additional time within which grantees could fulfill the conditions of their grants.[72] Why then, was the entire article deleted, instead of deleting only the objectionable part?[73] The latter course would have kept in the treaty a standard for later use in land grant adjudication. Apparently U.S. authorities did not want a clear standard. This cynical position is illustrated by the story of the protocol to the treaty.

In order to allay the concern of the Mexican government over the deletion of Article 10, as well as the deletion and modification of several other articles, the two American commissioners who replaced Trist were asked to sign, along with the Mexican representative, an explanation of the U.S. Senate amendments known as the Protocol of Querétaro. As to Article 10, the Protocol stated that the United States did not intend to annul legitimate grants by deleting Article 10. Legitimate titles, according to the Protocol, were those that were valid under Mexican law as of the cut-off date of 13 May 1846. With this written assurance to the government of Mexico, ratifications of the Treaty of Guadalupe Hidalgo were exchanged on 30 May 1848.[74]

While the government of Mexico considered the Protocol binding, the U.S. State Department refused to recognize its validity. Rumor had it that the Protocol had revived Article 10, but Secretary of State John M. Clayton, who had succeeded Buchanan, made the United States position crystal clear when he stated:

> It is believed that the Mexican government was not less prodigal in

> donations of its domains in New Mexico and California than it had been in disposing of Texas lands. . . . Could it however reasonably be expected that this government, in addition to the treasure and blood expended in prosecuting the war, would engage to pay fifteen millions of dollars for lands, the title to the most valuable part of which had been extinguished?[75]

In other words, the United States looked at the treaty as an enormous real estate deal; it expected to get clear title to most of the land it was paying for regardless of the property rights of Mexicans. It is not surprising then, that subsequent adjudication of land grants by the United States was often unjust.

To assess the fairness of land grant adjudication under the Treaty of Guadalupe Hidalgo, a comparison with the experience under earlier United States treaties involving land grants will be helpful. Spanish land grants were adjudicated in Louisiana under an 1803 treaty[76] and in Florida under an 1819 treaty.[77] In each state, land grant claims were filed with a board of commissioners which investigated them and then reported its recommendations to Congress for final action. A majority of these claims were confirmed,[78] partly because the amounts of land in question were relatively small; most claims did not exceed 640 acres.[79] But another factor of importance was the liberal nature of U.S. Supreme Court decisions on questions of land grant adjudication.

The treaty between the United States and Spain covering land grants in Florida contained a clause similar to those proposed by the Mexican commissioners negotiating the Treaty of Guadalupe Hidalgo. Article 8 of the Florida treaty said that land grants "shall be ratified and confirmed to those in possession of the lands. . . ."[80] Claimants argued before the U.S. Supreme Court that this language meant that the treaty itself confirmed land grants in Florida without the necessity for any further action by Congress or the courts. Thus, they argued, the treaty was self-executing and the land grant board did not have the power to reject grants, only to determine which grants were valid and to recommend those for confirmation. In 1829 U.S. Supreme Court Chief Justice John Marshall decided that Article 8 of the Florida treaty was not self-executing.[81] But in a landmark case in 1833, Marshall reversed his earlier decision, holding that the same clause of the same treaty was self-executing. The case was *United States v. Percheman.* Marshall changed his mind because the attorney representing Juan Percheman, the claimant, focused on the Spanish version of Article 8. It stated that land grants "quedarán ratificadas y reconocidas a las personas que estan en posesión de ellas. . . ." The verb *quedarán* had been mistranslated, said Percheman's attorney. It should have been translated, "[land grants] *remain* ratified" instead of "[land grants] *shall be* ratified," thus clearly signifying confirmation by the treaty itself. Justice Marshall agreed.[82]

This decision shows that both the English and the Spanish version of the treaty must be looked at to determine its meaning. Also, it provides a clue as to why the U.S. Congress deleted Article 10 from the Treaty of Guadalupe Hidalgo. Since the language of Article 8 of the Florida treaty was quite similar to Article 10 of the Treaty of Guadalupe Hidalgo, it is likely that the United States did not want to be fettered with the liberal precedent of *Percheman*'s construction of Article 8 of the Florida treaty in Article 10 of the Guadalupe Hidalgo Treaty. The Supreme Court took an extremely liberal approach to land grant adjudication in the *Percheman* case, but its decisions under the Treaty of Guadalupe Hidalgo would become progressively more conservative.

The first test of how the U.S. Supreme Court would treat the ill-defined obligation of the United States to protect the property rights of Mexicans under the Treaty of Guadalupe Hidalgo came after a board of land commissioners was established in California to adjudicate land grants there. Pressure on Congress to deal with the land title problem came first from California because of the discovery of gold there and its early admission as a state into the United States. The population increase due to the Gold Rush made land more valuable, and statehood gave California more leverage in Washington than was enjoyed by New Mexico.[83]

Before establishing the California Board of Land Commissioners, Congress attempted to learn something about the nature and extent of that state's land grants. In 1849 the Secretary of the Interior appointed William Carey Jones to make a detailed investigation, the results of which astounded many Congressmen.[84] Jones reported that a number of grants were made to the extent of the eleven-square-league limit (48,000 acres) of the Mexican Colonization Law of 1824. This was a far cry from the 640-acre grants the lawmakers were familiar with. Other problems with California land grants foreseen by Jones were "the loose designation of their limits and extent" and the likelihood of simulated grants.[85] He was right. Boundary problems, size limitations, and fraudulent grants would later plague those trying to settle land grant titles both in California and New Mexico.

The California Board of Land Commissioners was highly controversial when it was first proposed. Critics argued that the legislation establishing it was in violation of the property rights guarantee of the Guadalupe Hidalgo treaty.[86] After the deletion of Article 10, the only part of the treaty protecting land grant property rights was Article 8 which provided that "property of every kind now belonging to Mexicans . . . shall be inviolably respected."[87] Many questions were left unanswered by Article 8, but debate over the California law centered on the question of what procedures should be followed in implementing the remaining property rights guarantees of the Treaty of Guadalupe Hidalgo. The new law placed the burden on the land grant owner to file a claim with the land board by 1853 or have his or her property declared public domain of the United States. This burden of initiating and proving a claim required the claimant to hire an attorney and to gather all the documents and testimony needed to support the claim. After a hearing, the land board's decision could be appealed to the federal district court where a new trial would take place. The district court's decision could also be appealed to the U.S. Supreme Court. If the claimant was successful, he still had the burden of paying the cost of surveying his land and defending the survey before the Surveyor General's office.[88]

This procedure transformed the land grant owner into a claimant. It was a drastic change from the liberal self-executing treaty doctrine Justice Marshall had announced in the *Percheman* case. As Marshall interpreted the Florida treaty, the government had the burden of proving the invalidity of a land grant and had to take the initiative in doing so. Now the situation was reversed. The U.S. Supreme Court would soon have to decide whether the procedural burdens imposed by the California Act violated the promise of the United States to "inviolably respect" Hispanic property rights.

The test case came in the form of *Botiller v. Dominguez* involving the Rancho Las Virgenes grant made by the Mexican government in 1834. The grant was conceded to be a "perfect" grant in that all its conditions had been fulfilled. California Supreme Court decisions had held that such grant claims did not have to be submitted to the land board since "titles, such as were perfect under the former government, did not need any action of the new government for their protection."[89] This was very much like Marshall's self-executing treaty doctrine. In the *Botiller* case the California Supreme Court decided that the Rancho Las Virgenes grant did not need to be submitted to the land board; to the extent that the 1851 California Act required this, the Act was in violation of the Treaty of Guadalupe Hidalgo.[90] The government appealed this decision and the stage was set. Would the U.S. Supreme Court follow its earlier decision in the *Percheman* case?

The answer was a resounding no. The *Botiller* decision showed that the U.S. Supreme Court had changed its position dramatically since *Percheman.* In *Botiller* the court side-stepped the issue of what the treaty required of the United States in the way of land grant adjudication under the property rights guarantee. It held that if the 1851 statute conflicted with the treaty, then the statute must prevail. In the words of the court: "If the treaty was violated by this general statute . . . it was a matter of international concern, which the two states must determine by treaty, or by such other means as enables one state to enforce upon another the obligations of treaty."[91] In other words, the judicial branch of the government was washing its hands of any responsibility for interpreting the treaty. If the treaty was violated, said the court, it was up to Mexico to press the issue with the United States.

Although this was a harse appellate decision in relation to the earlier liberality of *Percheman,* the actual decisions under the California Act were relatively fair. It was the future effect of the *Botiller* decision that was so damaging. Having said that Congress was not bound by the Treaty of Guadalupe Hidalgo in its enactments of land grant adjudication schemes, the door was left open for more restrictive statutes in the future. In fact, the Court of Private Land Claims legislation for New Mexico was more restrictive than the California Act, and the decisions by the New Mexico Claims Court were even more limiting than was called for by the law. Moreover, without the regulating effect of the treaty, land grant decisions by the U.S. Supreme Court in the late 1800s circumscribed the rights of claimants to an ever-increasing extent.

The Treaty of Guadalupe Hidalgo was weakened from the beginning by the deletion of Article 10 and the disregard for the protocol; then it was ignored altogether. Since the courts have been unwilling to determine whether land grant adjudication was carried out in accordance with the treaty's requirements, the public must make its own judgment on this issue. Looking first at California and then at New Mexico, one might well ask the question, Has the government "inviolably respected" land grants in those states?

Early U.S. Supreme Court decisions on California cases gave substantial hope that a fair and just solution would be forthcoming for the land grant problem. These decisions, handed down before *Botiller,* contained magnanimous rhetoric:

> . . . the United States have bound themselves by a treaty to acknowledge and protect all bona fide titles granted by the previous Government, and this court [has] no discretion to enlarge or curtail such grants to suit our sense of propriety, or defeat just claims, however extensive, by stringent technical rules of construction to which they were not originally subjected,[92]

and

> They [the United States] have not desired the tribunals to conduct their investigations as if the rights of the inhabitants to the property which they claim depended upon the nicest observance of every legal formality.[93]

These high-sounding purposes were generally not followed in land grant adjudication. Especially in New Mexico in the 1890s, adjudicatory bodies were influenced by the size of grant claims, and they often held claimants to "the nicest observance of every legal formality" when the grants claimed were perfectly valid under Spanish and Mexican law.

In any case, the record of land grant adjudication in California was better than that in New Mexico. The statistics tell most of the story. In California approximately 12 million acres were claimed, of which 8.8 million were confirmed for a 73 percent confirmation figure.[94] In New Mexico this percentage was only 24 percent confirmation for both the Surveyor General and the Court of Private Land Claims; for the Claims Court alone it came to a surprisingly small 6 percent confirmation.[95]

Why were these percentages so small for New Mexico? To answer this question we must follow the winding path of land grant adjudication in New Mexico from the appointment of the first surveyor general in 1854 to the conclusion of the work of the Court of Private Land Claims in 1904.

The Surveyor General of New Mexico

California's status as a state with representation in Congress helped insure that the adjudication system established there would be relatively fair, though the California system was not without its critics. New Mexico, in contrast, did not become a state until 1912, and so was not able to vote on the method chosen by Congress to adjudicate land grant titles in New Mexican territory. Being a much poorer state than California, New Mexico found that Congress tended to minimize the importance of settling their land grant titles, so much so that the procedure first set up to New Mexico was wholly inadequate to deal with this vast and complicated problem.

Unlike California's situation, land grant adjudication in New Mexico was not undertaken promptly. When Congress established the office of Surveyor General of New Mexico in 1854, six years had passed since the signing of the Treaty of Guadalupe Hidalgo. This delay created uncertainty about New Mexican land titles which the surveyor general system never completely resolved. Moreover, when William Pelham was appointed the first surveyor general of New Mexico, he found that he had many other responsibilities in addition to the matter of land grants, making it virtually impossible to deal adequately with the land grant problem.

His primary duty was to extend the federal public land survey system which provided for a checkerboard of townships, each containing thirty-six 640-acre sections.[96] Once public land had been surveyed under this system, ownership could be obtained under the homestead and other laws which the surveyor general administered.[97] The boundaries of land grants were not to be surveyed until after they were confirmed; even today large areas within land grants have not been surveyed.[98] The American surveying system did not fit the arid Southwest, and Anglo property law was not understood by most Hispanos. Corruption of public officials and dishonesty of claimants under the United States land laws were additional factors preventing Hispanic land grant heirs from obtaining title, under the homestead and other similar laws, to the land grants they occupied. It was not unusual for enterprising Anglos to wrest from the Hispanos their land grant property through fraud or manipulation of the land laws.[99]

In addition to these problems, the scheme for adjudicating land grants under the surveyor general system was badly flawed. The Hispano did not understand or have any trust in the American system of landownership. Written evidence of title was not without importance under the Spanish and Mexican land systems, but to the Hispano, possession was indeed nine-tenths of the law. His use of the land was more important in establishing his ownership than were any documents. When called upon to bring his documents to Santa Fe and file a claim before the surveyor general, most Hispanos demurred.[100] Some feared that they would lose their documents if they turned them over to the surveyor general; others felt they were adequately protected by the Treaty of Guadalupe Hidalgo. Since filing a claim entailed considerable expense, it was the doubtful claim held by the speculator that was likely to be filed first.

The surveyor general's responsibility concerning land grants was to report his recommendation as to whether claims should be confirmed or rejected by Congress. In making this recommendation to the Congress, however, the surveyor general was severely hampered as to what investigation he could make. Surveyor General Pelham had at first taken the position that his responsibility to "ascertain the origin, nature, character and extent of all claims"[101] authorized him to tour the territory and investigate all land grant titles. But he was instructed by his superior that he was limited to dealing with those claims filed in his office. Moreover, he had no staff with which to attempt to corroborate the claimant's testimony and, though he was directed to summon witnesses, he had no funds for this purpose either.[102] Thus, the surveyor general was merely a passive agent of the government, and the procedure before his office was not really an adjudication at all.

This was surely the most serious defect in the surveyor general procedure: it lacked the essential element of all true adjudication—due process of law. To adjudicate titles is to determine landownership judicially, and the Constitution of the United States mandates that no one be deprived of property without a judicial determination that meets the requirements of due process of law. Due process requires that there be a hearing at which interested parties can present evidence and cross-examine opposing witnesses and that actual notice of the hearing be given to those whose property rights may be affected.[103] The failure to require a hearing with an adversarial procedure meant that most claims were decided solely on the affidavits of the claimant and his witnesses.

Potential adverse claimants were usually not even notified of the proceedings.[104]

Also, since the claims were not surveyed until after they were confirmed, the surveyor general and Congress had no idea how much land was being confirmed. Thus, after the Maxwell and Sangre de Cristo grants were confirmed, the Maxwell grant was found to contain 1,714,764 acres and the Sangre de Cristo grant 2,713,545 acres. These grants should have been limited to about 97,000 acres if the Mexican Colonization Law of 1824 had been applied (48,500 for each grantee). In fact, Congress did apply that law to the confirmation of the Las Animas and Rio Don Carlos grants, confirming the former at approximately 97,000 acres and the latter at 48,000 acres.[105]

The injustice of applying the eleven-square-league size limitation to some grants but not to others is apparent. Nevertheless, the U.S. Supreme Court upheld the confirmations of both the Maxwell and Sangre de Cristo grants, conceiving a novel theory to justify its action. Since it was obvious that the confirmations were in violation of Mexican law, the Supreme Court held that Congress had made a grant *de novo,* or a new grant, in its confirmation.[106] This was strange reasoning indeed, for under the surveyor general system, land grants were supposed to have been dealt with by the United States precisely as Spain and Mexico would have done.

Besides these grievous faults, the surveyor general system in New Mexico had no provision for the orderly determination of overlapping claims. Under the later Court of Private Land Claims, all possible overlapping claims to the same area were supposed to be joined in one proceeding that determined all rights to the disputed land. Not so under the surveyor general system. Since there was no provision for notifying adverse claimants, the surveyor general operated on a first come, first served basis. Often it was the large grant, overlapping several smaller grants, that came first and was confirmed. Then when the smaller grants sought confirmation, they were met with the answer that the United States had already confirmed the land to someone else.[107]

It was soon apparent that the surveyor general system was woefully inadequate. Surveyor General Pelham told his superiors in his first annual report that "the present law has utterly failed to secure the object for which it was intended."[108] Congress too despaired of a fair solution to New Mexico's land grant problem under the surveyor general system. In 1860, the Committee on Private Land Claims of the House of Representatives reported on the bill to confirm the first series of grants recommended by Pelham. In its report, the committee noted that it did not have time to properly review the proceedings in each case, "nor will it ever be in the power hereafter of this House to make such an examination as will be entirely satisfactory. . . ."[109]

But the surveyor general system, imperfect as it was, continued for two more decades, during which time opportunities were plentiful for individual speculators to enrich themselves, usually at the expense of the settlers living on the land grants. Often these speculators included the surveyor general himself. Of the nine men to hold the office, three were blatant land speculators: T. Rush Spencer (1869–1874), James K. Proudfit (1872–1876), and Henry M. Atkinson (1876–1884). Spencer and Atkinson each had land grant holdings while they were in office.[110] These conflicts of interest, in addition to the inherent defects of the surveyor general system, often guaranteed that land grant adjudications would be unfair.

As an example, Surveyor General Atkinson claimed to own most of the Anton Chico community grant at the same time he was making important decisions about its title. This story illustrates one of the two main methods used by speculators during the surveyor general period for acquiring land grants: purchase of the principal settler's interest in a community grant. The second method was the partition suit.

It was often the case that a community grant like Anton Chico was requested at the outset by one or two individuals on behalf of a group of prospective settlers. This individual was the *poblador principal* (principal settler).[111] Often a list of all the proposed settlers would be attached to the petition, but sometimes only the name of the *poblador principal* would appear on the grant documents. In the case of Anton Chico, the petition was lost, but the granting decree of Governor Facundo Melgares referred to "the petition of citizen Manuel Rivera, for himself and in the name of thirty-six men."[112] Thus, the only actual name of a grantee appearing on the grant document was that of Manuel Rivera.

Anton Chico was clearly a community grant for it was made to a group of settlers and there was provision in the granting decree for the establishment of common lands. Moreover, when the grant was recommended for confirmation by Surveyor General Pelham, it was determined to be a community grant, for Pelham invoked the rule that the existence of a community on the grant in 1846 was *prima facie* evidence of a grant to that community.[113] Nevertheless, the fact that only Manuel Rivera's name appeared on the original grant papers created enough ambiguity that the General Land Office was asked to decide whether the patent should be issued to the Town of Anton Chico or to Manuel Rivera and thirty-six unnamed others. It was decided that Manuel Rivera and the thirty-six others should be the patentees and the patent was so issued on 27 March 1883.[114]

By this time Surveyor General Atkinson had purchased all the interests of the heirs of Manuel Rivera in the grant. He then deeded these interests to the New Mexico Land and Livestock Company of which he was president. The stage was set for a hearing on 20 April 1883, when representatives of the Anton Chico grant applied to Surveyor General Atkinson for delivery of the patent as representatives of the residents of the Anton Chico grant. Not surprisingly, Atkinson ruled that the title was vested only in Manuel Rivera, his heirs and successors. In effect, Henry Atkinson was ruling that he himself owned the grant! Fortunately the Town of Anton Chico was later declared by the courts to be owner of the Anton Chico grant, and it finally received the patent.[115] Today the grant is still operated as a community grant. But Atkinson's attempt to wrest the grant from its rightful owners points to the corruption that prevailed in the surveyor general's office in the 1870s and 1880s.

The Tierra Amarilla grant was similar to the Anton Chico grant in respects which made possible its acquisition by Thomas Benton Catron, just as Atkinson had acquired Anton Chico. This case also illustrates the first method of land grant acquisition used by speculators. The Tierra Amarilla grant was a community grant, but the grant documents mentioned only the name of the *poblador principal,* Manuel Martínez. Because of the due process defects in the surveyor general system, it was an easy matter for Manuel Martínez's son Francisco to seek confirmation of the grant in his name alone, since notice of Francisco's claim was not given to the settlers living on the grant. After the grant was confirmed (apparently to the heirs of Manuel Martínez), Catron purchased all the interests of those heirs and was able to obtain a court decree stating that he owned the grant. He then sold it, and another land grant was dispossessed of its common lands. Although the Tierra Amarilla grant heirs have gone to court five times to regain their common lands, they have been unsuccessful in each case.[116]

The other device frequently used by land-grabbing speculators was the partition suit. In numerous cases attorneys like Catron took as their fee for representing land grant claimants a portion of the land confirmed. This was usually one-third of the total acreage—a substantial fee.[117] Once the grant was confirmed, the attorney became a co-owner of the grant along with the heirs. Under the partition statute, enacted by the New Mexico territorial legislature in 1876,[118] the lawyer was entitled to request a division of the grant among its owners and to then force a sale of the grant pursuant to a court procedure. The statute required a sale if the property could not be physically divided without decreasing its value. The courts uniformly found this prerequisite to exist and ordered the grant sold.

The partition law was usually applied to the common lands of community grants, in direct opposition to the Spanish and Mexican systems of land tenure.[119] Under those systems the common lands could not be sold—they were required to remain intact as a perpetual resource for the community.[120] But under the partition statute, common lands were sold, often at ridiculously low prices. Sometimes the purchaser was merely a front for the lawyer who forced the sale in the first place. The grantees would receive a small amount of money for their priceless resource and the attorney who had won confirmation of the grant would end up owning most of the grant himself. When the Las Trampas grant was sold at a partition sale in 1902, the purchaser was H. F. Raynolds, the law partner of the attorney who handled the partition proceedings, Alonzo S. McMillan. Fortunately for the Hispanic owners of the grant, the sale was set aside when it was proven that Raynolds and McMillan had already contracted to resell the grant for $1.50 per acre before buying it for $.18 per acre and had bribed a court official to go along with their scheme. The grant was eventually sold for about $.60 an acre.[121]

Lawyers occupied with land grant speculation, joined by judges, politicians, businessmen, and a friendly press, were known as the Santa Fe Ring—a network established for mutual gain. Besides the surveyors general mentioned earlier, nearly every governor of New Mexico from the late 1860s to 1885 was a member of the Santa Fe Ring.[122] It was no wonder that the average Hispanic land grant settler, unfamiliar with the Anglo laws and language and often not notified of court proceedings involving his land grant, had little chance of protecting his property.

Land grant speculation was not the exclusive province of the Anglo, however. Many Anglo speculators worked through Hispanic middlemen in acquiring land grants,[123] and some members of the Santa Fe Ring like Antonio Joseph of Taos, were themselves Hispanos.[124] In fact, land grant speculation by Hispanos was occurring in New Mexico as early as the 1820s. By this time there was a tendency among elite Hispanos such as Juan Estevan Pino and Donaciano Vigil "to regard land as an economic asset to be exploited for the capital it would raise, not for the crops it would yield."[125]

Even priests were involved with land grant acquisition and resale. For example, in 1879 Padre Thomas Aquinas Hayes purchased the Ramón Vigil grant for $4,000.00. Father Hayes was probably the most successful land grant speculator on record. Within a month of his purchase he sold the grant for $16,000.00, then later repurchased it at the same price, most likely to increase the paper value of the grant in preparation for his next transaction. In 1884, Father Hayes sold the grant again, this time for a whopping $100,000.00, thus turning a tidy overall profit of $96,000.00.[126] Most land grant speculators did not do as well as Father Hayes. Even Thomas Benton Catron, the most notorious Santa Fe Ring member, was never able to match the ease with which Hayes made a 2400 percent profit on his investment in five years.[127]

While the abuses of the surveyor general system and the machinations of the Santa Fe Ring were occurring in the four decades after the signing of the Treaty of Guadalupe Hidalgo, most land titles in New Mexico were still in a chaotic state. An attempt at reforming the operation of the surveyor general system took place in 1885 with the appointment of George Washington Julian as surveyor general.[128] Appointed by President Grover Cleveland, one of Julian's main tasks was to break up the Santa Fe Ring and other lesser rings operating in New Mexico.[129] He set out vigorously to do this, but his zeal to correct the abuses of land grant adjudication under the surveyor general system led him to an over-critical questioning of many perfectly valid grants. In response to instructions from his superior, Commissioner William Andrew Jackson Sparks of the General Land Office, Julian reexamined 35 claims covering 4,380,048 acres of land that had been recommended for confirmation by his predecessors and were pending before Congress for final action. He recommended the rejection of 22 of these grants embracing 2,155,883 acres. Of those grants he recommended for confirmation, almost every one was recommended for a smaller area than was claimed.[130]

In the process of his reevaluation of land grant claims submitted to the surveyor general, Julian revised both the procedural and the substantive rules that had governed land grant adjudication up to that time. The effect was to make confirmation more difficult. Singlehandedly, Julian reversed certain presumptions in favor of the validity of land grant claims and took the position that these claims should be strictly construed against the claimant.[131] He also initiated investigations on substantive legal issues like the ownership of the common lands of community land grants. In 1887, he sent investigators to San Miguel County to search for evidence in the deed books in Las Vegas to support his theory that the title to the common lands of the Las Vegas grant was retained by the Spanish and Mexican governments.[132] Although this investigation was never completed, it is evident that a restrictive, conservative approach to land grant adjudication by the Court of Private Land Claims began during Surveyor General Julian's administration.

The Court of Private Land Claims

By 1889 the complete breakdown of the surveyor general system was apparent. A backlog of 116 grants awaited Congressional action, while Congress had not confirmed any grants since early in 1879. The confirmation of the Maxwell and Sangre de Cristo grants had caused considerable embarrassment, both because the size of these grants was far in excess of the maximum provided under Mexican law and because fraud had been committed in their survey.[133] Most surveyors general had recommended that further legislation be passed to provide for the adjudication of New Mexico land grants before a commission or judicial tribunal,[134] but it was not until 3 March 1891 that a law establishing a five-judge Court of Private Land Claims was signed by President Benjamin Harrison.[135] As early as 1879, bills similar to the 1891 Act had passed the Senate but had foundered in disagreements between the Senate and the House over the proper method of adjudicating land grant claims under the Treaty of Guadalupe Hidalgo.[136]

The statute setting up the Court of Private Land Claims was not in itself a radical departure from the procedure followed in California to adjudicate land titles there. However, differences in language between the two statutes were used by the courts as a basis for a stricter, more technical approach under the 1891 Act. For one thing, the 1891 Act did not refer to custom as a factor to be considered by the court in making its decisions.[137] Additionally the Act provided that every condition of a grant must be shown to have been performed within the time allowed[138] and that only a grant "lawfully and regularly derived from the Government of Spain or Mexico" was entitled to be confirmed.[139]

It appears from the debate in Congress over the predecessors to the 1891 Act that some congressmen saw the law which led to the establishment of the Court of Private Land Claims as an overreaction to the abuses of the surveyor general system. In the debate, Senator Plumb remarked that "[the bill] is an illustration of the operation of certain mental characteristics which having been aroused upon a suggestion of fraud about to be committed, the result is an immediate loss of balance and a swinging to the farthest point on the other side, irrespective of the consequences."[140] This would be an accurate assessment of the effect of the claims court, but the cause of the swing is to be found more in the procedure followed under the 1891 Act, in the adversarial climate of the Court of Private Land Claims and the judicial climate of the Supreme Court, than in the statute itself. One effect of this movement toward a conservative approach to land grant adjudication was that the grants most deserving of confirmation were caught in the crunch, since many of the large speculative grants had already been confirmed.

The procedure before the Court of Private Land Claims heavily favored the government and resulted in numerous unjust decisions. As under the surveyor general system, the claimant before the claims court had the burden of proving the existence of the grant and the performance of all its conditions. Previously, however, the claimant was aided by certain presumptions which eased that burden of proof, such as the presumption of the existence of a community grant from the existence of a settlement on the grant in 1846, the presumption of the regularity of the grant, and the presumption of the authority of the granting official. Under the Court of Private Land Claims, these presumptions were eliminated.

Surveyor General Julian seems to have been responsible for the elimination of the first two presumptions during his overzealous crusade. The third, the presumption of the authority of the granting official, was established in 1832 by the U.S. Supreme Court in the *Arredondo* case.[141] This presumption was followed until it was eliminated in 1898 by the U.S. Supreme Court on appeal from the Court of Private Land Claims in the case of *Hayes v. United States.*[142] Some background will help in understanding the *Hayes* case.

As previously mentioned, it was the governor who made most land grants in New Mexico. But other officials and governing bodies like the lieutenant governor, alcaldes, ayuntamientos, and prefects had all made land grants during the Spanish and Mexican periods.[143] These grants were not invalid when they were made; rather their validity under Spanish and Mexican law depended on custom and on whether the governor knew of the grant and either ratified or revoked it.

All of these lesser officials and governing bodies were involved in the grant-making process, so it was not unreasonable to assume that they might have the power to make land grants under customary practice. In fact, an official of the Mexican government testified before the surveyor general that "the governors, prefects, and alcaldes, in conjunction with the ayuntamientos, had the authority to make grants of land" because it was the custom and usage.[144] Under Spanish and Mexican law, the custom of grant making by lesser officials and governing bodies might give legitimacy to such grants, especially if the grant was ratified by the governor, but if the governor later revoked one of these grants, it would no longer be valid and would not be entitled to confirmation by the Court of Private Land Claims.

As it happened, some of these grants were revoked by the governor. An example is the John Heath grant northwest of El Paso, made by the ayuntamiento of El Paso in 1823. When the grant papers were referred to the governor for approval, he consulted with the provincial deputation and together they decided to revoke the grant, partly because Heath was a foreigner and partly because the grant encroached on the common lands of El Paso. This was one of the cases where the Court of Private Land Claims was correct in rejecting a grant made by an ayuntamiento, not because the ayuntamiento did not have the power to make the grant, but because the grant had been revoked by the Mexican government.[145]

The *Hayes* case involved the Antonio Chávez grant made by a territorial deputation presided over by the governor. Moreover, Governor Bartolomé Baca recommended to the deputation that the grant be made.[146] Nevertheless, the Court of Private Land Claims rejected the grant on the ground that the territorial deputation did not have grant-making power, and the Supreme Court affirmed the decision, repudiating the presumption that the granting officials had the authority to make the grant.[147] From then on, the claims court would require the claimant to produce strict proof of the authority of the granting official, instead of placing the burden on the government to show that the granting official(s) did not have the power to make the grant. It would have made better sense to continue the presumption of the granting official's authority, for the government had the most archival expertise and could have discovered documentary evidence in the archives regarding the authority of a granting official more readily than could the claimant. Nonetheless, after the *Hayes* case, grants made by alcaldes, prefects, and ayuntamientos were usually rejected.[148]

The *Hayes* ruling was even extended to other situations, resulting in the rejection of a valid grant made by the governor in 1725—the Embudo grant. The claims court admitted that the grant was valid; the supposed defect was that, instead of presenting the original grant documents, the claimants submitted a certified copy made by an alcalde some thirty-odd years after the making of the original grant. The court had no doubt that this was a genuine copy, and it was proven that alcaldes customarily made such certified copies when the originals had become worn and torn from repeated handling. However, the government pointed out that under Spanish law the official authorized to make certified copies was the *escribano,* not the alcalde. But there were no escribanos in New Mexico at the time, so the practice of alcaldes making certified copies was legal under customary law.[149] The claims court's rejection of the Embudo grant because of the supposed lack of authority of alcaldes to make certified copies was outrageous.[150]

After the *Hayes* decision, the land grant claimant, carrying the burden of proof, had lost the benefit of the presumptions which had made this burden a little less onerous. Added to this situation was a climate in the Court of Private Land Claims that definitely favored the government.

The experts most familiar with the Spanish and Mexican archives all worked for the government. William (Will) M. Tipton, the government's most valuable expert, had acquired an intimate knowledge of the documents in the archives while working for the surveyor general starting in 1876. Tipton was often used by claimant's lawyers to authenticate documents, illustrating the lack of any similar experts working for the claimants.[151] (In present-day land grant litigation, each side typically has its own historical expert.) Then there was Henry Ossian

Flipper, who had earlier distinguished himself as the first Black cadet to graduate from West Point.[152] He researched and wrote most of the compilation of Spanish and Mexican laws published under the name of the claims court attorney Matthew Givens Reynolds.[153] Amazingly, even though the titular author was the government's chief attorney, Reynolds's book became the primary authority for both the claims court and the U.S Supreme Court on questions of Spanish and Mexican law. Unfortunately for land grant claimants, the compilation contains a bias in favor of the government, for it makes no mention of Spanish laws concerning custom[154] (evidence of custom usually favored the claimant), nor does it mention laws dealing with prescription (acquisition of title to land by continuous possession).[155] When the courts accepted Reynolds's book as the definitive statement of Spanish and Mexican law, they adopted this bias, giving the government still another edge over the claimant. In addition, the government had greater resources than did the claimant. This allowed the U.S. Attorney to hire investigators to go to the land in question and report on the boundaries of the grant and on any weaknesses of the claim, an activity seldom undertaken by claimants' attorneys.[156]

Faced with this formidable team of attorneys and experts, the claimants were often poorly represented. Since they usually did not have the funds to hire experts to research Spanish and Mexican land records or to survey their grant, land grant claimants were wholly dependent on the skill and honesty of the attorney they hired to represent them. An examination of the records of the Court of Private Land Claims shows that often this representation was inadequate, resulting in severe injustice to the claimants.

A case in point is the representation of the Pueblo Quemado grant claimants by Thomas Benton Catron. The claimants did not have any grant documents, but there were numerous references to the grant in the Spanish archives. Additionally, the Cundiyó grant to the south mentioned the Pueblo Quemado grant as its northern boundary. Catron filed a petition for confirmation of the grant in 1893 and then took no action on the case for the next seven years. During this time several grants without documents were confirmed. When the case finally came up for trial in 1900, Catron voluntarily dismissed the petition.[157] Thus the claimants never had their day in court, because Catron, like many other land grant attorneys, treated the representation of these claimants primarily as a business.

Land grant lawyers were often more concerned with their own interests than with their basic duty to pursue their clients' interests with vigor. They usually handled several land grant cases simultaneously, and since their fee was dependent on winning a confirmation, they tended to neglect or concede doubtful cases. At the same time, the government pursued every case assiduously, appealing many on highly technical grounds. As the government won more appeals, new precedents were established in its favor, making more of the claimants' cases doubtful. This resulted in the concession of many cases by claimants' lawyers near the end of the fourteen-year term of the Court of Private Land Claims.[158]

Although the adversarial climate favored the government in Court of Private Land Claims, the decisions of the claims court occasionally displayed a balanced approach that yielded a result favorable to the claimant. But in several instances, when the government appealed these decisions, the Supreme Court reversed, siding with the government and against the claimant. The most famous of these decisions, *U.S. v. Sandoval,*[159] concerned the ownership of the common lands of the San Miguel del Bado grant in San Miguel County. This case illustrates the negative judicial climate of the U.S. Supreme Court concerning land grants.

San Miguel del Bado was a community grant of 315,300 acres, according to a 1879 survey. Prior to United States occupation, seven villages had grown up on the grant in addition to the initial settlement at San Miguel.[160] When the inhabitants of these villages sought confirmation of the grant before the surveyor general, it was first recommended that the entire grant be confirmed. Later the General Land Office commissioner recommended that only the occupied lands on the grant should be confirmed. This would mean the rejection of the common lands—the bulk of the land within the grant. But the Court of Private Land Claims confirmed the entire grant, and the government appealed that decision to the U.S. Supreme Court.[161] This was an important case for the government, for if the common lands of this grant were rejected, hundreds of thousands—perhaps millions—of acres of other community grants not yet adjudicated would belong to the government, not to the land grant heirs.

The Supreme Court reversed the claims court decision, holding that the common lands belonged to the governments of Spain and Mexico when the grant was made and that title to the lands had then passed to the United States in 1848 under the treaty. It appears that the Supreme Court was in error on this point of Spanish and Mexican law,[162] but the Court of Private Land Claims was forced to confirm only the allotted lands of the grant, determined to be only 5,207 acres.[163]

After the 1897 *Sandoval* decision, the claims court rejected the common lands of every community grant that came up for adjudication. This vast acreage acquired by the United States now comprises most of the Carson and Santa Fe National Forests in northern New Mexico. The Court of Private Land Claims did, however, refuse to apply the *Sandoval* decision retroactively, so community grants confirmed before the *Sandoval* decision were able to retain their common lands.[164]

Several other technical grounds were used by the Supreme Court and by the Court of Private Land Claims to reject perfectly valid grants. These included requirements that the grant be recorded in the archives,[165] that the grant be approved by the territorial deputation if made during the Mexican Period,[166] and that there be strict compliance with each of the procedural steps of the grant: the petition, the grant, and the act of possession.[167]

However, these technical reasons were seldom if ever the basis for a land grant rejection by Spain or Mexico. The Mexican government specifically decided that failure to record a grant in the archives did not make it invalid.[168] One situation in which Spanish or Mexican officials did reject a grant due to a procedural defect was where notice to adjacent landowners (allowing them the opportunity to object to the grant) had not been given. But United States courts rarely looked to see how the Spanish and Mexican governments had treated land grants in New Mexico, despite the availability of cases in the archives involving land grant disputes.

There were several reasons which did justify the rejection of grants by Spanish and Mexican authorities. These included: (1) forgery of the documents,[170] (2) insufficient proof that a grant was made,[171] (3) failure to notify owners of land adjoining the grant,[172] (4) failure to meet a condition of the grant,[173] (5) revocation of the grant by Spanish or Mexican officials,[174] and (6) failure to settle the land within four years after the making of the grant and continuous possession thereafter.[175] These were grounds that would clearly justify United States courts in rejecting grants.

Under international law, United States courts should have adjudicated land grants in the same manner as Spain and Mexico would have done.[176] But instead of examining these questions in depth, the courts often found it more expedient to refer to an unused Spanish or Mexican law as the basis for a decision. We have seen how this was done in the Embudo grant decision, where a Spanish law that did not apply in New Mexico was used to reject the grant. And rather than seek the benefit of expert testimony on questions of Spanish and Mexican law, both the Court of Private Land Claims and the Supreme Court generally relied on Reynolds's compilation of Spanish and Mexican laws.

If Article 10 had been left in the Treaty of Guadalupe Hidalgo, its mandate to confirm all grants to the extent that New Mexico under Spain or Mexico would have confirmed them, might have provided a guide for land grant adjudication. As it was, the claims court followed no consistent principles; both it and the Supreme Court were highly erratic in their land grant decisions. But these courts did render a few well-reasoned decisions. These rarities stand out as beacons of fairness showing how all the cases should have been handled. One such case was *U.S. v. Chaves*.

The *Chaves* case involved a community grant made to the town of Cubero in present-day Valencia County in 1833. The Court of Private Land Claims confirmed the grant, though the claimants had no grant documents at all. The government appealed and the Supreme Court affirmed in a cogent opinion by Justice Shiras. The justice must have done a great deal of independent research, because there was no brief or court appearance on behalf of the claimants to aid him. Forced to do his own investigation, Justice Shiras examined many important questions addressed by few other cases.

The government's position, under its restrictive interpretation of the 1891 Act, was that the grant could not be confirmed since it lacked grant documents. Justice Shiras's opinion begins with an examination of the relevant rules. First he refers to the early Marshall decisions under the Florida treaty that had set a liberal tone for land grant adjudication. He then covers the rules of international law and the terms of the Treaty of Guadalupe Hidalgo, factors seldom mentioned in other decisions. Justice Shiras concludes that Congress did not intend to restrict the powers of the Court of Private Land Claims, and proceeds to discuss the facts of the case. He summarizes the testimony of several witnesses who had lived in the town of Cubero for varying periods from the time the grant was made in 1833. Many of these witnesses saw the original grant documents. Documents concerning a dispute between the town of Cubero and the Pueblo of Laguna are cited as evidence of a grant to the town of Cubero. But most important is the undisputed testimony that the claimants were in possession of the land since 1833. It was primarily on the basis of this evidence of possession that the lower court's decision confirming the grant was affirmed.[177]

Although the *Chaves* decision was in accord with the Spanish and Mexican law of prescription (gaining title by continous possession), it was rarely followed in other cases.[178] If there had been more Supreme Court decisions like *Chaves,* the six percent confirmation record of the Court of Private Land Claims would have been considerably higher. Matthew Reynolds was one of the attorneys who argued the *Chaves* case before the Supreme Court. He was in the habit of appealing almost every case the government lost, but after the *Chaves* decision he moderated this stance for a period. In a similar case involving the Doña Ana Bend Colony grant he recommended that a previously authorized appeal be dismissed. Reynolds apparently believed, after reading the *Chaves* opinion, that the Supreme Court was likely to overrule his admittedly technical objection to the Doña Ana Bend grant because of the long and continuous possession of that land by the claimants.[179] A few more Supreme Court opinions like *Chaves* would probably have caused fewer government appeals and more liberal opinions by the Court of Private Land Claims.

It seems apparent that the courts and Congress did not effectively discharge the obligations assumed by the United States under the Treaty of Guadalupe Hidalgo. They should have adopted a clear and consistent standard to use in judging the validity of Spanish and Mexican land grants, one that would have provided for rejection of grants only in cases where Spain or Mexico would have rejected the grant.

Because no such comprehensive standard was followed by United States courts in their adjudication of Spanish and Mexican land grants, property rights were not adequately protected. Thus the perception of injustice by many land grant heirs is largely justified. A few scholars have labeled the work of the Court of Private Land Claims as relatively fair,[180] but such a conclusion is not justified by the facts. This judgment seems to have been reached mostly through a face-value acceptance of the courts' reasoning without an independent in-depth analysis of specific land grants. Others have suggested that the Court of Private Land Claims should be judged by the more lax standards of its time.[181]

One thing is clear: Hispanic people have not been treated fairly in relation to the land grant issue. But the causes of this unfairness are not as clear. No one individual or group of individuals is to blame—not Matthew Reynolds, nor Thomas Catron, nor Henry Atkinson, nor even the Santa Fe Ring. They all played a part in the chicanery of land grant adjudication, but the drama was allowed to proceed by the United States government.

Some scholars have suggested steps the government can presently take to finally solve the problem.[182] The first step is to acknowledge the error of earlier court decisions. The U.S. Supreme Court has been wrong before. In 1896, a year before it decided the *Sandoval* case, the Supreme Court upheld racial segregation in the schools in *Plessy v. Ferguson.*[183] Now that decision has been overruled.

The basic injustices of land grant adjudication will not be simply forgotten. It is more likely that the controversies will continue to surface. (See the chapters by Hall, Rosenbaum and Larson, and Rodríguez.) New Mexico is a primarily rural state with many people still living close to the land. To many Hispanic residents, the land grant story is not simply a fading part of New Mexico's history. Rather, it is the story of their own families, going back many generations. And it is the story of a passionate and continuing struggle for the land their ancestors were promised when they became citizens of the United States in 1848. May that promise someday be kept.

Notes

*The author wishes to thank historians William B. Taylor and Daniel Tyler for reading portions of this chapter.

1. Javier Malagón-Barceló, "The Role of the Letrado in the Colonization of America," *The Americas* 18 (1961–1962): 1–17; E. N. Van Kleffens, *Hispanic Law Until the End of the Middle Ages* (Edinburgh: Edinburgh University Press, 1968).

2. J. H. Parry, *The Spanish Theory of Empire in the Sixteenth Century* (Cambridge, 1940), p. 2.

3. Van Kleffens, *Hispanic Law,* p. 34, 36–40.

4. Gustavus Schmidt, *The Civil Law of Spain and Mexico* (New Orleans, 1851), p. 15.

5. Richard L. Kagan, *Lawsuits and Litigants in Castile: 1500–1700* (Chapel Hill: Universtiy of North Carolina Press, 1981), p. 23; Colin M. MacLachlan,

Criminal Justice in Eighteenth Century Mexico (Berkeley: University of California Press, 1974), pp. 4–5 and Schmidt, *Civil Law,* p. 22, Note 8.

6. MacLachlan, *Criminal Justice,* p. 5.

7. Betty Eakle Dobkins, *The Spanish Element in Texas Water Law* (Austin: University of Texas Press, 1959), p. 69; Roque Bárcia, *Primer Diccionario General Etimológico de la Lengua Española* (Madrid: Establecimiento Tipográfico de Álvarez Hermanos, 1883), p. 632 (zanja).

8. Dobkins, *Texas Water Law,* p. 71.

9. David E. Vassberg, "The *Tierras Baldias:* Community Property and Public Lands in 16th Century Castille," p. 391.

10. J. M. Ots Capdequi, *España en América: El Régimen de Tierras en la Epoca Colonial* (México: Fondo de Cultura Económica, 1959), p. 50.

11. J. Richard Salazar, "Nuestra Señora del Rosario, San Fernando y Santiago del Rio de las Truchas: A Brief History," p. 8; and Spanish Archives of New Mexico, Vol. I (SANM I), State Records Center and Archives, Santa Fe, No. 771, the Truchas grant.

12. New Mexico Land Grants-Private Land Claims (NMLG-PLC), Case 107, reel 45, frames 9 and 14, the San Joaquin grant.

13. Elizabeth A. H. John, *Storms Brewed in Other Men's Worlds: The Confrontation of Indians, Spanish and French in the Southwest 1540–1795* (College Station: Texas A&M University Press, 1975), p. 9.

14. G. Michael Riley, *Fernando Cortes and the Marquesado in Morelos, 1522–1547* (Albuquerque: University of New Mexico, 1973), pp. 19–20.

15. John, *Other Men's Worlds,* pp. 9–10.

16. *Recopilación de las Leyes de los Reynos de las Indias,* third edition (Madrid, 1774), Preface and Book 2, title 1, law 1.

17. *Recopilación,* Book 2, title 1, law 2.

18. Weights and measures varied considerably throughout Spain and New Spain. The basic measurement—the vara—was for a long time the length of a specific staff kept in the town of Burgos to which all varas were supposed to correspond. The vara of Burgos measured 32.99 inches. Early Spanish kings and later the Mexican government tried to make the vara an even three feet, but the standard vara remained about 33 inches. Manuel Carrera Stampa, "The Evolution of Weights and Measures in New Spain," *The Hispanic American Historical Review* (*HAHR*) 29 (February 1949): 2–24; Mexican Colonization Law of 1823, Spanish Archives of New Mexico (SANM) Vol. 1, No. 1107.

19. François Chevalier, *Land and Society in Colonial Mexico: The Great Hacienda* (Berkeley, 1963), p. 54. Two of New Mexico land grants where the settlers were required to have firearms within two years of the making of the grant were the Arroyo Hondo (NMLG-SG, Reel 29, report 159, frame 44 *et seq.*) made in 1815 and the Rancho del Rio Grande grant (NMGL-SG, Reel 19, report 58, frame 2 *et seq.*) made in 1795.

20. Some of the regional studies that examine private and community landholdings of both the Spanish and the Indian populations as well as encomiendas are: William B. Taylor, *Landlord and Peasant in Colonial Oaxaca* (Stanford: Stanford University Press, 1972); José Cuello, "Saltillo in the Sev-

enteenth Century: Local Society on the North Mexican Frontier" (Ph.D. diss., University of California, Berkeley, 1981); Elinore Magee Barrett, "Land Tenure and Settlement in the Tepalcatepec Lowland, Michoacán, Mexico" (Ph.D. diss., University of California, Berkeley, 1970). For land measurements, see Thomas C. Barnes, Thomas H. Naylor, and Charles W. Polzer, *Northern New Spain: A Research Guide* (Tucson, 1981), p. 69. Also see Mariano Galván-Rivera, *Ordananzas de Tierras y Aguas* . . . published as a supplement to Joaquin Escriche's *Diccionario Razonado de Legislacion y Jurisprudencia* (Paris: Rosa y Bouret, [1863]), pp. 202–4.

21. Chevalier, *Land and Society,* pp. 134–39. Case histories of the expansion of the twelve haciendas in the Valley of Saltillo are found in Cuello, "Saltillo in the Seventeenth Century," pp. 112–35.

22. Chevalier, *Land and Society,* p. 142. The Aztec land tenure system at the time of the arrival of Cortés is described in Chevalier at pp. 16–23 and in George McCutchen McBride, *The Land Systems of Mexico* (1923; reprint ed., New York: Octagon Books, 1971), pp. 112–23.

23. William H. Dusenberry, *The Mexican Mesta: The Administration of Ranching in Colonial Mexico* (Urbana: University of Illinois Press, 1963), pp. 90–96.

24. Lesley Byrd Simpson, *Exploitation of Land in Central Mexico in the Sixteenth Century* (Berkeley and Los Angeles: University of California Press, 1952).

25. Vassberg, "The *Tierras Baldias,*" pp. 386–88; Barrett, "Land Tenure in Michoacán," p. 120; and Hall, *The Four Leagues of Pecos* (Albuquerque: University of New Mexico Press, 1984), pp. 167–68.

26. For example, Captain Juan Martínez de Montoya, who was named as interim governor when Oñate resigned, was granted one of the Jemez Pueblos in encomienda for three generations in 1606. "Conquistador of New Mexico," *New Mexico Historical Review* (*NMHR*) 19 (1944): 340. David H. Snow lists the known encomenderos together with their encomiendas in "A Note on Encomienda Economics in Seventeenth-Century New Mexico," in Marta Weigle et al. (ed.) *Hispanic Arts and Ethno History in the Southwest* (Santa Fe: Ancient City Press, 1983), pp. 354–56.

27. Snow argues that encomienda tribute was not initially an onerous burden but that it gradually became so. Ibid., pp. 353–54. Marc Simmons (ed. and trans.), *Father Juan Agustín de Morfi's Account of the Disorders in New Mexico* (Santa Fe, 1977), pp. 26–29. France V. Scholes, "Troublous Times in New Mexico," *NMHR* 12 (1937): 388.

28. France V. Scholes, "Civil Government and Society in New Mexico in the Seventeenth Century," *NMHR* 10 (April 1935): 105.

29. Although Vargas received a large encomienda grant as a reward for recolonizing New Mexico, the grant was never put into operation but was converted to money payments by his heirs. Lansing B. Bloom, "The Vargas Encomienda," *NMHR* 14 (October 1939): 371–72, 413.

30. Oakah L. Jones, Jr., "Pueblo Indian Auxiliaries and the Spanish Defense of New Mexico, 1692–1794" (Ph.D. diss., University of Oklahoma,

1964). Another reason for improved defense was the formation of presidial garrisons whose soldiers were paid from the royal treasury. The Santa Fe presidio, established in 1693, was supposed to be made up of eighty men according to the Reglamento of 1772, but was comprised of 120 men in 1783. Max L. Moorhead, *The Presidio: Bastion of the Spanish Borderlands* (Norman: University of Oklahoma Press, 1975), pp. 66 and 92. Max L. Moorhead, "Rebuilding the Presidio of Santa Fe, 1789–1791," *NMHR* 49 (April 1974): 124.

31. Marc Simmons, "Settlement Patterns and Village Plans in Colonial New Mexico," *Journal of the West* 8 (January 1969): 10–13; Simmons, "Disorders in New Mexico," pp. 11–14.

32. The royal cedula appointing Domingo de Cruzate governor of New Mexico in 1684 contains the first record of written authority to make land grants. White et al. and The New Mexico State Planning Office, *Land Title Study* (Santa Fe: State Planning Office, 1971), p. 10. A translation of this cedula is found at pp. 217–18. For a list of grants made in New Mexico by alcaldes and prefects, see note 43.

33. The first mention of a land grant to a Spaniard which I have found is the Cerrillos grant made to Ensign Alonzo Rael de Aguilar by Governor Vargas in 1692. SANM I, No. 14.

34. A reference to the provision for regranting lands occupied before the Pueblo Revolt is found in decree of Juan Páez Hurtado, Santa Fe, 10 March 1713, SANM I, No. 491. See also, petition of Maria and Juana Griego to Governor Diego de Vargas, Santa Fe, 2 December 1703, SANM I, No. 294.

35. Francisco de la Maza, *Código de colonización y terrenos baldíos . . . publicado según acuerdo del Presidente de la República, 1541–1892* (México, 1893), pp. 237–40. For a translation see, Frederic Hall, *The Laws of Mexico* (San Francisco, 1885), pp. 150–53.

36. The main difference between the regulation of 1828 and prior custom was the provision in Article 1 which authorized grants to foreigners. During the Spanish colonial period, foreigners were generally not welcome in New Mexico. Marc Simmons, *New Mexico: A Bicentennial History* (New York and Nashville, 1977), pp. 80–81 and 97–100.

37. See, for example, the Report of the ayuntamiento of Abiquiu concerning the Tierra Amarilla grant, New Mexico Land Grants-Surveyor General (NMLG-SG), Reel 12, report 3, frame 16 transcribed and translated in Ebright, *The Tierra Amarilla Grant,* p. 34.

38. Governor Bartolome Baca made the report in the case of the Antonio Chávez and Tecolote grants. SANM I, No. 218 (Antonio Chávez); Governor Baca to the *diputación,* Santa Fe, November 19, 1824, SANM I, No. 1009 (Tecolote).

39. The Picuris Indians were not given an opportunity to object to the Embudo grant until the delivery of possession. Malcolm Ebright, "The Embudo Grant: A Case Study of Justice and the Court of Private Land Claims," *Journal of the West* 19 (July 1980): 74. When the Jacona grant was made to

Ignacio Roybal in 1702, no opportunity was given to the adjacent San Ildefonso Pueblo to object to the grant. NMLG-PLC, Reel 36, case 35, frames 6–7.

40. The Picuris Indians objected to the Embudo grant and Alcalde Miguel José de la Vega y Coca settled the dispute, in favor of the Spanish, at the time of the delivery of possession. Ebright, "The Embudo Grant," p. 74.

41. Elizabeth Nelson Patrick, "Land Grants During the Administration of Spanish Colonial Governor Pedro Fermín Mendinueta," *NMHR* 51 (January 1976): 11–12. A grant in which a rudimentary survey was performed, with distances measured along the boundaries, is the Guadalupe Miranda grant made by the governor of the state of Chihuahua in 1851. J. J. Bowden, *Spanish and Mexican Land Grants in the Chihuahuan Acquistion* (El Paso, 1971), p. 6.

42. Such an argument occurred in 1818 when Juan de Aguilar complained to Governor Facundo Melgares about the measurement of the Pecos league. Aguilar, whose land was found to have been within the league, said that a fifty-vara cordel should have been used instead of a one-hundred-vara cordel. Alcalde Vicente Villanueva said that use of the shorter cordel would be prejudicial to the Indians because of the broken and irregular character of the ground. There is no record of how this dispute was settled. SANM I, No. 56; G. Emlen Hall, *Four Leagues of Pecos* (Albuquerque, 1984), pp. 26–29.

43. During the Mexican Period the grantees would shout "Long live the president and the Mexican nation." I have used the masculine singular in reference to recipients of land grants for simplicity although grants were often made to groups rather than individuals and were sometimes made to women. An example of a grant made to a woman is the Gijosa grant made in 1715 to Francisca Antonia de Gijosa. Bowden, "Private Land Claims," 4: 972–73, Myra Ellen Jenkins, "Some Eighteenth-Century New Mexico Women of Property," in *Hispanic Arts and Ethnohistory,* pp. 335–45.

44. Ebright, "The Embudo Grant," pp. 77–81.

45. The legal basis for the community grant is found in the *Recopilación,* Libro IV, titulo 5, ley 7. The adjudication of the Tierra Amarilla grant provides an example of the importance of the distinction between a private and a community grant. Malcolm Ebright, *The Tierra Amarilla Grant: A History of Chicanery* (Santa Fe: The Center for Land Grant Studies, 1980), *passim.*

46. Mariano Galván-Rivera, *Ordenanzas de Tierras y Aguas . . . y Vigentes Hasta el Dia en la Republica Mejicana,* published as a supplement to Joaquin Escriche's *Diccionario Razonado de Legislacion y Jurisprudencia* [Paris, (1863)], p. 166, Section 19. Mesilla Colony Grant, NMLG-SG, Reel 21, report 162, frame 2 (reference courtesy Daniel Tyler).

47. See, for example, the Arroyo Hondo grant, New Mexico Land Grants-Surveyor General (NMLG-SG), State Records Center and Archives, Santa Fe, Reel 29, report 159, frames 44–45.

48. The minimum four-year possession period is found in *Recopilación,* Book 4, title 12, law 1.

49. Galván, *Tierras y Aguas,* p. 166, Section 19; p. 187, Capitulo 6.

50. Patrick, "Land Grants of Governor Mendinuetta," pp. 10–11. See

also, Governor Vélez Cachupín's detailed instructions concerning the building of Truchas when that grant was made in 1754, in Richard Salazar, "Nuestra Señora del Rosario, San Fernando y Santiago del Rio de las Truchas: A Brief History" (Paper presented at the Annual Meeting of the Western Social Science Association, Albuquerque, April 1980).

51. Provisions for laying out of Spanish municipalities are found in the *Recopilación,* Libro IV, titulo 7, ley 7. See also, Simmons, "Settlement Patterns," pp. 12–13.

52. Benjamin M. Read, *Illustrated History of New Mexico* (1912; reprint ed. New York, 1976), p. 315; Marc Simmons, "Governor Cuervo and the Beginnings of Albuquerque: Another Look," *NMHR* 55 (July 1980): 189–207.

53. The 1790 census for Santa Fe lists a total of 130 artisans out of a total population of 4,346 for the villa. Among the occupations listed are *zapatero* (shoemaker), *sastre* (tailor), *tornalero* (woodworker), *herrero* (blacksmith), *tejedor* (weaver), and *albañil* (mason). Janie Louise Aragon, "The People of Santa Fe in the 1790s," *Atzlan* 7 (Fall 1976): 392, 404.

54. Complaints by Pojoque Pueblo against Captain Antonio de Salas for crop damage ca. 1660, Scholes, "Troublous Times," p. 389. See also SANM II, No. 361 for a complaint in 1731 by Taos Pueblo against Sebastian Martin, Baltazar Romero, and others, for crop damage.

55. Order of Governor Francisco Cuervo y Valdez, Santa Fe, 25 April 1705, SANM I, No. 1251; order of Lieutenant Governor Juan Páez Hurtado, Santa Fe, 27 March 1717.

56. For Ojo Caliente, see E. Boyd, "Troubles at Ojo Caliente: A Frontier Post," *El Palacio* 64 (November–December 1957): 347; for Abiquiu, see J. Richard Salazar, "Santa Rosa de Lima de Abiquiu," *New Mexico Architecture* 18 (September–October 1976): 16; Las Trampas, SANM I, No. 975; Ranchos de Taos, Declaration of Fray Miguel Menchero, Santa Bárbara, May 10, 1744, in Charles Wilson Hackett, *Historical Documents Relating to New Mexico, Nueva Vizcaya, and Approaches Thereto, to 1773* (Washington, D.C.: Carnegie Institution of Washington, 1937), p. 400; Tomé, Frank D. Reeve, *History of New Mexico* (New York: Lewis Historical Publishing Company, Inc., 1961), vol. 1, p. 319; Valencia, Marc Simmons, *Albuquerque, A Narrative History* (Albuquerque: University of New Mexico Press, 1982), p. 104; Belen, SANM I, No. 113.

57. Boyd, "Troubles at Ojo Caliente," pp. 347–60.

58. Jack August, "Balance of Power Diplomacy in New Mexico: Governor Fernando de la Concha and the Indian Policy of Conciliation," *NMHR* 56 (April 1981): 141–60. For the increase in the Taos Valley population see Adams and Chavez, *Missions of New Mexico,* pp. 112–13 for 1776 and SANM II, Reel 21, frame 545 for the 1796 census.

59. For a general survey of early population expansion, see Reeve, *History of New Mexico,* vol. 1, pp. 311–32.

60. David J. Weber, *The Mexican Frontier, 1821–1846* (Albuquerque: University of New Mexico Press, 1982), pp. 125–33. A good study of Anglo-

Hispano intermarriage is Rebecca McDowell Craver, *The Impact of Intimacy: Mexican-Anglo Intermarriage in New Mexico, 1821–1846* (El Paso: Texas Western Press, 1982). Land grants are dealt with at pp. 31–36.

61. Lawrence R. Murphy, "The Beaubien and Miranda Land Grant, 1841–1846," *NMHR* 42 (January 1967): 29–32. Marianne L. Stoller, "Grants of Desperation, Lands of Speculation: Mexican Period Land Grants in Colorado," *Journal of the West* 19 (July 1980): 26; Harold H. Dunham, "New Mexico Land Grants with Special Reference to the Title Papers of the Maxwell Grant," *NMHR* 30 (January 1955): 5; Bowden, "Private Land Claims," 4: 850, 885.

62. For an example of a lawsuit in which custom is referred to as the basis of decision, see Malcolm Ebright, "Manuel Martínez's Ditch Dispute: A Study in Mexican Period Custom and Justice," *NMHR* 54 (January 1979): 30.

63. Ebright, "Ditch Dispute," pp. 30–31.

64. Luis Maria Cabesa de Baca received what was later to become the Las Vegas grant in 1821, but was not placed in possession until at least 1825 due to the delaying and obstructionist tactics of local alcaldes. Statement of Tomás Sena, Santa Fe, January 13, 1826 and Juan Antonio Cabesa de Baca to Governor Antonio Narbona, NMLG-SG, Reel 15, files 6 and 12, frames 44 and 30–31.

65. Few decisions were appealed to the Supreme Court in Mexico City. When in 1830 such an appeal was made, the Mexican high court refused to get involved, stating that the litigation should be resolved by the local authorities. SANM I, No. 1369.

66. Kearny's proclamation to the people of New Mexico delivered at Las Vegas on 15 August 1846 is reproduced in David J. Weber, *Foreigners in Their Native Land* (Albuquerque: University of New Mexico Press, 1973), pp. 161–62. Similar addresses were delivered at the Santa Fe plaza on August 19 and 22, according to Weber.

67. Nicolas Trist was appointed Commissioner of the United States to the Mexican Republic on 15 April 1847 and on that date was given written instructions together with a draft treaty. For a copy of these instructions and the draft treaty see Hunter Miller (ed.), *Treaties and Other International Acts of the United States of America,* vol. 5 (Washington: Government Printing Office, 1937), pp. 262–67. The appointment of the Mexican commissioners was provided for in an armistice dated 24 August 1847. The Mexican commissioners were General José Joaquin de Herrera, José Bernardo Couto, Brigadier General Ignacio de Mora y Villamil, and Miguel Atristain. Miller, *Treaties,* vol. 5 (1937), pp. 279–80.

68. The instructions to the Mexican commissioners and the Mexican draft treaty are found in Miller, *Treaties,* vol. 5 (1937), pp. 299–302. Article 9 of this draft treaty deals with land grants. Another Mexican draft treaty was presented to Trist on 9 January 1848 containing in its Article 11 a similar proposed land grant guarantee; its text is in Miller, *Treaties,* vol. 5 (1937), pp. 309–13. Trist's rejection of this article and his drafting of a substitute is chronicled in Geoffrey P. Mawn, "A Land-Grant Guarantee: The Treaty of

Guadalupe Hidalgo or the Protocol of Queretaro?" *Journal of the West* 14 (October 1975): 52–53. Mawn includes the English text of Article 10 with the source of each portion at p. 53.

69. Luis G. Zorrilla, *Historia de las relaciones entre México y Los Estados Unidos de America, 1800–1958,* 2 vols. (Mexico: 1965), 1: 218, quoted in Weber, *Foreigners,* p. 141.

70. The phrase "manifest destiny" was coined by journalist John L. O'Sullivan who wrote in the New York Morning News for 27 December 1845 that "our manifest destiny is to overspread and possess the whole continent which Providence has given us for the development of the great experiment of liberty." Quoted in Frederick Merk, *Manifest Destiny and Mission in American History, a Reinterpretation* (New York, 1963), pp. 31–32. This book provides an excellent discussion of the effect of American journalism of this period on public opinion in the United States. For a study of Mexican attitudes toward the United States during the two decades prior to the war, see Gene M. Brack, *Mexico Views Manifest Destiny, 1821–1846* (Albuquerque: University of New Mexico Press, 1975).

71. Buchanan to Trist, 25 October 1847 in Miller, *Treaties,* vol. 5, p. 292. The Mexican commissioners were told on 22 January 1848 that further military occupation of Mexico would take place unless a treaty of peace was signed. Miller, *Treaties,* vol. 5, p. 314.

72. For a discussion of the instruction to Trist recalling him from his mission and of Trist's decision to remain in Mexico, see Miller, *Treaties,* vol. 5, pp. 289–93, 296–97. For a review of the Senate proceedings leading to ratification, including President Polk's message to the Senate, see Miller, *Treaties,* vol. 5, pp. 246–53. A brief discussion of the reasons for the deletion of Article 10 is in Mawn, "Land-Grant Guarantee," p. 54. Secretary of State Buchanan's note to the Mexican Minister of Foreign Relations, dated 18 March 1848, explaining the Senate amendments is in Miller, *Treaties,* vol. 5, pp. 253–57.

73. There was a precedent for revising rather than entirely deleting a treaty article in the treatment of Article 9; it was revised to eliminate certain objectionable parts while keeping other satisfactory portions with slight revisions. Buchanan's explanation to the Mexican government of the revision of Article 9 is in Miller, *Treaties,* vol. 5, pp. 254–55. Weber's *Foreigners* includes the text of Article 9 prior to amendment and as ratified, with comments on the reasons for the changes at pp. 162–68.

74. For the text of the Protocol in English and Spanish together with some of the extensive diplomatic correspondence concerning its validity, see Miller, *Treaties,* vol. 5, pp. 380–406. Miller includes excerpts from the Mexican and U.S. instruments of ratification at pp. 257–59.

75. Miller, *Treaties,* vol. 5, p. 401. Mawn discusses the political and diplomatic questions raised by the Protocol in his "Land-Grant Guarantee," pp. 59–60.

76. Louisiana Purchase, Treaty of Paris, April 30, 1803, Miller, *Treaties,* vol. 2 (1931), pp. 298–505.

77. Florida Purchase, Treaty of February 22, 1819, Miller, *Treaties,* vol. 3 (1933), pp. 3–64.

78. Most claims in Louisiana were confirmed by an Act of Congress that relinquished title to them, see Bowden, "Private Land Claims," 1: 106–18; adjudication of claims in the Florida Purchase is discussed in Bowden, "Private Land Claims," 1: 118–34.

79. Bowden, "Private Land Claims," 1: 155, note 135.

80. Miller, *Treaties,* vol. 3, p. 10.

81. *Foster v. Nelson,* 27 U.S. 253 (1829).

82. *United States v. Percheman,* 32 U.S. 50 (1833).

83. Two articles that deal with land grant adjudication in California from the point of view of the squatters rather than the land grant claimants are Paul W. Gates, "Adjudication of Spanish-Mexican Land Claims in California," *The Huntington Library Quarterly,* 3 (May 1958): 213 and Gates, "California's Embattled Settlers," *California Historical Society Quarterly,* 41 (1962): 99. For more balanced accounts of California land grant adjudication, see Bowden, "Private Land Claims," 1: 148–64 and William W. Morrow, *Spanish and Mexican Private Land Grants* (San Francisco and Los Angeles: Bancroft-Whitney Company, 1923).

84. Report of William Carey Jones, S. Exec. Doc. No. 18, 31st Cong., 2nd Sess., pp. 1–136 (1851).

85. Report of William Carey Jones, quoted in Bowden, "Private Land Claims," 1: 155.

86. Senator Thomas Hart Benton made this argument in Congress, Cong. Globe, 30th Cong., 2nd Sess., 237–54 (1849) cited in Bowden, "Private Land Claims," 1: 149. See also, John Currey, "Treaty of Guadalupe Hidalgo and Private Land Claims," in Shuck, *History of the Bench and Bar of California* (1901), pp. 57–71.

87. Miller, *Treaties,* vol. 5, pp. 217–18.

88. Bowden, "Private Land Claims," 1: 161–62.

89. *Leese v. Clark,* 20 Cal. 387 (1862).

90. *Botiller v. Dominguez,* 74 Cal. 457 (1887).

91. *Botiller v. Dominguez,* 130 U.S. 238 (1888).

92. *U.S. v. Sutherland,* 60 U.S. 363, 365 (1856).

93. *U.S. v. Auguisola,* 68 U.S. 352, 358 (1863).

94. Bowden, "Private Land Claims," 1: 162–63; Morrow, *Spanish and Mexican Grants,* pp. 14–15.

95. Between 22 December 1858 and 28 January 1879, Congress confirmed 8,636,673 acres of land in 46 grants. Grants not acted upon by Congress under the surveyor general system could be resubmitted to the Court of Private Land Claims. The Court of Private Land Claims confirmed 1,934,986 of the 34,653,340 acres submitted to it. The resulting 6 percent confirmation percentage for the claims court and the 24 percent for the claims court and the surveyor general is somewhat distorted by the inclusion of the notoriously fraudulent Peralta-Reavis grant (12,467,456 acres) which was rejected by the Court of Private Land Claims. If that acreage is subtracted from the total

acreage claimed, the confirmation percentages become 34 percent overall and 8 percent for the Court of Private Land Claims. For a list of the grants confirmed by Congress and for those grants submitted to the claims court, see White et al., and State Planning Office, *Land Title Study,* pp. 222–23, 228–34.

96. White et al. and State Planning Office, *Land Title Study,* p. 30. For a discussion of the public land survey system, see Land Title Study, pp. 94–96.

97. Victor Westphall, *The Public Domain in New Mexico: 1854–1891* (Albuquerque: University of New Mexico Press, 1965), discusses the Homestead Act of 1862, as well as the Donation Act of 1854, the Timber Culture Law of 1873, and the Desert Land Act of 1877, in chapters 3, 4, 6, and 7.

98. White et al., and State Planning Office, *Land Title Study,* pp. 30 and 70.

99. Westphall, *The Public Domain,* p. 19 and Victor Westphall, *Thomas Benton Catron and His Era* (Tucson: University of Arizona Press, 1973), p. 160.

100. On 18 January 1855 Surveyor General Pelham issued a notice to the inhabitants of New Mexico claiming land under the Treaty of Guadalupe Hidalgo to submit their claims as soon as possible. By the end of September only fifteen claims had been filed. Bowden, "Private Land Claims," pp. 182–83.

101. "An Act to Establish the Surveyor General of New Mexico . . ." 22 July 1854. Chap. 103, 10 Stat. 308 (1854), Section 8.

102. Bowden, "Private Land Claims," pp. 176–84.

103. *American Jurisprudence,* 2nd Edition, 16: 935.

104. The most unfair confirmation under the surveyor general system involved the Tierra Amarilla grant. It was confirmed to one individual as a private grant when it was actually a community land grant. Ebright, *The Tierra Amarilla Grant, passim.* Due process requirements are discussed at p. 20.

105. For histories of the Las Animas and Rio Don Carlos grants, see Bowden, "Private Land Claims," 6: 1794–1809.

106. *Tameling v. U.S. Freehold & Emigration Co.,* 93 U.S. 644 (1874).

107. The Juan José Lobato grant overlapped at least thirteen other grants, all but three of which were rejected because the Lovato grant had already been confirmed. Bowden, "Private Land Claims," 4: 1034. Another example is the Mora grant which partially overlapped five other grants, all of which were rejected. Bowden, "Private Land Claims," 4: 810.

108. Annual Report of the Surveyor General, 30 September 1855. H.R. Exec. Doc. No. 1, 34th Cong., 1st Sess., pp. 301–7, cited in Bowden, "Private Land Claims," 1: 183.

109. H.R. Report No. 321, 36th Cong., 1st Sess., pp. 1–2 (1860), cited in Bowden, "Private Land Claims," 1: 200–201.

110. Westphall, *The Public Domain in New Mexico,* pp. 21–32.

111. *Recopilación,* Libro IV, título 3, ley 24.

112. SANM I, No. 899.

113. The rule was established for California land grant adjudication, 9 Statutes 634 (1851), Section 14, and was followed by the surveyor general of New Mexico.

114. Michael J. Rock, "Anton Chico and Its Patent," in *Spanish and Mexican Land Grants in New Mexico and Colorado,* ed. John R. and Christine M. Van Ness, pp. 88–89.

115. Ibid., pp. 90–91.

116. Malcolm Ebright, *The Tierra Amarilla Grant, passim.*

117. Rock, "Anton Chico," p. 91. In the case of the Juan José Lobato grant, George Hill Howard, as attorney for the grant claimants, received one-half of the grant as his fee for getting the grant confirmed. Hutchinson abstract of Lobato grant, pp. 9–10.

118. New Mexico, *Laws* (1875–1876), chap. 3.

119. Michael J. Rock, "Partition," unpublished manuscript, pp. 1–3. Among the grants that were partitioned were Cebolletta, San Cristobal, Santa Barbara, Mora, Sebastián Martín, and Las Trampas.

120. Galván, *Tierras y Aguas,* p. 187.

121. William deBuys, "Fractions of Justice, A Legal and Social History of the Las Trampas Land Grant, New Mexico," *NMHR* 56: 71–97.

122. Howard Roberts Lamar, *The Far Southwest: 1846–1912* (New Haven and London: Yale University Press, 1966), pp. 146–48 and White et al., *Land Title Study,* p. 31.

123. For example, in the 1870s, Catron used Nicolás Pino, the son of land speculator Juan Estevan Pino, to help him acquire his interest in the San Cristobal grant in Santa Fe County. The grant was made to another early Hispanic speculator, Domingo Fernández, together with thirty associates in 1827. Westphall, *Mercedes Reales* (Albuquerque: University of New Mexico Press, 1983), p. 232.

124. Antonio Joseph was of Portuguese descent. Hall, *Four Leagues of Pecos,* p. 128.

125. G. Emlen Hall, "Juan Estevan Pino, 'se los coma': New Mexico Land Speculation in the 1820s," *NMHR* and Em Hall, "Giant Before the Surveyor General: The Land Career of Donaciano Vigil," in *Spanish and Mexican Land Grants in New Mexico and Colorado,* ed. John R. and Christine M. Van Ness, pp. 64–73.

126. Marjorie Bell Chambers, "Technically Sweet Los Alamos: The Development of a Federally Sponsored Scientific Community" (Ph.D. diss., University of New Mexico, 1974), pp. 27–28.

127. Catron spent twenty years acquiring the Tierra Amarilla grant for around $200,000. He was not able to sell it until 1909 at a price of $850,000 of which $495,000 was in cash. Westphall, *Thomas Benton Catron,* pp. 46–60 and Westphall, *Mercedes Reales,* p. 235.

128. For articles by and about Julian, see Julian, "Land Stealing in New Mexico," *North American Review* 145: 20 and R. Hal Williams, "George W. Julian and Land Reform in New Mexico," *Agricultural History* 41: 72.

129. Julian wrote that President Cleveland "asked me if I would accept

the office of Governor or Surveyor General of New Mexico and cooperate with him in breaking up the 'rings' of that Territory." Julian, "Land Stealing," *North American Review* 145: 17.

130. Bowden, "Private Land Claims," 1: 224–25.

131. Julian stated in 1887 that "the Surveyor-General [has] acted upon the principle that Spanish and Mexican grants are to be presumed, and all doubts solved in the interest of the claimant." Julian, "Land Stealing," *North American Review* 145: 18. Julian's policies reversed this approach.

132. Russell B. Rice, San Miguel County Surveyor, to J. N. Lamoreaux, Commissioner, General Land Office, 8 April 1893, cited in Clark S. Knowlton, "The Town of Las Vegas Community Grant: An Anglo-American Coup d'Etat," *Journal of the West* 19: 18.

133. Bowden, "Private Land Claims," 1: 214–16 and 229–30.

134. Bowden, "Private Land Claims," pp. 182–83 and 230.

135. Act of 3 March 1891, 26 Statutes 854.

136. White et al. and State Planning Office, *Land Title Study,* 34–38.

137. The Act establishing the California Commission provided that in deciding on the validity of any claim, the commission "shall be governed by the treaty of Guadalupe Hidalgo, the law of nations, the laws, usages, and customs of the government from which the claim is derived, the principles of equity, and the decisions of the Supreme Court of the United States." Act of March 3, 1851, Chapter 41, 9 Statutes 631–34, Section 11.

138. Section 13, clause 8, 26 Statutes 854.

139. Section 13, clause 1, 26 Statutes 854.

140. 18 Cong. Rec. 2490 (1887), cited in White et al. and State Planning Office, *Land Title Study,* p. 38.

141. *U.S. v. Arredondo,* 31 U.S. 691 (1832).

142. *Hayes v. U.S.,* 170 U.S. 637 (1898).

143. Grants made by alcaldes included: the Cañada de los Mestanos grant, made in 1828 by the Alcalde of Taos and the Guadalupita grant, made in 1837 by the Alcalde of Las Trampas. Bowden, "Private Land Claims," 4: 913 and 4: 824. Grants made by Lieutenant Governor Juan Páez Hurtado were: the Barranca, Manuel García de las Rivas, José Antonio Torres, Juan Estevan García de Noriega, and Antonio de Ulibarrí grants all in Rio Arriba County. Bowden, "Private Land Claims," 4: 1090, 4: 1117, 4: 1130, 4: 1132, and 4: 1134. The San Antonio del Rio Colorado grant was made by the prefect of the first district of the department of New Mexico in 1842. Bowden, "Private Land Claims," 4: 898.

144. The witness was Donaciano Vigil, who was military secretary under Governor Manuel Armijo. Hall, "Donaciano Vigil," p. 68. Vigil testified before Surveyor General Proudfit in the 1874 hearings on the Cañon del Rio Colorado grant. Bowden, "Private Land Claims," 4: 921.

145. J. J. Bowden, *Spanish and Mexican Land Grants in the Chihuahuan Acquisition,* pp. 77–79. MANM, Reel 42, frame 106. *Cessna v. U.S.,* 169 U.S. 165 (1898).

146. Governor Bartolome Baca to territorial deputation, Santa Fe, February 25, 1825, SANM I, No. 218.

147. *Hayes v. U.S.,* 170 U.S. 637 (1898).

148. See, for example, *Crespin v. U.S.,* 168 U.S. 208 (1897), in which the San Antonito grant was rejected because it was made by a prefect.

149. *Las Siete Partidas,* Partida I, título 2, leyes 4, 5, and 6.

150. Malcolm Ebright, "The Embudo Grant: A Case Study of Justice and the Court of Private Land Claims," *Journal of the West,* 19: 74–85.

151. Jacona grant, NMLG-PLC, Reel 36, case 35, frame 51.

152. Henry Ossian Flipper, *The Colored Cadet at West Point* (1878; reprint ed., New York: Arno Press and the New York Times, 1969), p. ii.

153. Matthew Givens Reynolds, *Spanish and Mexican Land Laws; New Spain and Mexico.* For pictures of Reynolds, Flipper, and Tipton, see Ebright, "The Embudo Grant," *Journal of the West* 19: 79–80.

154. *Las Siete Partidas,* Partida I, título 2, leyes 4, 5, and 6.

155. *Las Siete Partidas,* Partida III, título 29, leyes 18 and 21 provide for acquisition of title by prescription after periods of possession of ten or thirty years, depending on how possession was acquired.

156. "Report," Thomas B. Catron Papers, Section 301, box 38, case 211, folder 2, Special Collections, University of New Mexico Library, Albuquerque.

157. Jennifer Davis, "Perceptions of Power: The Court of Private Land Claims and the Shrinking of the Santo Domingo de Cundiyó Land Grant," unpublished manuscript; see also the chapter by Briggs.

158. See for example, NMLG-PLC, Reel 54, case 282, Rancho de Galván grant.

159. *U.S. v. Sandoval,* 167 U.S. 278 (1897).

160. These were the villages of San José, Las Mulas, Puerticito, Gusano, Bernal, La Cuesta, and Pueblo. Bowden, "Private Land Claims," 3: 737–38.

161. Bowden, "Private Land Claims," 3: 734–44.

162. Malcolm Ebright, "The San Joaquin Grant: Who Owned the Common Lands? A Historical-Legal Puzzle," *NMHR* 57: 5–26.

163. Bowden, "Private Land Claims," 3: 743.

164. See, for example, the Arroyo Hondo grant, confirmed as a community grant in 1892. After the *Sandoval* decision the government asked the Court of Private Land Claims to reverse its decision in the Arroyo Hondo case as to the common lands. The claims court refused, stating that the *Sandoval* decision was not retroactive. Bowden, "Private Land Claims," 4: 933–34.

165. *U.S. v. Pendell,* 185 U.S. 189 (1902), concerning the Santa Teresa grant.

166. *Whitney v. U.S.,* 181 U.S. 104 (1901), concerning the Estancia grant.

167. *U.S. v. Elder,* 177 U.S. 104 (1900), concerning the Cebolla grant; *Peabody v. U.S.,* 175 U.S. 546 (1899), concerning the Vallecito de Lobato grant, and *U.S. v. Bergere,* 168 U.S. 66 (1897), concerning the Bartolome Baca grant.

168. Decision of Licenciado Antonio Barreiro, 26 April 1832, NMLG-

PLC, Reel 45, case 107, frames 48–49, 262–63; cited in Ebright, "The San Joaquin Grant," *NMHR* 57: 18 (note 66).

169. Governor Pedro Fermín Mendinueta declared in 1767 that the Rito de los Frijoles grant made to Captain Andrés Montoya was void because no notice of the grant had been given to adjoining landowners. Bowden, "Private Land Claims," 5: 1230, SANM I, No. 1352.

170. Eleven grants were found to be or suspected of being forged: the Peralta-Reavis, Uña del Gato, Sopori, Oreja del Llano de los Aguajes, Corpus Christi, Sierra Mosca, Pueblo of San Cristoval, Medano Springs and Zapato, Ojita de Galisteo, El Paso de los Algodones, and the Pueblo of Laguna grants. The forgery of the Pueblo of Laguna grant casts doubt on the genuineness of the twelve other Cruzate Pueblo grants. Bowden, "Private Land Claims," 1: 305–6 (note 89).

171. In many cases, besides the absence of grant documents, there was no proof of settlement. See, for example, Chino Tejano Claim, Opinion of the Court of Private Land Claims, NMLG-PLC, Reel 36, case 36, frame 82.

172. Rito de los Frijoles grant, Bowden, "Private Land Claims," 5: 1230, SANM I, no. 1352.

173. An example of a grant made on a specific condition was the Ocaté grant, made in 1837 to Manuel Alvarez by Governor Manuel Armijo on the condition that within three years Alvarez settle the land and commence raising merino sheep. Alvarez did not fulfill this condition and the claims court properly rejected the grant. Bowden, "Private Land Claims," 4: 827–35.

174. Examples of grants revoked by Spanish officials are a series of grants made by Lieutenant Governor Juan Páez Hurtado in the absence of Governor Gervasio Cruzat y Góngora. On his return Governor Cruzat revoked the following grants: Baranca, Manuel García de Las Ribas, José Antonio Torres, Juan Estevan García de Noriega, and Antonio de Ulibarrí. Ibid., 4: 1090, 1118–19, 1131, 1133–34, and 1135–36. See also the John Heath grant, revoked in 1823 by the governor and the provincial deputation. Bowden, *Grants of the Chihuahuan Acquisition,* p. 79.

175. *Recopilación,* Libro IV, título 12, ley 1.

176. Under the acquired rights doctrine of international law, a land grant valid under Spanish and Mexican law must be respected by the U.S. Daniel Patrick O'Connell, *State Succession in Municipal Law and in International Law,* 1: 239–50. For an excellent discussion of the acquired rights doctrine and its application to numerous specific situations in international practice, see John L. Walker, "The Treatment of Private Property in International Law After State Succession," pp. 40–73, in unpublished manuscript.

177. *U.S. v. Chaves,* 159 U.S. 452 (1895).

178. One exception was *U.S. v. Pendell* that confirmed a grant where title papers were not produced. There the Santa Teresa grant was confirmed based on continuous possession since 1790. 185 U.S. 189 (1902).

179. Bowden, *Grants of the Chihuahuan Acquisition,* pp. 73–74.

180. Richard Wells Bradfute, *The Court of Private Land Claims: The Adjudication of Spanish and Mexican Land Grant Titles, 1891–1904* (Albuquerque:

University of New Mexico Press, 1975), pp. viii and 222–23. Bowden, "Private Land Claims," 1: 310.

181. Jill L. Marron, "The Court of Private Land Claims: Inviolate Protection or Inevitable Paternalism on the Frontier," unpublished manuscript.

182. Donald Cutter, "The Legacy of the Treaty of Guadalupe Hidalgo," *NMHR* 53 (October 1978): 305.

183. *Plessy v. Ferguson,* 163 U.S. 537 (1896).

Irrigation gate, Saguache, Colorado. Kathryn Nelson photograph.

TWO

The Pueblo Grant Labyrinth

TWO

The Pueblo Grant Labyrinth

G. Emlen Hall

The Context

Viewed from afar, the current land-status map of the state of New Mexico looks like the work of a quilter gone mad. A riot of colors marks patches of state land, federal land, military land, Indian reservation land, and grant land. There is no consistent order to either the size or shape of the different patches. In the Midwest, the Northwest Ordinance imposed its own regularity on the land. There all fences run due north and south, straight east and west, each delineating a square block of land. For the most part, those symmetrical rectangles cannot be found in New Mexico's chaotic scheme of land ownership.

Pueblo Indian land grants seem to provide the only relief. Colored orange and marked off in neat, striped east-west, north-south squares 5.2 miles on a side, the nineteen Pueblo grants that survive today each delineate approximately 18,000 acres of land which form the core (but not all) of the Pueblos' present holdings. The Pueblo grants extend from the Zuni Pueblo on the west to the extinct Pecos Pueblo on the east and from the Taos Pueblo on the north to the Isleta Pueblo on the south. Together, the Pueblo grants hover around New Mexico's principal water sources and appear to offer an anchor of order in the state's otherwise chaotic landownership and status pattern.[1]

In fact, however, New Mexico's regularly shaped Pueblo grants represent New Mexico land status at its most chaotic. The Pueblo grants do not so much anchor the history of New Mexico land as show the shifting, chaotic foundations on which the whole system is built. To understand Pueblo Indian land grants is to come to grips with why land is still such a problem here. But to reach that understanding, one must take a closer look on the ground.

Imagine the highway running north from Santa Fe to Taos. The towering Sangre de Cristo mountains to the east and the Jemez mountains to the west pinch the highway between them. The surrounding mountains also contain the north-running Tesuque Creek and, after its confluence, the west-running Nambe-Pojoaque stream. Together, the two streams meander down to the much larger south-running Rio Grande, the real spine of these two mountain ranges. Along the parallel highway, road signs mark the boundaries of first the Tesuque and then the Pojoaque Indian reservations. On the south side of the confluence between the Nambe-Pojoaque River and the Rio Tesuque, the Taos highway divides. The right fork leads east along the Nambe-Pojoaque, through the Pojoaque Pueblo to the Nambe Pueblo, perched on the creek's headwaters. The left fork leads downstream through, again, the Pojoaque Pueblo and then into the lands of the San Ildefonso Pueblo. From there, this road crosses the Rio Grande and then climbs to Los Alamos. Here in the valley three Pueblos—Nambe, Pojoaque, and San Ildefonso—lie like closely placed beads along the narrow, short string of the ten-mile Nambe River. The fourth Pueblo, Tesuque, sits in the middle of the shorter, more modest, but the only tributary to the principal Nambe River. In the wider world of watercourses neither of these streams would even pass for a brook. In water-short New Mexico, these "rivers" are the only sources around. The Pueblos sit on them all. Take the left fork west along the Nambe river and follow directions to Jacona. Slowly you begin to understand why the Pueblos' position is so strategic.

Less than a mile from the intersection of the Taos and Los Alamos highways, a small sign directs travelers to Jacona and a new world. The Jacona road is dirt and narrow. Now, in the summer, heavy vegetation presses in from the crude wooden fences that bound the road. The expansive desert vistas of the surrounding terrain, running from one mountain range to the other, give way to a compressed, enclosed jungle of overgrown foliage. A mile and a half later, the road opens into the ancient, still open plaza of Jacona, canopied by the huge old cottonwoods around it. A large, rambling, flat-roofed adobe sits on the plaza's southeast corner. The house bears a plaque attesting to its place on the New Mexico State Register of Cultural Properties.

Now the house belongs to a Los Alamos physicist and, among other members of his family, a son who enjoys a world ranking among teen-age chess players. But the house was first built in the early eighteenth century by Don Ignacio Roybal, one of the gentleman farmers recruited by Diego de Vargas in 1693 for the reconquest of New Mexico after the Pueblo Revolt. Don Ignacio was a high-level local officer of the Spanish Inquisition, and himself something of a Bobby Fisher in the early New Mexico games centering on land, particularly Pueblo Indian land.[2]

As the Roybal house did in the beginning, the Fisher house occupies a tract of land shown on the land-status map as within the Pojoaque Pueblo grant. If you look closely today you can still find the beginnings of a long *acequia* (irrigation ditch) that begins just east of the Fisher house and flows west almost two and a half miles toward the Rio Grande, carrying in it precious irrigation water. That ditch too probably began in Ignacio Roybal's day and served the increasing number of non-Pueblos located along it. That ditch, the Acequia Larga de Jacona, heads on Pojoaque Pueblo grant land, quickly leaves it, and runs most of its long course on the lands of the San Ildefonso Pueblo grant.[3]

Obviously, Robert Fisher inherited more than Ignacio Roybal's house. He has taken as well land and water within the formal boundaries of the neighboring Indian Pueblos. Appropriately enough, Robert Fisher has also inherited from Ignacio Roybal a lawsuit that has dragged on for almost three centuries. In one form or another that ongoing litigation has pitted non-Pueblos—like Roybal in the eighteenth century and Fisher in the twentieth—against their neighbors to the east and west—the Pojoaque and San Ildefonso Pueblos—in a fight for a share of the extremely limited natural resources of this resource-poor, scenery-rich area. The suit arose under New Mexico's first sovereign, Spain. Phoenix-like, it reared its head under Mexico and then again as New Mexico settled into the United States federal system of government, first as a military enclave from 1846 to 1851, then as a territory from 1851 to 1912, and, finally, after 1912, as a full-fledged state. Each change in sovereign, even each change in governmental status under the same sovereign, brought the two sides back to the first and fundamental issue: Did Ignacio Roybal or his successors have any right to be on Pueblo land, using Pueblo land grant water? The ruling nations changed and, with them, the laws; but the question remains the same.

The most recent suit raising the issue started in 1967 as a straightforward adjudication of the Nambe-Pojoaque stream system's water rights. In 1986 it has become one of the oldest pending lawsuits in the federal judicial system, as court administrators in Washington point out with chagrin. Imagine their horror if they knew that this same question had gone unresolved since 1703 in this small valley and in every other New Mexico valley settlement since then. Ignacio Roybal's precarious position was no different than that of Taos Plaza residents, living and working on land still shown on your map as Taos Pueblo grant land. Ignacio Roybal's successors shared a common plight with those residents of Española whose houses sit on San Juan and Santa Clara Pueblo grant lands. The Cochiti Pueblo has its Peña Blanca; the Picuris Pueblo, its Peñasco. Indeed, each of the nineteen Pueblo grants confirmed by the United States has its Ignacio Roybal.

In most cases the non-Indian hold on Pueblo natural resources—including land—has not been as tenacious as has Ignacio Roybal's. But time has added to the complexity of the problem whatever may have been initially lacking in assertiveness. Even at San Ildefonso Pueblo, the problem began as a contest between a formal community—the Pueblo—and an individual family—the Ignacio Roybals. By 1776, a couple of years after Ignacio's death, an astute and nosy cleric found five Hispanic families operating farms on the Roybal ditch. By 1874, roughly fifty families used the same acequia, then known as the "Acequia Madre de los Senores Roybales," not the "Acequia Larga de Jacona" as it is known today. A little less than fifty years after that, federal investigators found almost 150 non-Indian families dependent on the same ditch. Meanwhile, the Pueblos, by and large, have maintained both their identities and their populations.

In other words, what started as the large estate of a single rich Hispano became over the centuries the many tiny farms of numerous families. Like their Pueblo neighbors, most of the successors to Ignacio Roybal's huge estate are very poor, still tied to their land and their irrigation ditch, and reluctant to acknowledge the continued existence of a lawsuit that once threatened to eject Ignacio Roybal from his home and now threatens the same fate for them. After all, the Acequia Larga de Jacona still serves the same land it served in 1723–1725 when Ignacio Roybal went to the extraordinary trouble of securing formal governmental permission to begin construction of the ditch that still exists today.[4]

But the current litigation threatens the present residents of Jacona just as the eighteenth-century litigation threatened their predecessors. None of the lawsuits has yet clarified the full legal status of New Mexico's nineteen Pueblo Indian land grants.

Obviously, this two-and-a-half-century failure is tragic at several levels. What kind of legal systems have failed to set to rest the nature and extent of Pueblo claims to land? How do you measure the human effect of Indian and non-Indian people living together in the same small valley for 250 years, neither feeling comfortable with the other's presence, each constantly on the lookout for an institutional means of getting rid of his neighbor? How can you allocate equitably between two people resources that simply do not exist?

But, in the final analysis, all of these more or less ethereal problems pale when compared to the ultimate tragedy of Pueblo Indian land grants. The lingering ambiguity about what Pueblo land grants are and what rights they confer has left New Mexico's two oldest, poorest, and most vulnerable populations—Pueblo Indians and Hispanos—pitted against one another in a never-ending battle for the extraordinarily pinched natural resources of what one Spanish priest correctly called "this miserable kingdom." The combatants cannot afford the battle. The prize is not worth much on a national or even on a statewide scale. But for more than 200 years, the all-important local battle has raged on.

As a result, Pueblo Indian land grants epitomize the tragedy of New Mexico land grants. Those Indian grants are the most ancient in their origins and the most volatile in today's world. The ultimate irony is that they are not based on grants of land at all. Except for the formal grant in 1745 from the Spanish governor of New Mexico to the just reestablished Pueblo near present-day Albuquerque, there are no known authentic grants to any of New Mexico's eighteen other Pueblos.[5] Instead, the source of their title to lands remains shrouded in other Spanish policies, as those policies were filtered through and changed and distorted by succeeding sovereigns—Mexico and the United States—on their way to the still ambiguous present. To understand the problem of Pueblo Indian land grants, one must begin with Spain in New Mexico.

The Spanish Basis for Pueblo Indian Land Grants

> The Bull was not—and could not be—an altogether adequate charter. Of its three most important provisions, the unequivocal grant of

> "islands and mainlands towards the west and south" was held invalid by many Spaniards and by most foreigners. . . . Francis I, in a moment of defiance, demanded to be shown the "testament of Adam" which had bequeathed a hemisphere to the Spanish and Portuguese Crowns.
>
> —J. H. Parry, *The Spanish Theory of Empire*

Spanish law, and particularly the law of conquest, could be highly, almost painfully theoretical. But, conveniently enough, all sources available to the Crown at the time Spain discovered the New World indicated that all the property so discovered belonged to the Crown. The rights of conquest, the law of nations, and even the pope (with some dissent from non-Catholic European monarchs) agreed that the land of New Mexico belonged to Ferdinand and Isabella by virtue of their underwriting Columbus's voyages of discovery.

From that proposition, absurd as it may now sound, it followed that all claimants to private lands in the New World had to trace their titles to the original owner, the Crown. True enough, Spanish real property law gave great respect to nothing more than possession. The great Crown investigations into New World titles, called *composiciones,* revealed a remarkably lenient royal owner, particularly if the claimant without a crown grant was willing to pay. But still, all titles stemmed from the Crown because all land originally belonged to it.

This principle applied to Indian and non-Indian land alike in the New World. Spanish law dubbed crown grants *mercedes reales* (royal gifts) to emphasize the fact that private acquisition of land depended entirely on royal goodwill. But new Indian communities, formed as a result of the Crown policy favoring centralization of Indian towns (*reduciones*), also required a royal grant.

Property acquired prior to the royal discovery provided the only exception to this general rule. In subsequent centuries, first Mexico guaranteed by treaty that it would respect property acquired under Spanish rule. Then the United States, by treaty again, guaranteed that it would not disturb existing property rights at the time of its acquisition of New Mexico. But Spain, lying at the bottom of this pyramid of self-proclaimed sovereigns, had guaranteed nothing to occupants of the discovered territory by treaty.

Instead, Queen Isabella did it by will and the Royal Council did it by formal debate. In her 1493 will, Isabella directed her successors to respect, and therefore not claim as royal property, the already acquired rights of indigenous people found in lands discovered by Spain. By the mid-sixteenth century, Iberian intellectuals, after decades of ferocious debate, decided that indigenous people in the Americas had the requisite capacity to own property. Combined with the Crown's intent to recognize already acquired rights, this recognition meant that "civilized" native Americans, like the Pueblos, "owned" what they had at the time of the European discovery.[6]

To the extent that the Crown imposed on itself the restrictions of what later came to be known as the "doctrine of acquired rights," Spain showed the best side of its Catholic drive to world dominion. But what real property did the Pueblos "own" at the time Coronado "discovered" them?

Anthropologists, including one Pueblo Indian, now tell us that enclosed blocks of space designed to wall some people in and others out—one essential of Anglo-Saxon private property—do not fit the Pueblo world view very well. The Pueblos lived in a "relentlessly interconnected" world that had definite limits. But the limits served what Anglos would call a religious, not a legal, function. So, while the Pueblo world had boundaries before the incursion of the Spanish, and while that world was rigorously organized to reflect those boundaries, and, finally, while the Pueblo world used land, especially near the center of the Pueblo itself and its irrigated fields, in a way that resembled European notions of private property, still it was hard to tell what the Pueblos "owned."[7]

The Pueblos themselves advanced different theories at different times. For example, they told the United States's first Indian agent in New Mexico that they literally owned the whole territory before the Spanish arrival and that Spanish recognition of their titles in fact reduced the amount of property each owned. At other times, particular Pueblos specifically acknowledged that they had recognized boundaries between adjoining Pueblos, establishing in effect the fixed external property lines the anthropologists say never existed in the Pueblo world view until the Spanish came. As we shall see, the possibility that the Pueblos themselves put boundaries between each other had unique, confusing, and ironic results in the case of Ignacio Roybal and the Pueblo of San Ildefonso. For the moment, it is enough to note the problem of determining what real property the Pueblos owned on their own terms.[8]

That dilemma posed no problem to Spain, however, because, while the Crown recognized the "acquired rights" of indigenous Pueblos, it assumed that those rights conformed to the Spanish concept of real property ownership. Fundamentally, Spanish land law was based on two alternative possibilities: private use or public ownership. The public owned everything except that property which a private entity—an individual, a town, or a pueblo—actually used. To use property, according to the Spanish view, meant to make it produce something that nature itself would not have produced alone. Technically, the principle meant that farmed, irrigated land could be considered private property only during the growing season and that fallow or unplanted land could only be public and accessible to whoever wanted to use it. Applied to the Pueblos, the principle would have restricted the Pueblos' acquired rights to those lands they farmed at the time of the Spanish arrival and the houses in which they lived. Grazing land, forage land, open land would have had to be shared with non-Indian neighbors.[9]

Parts of formal, quasi-codified Spanish law reflect this restrictive view of the acquired rights of the New Mexico Pueblos. For example, in one key section dealing with Spanish colonial treatment of indigenous people, the magnificent 1681 *Recopilación de las Leyes de los Reynos de las Indias* states that

> the Indians shall be given all the land with an excess that belongs to them, both to individuals and communities, and especially those lands where they may have made irrigation ditches or any other improvement made by their own industry. This is to apply particularly with respect to water and irrigation. And for no reason can these lands be sold or taken away.

The initial chapter of the San Ildefonso Pueblo-Ignacio Roybal battle could have taken this lesson as its text. Applied to all New Mexico Pueblos, the law suggests that, in the Spanish view of Pueblo property, Pueblo rights were not to be measured by any arbitrary quantity of land laid out mathematically on the New Mexico earth. Instead, actual Pueblo use would measure each Pueblo's acquired rights.[10]

But Pueblo Indians were wards of the Crown as well as property owners with acquired rights at the time of the conquest. This wardship status added a dimension to Pueblo acquired rights. Crown guardianship expressed itself not as an additional grant of rights and privileges to the indigenous Pueblos, but rather as a restriction on the ability of non-Indians to encroach on "owned" Pueblo natural resources. For example, the *Recopilación* prohibited Spaniards from buying Indian real property, except under certain prescribed conditions; the statute simply voided any nonconforming sale and did not define what real property the Pueblos owned.[11]

Similarly, the Crown's guardianship interest in Pueblo lands expressed itself as a restriction on the authority of local Spanish administrators to grant land from the public domain to non-Indians in such a way that would prejudice the rights of any third party, Indian or non-Indian. Before a grant from the surrounding public domain was made, Pueblos residing in the vicinity were summoned and asked if the proposed grant would harm them. Sometimes the local Spanish alcaldes swore the neighboring Pueblo agreed to the proposed grant. Other times, the affected Pueblo would protest the new grant and officials either denied or drastically amended it. In one dramatic instance, the New Mexico governor revoked a grant previously made to non-Indians simply because the Indians had not been given the opportunity to make any protest at all. However, in at least two other instances, Pueblos protested and the granting officials dismissed the allegation of prejudice as groundless. In any case, the process protected Pueblo property rights without defining them. These were boundaries created by consent, not survey.[12]

A second aspect of this Crown guardianship interest did express itself in terms closer to common notions of property definition. In different places and at different times, for example, the codified Spanish law specified how close non-Indian grants could come to established Indian Pueblos. Spanish cattle ranching grants (*estancias de ganado mayor*), for example, "may not be situated within a league and a half of existing Indian communities and sheep ranches [*estancias de ganado menor*] within a half a league." In another section, the *Recopilación* specified that new Indian towns (*reduciones*) were to have a league of commons (*ejidos*) for livestock in addition to other lands in the town. Obviously the terms of the formal law varied from section to section in specifying the distance between Hispanic settlements and Pueblos.

Settlement practices varied even more. In the crowded central valley of Mexico, indigenous Indian towns left each other insufficient space by any measure to meet whatever spread the law required. In the sparsely populated northern provinces around Chihuahua, indigenous Pueblos often were separated by as much as sixteen leagues from the nearest non-Indian settlement.

Even in New Mexico, Pueblos were occasionally bunched so tightly together along stream systems that none could claim the full measure of their government-enforced right to be left alone. In pre-Pueblo Revolt days, there was not enough land along the stream for the Pueblos of Nambe, Pojoaque, Jacona, and San Ildefonso to leave the requisite distance between each one. Even after the Revolt, when Jacona Pueblo abandoned its ancestral home never to return, the Nambe and Pojoaque Pueblo leagues still overlapped each other in terms of the provisions of Spanish law that guaranteed all Pueblos a corridor of isolation from encroachment. Only the more isolated Pueblos—Taos, Pecos, Jemez, Zuni for example—had sufficient vacant space between Pueblos to fully enforce government-imposed restrictions on the proximity of new grants from the Crown's public domain.[13]

But, by the mid-eighteenth century, New Mexico practice and custom made it clear that local officials, citizens, and the Pueblos themselves all believed that each of the New Mexico Pueblos actually owned four square leagues, usually measured from the cross at the center of the Pueblo cemetery. The configuration of the Pueblo four square leagues was easier to identify than its source. Each league measured 5,000 Castilian varas, and each vara measured between 32 and 33 inches. So the Spanish league applied to the Pueblos became a linear measure of about 2.3 miles. From that, surveyors could easily construct the 18,000-acre squares that contained the basic Pueblo land base under Spanish, Mexican, and American rule.

Measuring the boundaries of this Pueblo league, not verifying its existence, became the focus of much New Mexico litigation in the late eighteenth and early nineteenth centuries. Officials, summoned to determine whether non-Indians had encroached on what was regarded as the Pueblo league, usually used a rope (*cordel*) to establish the legitimate boundaries. The rope stretched in the morning, when the grass was wet, and shrank in the afternoon, when it had dried out, so the league was longer early in the day than it was later. Naturally, the Pueblos favored measuring at dawn while the neighboring Spaniards fought for delay. Bitterness over the niceties of measuring the league became so pronounced that, in at least one instance, the Santa Clara Pueblo insisted on using a stick, rather than the more flexible rope, to measure its league and the San Ildefonso Pueblo buried a secret cross to mark the terminal point of its league because, according to the Pueblo, Hispanos kept moving the government-established markers.[14]

In the intricacies of these bitter but esoteric New Mexico battles, the source of the league as a definition of Pueblo boundaries itself got lost. In addition, there disappeared as well any distinction between the Pueblo league as a government-imposed measure designed to separate Pueblos and Hispanos and to protect one from the other, and the Pueblo league as the actual measure of Pueblo-owned property in the Spanish view.

Clearly, the Pueblo league came to New Mexico from the aspect of Spanish legal tradition that was based on societal welfare, not property ownership, on the beneficent protection of a vulnerable indigenous people rather than the recognition of a previously acquired property right. The distinction is critical, perhaps in Spanish and certainly in United States jurisprudence. The right to property, such as the right an owner conveys to his successor, vests in the new owner and cannot be taken from that new owner except under certain specified and generally limited conditions. On the other hand, the protection extended by the state to those it views as its wards exists entirely at the sufferance of the state. Guardianship of this kind can be altered at any time without affecting "vested" rights. If the Pueblo league reflected the Crown's interest in protecting the Pueblos, rather than the Crown's recognition of what the Pueblos owned, then clearly the Pueblos never owned their leagues under Spanish law.

But by the end of Spanish rule in the New World all New Mexicans regarded the Pueblos as the owners of their four-square-league tracts on the basis of those property-like transactions, land grants made in 1689 by the Spanish governor, acting for the Crown, to each Pueblo. It made no difference that the four square leagues these grants called for were wrenched out of the Spanish tradition tying land and use. It made no difference that the Pueblos never produced one of these so-called Cruzate grants until very late in the eighteenth century, despite the fact that traditional practice in land disputes called on the competing parties to produce their grant documents as the first step in litigation. Obviously, during the Spanish period it made no difference that late in the nineteenth century, a United States handwriting expert for the Court of Private Land Claims would show these 1689 grants to be clumsy and relatively modern forgeries. Two late Spanish period (1815) Pueblo-Hispanic lawsuits, one involving Taos Pueblo, the other Santa Clara Pueblo, made it clear that the Pueblos as communities possessed the lands they occupied. By 1821 in New Mexico, the Pueblos each owned four square leagues.[15]

But, obviously, on the eve of Mexican independence, the exact practical status of Pueblo lands under Spanish law was anything but clear. The situation at Taos and Santa Clara was mirrored by the other eighteen New Mexico Pueblos. The extent of Hispanic penetration generally determined the depth of the problem at a particular Pueblo. The Jemez Pueblo remained relatively untouched; the Sandia Pueblo already had been hard hit. Every Pueblo grant was different. But every Pueblo and every Hispano living in the vicinity of a Pueblo had the same problem. As time passed, that problem became more vexatious, rather than less, and more difficult to answer.

What had happened to Pueblo land grants in New Mexico in 125 years of recorded Spanish rule is best shown by the tortured, bitter, and unresolved relationship between Ignacio Roybal and the Pueblos of Pojoaque and San Ildefonso. Remember that by 1750 Roybal's estate overlapped the western part of the Pojoaque Pueblo league by a little less than half a mile and the eastern part of the San Ildefonso league by the same amount. That overlap came to pass in essentially two transactions, the validity of which were upheld in two lawsuits. The transactions and the lawsuits together suggest the symbiotic relationship between Hispanic- and Pueblo-held land under Spanish rule, a relationship that by the time of Mexican independence in 1821 had already become so tortured, complex, and unresolved that no amount of tinkering could untangle it.

Ignacio Roybal appeared on the Pojoaque River scene innocently enough in 1702 when he applied to Governor Cubero for the large part of the abandoned Jacona Pueblo land that had not previously been granted to another Spaniard. (Later Roybal would purchase the already granted area too.) This land was not exactly unappropriated royal domain. Prior to the Pueblo Revolt of 1680, the small Jacona Pueblo and its forty members were sandwiched along the stream between the Pueblos of Pojoaque on the east and San Ildefonso on the west. Even when entirely Pueblo occupied, there was not enough space along the Nambe-Pojoaque stream to allow a league in each direction for each Pueblo. The San Ildefonso Pueblo itself identified a deep arroyo on the south side of the river as the boundary between its lands and those of the Pueblo of Jacona. That arroyo, as a 1763 survey (*vista de ojos*) showed, lay 1,150 varas (more than half a mile) within the eastern boundary of the San Ildefonso Pueblo's 5,000 vara (2.6 mile) league. As a result of the grant from Governor Cubero to Ignacio Roybal of the abandoned Jacona Pueblo lands, that arroyo became the western boundary of the Ignacio Roybal estate.

Clearly, the use of that boundary, even though it overlapped the San Ildefonso league, did not deprive the San Ildefonso Pueblo of acquired rights. The grant to Roybal simply replaced a previous private (albeit Pueblo) owner. Unless the San Ildefonso Pueblo had a preemptive claim to the already privatized, then abandoned Jacona Pueblo property, Roybal simply stood in the shoes of the old Pueblo.

Such a San Ildefonso claim to additional lands might have come from two possible sources. It might have arisen by simple application of the *sin perjuicio* restriction on other grants from the royal domain. The more complex right-of-first-refusal principle by which Pueblos sometimes were given first shot at surrounding vacant land might have applied in this instance as it appeared to have at the Nambe Pueblo in 1739. But initially the San Ildefonso Pueblo never had the chance to say anything about the grant of the abandoned Jacona Pueblo's lands to Ignacio Roybal. From the Roybal grant on, the Pueblo accepted Roybal's west boundary while simultaneously insisting on its right to its league.

Two subsequent eighteenth-century lawsuits brought by the San Ildefonso Pueblo, one directly concerning land claimed by Ignacio Roybal, the other involving him indirectly, suggest the then current status of the San Ildefonso league.

In the first suit, the San Ildefonso Pueblo, through its government-provided protector of the Indians, in 1704 challenged a grazing grant Roybal had applied for and received on the west side of the Rio Grande, opposite the Pueblo proper. The protector offered two alternative explanations for why the land belonged to the Indians. First, Protector Rael de Aguilar said that at that time the Indians had planted squash and watermelons (*calabasitas y sandias*) on much of the land claimed by Roybal. Second, suggested the protector, the New Mexico governor should mark out the boundaries "of the four leagues, one to each point of the compass, according to the Will of his Majesty . . . so that disputes and litigation will cease." In those two possibilities Protector Rael de Aguilar had expressed the alternative bases for Pueblo property ownership: one based on rights acquired by Indian use according to Spanish definition, the other based on protective largesse afforded by the Crown.

Of course, Ignacio Roybal would have none of it. He presented his grant made by another governor in the spring of that same year. In response, Governor Hurtado ordered an investigation. He did not at that point direct any league to be measured. Instead he directed the local alcalde and two assistants to "examine with their own eyes and ascertain if the natives of said Pueblo do have now or have had cultivated lands and an acequia on the other side of the Rio del Norte. . . ." Hurtado did not cite *Recopilación* IV–12–18. He may not even have had a copy. But he might as well have taken his text from that law's explicit direction to respect Indian-acquired rights to improved property, including specifically land on which Indians had built irrigation ditches.

When, on 22 September 1704, at Hurtado's direction, the San Ildefonso Indians, Ignacio Roybal, and the local officials rode out west of the Rio Grande to look for the Indian ditch, they found it about three-quarters of a league west of the Pueblo. The ditch had not been used and the land had not been planted since the Pueblo Revolt of 1680 but there it was, an embodiment of the *Recopilación* itself.

That discovery was all Governor Hurtado needed to start issuing orders. He directed measurement of the San Ildefonso league to the west and ruled that Ignacio Roybal's holdings west of the river had to begin, if at all, at that western Pueblo boundary. Then he ordered the local alcalde to establish as well the San Ildefonso league to the north, south, and east, up the Pojoaque River. But, directed Hurtado, if, in those full measurements, the alcalde should encounter cultivated land of Hispanos, he should stop there. Clearly, the governor felt that the law's preference for cultivated property should refer to Indians and non-Indians alike.

When it actually became time to measure the San Ildefonso league in 1704, the picture became more complex. The Indians told the alcalde they were interested only in farming land, and the alcalde located a cultivable league to the Pueblo's north. But topography constrained him on the south and on the west. In those directions, he measured off only half a league for the Pueblo. To the east, up the Pojoaque River, he measured off only a half a league as well, not because the terrain made farming impossible as it did on the south and west but because he ran into the cultivated lands of the Hispano Matias Madrid, and Hurtado had told him specifically to stop there. As it turned out, Madrid's eastern boundary was the western boundary of Ignacio Roybal's Jacona grant. Both were inside the eastern extension of the San

Ildefonso league up the Pojoaque River. But if Madrid could stay, certainly Roybal could as well.[16]

In 1704 the San Ildefonso Pueblo accepted this victory over Ignacio Roybal's claim to lands west of the river and these determinations of the Pueblo boundaries in the other three directions. Neither the Pueblo nor the supervising government officials sought mechanical application of any four-square-league rule. Instead, the Pueblo and the government accepted Hispanos who were living, procreating, dying, leaving heirs well within the eastern league, and using the Pojoaque River as a common source of life-giving irrigation water.

Well before the end of the eighteenth century, however, the San Ildefonso Pueblo raised once again the issue of the presence of Hispanos along the Pojoaque River within the boundary of its eastern league. By 1763, Juana Lujan and her progeny had replaced Matias Madrid, and the heirs of Ignacio Roybal just upstream had dug further in with their settlements. In his petition that year to Governor Tomas Velez Cachupin, one of the strong legalists on the roll of Spanish New Mexican governors, Pueblo Protector Felipe Tafoya complained specifically about what he called the Juana Lujan "encroachment" on Pueblo lands to the east. (Tafoya also complained about problems in other directions from the Pueblo.) The Lujan "encroachment," alleged Tafoya, had resulted from some earlier, Byzantine, and very shady dealings of Matias Madrid by which the San Ildefonso Pueblo had been dealt out of its lands. Now Tafoya asked that the full San Ildefonso league be measured to the east and that the lands within it be restored. To hear Tafoya tell the San Ildefonso story, the actions of Matias Madrid and Juana Lujan merited jail.

However, in response, on 17 February 1763, the heirs of Juana Lujan provided the investigating alcalde with a deed for the lands to their mother from Matias Madrid, the original 1702 grant for the lands from Governor Cubero to Madrid, a couple of official revalidations of the grant to Madrid and the sale to Lujan, and, finally, a copy of the 1704 Hurtado decision directing the eastern extension of the San Ildefonso lands to stop at the Matias Madrid cultivated lands. Whatever else one might say about the Juana Lujan estate as of 1763, it had been assembled with genuine attention to legal procedure and detail.

Next, Governor Cachupin directed Alcalde Carlos Fernandez to measure the distance ". . . from the church of said pueblo up to the location of said (Lujan) ranch in order to judge the damages which are reported."

Fernandez did so on 17 February 1763. First, Fernandez measured off a 100-vara rope so that the San Ildefonso 5,000-vara eastern league would consist of 50 cord lengths. Then he set off from the gate of the San Ildefonso Pueblo, calling the vara count length by length in the presence of Pueblo leaders, the protector of the Indians, and the heirs of Juana Lujan.

What he found on this shot of the San Ildefonso Pueblo league in 1763 measured quite precisely the same problem with the Pueblo league that had existed earlier in the century. At 2,200 varas, less than half of the 5,000-vara Pueblo league, Fernandez came to the western boundary of the Lujan property. This would place the Lujan boundary 300 varas nearer to the Pueblo than the half-league that had been assigned to it on the east in 1704, and 2,800 varas short of the full league the Pueblo now claimed on its east.

Continuing east from this 2,200-vara mark, Fernandez proceeded another 1,650 varas to a dry arroyo that marked the eastern boundary of the Lujan property, the western boundary of the Ignacio Roybal property, and, according to the San Ildefonso Pueblo, the old, common boundary between the Pueblos of San Ildefonso and Jacona. There remained 1,150 varas to the 5,000-vara San Ildefonso league, and this land belonged to the Roybal heirs.

Fernandez's shots of the San Ildefonso league in the other three directions revealed different, equally complex land problems. But the eastern shot, along the Rio Pojoaque and into the heart of Hispanic settlement within the San Ildefonso league, set the legal wheels in motion. Hispanos and Pueblos, each armed with the Fernandez measurements, responded in different ways. Indian Protector Tafoya, complaining as the Pueblo had in 1704 about the lack of water and tillable land, denied the validity of the original grant to Matias Madrid. He did so, however, by confusing the already invalidiated grant to Ignacio Roybal west of the Rio Grande with the subsequent, and never before challenged, grant to Madrid.

For their part, the heirs of Juana Lujan countered in three ways. First, they pointed to the formal proceedings by which their title had been created, validated, revalidated, and reconfirmed. If there was blame, "the fault was not the possessors [Matias Madrid] nor ours [the Lujans] but his who made the grant and the one who gave possession." Second, in a refrain that would become increasingly familiar and compelling in these Pueblo-Hispano contests, the heirs of Juana Lujan pointed to the length of time, nearly seventy years, that they had possessed the land in question. Finally, the Lujans suggested that the small population of the San Ildefonso Pueblo did not justify a claim to this land.

Governor Cachupin gave the Indians the last move in the litigation. In the late fall of 1763, San Ildefonso Protector Tafoya responded to the Lujan heirs. He said the Fernandez measurements, which no one had challenged, spoke for themselves. The Lujan estate was inside the San Ildefonso league, and that was that. Then, confusing the adjudication of the Ignacio Roybal claim west of the Rio Grande with the Roybal claim to the Jacona grant east of the river, Tafoya said that prior determination of prejudice on the part of the Roybal grant proved that the Lujan claim also prejudiced the Pueblo since it lay even closer to the San Ildefonso center than the Roybal tract. Finally, for the first time in the litigation, Tafoya referred to codified Spanish law and cited provisions from the *Recopilación*.

Faced with this flurry of legal activity and the obvious importance of the issue, Governor Cachupin, a man who had shown mettle in Pueblo land affairs, this time ducked the issue. He sent all the relevant papers on 12 November 1763 to Don Fernando de Torija y Leri, royal attorney and magistrate of Chihuahua, for his opinion on the matter. A year later, on 27 October 1764, Torija y Leri responded. "Almost the same right," he wrote, "attends the Hispanic residents [*vecinos*] who defend their old possession of the houses and lands which they possess as that [right] which is maintained by the natives of the Pueblo of San Ildefonso." In addition, he continued, he could not tell whether the Madrid and Jacona grants to Hispanos had impinged on the needs of the Pueblo, in either 1702 or now in 1764, because no one had told him whether the Pueblo had grown or shrunk in population in the intervening years. In other words, neither legal right nor need, the two principal factors to be considered, gave a categorical answer to the problem of the Hispanic presence within the Pueblo league. However, the royal attorney from Chihuahua had a practical solution. Leave the Hispanos in place east of the San Ildefonso Pueblo, he said, and grant to the Pueblo from the vacant public domain additional lands adjoining the Pueblo.

On receiving this answer, Governor Cachupin endorsed the analysis and solution, writing that he ". . . agreed entirely with his [the royal attorney's] opinion, which is in conformity with the law, in the lawsuit instituted by the representative of the native Indians [*naturales*] of the Pueblo of San Ildefonso against the heirs of Juana Lujan, leaving the latter in the quiet and peaceable possession of their house and lands for the reasons alleged and those set forth by the said counselor." If the heirs of Juana Lujan could stay, then, of course, the heirs of Ignacio Roybal could stay as well. Informed of this decision, the San Ildefonso Pueblo accepted.

The arrangement left non-Indians in possession of the eastern 2,800 varas of San Ildefonso's 5,000-vara eastern league. The Spanish government had created, blessed, baptized, confirmed, reconfirmed, and confirmed yet again the possessions of the heirs of Juana Lujan and Ignacio Roybal. The Pueblo had agreed to the Spanish presence; the government had sanctified the union. By 1765 all reasonable men must have thought that the San Ildefonso problem on the east had been laid to rest once and for all.[17] The heirs of Juana Lujan and Ignacio Roybal could rest assured. To put the icing on the cake, in 1782 Governor Anza reconfirmed the title of the Roybal heirs.

Yet this was just the beginning of the problems the Roybals would have. On the east, where the family's principal residence stood, the Roybals would discover that the Juan de Mestas grant purchased by Don Ignacio—a grant that like Jacona had been approved time and time again—lay in a part of the western 5,000 varas of the Pojoaque Pueblo's league. Like the problem of the eastern San Ildefonso league, the problem of the western Pojoaque Pueblo league never went away.

A large part of the problem had to do with the sovereign's failure to establish from the beginning simple and easily understood rules about Pueblo Indian land. There was a world of difference between the 1765 view of San Ildefonso's entitlement to four square leagues and the 1815 view of the Taos Pueblo's entitlement to the equivalent area. The one represented a pragmatic view of Pueblo rights to land, the other a form of what one astute historian has called the kind of absolutist Hapsburg legal principle never applied in New Mexico. No change in the law between the two decisions could explain the difference between them. They simply reflected an underlying confusion about the nature and extent of Pueblo claims to land, particularly in conflict with already long-standing Hispanic claims to the same area, at the end of 300 years of Spanish rule and on the eve of Mexican independence. That independence simply added another layer of confusion to the existing Spanish view of Pueblo Indian land grants.

Pueblo Indian Land Grants under Mexican Rule

> Haciendoles saber a dichos Naturales que asi como cesaron sus antiguas cargas, han terminado sus antiguas privilegios, quedando igual, unos y otros, a todos los demas ciudadanos que con ellos forman la gran familia mejicana.
>
> —Diputacion Territorial to Pecos Pueblo 1825
>
> [Making these Natives understand that just as their old burdens have ceased, so also have their old privileges ended, leaving equal, one to another, all the additional citizens who with them make up the great Mexican family.]

The Spanish ruled New Mexico Pueblos for 300 years. The Republic of Mexico held sovereignty for only 25 years, from 1821 to 1846. Yet, Mexican rule had critical importance for Pueblo Indian land grants in New Mexico. Mexican rule determined what rights the United States agreed to respect when it succeeded as sovereign in 1846. To that extent, Mexico, not Spain, controlled the rights that were passed on to the United States and guaranteed recognition and protection under the Treaty of Guadalupe Hidalgo. The point would be academic except that during its sovereignty over New Mexico, the Republic of Mexico exercised its short-lived but very real power to change the legacy it received from Spain and so alter the obligation it forwarded to the United States.

Mexico did so in three ways. First, the new sovereign used its sovereign legislative power to redefine the legal status of Pueblo Indians by specifically altering their wardship status under Spanish law. Most apparent was the immediate problem of whether or not the previous Spanish prohibition against Indian sales of land to non-Indians still applied under Mexico. But, more fundamentally, the change in status raised the question of what was left of the Pueblo league if that league had arisen from and depended on that Pueblo wardship status.

Second, Mexican sovereignty over Pueblo lands brought with it new legislation designed to free unused communal lands of both Indians and Hispanos and redistribute them among private, productive hands. This new legislation brought intensified Hispanic pressure on limited Pueblo resources and offered a new potential route for Hispanos onto Pueblo lands.

Finally, Mexican sovereignty raised once again the question of the status of Pueblo lands within the Pueblo grants. The 1815–1816 Santa

Clara decision had implied that no individual Pueblo Indian had title to any tract within the grant where he resided. Spanish law forbade Pueblo sales of land to non-Indians without government approval. Mexican sovereignty may have removed that impediment to Indian sales but, if so, could an individual Pueblo Indian sell a tract of land within the Pueblo grant or did the sale require the approval of the Pueblo as a whole?[18]

None of these issues were immediately apparent at the beginning of Mexican independence in 1821, particularly in far-off New Mexico. They emerged only over the next three decades of Mexican rule. Then, before the Mexican government could fully resolve them in New Mexico, sovereighty changed again with the entrance of General Kearny and the United States in 1846. In the end, Mexican rule contributed yet another layer of unresolved ambiguity to the Pueblo land grant problem the United States inherited.

No one would have guessed that so many Pueblo problems could have arisen from Mexico's goal of eliminating all racial distinctions between Indians and non-Indians. As elsewhere in the new Mexican nation, New Mexico officials were directed to drop any reference to race in official documents. Church books, census records, and tax rolls no longer designated entries by Indian and non-Indian status. All now belonged to what one New Mexico official called *la gran familia mejicana,* in which no distinctions were supposedly allowed. Now, under Mexican rule, the Pueblos operated their own municipal governments, paid taxes, and served in the militia along with non-Indians. The Pueblos were full citizens for the first time.

New Mexico Governor Facundo Melgares, the transitional leader between the two sovereigns, declared the Pueblos' "minority" status finished under Mexico. But it was never quite clear exactly where this left their former wardship status under Spanish rule. Mexico never provided a special attorney to defend Pueblo interests as Spain always had. As an early California court pointed out, the fact that Pueblos became citizens under Mexican law did not necessarily mean that all the special status attached to them and their affairs under Spanish law automatically disappeared as well. After all, minors were citizens and there were many things they could not do with their property without official sanction.

In the first, heady days of Mexican rule in New Mexico, officials tended to overlook these more subtle problems. In response to the elimination of racial classifications and the emphasis on the new, national Mexican enterprise, New Mexico officials stressed cooperation and sharing between Pueblo and non-Indian neighbors rather than the separation of the two worlds that Spanish policy had sometimes tried to impose.[19]

But did this combined elimination of special status and new emphasis on national unity extend to the ability of Hispanos and other non-Indians to acquire the land and water of New Mexico Pueblos? Formal Spanish law had sharply restricted the conditions on which such acquisitions could occur. Administrators like Maynez had extended those restrictions to a near prohibition. Now, with the advent of Mexican sovereignty and the explicit changes that it heralded, many New Mexicans, both Pueblo and Hispano, believed that Pueblo citizens could convey to Hispanic citizens land and its associated resources within the boundaries of the formerly restricted Pueblo grants.

No formal depository for private transfers of real property existed in New Mexico before United States rule. It is difficult to quantify the number of land sales by Pueblos to non-Indians during the Mexican Period. But surviving documentation suggests that the number of real property transfers from Pueblo Indians to non-Indians increased markedly during the period of Mexican rule.

These sales usually involved the small, irrigated farming plots that Pueblo families had held within the external boundaries of the Pueblo grants. To the outside world, these tracts had all the attributes of private property: single Pueblo families worked them for many years, passed them by inheritance from one generation to the next, and kept the entire produce from the individual tracts. From time to time Spanish law had suggested, as in the Santa Clara-Roque Canjuebes battle, that this tradition did not imply ownership or that Pueblo families could, therefore, convey their tracts outside the Pueblo. But, surely, the arrival of Mexican law, with its emphasis on the individual and privatized property, had also altered whatever restrictions there might have been.

The debate on the status of Pueblo land continued through the Mexican Period.[20] But it proceeded in, and was informed by, a parallel debate that raged throughout the first decade of Mexican rule in New Mexico about the power of the Mexican government to break up unused, already privatized communal lands belonging to Indian and Hispanic communities and redistribute them for more productive uses among private individuals.

The impetus for the debate came from the liberal philosophers of Mexico with their bent for individualism and their passion for private property. In their eyes, Pueblo communalism was anathema. The legal source for the debate came from two obscure acts of the Spanish Cortes in 1812 and 1813—acts, curiously enough, which were repealed before they reached New Mexico under the old Spanish regime and then were readopted under the Mexican government after 1821.

The issue the philosophy and the acts raised was only indirectly concerned with whether Pueblos could sell their land. Instead, the question became whether the Mexican government could simply grant it to others. Specifically, the act of 9 November 1812, effective in New Mexico after 1821, provided:

> If the common lands are very numerous in respect to the population of the pueblo to which they belong, the lands will be divided up to half of these lands at the most. It should be understood that in any of these divisions [*repartimientos*] the legislatures [*las diputaciones provinciales*] will designate the parcel of land that belongs to each individual according to the particular circumstances of that individual and of each pueblo.

The issues raised by this law began to surface in New Mexico in the water-rich but then unused fields of the Pecos Pueblo, just east of Santa Fe. There, between 1824 and 1829, the new government in Santa Fe embarked on a tortured journey, full of false starts and stops, much local, esoteric politics, and great bitterness, in an attempt to define the status of Pueblo Indian grants under Mexican law. The battle pitted sophisticated, water-hungry Hispanos from Santa Fe, armed with an arsenal of new laws, against a once great but now diminished Pueblo, still fully capable of fighting with real vigor and sophistication against the effort to expropriate its lands.

The fight began in 1823 when astute land speculator Domingo Fernandez and other Hispanos from Santa Fe applied under the act of 9 November 1812 for portions of the unused Cienega de Pecos, well within the Pecos Pueblo's four square leagues. By the time the Pecos request received serious consideration by the New Mexico governor and his quasi-legislative advisors of the new *diputacion teritorial,* it was accompanied by similar applications for unused common lands of the Pueblos of San Felipe and Santo Domingo.

At that time, all three Pueblos protested that they needed the lands which the Mexican government proposed to privatize and place in the hands of non-Indians. In 1824, the Santo Domingo and San Felipe Pueblos lost their arguments based on need but, surprisingly, the Pecos Pueblo won on the same grounds.

Less than a year later, the Hispanos were back, knocking on the Pecos Pueblo's doors once again. The Pueblo protested the plan to put some of its lands in non-Indian hands, this time arguing not on the basis of need but on the basis of "the league of land that it had in the time of the Spanish government." In response to this argument, government officials were told to tell the Pecos Pueblo that under Mexican rule the Pueblo no longer enjoyed a special status. Clearly, these Mexican officials thought that the sacrosanct Pueblo league was not acquired property but the simple (and alterable) result of government largesse, a largesse that Mexico was not obligated to either respect or follow. The officials rejected the Pueblo's argument and awarded Pecos land to non-Indians.

That policy, however, was not immediately followed at other Pueblos. Late in 1825, the Santa Fe government denied a similar request for unused communal lands at the San Juan Pueblo. Showing a new caution, the government justified its earlier Pecos Pueblo action on the "very small number of persons who make up the ancient Pueblo of Pecos" and held all future applications for unused Pueblo land in abeyance, pending clarification from Mexico City of the Santa Fe government's actual authority in the matter.

That clarification never came. Instead, in the next year, the Pecos Pueblo protested for the third time the taking of their lands. In 1824, they had tried need as the basis for their argument and won. In 1825, they had tried the Spanish league and lost. Now in 1826, they turned to private property as the legal grounds on which the Pueblo's land could not be granted to non-Indians.

The Pecos Pueblo, said its leader, owned its own lands including the lands the new government wanted to give away. If the government wanted to give lands away, it could grant those public lands farther from the Pueblo that were not private (*"las que no tienen dueños"*) in frontier places like Mora, Sapello, and Coyote. But the Pueblos, said the Pecos leader, were sons of God and the Mexican nation, just like everyone else. They enjoyed "all the laws and rights of citizens." The New Mexican government could not just come in, expropriate Pecos Pueblo land without the Pueblo's consent, and give the land to others.

The three different positions taken by the Pecos Pueblo in 1824–1826 reflected a real uncertainty about the underlying basis for Pueblo claims to land under Mexican rule in New Mexico. The response of the government in Santa Fe reflected that uncertainty and an additional uneasiness about the exact meaning of the old laws of the Spanish Cortes of 1812 and 1813 in the Mexican context. As Governor Cachupin had done in the 1760s with the San Ildefonso case, New Mexico officials, caught in a difficult and bitter political situation, ducked and passed the issue higher up. This time no definitive answer came down.

That impasse left forty Hispanic families in the middle of the Pecos Pueblo grant, living and farming land in the water-rich Cienega de Pecos. They surrounded the few remaining Pecos Pueblo families to whom the Santa Fe government also had apportioned small privatized and irrigated tracts. The situation at Pecos was still volatile. Hispanos, now legally in the grant, began to buy and sell the tracts they had been given. Apparently, the individual Pecos Pueblo Indians, who also had received private tracts within the Pueblo lands, did the same.

But the issues underlying the matter did not rest there. The Pecos Pueblo itself never fully accepted the basic application of the new policy to its lands. In 1829, the Pueblo leaders seized the opportunity presented by an internecine fight that developed between Pecos Hispanos. Once again the Pueblo challenged the authority of the government to rearrange landownership inside Pueblo grants.

Surprisingly enough, this time the Pecos Pueblo prevailed. The local Mexican government in Santa Fe reversed itself and declared that the Pecos Pueblo grant was the private property of the Pueblo and, therefore, not subject to forced government transfer of Pueblo land from Indians to non-Indians. In an addendum to its decision, Santa Fe officials explicitly stated what the initial decision implied: while the government could not give away Pueblo land to Hispanos, the Pueblo itself could sell its private property.

Among New Mexico's twenty Pueblos, the Pecos Pueblo experience and ultimate victory had been unique. The Mexican government in Santa Fe had never before gone so far as to actually impose, even if temporarily, a redistributive policy on Pueblo lands. Santa Fe officials may have regarded the Pecos Pueblo itself as unique, since it was failing and nearing extinction (complete by 1837).

In addition, the Pecos Pueblo victory in 1829 was ambiguous. Did the Santa Fe government uphold the right of individual Indians to sell land within a Pueblo grant or just the right of the Pueblo as a whole? If the government meant to uphold the individual right to sell, did that apply to all Pueblo Indians in possession of particular tracts of lands within the grants, a situation obtaining at all Pueblos, or did it just apply to those individuals who had received from the government private titles to their tracts, as had occurred only at the Pecos Pueblo? The victorious Pecos Pueblo itself solved that dilemma when the leaders sold, in the fall of 1830, the land they had rescued from the Santa Fe politicians.[21]

What had started as a case to test the limits of Mexican authority over Pueblo grant lands ended up as a test case on the power of Pueblos under Mexican law to treat their grants as private property, including the power to convey to whomever they, as owners free and clear, chose. Despite the ambiguities that lurked in the Pecos Pueblo grant resolution, existing records show after 1829 a quantum leap in the number of sales from individual Indian members of Pueblos to non-Indians. The transfers took all forms. Some were executed by the Pueblo as a formal organization. Others were signed by both an individual Indian and acknowledged by Pueblo officials. Still others were only executed by the individual Indian who claimed to own the tract he was selling. Finally, some deeds from Indians to non-Indians probably failed to identify by ethnicity either party to the transaction. The lack of conformity reflected a remaining uncertainty about the form Pueblo sales should take and, ultimately, the nature of Pueblo ownership of land. But one thing was clear to New Mexicans after 1830. The Pueblos could sell and Hispanos could buy, without the bother of government supervision and without the worry of government interdiction.[22]

The result, of course, was a further mixing of Hispanos and Pueblos on what formally may have been Pueblo land. The mixing was not very pronounced in the outlying Pueblos. But in those Pueblos near urban areas, the balance between Indians and non-Indians grew more equal. In fact, in the four Pueblos of the Tesuque-Nambe-Pojoaque stream system, non-Indians outnumbered Indians by the end of Mexican rule.

Curiously, none of this mixing from within meant the abandonment of the Pueblo league as the boundary of Pueblo land from without. During the Mexican period, no Pueblo challenged the presence of the large number of non-Indians living within its borders. But the Pueblos continued to defend those one-league, external borders against out-

and-out encroachments on them. Until the mid-1840s, the Mexican government continued to measure the Pueblo leagues and to exclude non-Indians whose boundaries, derived from other sources, overlapped the Pueblo league. Those non-Indians who claimed a right to be inside the Pueblo boundaries by virtue of a common source—the Pueblo grants now conveyed in part to them—remained where they were, unchallenged by either the Pueblos or the government.[23]

In microcosm, the situation at the San Ildefonso Pueblo and on the grants of Juana Lujan and Ignacio Roybal between 1821 and 1846 showed in detail what was happening to Pueblo land grants during the Mexican Period. To begin, the San Ildefonso Pueblo took its place in the governmental structure of New Mexico. It had a council (ayuntamiento) that ministered to both Indians and non-Indians within its jurisdiction and that was subject to the general power of the clearly non-Indian ayuntamiento of Santa Cruz de la Canada. The Pueblo acknowledged its subordinate position in that governmental structure by, among other things, seeking permission to institute land and water changes. For example, in 1832 the San Ildefonso Pueblo applied to the New Mexico governor for permission to take a new acequia out of the Rio Grande even though the Pueblo itself had demonstrated as early as 1704 that it had had such an acequia prior to 1680. The governor urged the alcalde constitutional of Santa Cruz de la Canada to grant the San Ildefonso request, but only if it could be shown that it would not injure anyone else, Indian or non-Indian. Here was the San Ildefonso Pueblo behaving as a group of ordinary citizens, with no special rights or privileges.[24]

Similarly, the San Ildefonso Pueblo entered into the real estate market during these troubled years and sold portions of its grant to non-Indians. On 23 November 1820, a few months before Mexican independence, officials of the Pueblo sold a large tract of land south of the Pueblo itself but well within its southern league to Francisco Ortiz, a prominent Santa Fe merchant. With the approval of San Ildefonso Governor Juan Jose and six other Indians, the Pueblo conveyed 1,416 varas east of the Rio Grande near the present site of the bridge to Los Alamos. An 1826 map indicates a large hacienda south of the San Ildefonso Pueblo which may have become the Ortiz ranch headquarters.

In any case, seven years after the first transaction and well into the period of Mexican sovereignty, Ortiz bought a second piece of real estate from the pueblo on 6 June 1827. Lying north of the first purchase, this second piece consisted of 238 varas bounded on the west by the Rio Grande, on the north by remaining Pueblo lands, and on the east by an acequia. This tract too lay clearly within the southern San Ildefonso league.

With his position consolidated, Ortiz quickly moved to secure official approval of his Indian land purchases. On 23 June 1827, he requested that New Mexican Governor Manuel Armijo certify the sales and confirm his title. On 27 June, Armijo forwarded Ortiz's request to his advisors. After receiving a favorable report, the advisors and the governor approved Ortiz's acquisition of the two ranches. The caution with which Ortiz proceeded reflects his uncertainty about the purchase. But in 1827, the government placed its imprimatur on the transaction.[25] Who could object?

The San Ildefonso Pueblo did not. The Pueblo's active participation and acquiescence in the transfer of its southern league to Francisco Ortiz was accepted by all as an accurate statement of what New Mexico Pueblos could do with their land. The Ortizes retained the ranch along the river for at least several decades without complaint from the Pueblo.[26]

Of course, the same was true with respect to the Juana Lujan and Ignacio Roybal tracts on the Pueblo's east. No one, Indian or Hispano, ever conceived of these long-standing non-Indian settlements as possibly belonging to the San Ildefonso Pueblo by 1846. The two Hispanic communities were increasing in numbers, deepening their historic attachment to land that they and their families had possessed for more than a century, and becoming Hispanic towns: "El Rancho" on the site acquired by Juana Lujan, "Jacona" on the site acquired by Ignacio Roybal.

On the eve of the arrival of the United States in New Mexico in 1846, existing Mexican rule had only deepened and widened the confusion about Pueblo land grants in New Mexico. Under its rule, Mexico had altered the status of Pueblo lands, now authorizing the sale of Pueblo lands to non-Indians, now permitting individual Pueblos as well as the community as a whole to convey land. Clearly, Mexican rule had not altered the status of Hispanic holdings on the Pueblo leagues that were granted by the Spanish Crown. During the period, Hispanic purchasers and Hispanic grantees of lands witin the formal boundaries of the Pueblo leagues became more entrenched in what they regarded as their homes by birthright. The Hispanic homelands swelled; the Pueblo land base shrunk; the meager resources of the hard terrain from which both Indians and non-Indians struggled to wrest a living remained the same. By 1846, the Pueblo land grants, particularly those near the settled areas of Albuquerque, Santa Fe, Española, and Taos had become the homes of Hispano and Indian alike.

The Pueblo Grants under New Mexico Territorial Law and the United States

> There are some considerations higher than the merits of the equities of any particular case. . . . The faith and credit which are due to the government's public acts ought not to be lightly impugned. And when so solemn an instrument as a Patent, signed by the highest officer of the Nation . . . is duly and regularly given out as evidence of title . . . it ought to be regarded as sacred.
>
> —New Mexico attorney Frank Springer, oral argument in the Maxwell Land Grant Case before the United States Supreme Court

With its acquisition of New Mexico in 1846, the United States inherited the already confused Pueblo Indian land grant situation from Mexico and guaranteed by treaty to respect the quagmire of property rights that had already bogged down the question of who owned what within the Pueblos' "four square leagues." The United States responded to this confusion by simplifying its vision of Pueblo Indian land grants beyond any semblance of historical reality, then insulating that vision within the constraints of the federal system brought by the new sovereign to New Mexico, and finally washing its hands of that new insulated vision by its own carelessness. The result, of course, was a hydra-headed monster, simply waiting for the chance to emerge.

The United States laboratory for the creation of the monster that Pueblo Indian land grants became under United States law combined three elements. First, Pueblo Indian land grants under United States law were filtered through the Treaty of Guadalupe Hidalgo by which the United States promised to honor the acquired rights of all citizens of the transferred Mexican territory. Pueblo Indian lands at one level were treaty-covered lands just like all New Mexico land grants in existence as of 1846.

At a slightly different level, the United States also brought to the problem of Pueblo Indian land grants its own version of Indian law and its own vision of whether that law would or would not apply to the New Mexico Pueblos and their land. This decision posed a problem not of acquired rights but of newly conferred status. But the extent to which the United States adopted or revised the previous governmental treatment of Pueblo Indians would say a lot about the continued status of their lands.

Finally, the United States brought to the acquisition of New Mexico its own peculiar system of federalism, a system that controlled power through a delicately balanced separation of powers between coordinate branches of government. The system offered in those coordinate branches of government many different avenues for political meddling and dispute resolution.

Unfortunately, in the area of New Mexico Pueblo land grants, each of these factors only further muddied the nature and extent of Pueblo claims to land in New Mexico. Pueblo Indian land grants were treated no differently from Hispanic grants with disastrous results for both. Federal Indian law was awkwardly and only slowly applied to Pueblos and their land. Confusion resulted in New Mexico land titles. The otherwise magnificent federal system merely created multiple fronts on which to wage the endless battles that all this confusion caused.

Nothing about the Treaty of Guadalupe Hidalgo itself would have suggested the problems with which Pueblo Indian lands would plague the new United States sovereign. The treaty made no special mention of any New Mexico Indians and required nothing particular about their lands. Articles 8 and 9 required the United States to honor the acquired property rights of citizens of Mexico now residing in New Mexico. The Pueblo Indians had been citizens of Mexico and now were citizens of the United States. Everyone agreed that the United States was bound, as its first official instructions said, "to deal with private land titles and the 'Pueblos' precisely as Mexico would have done had the sovereignty not changed. We are bound to recognize all titles, as she would have done, to go that far, and no further."[27] That left the United States in Mexico's (and Spain's) shoes, applying Mexican and Spanish law to the New Mexico Pueblos. That job would have stumped a Mexican jurist intimate with the previous confusion over the nature and extent of Pueblo claims to land in New Mexico. It should have stopped altogether an American adjudicatory system entirely ignorant of that already tortured 300-year tradition.

In the beginning of United States rule in New Mexico, government officials knew nothing of Pueblo Indian land grants. They hardly knew about, let alone had investigated the rich Spanish and Mexican archives they inherited with the territory. But they learned quickly about Pueblo land grants from the Pueblos themselves. In 1847 the Pueblos told New Mexico's first Indian agent, James C. Calhoun, that they owned their lands by grant from the Spanish Crown and that no grant measured less than eight miles on a side. They complained bitterly about loss of those grant lands to Hispanos and asked the new sovereign to "restore their ancient boundaries."

Calhoun knew nothing of the already official steps taken by Spain and Mexico to sometimes adjust and even diminish the basic four-square league blocks the Pueblos told him about. Calhoun had no time to investigate. Before 1851 and the end of his short stay in New Mexico, Calhoun recommended, in response to the Pueblos' complaints, that the United States investigate, confirm, and survey the Pueblo grants to prevent further depredation of the kind the Pueblos said they already had suffered. In addition, Calhoun recommended a determination of the previous legal position of the Pueblos so that the government could determine the status of non-Indians residing within the Pueblo borders.[28]

The United States took until May 1877 to complete what was essentially the course recommended by Calhoun between 1848 and 1850. (Even then, the results would not prove final and, in fact, would undergo fundamental alterations in the 1910s and 1920s.) For the quarter-century immediately following the Calhoun recommendations the United States moved slowly but inexorably down the path he had suggested. But, despite subsequent accusations of a complete federal neglect of the Pueblo land dilemma, the record shows a consistent, but almost glacial, federal effort to resolve the enigma of Pueblo land grants between Calhoun's initial reports in 1848–1850 and the U.S. Supreme Court's *Joseph* decision in May 1877.

In 1851, the Pueblo land problem was just beginning to come into focus. In the meantime, the various levels of United States government that came to New Mexico acted on the vague American ideas of the Pueblo situation in a variety of ways. The military government established by the conquering U.S. Army immediately passed a law, partly at the Pueblos' request, making the Pueblos formal, if involuntary, corporations, with the power to sue and be sued. By 1851, the Pueblos and their lands had emerged in New Mexico with a formal identity that made their lands more visible.[29]

In that same year, Congress perfunctorily extended the 1834 Trade and Intercourse Act, the single major piece of federal Indian legislation, to the "tribes" in the newly acquired Territory of New Mexico. The 1834 act prohibited non-Indian acquisition of Indian land except under certain tightly controlled circumstances. But in 1851 the United States had not yet defined what lands the New Mexico Pueblos owned and, indeed, Congress had not made it very clear about whether or not the 1851 act applied to the Pueblos (as opposed to "genuine" tribes like the Jicarillas and Navajos). Even if the 1851 act applied to the New Mexico Pueblos, it applied prospectively only.[30] Nothing about the 1851 act would reveal what to make of Pueblo landholdings prior to 1851 or, indeed, 1846. That aspect of the dilemma of Pueblo landownership was simply a land grant problem arising under the law of New Mexico's antecedent sovereign—Mexico—and governed by the Treaty of Guadalupe Hidalgo.

That is exactly the way the United States treated it. The new sovereign filtered Calhoun's three-step program for Pueblo land relief through the same system it used to adjudicate all New Mexico land grants—first through the surveyor general system and then, after 1891, through the Court of Private Land Claims. The 1854 act established the office of Surveyor General for New Mexico and fixed the procedures for adjudicating claims to land in the newly acquired New Mexican territory. In claims originating under the United States' antecedent sovereigns the act made no distinction between Pueblo and Hispanic land grants. The first surveyor general knew nothing about either. But the first official instructions to Pelham in August 1854 directed him to pay early and special attention to the urgent need, as expressed by Calhoun, among others, to confirm the Pueblos' land grants.

As a result, the initial validation of the Pueblo grants came at the initiative of the surveyor general himself and at such an early time that he was entirely ignorant of the general land grant conditions that would confront the office. Of the twenty supposedly active Pueblos in New Mexico at the time of the surveyor general's arrival in Santa Fe in the fall of 1854, Pelham had approved four by the time of his first annual report in September 1855 and fourteen more by the time of his next annual report in September 1856.

There is no evidence that the Pueblos themselves either filed or pushed these claims. Apparently, Pelham acted on his own. He took as valid the eleven so-called 1689 Cruzate grants to different Pueblos which the archives yielded, even though a casual look at the documents would have raised doubts about their authenticity. For seven additional

Pueblo claims, Pueblo leaders universally testified that their landownership was based on the same Cruzate grants and the documents had been lost or stolen. All the Pueblos agreed that these grants provided both the basis and the measure of their entitlement to land: 18,000-acre square blocks at the heart of New Mexico. On that basis Pelham ruled that eighteen Pueblos had proved their entitlement under Spanish and Mexican law to their four square leagues.[31]

Pelham never gave notice of the nature and extent of his proposed Pueblo grant confirmations to the Hispanos then residing within the boundaries of the four square leagues. They neither appeared nor protested. His primary job was to segregate already acquired property from the public domain which the United States had won in conquest, not to determine competing private claims to land that clearly was not public. His disregard for the complex actual status of the land did not reflect any conscious federal Indian policy. Instead, it reflected the surveyor general's casual ignorance of the actual situation within the Pueblo land grants that he recommended for congressional confirmation. Among the recommendations was the Pecos Pueblo grant, the ancestral home of an Indian people who had not lived there since 1837 and now, in 1855, the location of a growing Hispanic community.

In the course of the procedure established for that confirmation, the 1854 act called for review at various levels of the surveyor general's initial recommendations. The commissioner of the General Land Office, to whom Pelham's Pueblo reports were first sent for review, simply reprinted them as his own and sent them to the U.S. House Committee on Private Land Claims. By early 1858 Committee Chairman Sandidge admitted that Congress could not fairly assess land claims in New Mexico. Sandidge also frankly stated that the surveyor general for New Mexico was not suited by training or profession for the essentially adjudicatory function the 1854 act called on him to perform. Congress itself showed little knowledge and less interest in Pueblo or New Mexican affairs. Yet out of this series of federal admissions of inability there came in 1858 congressional confirmation of land grants, based on written conveyances from the Crown of Spain, to seventeen of New Mexico's twenty Pueblos.[32]

In addition, the confirmation process obscured the exact areal extent of the claims considered. Formal surveys came after, not before, the crucial act of congressional confirmation. When it confirmed the Pueblo grants, Congress may have had no idea that large parts of Hispanic

Taos, Española, Peñasco, Nambe, Pojoaque, Jacona, El Rancho, Pecos, Angostura, Peña Blanca, and Bernalillo, to name a few long established non-Indian communities, lay within the bounds of the grants it had just confirmed exclusively to the Pueblos. But, in 1858 and 1859, when federal surveyors set out to establish the boundaries so confirmed, there was no question that those boundaries would include a large number of non-Indians.

The newly acquired knowledge, brought home by the surveys, gave the federal government no pause. In response to continued pressure from the Pueblos—while overcoming the crippling inertia of the Civil War—the United States completed the confirmation process by issuing United States patents in 1864 to each of the seventeen Pueblos whose titles Congress had confirmed in 1858. Each patent read like a deed from the United States to the Pueblo. Each patent recited the endless bearings and distances which located the confirmed Pueblo grants on the face of the New Mexico earth. President Lincoln himself signed each patent and sent along with it a silver cane as a testimony to the new sovereign's goodwill.

Each patent issued in 1864 ended with a disclaimer as to its effect which would haunt land grants in general and Pueblo land grants in particular from that moment on. The disclaimer read: "This confirmation shall only be construed as a relinquishment of all title and claim of the United States to any of the said lands and shall not affect any adverse valid rights, should such exist." At the time no one made much of the disclaimer. Hispanos holding land within the confirmed, surveyed, and patented Pueblo grants under titles that had been formally blessed by the governments of either Spain or Mexico could have believed that their claims to patented Pueblo land would survive. None expressed any worry about the effect of the Pueblo patents on their lands.[33]

But two other tangential concerns—the finality of congressionally issued patents and the status of Pueblo Indians under United States Indian law—might have given pause to the more farsighted. The first problem emerged slowly from the tangle of New Mexico land grant adjudication. Suddenly faced with conflicting and overlapping claims to New Mexico grant land, Congress adopted a variety of interim solutions to reflect the fact that it could not resolve the esoteric disputes. In one early instance where two claimants petitioned for the same land, Congress confirmed the claim of one and allowed the other to select equal acreage elsewhere in the New Mexico public domain. When that solution promised to exhaust the public domain, Congress for a short time took to confirming, surveying, and patenting overlapping claims and leaving it to the local courts to decide the issue. And when that solution promised to leave the New Mexico land situation as confused as it had ever been, Congress stood on its initial decisions and let adverse claimants find some other route to relief.

Quite quickly, the courts washed their hands of the matter too, holding the initial congressional determination of ownership final and not reviewable by the courts as a matter of judicial deference to legislative fact finding.[34] As a matter of general land grant law, that doctrine tended to insulate the congressional confirmation of New Mexico land grants from any subsequent review. Applied to the Pueblo land grants as such, the doctrine guaranteed that the initial 1858 confirmation of the Pueblo grants to the named Pueblos determined that, as of 1858, those Pueblos owned all of the lands patented to them despite the presence of non-Indians within those boundaries for hundreds of years.

The second lurking problem, that of the status of Pueblo Indians under United States law, revealed the reverse side of this emerging land grant issue. If land grant law prevented non-Indians from claiming acquired rights in lands confirmed by the United States to the Pueblos, then general New Mexico law, applicable after 1846 even to lands acquired prior to that year, would have protected non-Indian holdings within confirmed Pueblo grants on the basis of adverse possession. This common law principle, codified in New Mexico for the first time in 1857, gave rights to the possessor of land after a certain number of years, no matter who held the title. With the help of the doctrine, non-Indians who had held land confirmed by the Spanish government within the areas now patented to the Pueblos, could make their claim stick, not on the basis of approved possession by the Spanish or Mexican government, but by virtue of only ten years possession since 1846.[35]

Such a possibility held only as long as United States and territorial laws of adverse possession could be applied against the Pueblos. The chief effect of the 1834 Trade and Intercourse Act, extended to the "tribes" of New Mexico in 1851, was to prohibit any limitations against recognized Indians. The answer to Indian agent Calhoun's third concern—the status of Pueblo Indians under United States Indian law—finally would determine that issue. But if the congressional determination of Pueblo ownership of lands patented to each of them was final, and if local laws of adverse possession did not apply to those lands, then the Hispanos living within the borders of the confirmed, surveyed, and patented land grants were completely out of luck. On the other hand, if the laws of adverse possession did apply, then the land grant question was moot anyway, since without a confirmed grant the Hispano would still own the land on the basis of his possession existing since the advent of United States sovereignty.

The judicial battle over the legal status of Pueblo land grants dominated the New Mexico legal scene between 1864 and 1877. The battle took place within the esoteric limits of these then well-understood issues. Shrouded in obscure local politics, managed by United States district attorneys with their own political axes to grind, and decided at first by local territorial judges with their own biases and then by a United States Supreme Court looking down the business end of a new federal Indian agenda, the Pueblo Indian lawsuits between the first local decision in 1867 and the final Supreme Court decision in 1877 were sometimes difficult to follow. But clearly those lawsuits represented the third and final prong of the Pueblo land program formulated by Indian agent Calhoun in 1848–1850. In addition, the Pueblo lawsuits involved the fundamental determination of the status of non-Indians within the boundaries of confirmed Pueblo land grants as well as the continued status of those grants themselves.

Territorial District Judge John B. Slough decided the first Pueblo case in 1867. He ruled that the 1834 Trade and Intercourse Act as extended to New Mexico in 1851 did not apply to New Mexico Pueblos or their lands, because the Pueblos were too civilized to fall into the category of "tribes" to which the act was directed. In 1869 the territorial supreme court affirmed that decision. The United States District Attorney failed to appeal, and there the matter lay. The decision seemed a victory for the advanced state of the Pueblos. But the result deprived the Pueblos of the only federal act that prohibited the laws of adverse possession from favoring of non-Indians against the Pueblos and allowed Hispanos residing within the Pueblo grants to solidify their ancient possessions through territorial law in a way which they could not have done either through federal land grant law or through federal Indian law.

Federal Indian agents in New Mexico basically agreed with the 1869 decision of the territorial supreme court but their superiors in Washington wanted a definitive decision on the issue from the United States Supreme Court. So in late 1872 and early 1873, United States District Attorney Thomas B. Catron reopened the issue of the applicability of the Trade and Intercourse Act to the Pueblos by filing more than 200 suits against Hispanos living within the patented boundaries of Pueblo grants.[36]

This time the non-Indians defended themselves in a variety of ways. They hired lawyers to prove once again that the act simply did not apply to the New Mexico Pueblos and their lands. But, in addition, they took a new tack and finally tried to reopen the question of the validity of their land claims that had originated under the laws of Spain and Mexico, that had been guaranteed by the Treaty of Guadalupe Hidalgo, and that happened to either overlap or lie entirely within the land already patented by the United States Congress to the New Mexico Pueblos.

Between April 1872 and January 1874, while the second Pueblo litigation worked its way through the courts, the surveyor general of New Mexico issued reports recommending congressional confirmation of at least eleven Hispanic land claims that overlapped in whole or in part land grants already confirmed to New Mexico Pueblos. Five of those claims lay in the Nambe-Pojoaque stream system, dated from 1699 at the earliest to 1731 at the latest. These claims, when combined with a sixth unadjudicated claim filed earlier, would have occupied the western quarter of the confirmed Nambe Pueblo grant, almost all of the Pojoaque Pueblo grant, a northern portion of the Tesuque Pueblo grant, and the eastern half of the San Ildefonso Pueblo grant.[37]

Unsure of the outcome of the second effort to bring the Trade and Intercourse Act prohibitions to bear on New Mexico Pueblo land grants, Hispanos remaining within the Pueblo borders were hedging their bets. If the Supreme Court said that they could not use the local law of adverse possession to justify their ancient landholdings, then perhaps Congress would confirm those holdings on the basis of the Treaty of Guadalupe Hidalgo and Spanish and Mexican law.

As things turned out, the Hispanos need not have worried. In May 1877 the Supreme Court announced in *United States v. Joseph* that it agreed with the initial 1867 decision that the Trade and Intercourse Act did not apply to the lands of New Mexico Pueblos. Supreme Court Justice Miller concluded that if the defendant were

> on the lands of the Pueblo without the consent of the inhabitants, he may be ejected or punished civilly by a suit for trespass according to the law regulating such matters in the Territory. If he is there with their consent or license, we know of no injury which the United States suffers by his presence, nor any statute which he violates in that regard.[38]

The *Joseph* decision conveyed many unstated messages. Clearly the Supreme Court held that the Pueblos could defend themselves under local law. But even in 1877, local law could not reach those non-Indians who had lived in good faith on patented Pueblo land for more than ten years or since 1866. Because many of them had been there for a century before that, they no longer had to worry about their homes or, they thought, their land grants. As for the Pueblos, the *Joseph* decision simply told them how to prevent future land loss. There was no remedy for past Pueblo land losses.

Congress could have amended the Trade and Intercourse Act specifically to include the Pueblos after the extension of United States sovereignty. It did not. Congress also could have confirmed, surveyed, and patented the overlapping claims approved by the surveyor general of New Mexico. It did not do that either, and Hispanos residing within Pueblo boundaries did not force the issue. They may have lost the grant battle but they had won the adverse possession war, and either route promised them the protection they needed. In effect, by 1880 the federal government had declined any further responsibility for the additional mess it had created with its handling of Pueblo Indian land grants.

As of 1880 that benign neglect left New Mexico just about where it had always been with its Pueblo land problem. New Mexico was changing from the inside, however, while federal Indian policy was changing from the outside. The Pueblo grant problem was hardly over yet. The arrival of the railroad from the east in 1879–1880 brought a series of new connections to the hitherto isolated territory. For one, the railroad literally brought trained anthropologists and other intellectuals interested in primitive cultures to New Mexico. Adolph Bandelier and others like him "discovered" the Pueblos in the 1880s. From that point on, the Pueblos' stock started to soar in the national arena.

Congressional legislative proposals slowly started to reflect the rise. An 1888 federal act setting out the terms and conditions on which New Mexico might be admitted as a state to the union required that the proposed new state disclaim all jurisdiction over the Pueblos and their lands. Although statehood did not come to pass at this time, the federal condition for entrance suggested a new, as yet unexpressed, federal concern with the Pueblo Indians. Early in the 1890s, Congress began appropriating money for a special attorney to represent the Pueblos in their legal affairs. Cassandra-like, the attorneys began to foward to Washington horror stories of Pueblo land losses to non-Indians as if the losses had just happened. In the first decade of the twentieth century, Congress quietly but finally halted territorial taxation of Pueblo land, a taxation that had resulted in massive paper losses of Pueblo grant land for failure to pay local taxes. By exempting Pueblo grant land in 1905, Congress announced a new, special interest in Pueblo grant land that belied the earlier implication of the *Joseph* decision that Pueblo land was just like any other private land in New Mexico. All of these harbingers of change suggested that in the New Mexico railroad era, Pueblo Indian grant land would differ fundamentally from non-Indian land of all kinds.[39]

In addition, the changes brought by the railroad increased pressure to finally dispose of all lingering land grant problems in the state. Those lingering problems, it was said, prevented the federal government from fully developing its public domain. Land officials could not even tell where the public domain was until the land grants originating under Spain and Mexico had been disposed of; this uncertainty also prevented the full exploitation of private property since titles were so unsure. After years of listening to constant suggestions, Congress finally in 1891 established the Court of Private Land Claims and directed it to conclude the business begun by the surveyor general of New Mexico in 1854.

The surveyor general and Congress had already adjudicated all but one of the Pueblo land grants. The 1891 act establishing the Court of Private Land Claims reflected the new, growing preference for the Pueblos and their lands when it specifically limited the court's jurisdiction to unadjudicated grants that did not overlap already surveyed, patented, and thereafter unextinguished Pueblo Indian lands. In other words, the 1891 act offered no possibility of land grant relief to those Hispanic grant claimants whose petitions for confirmation the surveyor general had approved between 1872 and 1874, but which Congress itself had never acted on. The adverse possession blessed by the *Joseph* decision left them with their only alternative.

As a result, the Court of Private Land Claims had little legal impact on the ongoing problem of Pueblo land grants and the status of Hispanos claiming land within them. Ironically, however, the work of the court added considerably to the historical confusion about the status of the Pueblos and the basis of their land claims.

Of all the Pueblos, only Laguna was left without a patent when the Court of Private Land Claims began its work. So Laguna went before that body for confirmation of its grant from Spain. A government handwriting expert demonstrated, however, that the grant document offered by Laguna was a clumsy and inexpert forgery. Parts of that forgery had appeared in the other 1689 grants presented earlier to and approved by the surveyor general and Congress. Since Congress had already approved the land grant claims of other Pueblos who said that they had had grants and lost them, the Court of Private Land Claims approved the Laguna "grant" as well. But the Laguna discovery demonstrated that the United States had badly misunderstood Pueblo claims to land.[40]

Instead, the simple-minded assertion that the Pueblos absolutely owned the four square leagues Congress had confirmed to each became louder and more definite on the national scene while the concomitant and sometimes long-standing claims of non-Indians to the same land continued to recede into the national background. By 1904 the Court of Private Land Claims had finished its work in New Mexico. The land grant problem was supposed to be over. By 1910 Congress determined that New Mexico was ready to come into the federal union as a full-fledged state. But no one had resolved the ancient and continuing problem of Pueblo land grants. When statehood finally came on 6 January 1912, that problem quickly became worse, not better. As lawyer-historian Ralph Emerson Twitchell described the Pueblo land grant problem to Congress in 1923, "I have stated all along there are so many things in connection with this entire business that twenty King Solomons can not unravel the knot."[41]

Once again, the relationship between the San Ildefonso Pueblo, the Pojoaque Pueblo, and the heirs of Ignacio Roybal at Jacona provides a paradigm for the new problems that United States sovereignty brought to the already confused Pueblo land grant scene under Spain and Mexico.

Appearing before Surveyor General Pelham in 1856, the San Ildefonso and Pojoaque Pueblos could not produce the 1689 Cruzate grants that other Pueblos had introduced and that all Pueblos asserted were the basis for their land claims protected by the Treaty of Guadalupe

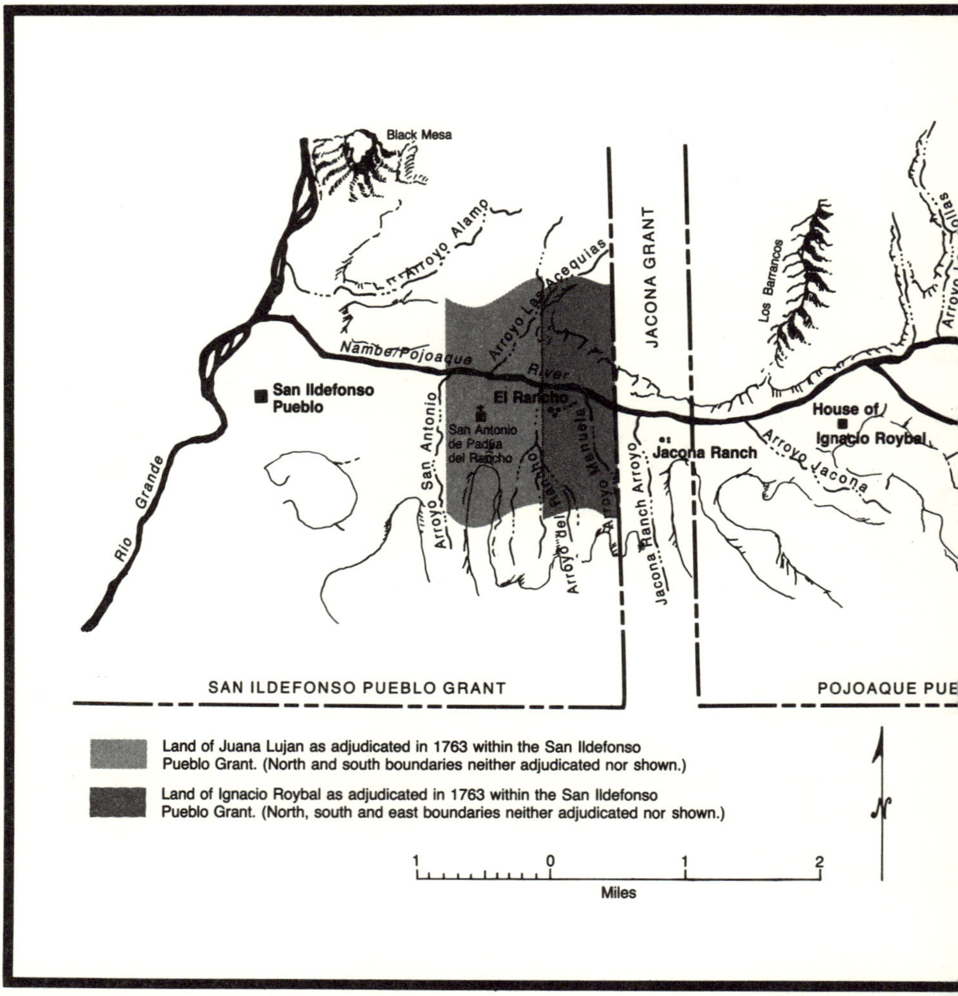

MAP 3. Juana Lujan and Ignacio Roybal grants.

Hidalgo. On 16 June 1856, the San Ildefonso Pueblo leaders told Pelham that the Pueblo had received such a grant but that a priest had taken it to Santa Fe "many years ago" to have a certified copy made and had never returned. When asked about the extent of the land conveyed by the grant, the San Ildefonsans responded, "the grant called for one league from the church towards the four cardinal points. We

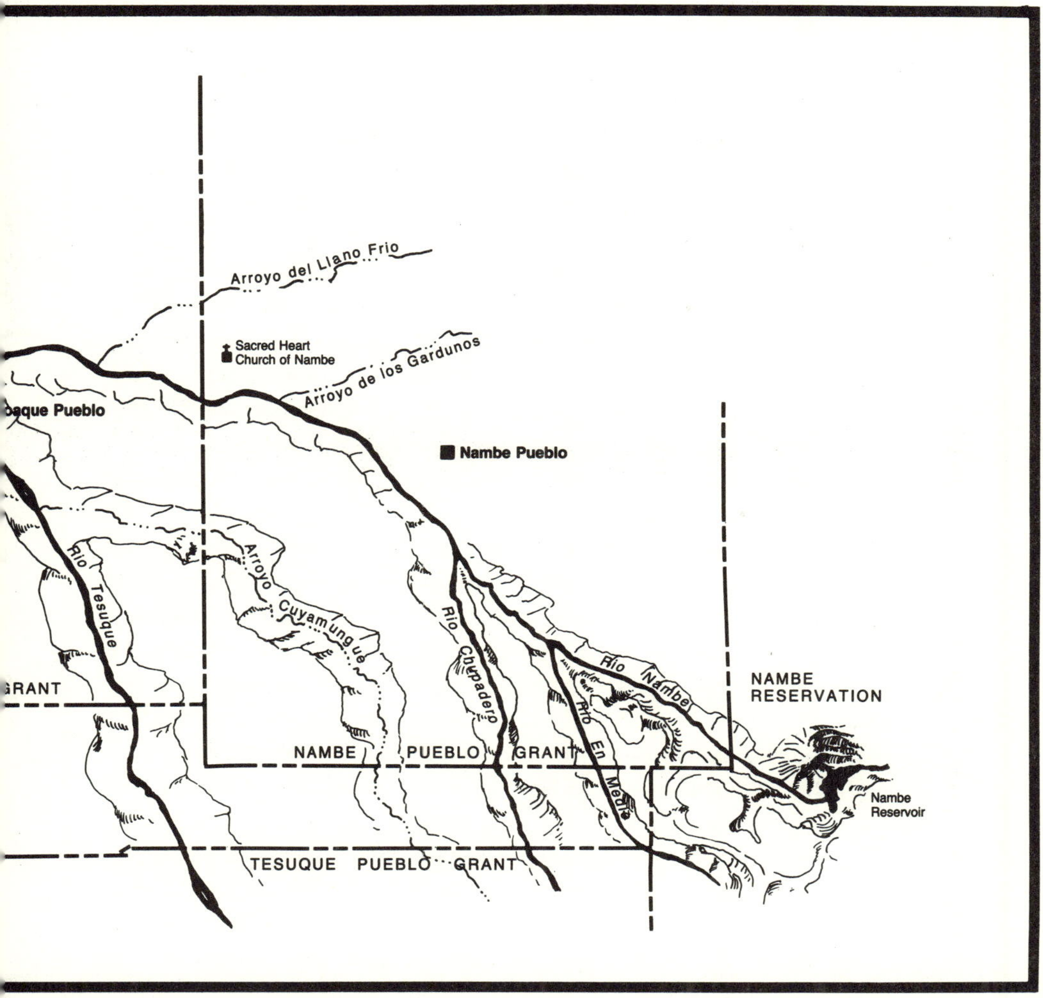

claim the same amount of land the other Pueblos have." Two weeks later, on 28 June 1856, the Pojoaque Pueblo leaders told Pelham the same story, changing it only to attribute the loss of the 1689 grant document to a corrupt Hispanic alcalde from nearby Chimayo.[42]

Less than three months later, Surveyor General Pelham forwarded his recommendation that Congress confirm the full four square leagues to each of the Pueblos. In addition, Pelham urged Congress to act "as speedily as possible" in the matter. Congress responded by confirming the San Ildefonso and Pojoaque Pueblo grants in 1858, surveying them in 1858–1859, and patenting them in 1864. The Pueblo patents included the homes of the heirs of Juana Lujan and the heirs of Ignacio Roybal.

Neither Hispanic family had any notice of the actions taken by Pelham and Congress. By September 1856, Pelham and his assistants had chronologically organized the 1,014 documents they had inherited from the Spanish and Mexican archives of New Mexico. Buried in them was the actual history of the land jointly occupied by the Hispanos and the Pueblos of San Ildefonso and Pojoaque. But Pelham could not even read the documents, and his assistants clearly had not had time to digest them.[43]

Despite the patents and the increasingly accepted legal view that determination of title to Pueblo grants was final under United States law, Hispanic residents still could count on their ancient possessions to defeat the formal Pueblo title so long as the law allowed that possession to count for something in the world of federal Indian land titles. That was what the *Joseph* litigation was really about. The residents of El Rancho and Jacona must have watched anxiously between 1867 and 1877 to see what would happen, even though they formally were not involved.

But in addition, while they awaited formal determination of the adverse possession issue, the heirs of Ignacio Roybal explored the alternative possibility of getting the United States to confirm their land grant. The Roybals' grant, like the Pueblo grants, had originated under the laws of New Mexico's antecedent sovereigns and was equally entitled to protection. On 5 January 1874, while the United States Supreme Court waited for final briefs in the *Joseph* case, attorney Samuel Ellison petitioned Surveyor General Proudfit for congressional confirmation of the Jacona grant. The petitioners were the heirs and legal representatives of both Ignacio Roybal and Jacinto Pelaez from whom Roybal had purchased that part of the grant not given to him in the early eighteenth century. Several witnesses supported the petition in affidavits. Neither the San Ildefonso or Pojoaque Pueblos received notice of its filing or the potential conflict the Jacona petition might involve with the leagues already confirmed and patented to the two Pueblos. But on 10 June 1874, less than six months after the petition had been filed, Surveyor General Proudfit recommended confirmation of the grant to the legal representatives of Ignacio Roybal.

A preliminary survey of the recommended Jacona grant in September 1878 showed it to contain an astounding 46,341 acres. Most of these acres lay within grants already confirmed and patented to the Pueblos of Pojoaque, San Ildefonso, and even Tesuque. If Congress had acted on Proudfit's favorable recommendation of the Jacona grant, there is no telling how it would have handled the conflict. But as was the case with all other recommendations forwarded by the surveyor general of New Mexico after 1870, Congress did nothing.[44]

Inaction left in limbo, however, that small portion of the Jacona grant that lay between the confirmed, patented, and surveyed boundaries of the Pueblos of Pojoaque and San Ildefonso on the east and west and the Tesuque Pueblo on the south. In enacting in 1891 the bill establishing the Court of Private Land Claims, Congress specifically restricted the power of the court to approving those Spanish and Mexican land claims which did not conflict with either land already patented to Pueblos or any other just and unextinguished Indian title. To those portions of the Jacona grant that overlapped the three Pueblo grants, the 1891 act offered no relief.

Still, the heirs of Ignacio Roybal tried to use the 1891 act for the limited help that it offered. On 21 September 1892, their attorneys petitioned the Court of Private Land Claims for confirmation of the Jacona grant. The government denied the validity of the grant altogether, but the Court of Private Land Claims agreed with the petitioners on several alternative grounds. The court's decree confirming the Jacona grant specifically excepted from its operation lands lying within the Pueblos of San Ildefonso, Tesuque, and Pojoaque.

The July 1898 survey of the confirmed Jacona grant showed just how pinched that victory was. According to the official survey, the Jacona grant contained 6,952 acres after excluding the following overlaps with the already patented Pueblo grants: Tesuque, 1,163 acres; San Ildefonso, 901 acres; and Pojoaque, 2,775 acres. Nobody knew what had happened to the additional 35,000 acres shown by the 1878 preliminary survey as being contained in the Jacona grant. Still on 15 November 1909, the United States patented the confirmed 6,952 acres of the Jacona grant to the heirs, successors, assignees, and legal representatives of Ignacio Roybal, his wife, Francisca Gomez, and their children.[45]

The Roybal heirs had not rescued much from the United States's grant confirmation process. They had not formally straightened out with their Pueblo neighbors the significant portions of the patented Pueblo lands that they used and occupied. But at least they had finally gotten the United States to recognize those portions of land that did not conflict with the Pueblos. That recognition extended to almost 1,000 acres of Jacona grant common lands, lands owned by no individual resident of the grant but used by all. It was a small victory. But, as things turned out, it was more than any of their kinsmen to the east in San Ildefonso Pueblo grant lands and to the west in Pojoaque Pueblo lands were finally able to save.

In 1910, Jacona slid back into the obscurity from which it had come, and the plight of the San Ildefonso Pueblo started to rise to national attention. Indian agents and Anglo visitors to New Mexico with easy access to wider audiences began to publicize San Ildefonso Pueblo land lost by "encroachment" to Hispanos as if those "losses" had just recently happened. Horrified publicists blamed recent upstream trespassers for acute water shortages at the Pueblo itself. The shortages were real enough—San Ildefonso could not produce enough food at the turn of the century to support itself—but by the Indians' own account, San Ildefonso had also been water short in the 1680s, a time when only Pueblos shared the water of the Nambe-Pojoaque stream system. San Ildefonso Pueblo had a problem: it was very old.[46]

In the seventy years before New Mexico statehood, the United States had done nothing through either its land grant or Indian policy to alleviate the Pueblo's problem. The Pueblos were left with a significant number of technical intruders within their United States-created borders. Those technical intruders found no relief in Congress or the federal government either. On the eve of New Mexico statehood in 1912 those Hispanic "trespassers" were left hanging on the thin thread of adverse possession. In the *Joseph* decision, the United States Supreme Court had read one particular federal statute to imply that state-ordained title by possession might work against the Pueblos. But courts could always maneuver around legislation if they chose. In addition, Congress could amend the statute. For seventy years, neither branch of the federal government had taken such options. Within a little more than one decade of New Mexico statehood in 1912, the coordinate branches of federal government took both. In the name of clarity, the confusion over the nature and extent of Pueblo Indian land grants only deepened.

When the chaos finally cleared around the mid-1930s, there remained a few problems that still return to haunt the Pueblos and their neighbors.

Pueblo Land Grants in the Hands of the New Federal Government

> The people of the Pueblos, although sedentary rather than nomadic in their inclinations and disposed to peace and industry are nevertheless Indians in race, custom and domestic government. Always living in separate and isolated communities, adhering to primitive modes of life, largely influenced by superstition and fetishism, and chiefly governed according to the crude customs inherited from their ancestors, they are essentially a simple, uninformed, and inferior people.
>
> —Mr. Justice VanDevanter for a unanimous United States Supreme Court in *United States v. Sandoval,* 1913

In the fifty years of the nineteenth century during which the United States held sovereignty over the New Mexico Pueblos, Congress intensified the dilemma of non-Indians on Pueblo grant lands, and the Supreme Court washed its hands of the matter. Now, at the beginning of the twentieth century, the two institutions reversed roles. The Supreme Court breathed new life into a problem it had laid to rest, and Congress tried once again to purge the Pueblo grant problem from the national mind. In the ultimate irony, the Supreme Court left open a narrow gap through which the Pueblo land grant problem threatened to sweep, hoary, unresolved, and more difficult than ever.

The beginning of this new round of false starts and incomplete finishes was played out against New Mexico's final drive to statehood between 1910 and 1912. That process set into motion a new, deepening confusion about the nature and extent of Pueblo claims to land. The process also unleashed a cancerous growth of ironies, feeding on each other, growing exponentially, and heading for certain disaster.

The majority of New Mexicans, with the Pueblos and their supporters as notable exceptions, favored statehood as the only means in the federal system of achieving a full measure of sovereign control over local affairs. Territorial status, to which Congress had consigned New Mexico in 1851, left New Mexico laws, literally and practically, at the whim of a national Congress serving a national constituency. Territorial status reversed the balance of power at the heart of a fully federal system of government and gave general powers to the national government while limiting powers of the local government. Statehood promised to give to New Mexico for the first time the full range of general governmental powers, and limited the federal government's powers to those expressly reserved.

Ironically, under the *Joseph* rule and Congress's lack of response to it, the limited power of territorial status had given New Mexico general power over the lands and resources of New Mexico Pueblos. Now, in the first two decades of the twentieth century, as New Mexico strove to become a state with general governmental power, Congress attempted for the first time to limit that general state power. In 1888, Congress had demanded as a condition to New Mexico's entry to the union as a state that the new state disclaim any jurisdiction over New Mexico Pueblos or their lands. In 1910, as the Territory of New Mexico made its final push to statehood, Congress upped the Pueblo Indian ante again.

This time Congress demanded as a condition to New Mexico's statehood additional renunciations of state jurisdiction over Pueblo Indian affairs. The conditions, written into the 1910 Federal Enabling Act, grew out of the increasing national attention on Pueblo affairs in New Mexico and reflected the concern and power of Senator Alfred Beveridge. The enabling act's conditions were directed at specific post-*Joseph* decisions of the federal territorial courts in New Mexico, at the underlying applicability of the 1834 Trade and Intercourse Act to the Pueblos, and, finally, at the jurisdiction of the proposed new state over the Pueblos. In effect, the conditions offered New Mexico the general powers of a state government only if the new state would agree to limit those powers by excluding control over the Pueblos.

Without a whimper and, indeed, without any discussion at all, New Mexico accepted. The constitution adopted by the new state contained all the disclaimers Congress had insisted on. On 6 January 1912, New Mexico became a full-fledged state with diminished power over the Pueblos, whereas from 1851 to 1912 New Mexico had been a diminished territory with full-fledged power over the Pueblos.[47]

At the time, no one knew precisely what this curious turnabout in local affairs meant, but everyone anxiously wanted to find out. The Federal Enabling Act of 1910 and the New Mexico State Constitution of 1912 specifically provided that the state would not contest the applicability to the Pueblos of general federal prohibitions against liquor in Indian country. The state of New Mexico also agreed to accept in principle the same prohibitions in the general 1851 Trade and Intercourse Act and an 1897 special act bearing specifically on the Pueblos, the earlier of which the United States Supreme Court had held did not apply to the Pueblos and the later of which the territorial courts of New Mexico had held inapplicable to the Pueblos. Clearly, the enabling act meant to reverse something. Almost immediately everyone set out to discover just what.

Within a couple of months of statehood and as if according to a plan, Indian agent "Pussyfoot" Johnson arrested a Hispano named Felipe Sandoval for selling liquor on the Santa Clara Pueblo grant. That mundane event set the stage for a monumental battle between the federal government and the new state of New Mexico over the power to control affairs on Pueblo land grants. Enter stage left Santa Fe lawyer A. B. Renehan in defense of Sandoval and state sovereignty over all New Mexicans, including Pueblos. Enter stage right Santa Fe attorney Francis C. Wilson as special prosecutor for the United States, who argued for the exclusively federal status of Pueblo affairs. The two protagonists over the next decade argued over the status of Pueblos and their land before Judge William H. Pope, a former special attorney for the Pueblos, but also the same judge who had previously ruled that the 1897 federal liquor prohibition could not apply to the Pueblos.

In what every New Mexican lawyer must have regarded as a masterful, exhaustive opinion, Judge Pope ruled in late July 1913 that Congress had no power to insist that New Mexico pay as a price for statehood the loss of power over the state's Pueblo Indians. The enabling act's restrictions on New Mexico's control over pueblos were void; no legitimate federal act prohibited Felipe Sandoval from selling liquor at the Santa Clara Pueblo. New Mexico attorneys doubted there was any chance that Judge Pope could be wrong or that a higher court might reverse him.[48]

When the Supreme Court decision came in October 1913, it should have raised even more eyebrows. Associate Supreme Court Justice VanDevanter reversed Pope's decision and sustained the constitutionality of the enabling act's requirements regarding state involvement with New Mexico Pueblos. The federal government, he ruled, retained the power to decide who was or was not an Indian under federal law. Congress had exercised that retained power in the 1910 enabling act. Now the new state was stuck with Congress's decision that New Mexico Pueblos were federal wards under the control of the federal government.

If that were all VanDevanter and the Supreme Court said in *United States v. Felipe Sandoval,* there would not have been much of a problem. New Mexico simply would have to change its ways in the future; nothing would affect rights established under the previous regimes. But VanDevanter in *Sandoval* went on to suggest that the previous *Joseph* view of the Pueblos as too "civilized" to be "Indians" was incorrect and that, in fact, the Pueblos always had been the wards of the guardian federal government.

This was strange, gossamer stuff coming from the Supreme Court, even though the tantalizing talk was characteristic of VanDevanter's opinions in general. Formally, the view of Pueblos as wards probably was not necessary to the *Sandoval* opinion, but the implications were clear enough: if the Pueblos had been wards since the beginning of United States rule in New Mexico, then no non-Indian could acquire rights to Pueblo land without the permission of the guardian federal government. That permission the United States had never given. In fact, the United States had confirmed to each Pueblo the full measure of their "leagues" as provided under Mexican law, despite the presence of many non-Indians within those borders. Clearly *Sandoval* and the previous actions of the federal government confirming the Pueblo grants had started events on a collision course with a couple of centuries of New Mexico history.

Surprisingly, at the outset no one paid much attention to these implications for the new state of New Mexico. Some attorneys wrote *Sandoval* off as "that liquor case." Others went ahead with business as usual. For example, Francis Wilson's victory in *Sandoval* did not stop him from arranging the sale of a large piece of the Pojoaque Pueblo grant, including those parts claimed by the great-grandchildren of Ignacio Roybal, to a California promoter.[49]

Indeed, *Sandoval*'s 1913 declaration of wardship status for the Pueblos neither changed much in their existing relationship with the federal government nor offered much immediate relief. At least since 1900, the Indian Service had made numerous expensive and unsuccessful efforts to develop an adequate supply of water for the San Ildefonso Pueblo, situated, as it was, at the tail end of the Nambe-Pojoaque stream system. Pipes, wells, infiltration galleries, a main stem diversion in the Rio Grande—each financed by the United States before 1913—all failed. Nothing about *Sandoval*'s abstract declaration promised the San Ildefonso Pueblo a new source of funds or any more water. At the time, no one considered San Ildefonso's salvation to lie in clearing their league of the El Rancho and Jacona settlers, since no one considered wholesale eviction a viable option at any other New Mexico Pueblo.[50] Yet slowly, between 1913 and 1924, the *Sandoval* train started in that direction and began to pick up speed. In 1914 the United States began the long, tedious, and controversial task of identifying by survey all the tracts of land within confirmed Pueblo grants then held by non-Indians. Responses differed as bitterness grew and the survey progressed. The Pueblos said claimants, largely Hispanic small farmers, exaggerated the nature and extent of their holdings. For their parts, the claimants, more than 3,000 of whom the Joy survey eventually identified on seventeen Pueblo grants, did what they could to shore up claims to land on which their ancestral homes had stood, sometimes for generations. Some went to Congress. Others, using an older VanDevanter Pueblo case, went to state court.

But now, the federal government began to take an active role in local Pueblo litigation. The United States, on behalf of the Pueblos, argued that the new state courts had no jurisdiction over Pueblo land and resources, particularly if the United States was a party. By and large, the courts agreed and the suits were dismissed.

But rather than let the matter rest there, a new and initially aggressive federal attorney, Richard Hanna, refiled the same suits on behalf of the Pueblos in the New Mexico federal courts. The so-called "Hanna ejectment suits," begun in 1919–1920, each addressed a particular situation. But, in addition, Hanna added to each suit another claim based on the new status of New Mexico Pueblos and the *Sandoval* decision: no non-Indian claim to land within the boundaries of the Pueblos as patented by the United States had any validity, no matter how long it had existed or what its source had been. To the humble beginnings of these relatively banal disputes, Hanna had added the ultimate Pueblo conundrum.[51]

The situation at the San Ildefonso Pueblo again illustrated both the peculiarities and the general Pueblo situation at the time. San Ildefonso's oldest, deepest, and most perplexing resource problems came from upstream, from the east and the communities of El Rancho, Jacona, and beyond. But for years Hispanic ranchers on the west side of the Rio Grande had plagued the Pueblo with their wandering herds. What began as a relatively minor dispute over cattle trespass west of the Rio Grande escalated under Hanna's aggressive tactics into a general attack on all non-Indians within the confirmed San Ildefonso grant in the case of *United States v. Rupert Archuleta, et al.*

By 1923 the more important issue of San Ildefonso's claim to water from the sparse Rio Pojoaque had also emerged. Once again trouble started in state court litigation begun by non-Indians on the stream system. Once again federal attorneys succeeded in having the initial suit thrown out of court. And, once again, they turned around and refiled the dismissed suit in federal court under their view of the new federal law.

The so-called *Exon* suit (*United States v. Guy S. Exon et al.*) named the Pueblo of San Ildefonso as plaintiff. The other upstream Pueblos in the Nambe-Pojoaque system did not join them as plaintiffs. Indeed, the names of the Pojoaque, Nambe, and Tesuque Pueblos did not even appear in the pleadings. But the list of defendants swelled between 1923 and 1925 to more than 850 and came to include both individual non-Indian irrigators and individual Pueblo irrigators upstream from San Ildefonso. What the *Exon* suit seemed to contemplate was nothing more than a formalization of that informal agreement Indian officials had worked out in the summer of 1923 whereby upstream Indian and non-Indian irrigators voluntarily let some of the Nambe-Pojoaque water flow down to San Ildefonso for that Pueblo's use. From San Ildefonso Pueblo's point of view in 1923, increased use by the upstream Nambe Pueblo posed as great a threat to its water supplies as similar use by any Hispano. A fair sharing of that limited supply by all promised some practical relief for San Ildefonso, at least in normal years.[52]

But by 1923 the war over Pueblo land and water had escalated to the point in New Mexico where racial status had become critical. United States law had divided long-time neighbors into mutually exclusive categories. Pueblo supporters saw the Hanna ejectment suits, despite their humble beginnings, as the brightest hope of fulfilling the nation's responsibilty to the Pueblos as American Indians. To those supporters, increasingly drawn from a national constituency of concerned citizens, that hope translated into an expectation that the Hanna suits would end in the federal court ordering that all Pueblo grants, as confirmed and patented by the United States, be cleared of all non-Pueblos and that suits like *Exon* would result in the restoration of all water rights to the Pueblos.

None of the suits reached that result or, indeed, any judicial end at all. In one sense, politics headed the suits off. In another sense, a different governmental entity simply intervened. Both Indian and non-Indian proponents in the escalating and looming Pueblo war feared the all-or-nothing result that the Hanna ejectment suits promised, and elected instead to hammer out a compromise in what was viewed as a more promising political arena: the United States Congress. After all, Congress had created part of the confusion by failing to respond to the open invitation of the 1877 *Joseph* decision until the 1910 Federal Enabling Act. Congress had also exercised its guardianship power over the Pueblos in the enabling act, and the Supreme Court had approved that exercise in the *Sandoval* case. Now, Congress could work out as well a final solution to the dilemmas created by its own inaction.

Of course, legislation, rather than litigation, meant politics. Everybody admitted that. But the course Congress charted over the next four years to solve the Pueblo problem became so contorted, and the battles of the larger-than-life combatants, including John Collier, A. A. Berle, A. B. Renehan, and Francis C. Wilson, among other national and local luminaries, became so intense that it was hard for even the participants to navigate. Often, from the perspective of the Pueblos, Congress itself seemed lost in a fog.[53]

To many, that fog extended to the bill which finally emerged on 6 June 1924. The Pueblo Lands Act represented Congress's effort to amalgamate at least six previous formal proposals, many of which took diametrically opposed positions with respect to the Pueblo and non-Indian rights they were supposed to adjust. Pro-Pueblo proposals were all based on the assumption that legally, at least, all non-Indians attempting to use Pueblo resources, basically defined as all land within the confirmed and patented Pueblo grants and all the water necessary for that land, were mere trespassers who had no rights to the lands they had been using, in some cases for generations. Pro-settler (as the Hispanos came to be called in the course of the battle) proposals were primarily based on the opposite assumption, that the non-Indians, not the Pueblos, had acquired rights that Congress could not take away. No court had ever determined which of these contradictory assumptions was correct. No court ever would. Instead, Congress took it on itself to adjust politically the claimed rights.

In doing so, Congress clearly favored the assumptions underlying the settlers', not the Pueblos', side. The 1924 act provided that the United States would recognize non-Indian claims to land within Pueblo grants if those claims had begun prior to one of two specified dates—

1899 or 1889—depending upon the nature of the claim. In itself, the fixing of permissible dates for recognizable non-Indian title represented a rejection of the basic Pueblo position that no non-Indian claim had any validity. But, in addition, the two effective dates in the 1924 legislation tracked to the day the history of local laws governing acquisition of real estate by adverse possession. The dates suggest that Congress meant to adopt the local law that the Pueblos claimed did not apply to them. If the choice of dates was intentional, it measured the extent to which Congress had rejected the Pueblos' claim of always having been free of territorial and state law. Clearly, in the 1924 act the Pueblos had not succeeded in wresting from Congress the results they had hoped to obtain from the Hanna ejectment suits, then still pending.

However, the Pueblos and their supporters did manage to salvage some of what they hoped would prove real concessions. For one, they forced a reluctant Congress to add compensation provisions to the 1924 act guaranteeing money at least for land the Pueblos might lose under the act. This late addition to what finally emerged as the law brought water to the surface for the first time. Prior to this legislation, Pueblo opponents shared a common assumption that if the Pueblos ended up losing land within their grants, they would also lose the water needed to irrigate that land. Now, late in the legislative game, the compensation provisions made this assumption explicit when Congress directed the United States to compensate for lost water as well as lost land.

In addition, Pueblo supporters managed to force Congress to add a requirement that non-Indians must have paid taxes on their claims within the pueblo grants in order to sustain that claim. New Mexico law had only recently added the tax requirement to one of its two adverse possession statutes. Pueblo advocates were informed that almost no one in New Mexico could prove he had paid the taxes for the requisite period. They regarded the addition of the requirement as a powerful tool in insisting that most land within the Pueblo grants be returned to the Pueblos. In the end, the tax requirements simply added another confusing issue to an already confused bill.

Finally, Pueblo supporters managed to salvage two additional procedural benefits from the 1924 act. From the beginning, the Pueblos had wanted a quasi-judicial body to make the numerous factual determinations on individual claims that the Pueblo problem would require. They got just such a body when the 1924 act created the

Pueblo Lands Board and directed it to consider particular non-Indian claims against the standards provided for by the act itself.

In a related, late-hour victory, the Pueblos got Congress to protect their right to complete the Hanna ejectment suits and others like them if they did not approve of the Pueblo Lands Board's handling of their case. The 1924 act never guaranteed that the unsatisfied Pueblo would win any resurrected case. It only guaranteed the Pueblo right to argue a case in court so long as the suit was filed within two years of the completion of the board's deliberations.

In this sense, the 1924 act offered no final solution to either the unresolved Hanna ejectment suits or the fundamental issue about who had what rights to which land within the confirmed Pueblo grants. Statutes of limitation and compensation, administrative determinations, and independent lawsuits were all played off against each other in a legal world that never got down to determining—and setting to rest—legal rights.[54]

Operating in this kind of vacuum, the quasi-judicial, quasi-administrative Pueblo Lands Board, called on by the 1924 act to administer its terms, was probably doomed to controversy from the very beginning. The oppositional characters of the board members and of the Pueblo, United States, and "settler" advocates who appeared before the board made its work even more bitter and the results it reached more obscure. For example, at the beginning of the board's operations in the summer of 1925, Board Chairman Herbert J. Hagerman candidly admitted that the Pueblo Lands Board had no idea how it was supposed to proceed or where it was to go. Immediately put on the defensive by Pueblo advocates anxious to know how the board would interpret the law under which it operated, the board officially declined to comment. The Pueblo Lands Board never recoverd from its initial problems in the nine years of its existence.

But the almost constant charges and countercharges, recriminations and rejoinders could not obscure the fundamental fact that the relatively recent recognition periods adopted by the act itself, when combined with the long presence of Hispanos in the federally recognized Pueblo grants, guaranteed that the Pueblo Lands Board would have to confirm in non-Indians many small tracts of the Pueblos' best irrigable land. Once the Pueblo Lands Board had laid the tax issue to rest, and the courts had confirmed the board's view of the matter, the battle to recover Pueblo lands, long in the hands of non-Indians, was lost.[55]

Various less essential issues, however, continued to provide the vessel into which interested parties could pour their strong feelings about the Pueblo grant issue. Compensation provided one. As the board's work wound down and the controversy surrounding it heated up, the erratic and increasingly niggardly board compensation recommendations became more and more controversial.

So did the Pueblo Lands Board's involvement with Pueblo water issues. Here also the board waffled in its approach. Initially, the board found that the Pueblos had lost both land and water if the non-Indian possession of an irrigated tract met the 1924 act's standards. The board recommended compensation for the loss of both. This system worked well enough in the first board determinations for the Tesuque Pueblo. But by the time the board moved on to consider the Nambe, San Ildefonso, and Taos Pueblo grants, where a great many non-Indians held more tracts than had been held at Tesuque, it became apparent that full compensation for both land and water would be very expensive indeed. The board began casting about for alternative water theories. By the late 1920s, the board had revised its original theory. It now held that in fact none of the Pueblos had lost any water when they lost their land, because the Indians retained a water right prior and paramount to any water right that might be appurtenant to lands within the Pueblo grants now confirmed in non-Indian ownership. This new theory represented a radical departure from existing practice and, indeed, from the theory put forward in *Exon* or any previous suit involving the nature and extent of Pueblo water rights. But, for the moment, the theory served the board's purpose of justifying the much-reduced awards it recommended for Pueblos after the initial Tesuque recommendation.[56]

All the while, Chairman Hagerman and the other board members cast about for what they considered practical solutions to the dilemma of the Pueblos in the third decade of the twentieth century. They made deals in New Mexico and in Washington to expedite the tedious work of the board. They tinkered with the tax and compensation provisions of the 1924 act to fashion what they regarded as an acceptable result. They made suggestions which went well beyond the board's formal jurisdiction in a political effort to bring the Pueblo matter to a final close.

By 1931, after almost six years of work and turmoil, the board thought it had succeeded. Altogether, during the time of its existence, the Pueblo Lands Board passed on 5,545 parcels of land claimed by non-Indians within the boundaries of Pueblo grants confirmed by the United States. These claims involved 98,000 acres, of which the board approved about 52 percent. But because the courts reversed some of the board's initial rejections, the net result was that about 80 percent of the non-Indian claims were finally approved, amounting to "something over 50,000 acres."[57]

The board solutions for the San Ildefonso and Pojoaque Pueblo grants were typical. The board considered as its fourth case the status of non-Indian claims to San Ildefonso grant lands, after having reviewed the status of Tesuque, Nambe, and Taos Pueblo lands. In its San Ildefonso report, issued 22 July 1929, the board found that non-Indians claimed to own 1,616 acres of the total 16,199 acres in the patented San Ildefonso Pueblo grant. Of the 455 claimants to these acres, the board approved the claims of 293 non-Indians to 863.3 acres, mostly in the El Rancho and Jacona areas settled in the early eighteenth century by Juana Lujan and Ignacio Roybal. Title to the balance of the San Ildefonso grant, some 15,336 acres, was reconfirmed to the Pueblo itself.

The story of the moribund Pojoaque Pueblo grant told a different tale, but the final numbers sounded a familiar tune. Uncertain at first as to whether the Pojoaque grant had not been entirely abandoned, the board nevertheless proceeded to determine the status of Pueblo claims to it. In its investigation, the board ascertained that 472 claimants had adverse claims totaling 2,084 acres and decided that, out of those claims, it would recognize those of 405 non-Indians to 1,722 acres. As at the San Ildefonso Pueblo grant, the practically nonexistent Pojoaque Pueblo gained reconfirmed title to the remaining 13,000 acres of the grant as confirmed and patented by the United States.[58]

The ecological facts of New Mexico agrarian life belied the relative story that these distributions seemed to tell. It was true enough that the Pueblos came away from the Pueblo Lands Board's determinations with a large part of their grant acreage intact. But the small percentage of lost land was composed almost entirely of irrigated, river bottom soil, while what they retained was composed of barren dry lands, suitable for, if anything, nonintensive grazing.

On the other hand, while the non-Indians wrested from the Pueblo Lands Board proceedings those small, intensively used irrigated tracts that they had farmed for generations, they lost all access to common grazing lands in the uplands of the grants. Access to these lands was as critical to the maintenance of traditional and essential subsistence livestock operations as were the irrigated lands to the maintenance of traditional, subsistence agricultural operations. For both Pueblos and non-Indians in the Nambe-Pojoaque valley, the Pueblo Lands Board determinations promised to alter fundamentally the relationship between two ethnic groups and one land base.

Some of these harbingers were dimly perceived at the time. Pueblo Lands Board Chairman Hagerman very quickly understood that the San Ildefonso Pueblo's primary problem was not land lost to non-Indians, but water claimed by Indians and non-Indians east and upstream from the Pueblo. His initial proposal for solving the San Ildefonso Pueblo's chronic water shortage involved physically relocating the Pueblo from the east to the west side of the Rio Grande; Hagerman reasoned that the Pueblo would never receive an adequate supply of water from the Nambe-Pojoaque. Thus, the Pueblo's only hope lay in the much more bountiful and less developed Rio Grande.

Thereafter, however, Hagerman and the board developed a new legal theory that promised to make up in water rights for what the San Ildefonso lacked in wet water. Fully articulated for the first time in the board's July 1929 San Ildefonso report, the theory would have guaranteed to each Pueblo the same kind of water rights that reservation tribes enjoyed, a paramount and prior right in the Pueblo against any non-Indian drawing water from a common water source. In other words, according to the board, the San Ildefonso Pueblo could get the water it needed but never had simply by shutting off all non-Indian irrigators upstream on the Nambe-Pojoaque.[59]

The board's theory overlooked the fact that the upstream Pueblos of Pojoaque, Nambe, and Tesuque threatened the San Ildefonso supply as much as any non-Indian. But at the time no one paid too much attention to either this irony or the general threat of the board's theory because everybody understood and steadfastly maintained that land lost to the Pueblos under the 1924 act had to mean lost water as well.[60]

The water issue became more acute as the administrative and judicial construction of the 1924 act's terms guaranteed greater and greater land losses to the Pueblos. Remember that in 1923, Collier and his advisors had counted on the 1924 act's requirement of real property tax payments to yield much returned land to the Pueblos. By 1926 the Pueblo Lands Board had taken all the teeth out of that requirement and, by 1929, the local New Mexico federal district court had approved the board's approach. By 1931 the court of appeals had agreed. Whatever promise the taxpaying provisions of the 1924 act may have held for Pueblo land recovery had all but disappeared.[61]

Two potentially ironic developments in the first years of the 1930s clouded the issue of how badly the Pueblos had fared under the 1924 act. First, appeals from the board's administrative determinations began to reach the circuit court of appeals between 1931 and 1933. That court uniformly upheld the pre-1924 Pueblos' assertion that their grant land had been inviolate during the whole period of United States sovereignty. Prior to the 1924 act, this holding would have resulted in the restoration of all the land within the Pueblo grants to the Pueblos. After the 1924 act, the holding meant that the act's specific terms provided the only means for non-Indians to gain title to Pueblo grant land. The Pueblo Lands Act of 1924 produced massive land losses to the Pueblos. The after-the-fact vindication of Collier's initial opinion in the court of appeals decisions of the 1930s proved a Pyrrhic victory of the most ironic kind.[62]

By the early 1930s, the Collierites found themselves hemmed in on all sides by these Pyrrhic victories. Hagerman promised the Pueblos more water rights and less water; the Pueblo Lands Board and the courts guaranteed them more rights to land and fewer acres left in their ownership. In increasing desperation, the Pueblos returned to the only remaining weapon left to them in their Pueblo Lands Board arsenal and filed a couple of those independent suits that the act itself allowed them if, in the end, they were not satisfied with the Pueblo Lands Board's work. In those suits the Pueblos returned to their earliest and most radical assertions: each Pueblo owned all the land patented to it by the United States government in the mid-nineteenth century, and no non-Indian could have acquired any title to those acres.

Shouts arose from all sides in New Mexico, decrying the Pueblos' efforts in these suits to upset all the previous work of the Pueblo Lands Board. But before any court could rule on the merits of the new claims, the Collierites made it clear that they regarded these independent suits as legal pawns in a larger political game whose aim was not restoration of lost Pueblo land, but increased Pueblo compensation for it. Between 1919 and 1924 the Hanna ejectment suits had set the stage for the political compromises embedded in the congressional Pueblo Lands Act. Now, between 1930 and 1933, the Pueblo independent suits provided the impetus for the final political intervention in the affairs of the Pueblo Indian land grants. Once again, the judicial branch of government gave way to a legislative solution. Once again, legal rights gave way to political compromises.[63]

Before Congress, the increased compensation issue, pushed by Collier and the Pueblos as the only alternative to the independent suits, rested on Hagerman's water theory. Oddly enough, the Pueblo advocates insisted that the Pueblos had lost water to non-Indians under the 1924 act and that Congress had to compensate them for the water loss before they would drop their meddlesome independent suits. Hagerman, hounded on all sides, stuck to his theory. To an extent, the Indian Bureau supported him. A young, western, special assistant to the Secretary of Interior adamantly agreed that the Pueblos should retain a prior and paramount right to water for lands remaining in their ownership even after the Pueblo Lands Board determinations. The Department of the Interior did not object to increased compensation, he argued, but the additional money should not be taken to confirm the view that the Indians did not retain superior water rights.

Finally, in early 1933, Congress approved the additional awards. Good to their words, the Pueblos withdrew the pending independent suits that attacked the very basis of the Pueblo Lands Board work. By late 1933, it looked as if the long war over the Pueblo land grants might have come to an end.[64]

Over the next decade, the money appropriated by Congress to compensate the Pueblos for the land lost to non-Indians within the boundaries of congressionally approved Pueblo grants went for a variety of purposes. In some instances, Pueblos and their guardians, the United States government, used the proceeds to purchase additional lands outside the original Pueblo grant boundaries. In other cases, the Pueblos used the funds to develop new, more sophisticated ways of tapping water supplies. Finally, in still other instances the Pueblos used the compensation to repurchase the same land that Congress had just awarded to non-Indians.

At the San Ildefonso Pueblo, the Indians and the United States pursued all three uses for the compensation funds. The Pueblo bought some land on the west side of the Rio Grande, outside the original grant. After negotiation, the Pueblo repurchased some lands awarded to non-Indians that lay very close to the Pueblo village itself. Finally, the Pueblo continued to search, largely unsuccessfully, for new sources of supply on the Nambe-Tesuque stream system.[65]

These activities at San Ildefonso and elsewhere implied that the Pueblo Lands Board Act of 1924 and the supplemental act of 1933 really had laid to rest more than two centuries of legal and political trouble caused by Pueblo land grants. Confirmation of non-Indian holdings within the Pueblo grants seemed to have settled an issue that had harried the courts of New Mexico since the San Ildefonso Pueblo first took Ignacio Roybal to court.

In the process, the United States government seemed to imply that that final solution included water as well. If the Pueblos had to repurchase land from recognized non-Indians in order to reduce competing claims to water from a shared source, then surely the Pueblos could not claim that the Pueblo Lands Board adjudications had left them with a superior right to water.

The solution gave to the Pueblo land grant picture a very different appearance than that of the twentieth-century situation with non-Indian Spanish and Mexican land grants. The United States had subjected non-Indian grants to an adjudication of their very identity. The federal government confirmed a few. The United States rejected others; they simply disappeared from the face of the New Mexico earth. In still others, the United States recognized the validity of a grant but sharply reduced its exterior boundaries. In the case of the Pueblo grants, however, the United States confirmed the grants and recognized the farthest limits of their exterior boundaries. Then, with the 1924 and 1933 acts, the United States reduced the grant base from within by confirming the landholdings of non-Indians within the grants, rather than reducing them from without by contracting their exterior boundaries.

Entire non-Indian grants came and went as a result of the actions of the United States government. The confirmed Pueblo grants became hodgepodges of Indian and non-Indian ownership. At the least, the Pueblo Lands Board Act promised to put to rest, once and for all, the vexing problem of shared resources within the Pueblo grants. But had it? All parties had turned to Congress itself for the final solution to the lingering water problem accompanying the more obvious land problem. Congress responded with the 1933 act; it solved the water problem by ducking the water issue. After fifteen years of constant battle, no one wanted to raise the water cry. But the issue of what to make of the existing rights of non-Indians to water shared with their Pueblo neighbors lurked beneath the uneasy silence that the congressional truce imposed on the weary combatants.

If nothing else was clear from the two-century hullabaloo, it was certain that the Pueblo Lands Board Act had meant to stop once and for all any non-Indian acquisition of Pueblo resources after 1924. Congress had faced an existing, historic problem in the 1924 act. It had made its adjustments. But, in the process of doing so, Congress had also indicated as clearly as it could that there would be no further adjustment in favor of non-Indians of future encroachments on confirmed Pueblo lands or related resources. Non-Indians within the Pueblo grants would have to work thereafter with what the United States had approved in the 1924 act.

As the Pueblo land grant war quieted through the decades of the 1940s, 1950s, and 1960s, both sides forgot even the prospective rule laid down in 1924. The areas around Pueblo grants and the areas within them that had been confirmed in non-Indian ownership under the Pueblo Lands Act continued to attract new residents. Those new residents had to divide and redivide among them Pueblo grant land already confirmed in non-Indian ownership. Everybody understood that no non-Indian could acquire new lands in the Pueblo grants. But this understanding did not extend to water. New Mexico was rediscovered, bringing many new residents to Pueblo grants. Each took a new, additional share of the existing water that may or may not have been apportioned between existing users in 1924.

The Wages of Legal Indecision and Historiographic Periods

The years 1540, 1821, 1848, and 1912 mark critical breaks in the legal systems which surrounded and controlled the land originally occupied by the Pueblos. First Spanish, then Mexican, United States territorial, and finally federal and New Mexico state law have changed and measured the legal space within which the Pueblos have had to fit their land.

To date, most studies of the status of Pueblo lands have sliced the problem along the divisions that changes in sovereignty provide and have focused on particular problems under particular regimes. We have had, for example, studies of particular Pueblo lands under Spanish rule, general investigations of the effect on Pueblo grants of the change to Mexican sovereignty, reports on the role of the Pueblos in the formation of the Pueblo Lands Board under United States rule, and even studies on the role of agricultural enterprises in recent Pueblo land use.[66]

These historically discrete studies beg for more, detailed work and show how little is known about Pueblo legal history at any particular time. We need to trace, document by document, law by law, the rise of the mysterious Pueblo league between 1700 and 1821 as the basis, measure, and limit of the Pueblos' claim to land under Spanish rule. We need a detailed, exhaustive analysis of Pueblo lands between 1821 and 1848 to determine how in fact the Pueblos and their non-Indian neighbors reacted to the change from Spanish to Mexican sovereignty. We need specific studies detailing the changes in Indian policy in the late nineteenth and early twentieth centuries that both foreboded and predicted the fundamental changes in Pueblo land status that the *Sandoval* decision and statehood brought. We need to know more specifically than we do now the precise legal state of affairs in New Mexico that preceded passage of the 1924 Pueblo Lands Act. In short, every segment of Pueblo land history requires additional basic work.

But to get a complete picture of the rule of law over Pueblo lands, legal historians must cut across the sovereign seams of New Mexico history, not along them. There are only three serious studies that try to take in the length of Pueblo legal history. All three are devoted to particular Pueblos. Ward Alan Minge's *Acoma, Pueblo in the Sky* and Joe S. Sando's *Nee Hemish, A History of the Jemez Pueblo,* both fine works, encompass a scope much broader than Pueblo land under successive sovereigns. My own *Four Leagues of Pecos* suffers from special problems, including the uniqueness of the Pecos Pueblo itself and the fact that the work barely scratches the surface of available documentation. Be that as it may, these three works represent the only efforts to see Pueblo land history as a whole.[67]

Viewed in that long perspective, a new image emerges of Pueblo land tenure under Spain, Mexico, and the United States. The different legal systems of the succeeding sovereigns were used in relentless, centuries-long efforts to wrest from the Pueblos the extraordinarily limited and, therefore, extraordinarily valuable, land and water resources that the Pueblos were using when the first European sovereign arrived. The long view of the Pueblos' response to this relentless pressure shows a relentless, resourceful, and entirely pragmatic defense of their homelands. Using whatever laws whichever sovereign offered, the Pueblos resisted impositions on their land and water for 400 years.

This perspective shows a consistency to Pueblo land grant history that belies the chaos and scrambling for survival characteristic of particular shifts in legal systems. Without such a long view, New Mexicans will be left, as they are today, with a series of broken images representing the fragmented story of particular eras.

Picture then the gymnasium of the Pojoaque High School on a Sunday afternoon in December 1979. The furor of last night's bitterly contested basketball game is over. Normally, this would be a dead time for this largest of public facilities in the Tesuque-Nambe-Pojoaque-San Ildefonso valley. But this afternoon, most of the valley property owners and irrigators have come to a valley meeting, called at the traditional northern New Mexico time, after Mass and before Monday morning.

Many Roybals, Lujans, Gabaldons, and Ortizes come from El Rancho, Jacona, Pojoaque, and Nambe, most of them direct descendants of the first Spanish settlers in this predominantly Pueblo land grant area. Now, in addition, plenty of Fishers, Herters, Triggs, and Owenses arrive, silent testimony to the fact that many changes have come to this valley in the twentieth century, including the elite from other well-watered parts of the country. Even a Pueblo Indian is attending. He's Ernest Mirabal, one of the most respected leaders of the San Ildefonso Pueblo and the liaison for the Northern Pueblos Tributary Water Rights Association, a loose federation of northern Pueblos organized to present a united Indian front on local resource issues.

The grandstands on the south side of the gymnasium look down on a table near the center of the room. There sit New Mexico's United States Senator Pete Domenici, New Mexico State Engineer Steve Reynolds, Santa Fe attorney Peter Shoenfeld, and a couple of administrative aides. They have come to spend Sunday afternoon talking to this large, angry crowd about Pueblo Indian rights to land and water.

This time the explosive meeting is occasioned by the latest, but no means first, eruption in the *Aamodt* litigation. State Engineer Steve Reynolds instituted the lawsuit in 1966 as a statutory stream system adjudication of water rights in the Nambe-Pojoaque stream system. Ironically, importation of what water engineers called "foreign" water from the San Juan Basin to supplement the already overburdened flows of the "native" Rio Grande and its tributaries had brought on the adjudication. Neither the Pueblos nor the non-Indians in the Nambe-Pojoaque stream system had asked for it, but getting the new water to the burgeoning city of Albuquerque meant making sure that "native" water rights owners did not use the water first. To save Albuquerque growth, Reynolds resurrected the *Exon* suit that had been started and aborted in the 1920s.

Reynolds's lawyers knew that the *Aamodt* suit would judicially define for the first time Pueblo Indian water rights, especially relative to non-Indian water rights in general and, in particular, to non-Indian water rights within the confirmed Pueblo grants. But, despite the recognition that the proposed adjudication would open once again the old sores between the Pueblos and their neighbors over an issue—water—close to every New Mexican's soul, Reynolds's legal staff did not do a lot to prepare. The state engineer hired a Chihuahua, Mexico banking attorney with a large library to testify on the water law of Pueblos under New Mexico's antecedent sovereigns. The state engineer's own staff determined, pretty much ex cathedra on faith and morals, that the 1933 Pueblo Supplemental Compensation Act in fact sealed the state's case: Pueblo Indian water rights were the same as state water rights, governed by and limited to a special federal law of prior appropriation.

At first the San Ildefonso, Pojoaque, Nambe, and Tesuque Pueblos were all represented only by the United States Department of Justice. Justice Department lawyers prepared to argue that their clients, the Pueblo wards, enjoyed the same kind of special preemptive water rights as any other Indian tribe. The lawyers hired a whole battery of translators, historians, hydrologists, economists, and planners to prove their point in a general way and got ready to try their case in early 1974.

But before anything had a chance to get underway, the Pueblos revolted. In the increasing strain between Indians and their protectors, the Pueblos and the United States, the four Pueblos involved in the *Aamodt* litigation accused their own federal attorneys of inadequate representation and asked the United States to provide funds so the Pueblos could hire lawyers of their own. In the brouhaha that ensued, everyone forgot for the moment that most of the 2,000 non-Indian residents of the Pueblo grants involved in the adjudication had no lawyers at all, with or without conflicts of interest.

The first *Aamodt* hearings began in this bellicose atmosphere in early 1974. The federal judge in charge quickly ruled that the Pueblos could not have their own attorneys and had to accept the exclusive services of the United States. On that basis, he heard a couple of days' testimony from the state's Chihuahua expert and then, in a surprise move, cut the trial off early and ruled that the Pueblos were governed by the law of prior appropriation, not by general federal Indian law as the United States had maintained.

The non-Indian residents of the Nambe-Pojoaque-Tesuque stream system breathed a sigh of relief and went back to watching for further developments. The Pueblos and their private attorneys, whom the judge had kept out of the lawsuit, all appealed to the Tenth Circuit Court of Appeals in Denver. In 1976, ten years after *Aamodt* had begun, the court reversed the district judge's hasty decision on all scores. The United States did have a conflict of interest, ruled the court, when it represented the Pueblos. The Pueblos were entitled to have private attorneys, paid for out of government funds, to represent them. The state law of prior appropriation, ruled the appeals court, did not govern the water rights of Pueblos. With a fairly clear laundry list of what yet needed to be done, the court sent the case back to the New Mexico federal district court for further proceedings.

Back in New Mexico, everyone ignored the Tenth Circuit Court's directions. Some parties prepared to proceed with the case that had been interrupted in 1974. But now each of the four Pueblos involved had a private attorney of its own in addition to the Department of Justice representation. Costs escalated. (Between 1974 and 1983 the United States paid the Pueblo private attorneys $1.1 million in fees.) The legal theories put forward by the new Pueblo attorneys changed and multiplied. (The Nambe Pueblo attorney took the state's position that Congress had subjected Pueblo water rights to the doctrine of prior appropriation, and stood it on its head. Now the Nambe Pueblo argued that the same 1933 act had given to the Pueblos expansive and very different water rights.) Esoteric hydrology (How much groundwater under the Nambe-Pojoaque valley could be safely pumped?), esoteric agronomy (Could strawberries be raised at the Pojoaque Pueblo?), and esoteric history (What did Queen Isabella's 1493 Will really mean?) all surfaced and produced expert witnesses. The non-Indian defendants turned their backs on a lawsuit that already had been going on for so long that it did not seem real.

In all the jockeying for positions, it finally emerged that the Pueblos theory of the case rested on the assertion that all non-Indians then residing within the borders of the Pueblo grants were absolute trespassers on Pueblo lands until at least the 1924 passage of the Pueblo Lands Board Act. If this assertion were true, then non-Indian water rights in the Nambe-Pojoaque stream system had just dried up and turned to paper. In effect, the "new" Pueblo theory resurrected the issue raised but never decided in the *San Ildefonso* suit in 1763, the *Joseph* suit in 1876, and the Hanna suits in the 1920s. The non-Indian defendants in the suit continued to sit back.[68]

Beginning in early 1980 and continuing sporadically over the next year, the state, the United States, and the Pueblos presented esoteric historical and hydrological evidence to a special master sitting in place of the district judge. Whatever the master recommended the judge himself still had to approve. But no one was quite prepared for the master's preliminary findings, released in late 1980. Under them, the master found that no matter what the theory of Pueblo water rights, the Pueblos still had enough rights to entirely consume the constant water supply of the Nambe-Pojoaque stream system.

Word of the proposed decision reached the press and all hell broke loose. Bumper stickers appeared around Pojoaque saying, "La agua es vida: Let's share." Other residents were not so restrained. One Roybal resident of Tesuque warned of potential violence. Another Roybal from El Rancho told a *New York Times* reporter that he wished his ancestors had killed all the Indians when they first settled in the Nambe Valley "just like they did back east." Calmer voices called for a more gentle response.

This Sunday afternoon meeting resulted. State Engineer Reynolds equivocated, sticking to his position that this is a matter for judicial solution despite accusations from the audience that he, not the Pueblos, brought this awful mess to the courts. Senator Domenici was noncommittal. When a question from the audience implied that Congress ought to solve the problem since Congress created it, Domenici allowed it would be politically impossible to pass yet another Pueblo Lands Act. Domenici did state that it may be possible to drum up a little money to pay some of the non-Indians' costs of defending themselves, thus equalizing the war chests of the Pueblo and non-Indian litigants. Most residents left confused but happy that the confusion may not cost them an arm and a leg. Ernest Mirabal left with incredible dignity in the face of palpable hostility.

Sure enough, shortly after the meeting, Washington announced that Congress had appropriated $400,000 to help defray non-Indian legal costs in defending their interests in the *Aamodt* suit. A new set of private attorneys got new theories and new experts together for yet another round of trial.

Another week of hearings before the special master ensued. The evidence primarily involved the status of the Pueblos under Mexican law and the effect that changes made then may have on present Pueblo water rights. Well after the conclusion of the hearings, the special master reversed his position on the water rights of the Pueblos under Spanish and Mexican law. Where first he ruled that the Pueblos had a prior and paramount right to water under Spanish and Mexican law, he now held that Pueblos and non-Indians had to share water equitably under the law of New Mexico's antecedent sovereigns. Some parties cheered. Others wept. All appealed to the United States district judge under whose authority and by whose direction the special master has conducted these seemingly endless proceedings. They waited as the contestants had waited for 400 years.

Finally, on 18 September 1985, Federal District Judge Edwin Mechem entered a thirty-five-page decision. The Pueblos and non-Indians each heralded the decision as an absolute victory for their positions. The decision was obscure enough to all parties to support either view. In the end, only two things remained clear about the long-awaited ruling.

First, it was not the end. Judge Mechem had certified his decision for interlocutory appeal. In lawyer's jargon, this meant that he had decided some, but by no means all, of the issues in the case and wanted appellate review of his interim ruling. In any case, the Tenth Circuit Court of Appeals could only review the partial record and send it back to the New Mexico District Court with instructions on how to proceed as it already had once done ten years before in 1976. Rather than promising an end to the litigation, Judge Mechem's ruling only guaranteed that the case would go on and on.

Second, if Judge Mechem's ruling on the law meant anything, it only meant that he had rejected the absolutist position of the Pueblos, which demanded all the Rio Pojoaque water, and the equally absolutist position of the non-Indians, which would have restricted the Pueblos to a minimum amount of water.

Neither side had won. Both sides accepted Judge Mechem's invitation and appealed to the Tenth Circuit Court of Appeals. Another interim ruling in a couple of years would be the best that could come of that.

In the meantime, at this February 1986 writing, there is a strong sense of *deja vu* that comes out of these recent complex proceedings. Surely this procedure is the same one that was held in Tesuque in 1920 when local Hispanic residents met with members of Congress to describe the Tesuque Pueblo "rebellion," which consisted of some fence cutting. Surely, angry Indians and non-Indians must have expressed some of the same sentiments in the 1870s when both sides awaited the outcome of the *Joseph* litigation and considered their alternatives to the possible outcomes. Surely, Santa Clara Hispanos felt the same way in 1815–1816 when they accused Governor Maynes of stirring up all the Pueblos with grandiose (although uneffectuated) pronouncements on the rights of the Pueblos to their complete leagues and ended up having to walk to Durango, Mexico, to get some relief. And surely the line of Ignacio Roybal and the San Ildefonso Pueblo felt the same biting issue, again and again and again and again.

The Nambe-Pojoaque river hardly runs at all but it runs very deep, back into the tortured history of land grants in New Mexico. It is a history that oozes bitterness of the worst racial kind out of its every pore. It is a legal history full of problems that the law has never had the courage to resolve.[69]

Notes

1. White et al., *Land Title Study* (Santa Fe: State Planning Office, 1971) 223; Westphall, *The Public Domain in New Mexico: 1854–1891* (Albuquerque: University of New Mexico Press, 1965); USGS, State of New Mexico: Land Status Map, 1982 (Santa Fe: BLM, 1982).

2. Fray Angelico Chavez, *Origins of New Mexico Families* (Santa Fe: Gannon, 1975) 273–75; Spanish Archives of New Mexico, Vol. 1 (SANM I), pp. 487, 488.

3. Map Sheet No. 1, State of New Mexico Hydrographic Survey, 1967.

4. Adams and Chavez, eds., *The Missions of New Mexico, 1776* (Albuquerque: University of New Mexico Press, 1956) 71–72; Affidavit of Jesus Maria Ortiz, 5 June 1874, Records of Surveyor General of New Mexico (SGNM) R. 22, Fr. 14–15; Referee's report, 26 March 1909, Santa Fe County No. 6323, SRCA, Santa Fe; Roybal to Bustamante, SANM I, 745; Santa Fe County Deed Book G-1, pp. 20–21, recorded in Office of the County Clerk, Santa Fe, 28 June 1899. See generally Baxter, *Spanish Irrigation in the Pojoaque and Tesuque Valleys During the Eighteenth and Early Nineteenth Centuries* (Santa Fe: State Engineer's Office, 1984), pp. 9–12.

5. Grant to Sandia Pueblo, 23 January 1745, SANM I 1347; Myra Ellen Jenkins, "Spanish Administration of New Mexico and the Tewa Indians," 22–25 (Unpublished ms., SRCA, Santa Fe, 1968).

6. J. H. Parry, *The Spanish Theory of Empire in the Sixteenth Century* (Cambridge: The University Press, 1940), pp. 1–26.

7. Alfonso Ortiz, *The Tewa World: Space, Time, Being and Becoming in a Pueblo Society* (Chicago: University of Chicago Press, 1969), pp. 20–23; Alfonso Ortiz, "Ritual Drama and the Pueblo World View," in Ortiz, ed. *New Perspectives on the Pueblos* (Albuquerque: University of New Mexico Press and School of American Research, 1972).

8. Abel, ed., *Correspondence of James Calhoun,* Calhoun to Medill, 1 Oct., 15 Oct., and 10 Dec. 1849. Testimony of "governor and chiefs" of San Ildefonso Pueblo before Surveyor General, 16 June 1856, in Report of the Secretary of Interior, 1856, pp. 516–17.

9. David E. Vassberg, "The Tierras Baldias: Community Property and Public Lands in 16th Century Castile," *Agricultural History* 48 (July 1974): 384.

10. *Recopilación de las Leyes de los Reynos de las Indias* (Madrid, 1792), IV: 12–18.

11. For example, Myra Ellen Jenkins, "The Baltasar Baca 'Grant': History of an Encroachment," *El Palacio* 68 (Spring 1961): 47.

12. Malcolm Ebright, "The Embudo Grant: A Case Study of Justice and the Court of Private Land Claims," 19 *Journal of the West,* No. 3 (July 1980) 74; Myra Ellen Jenkins, "Taos Pueblo and Its Neighbors, 1540–1847," 41 *New Mexico Historical Review* (*NMHR*) 2 (1966), 85–14; 1704 proceedings with respect to land near the Pueblo of San Ildefonso on the west side of the Rio Grande, SANM I: 339.

13. *Recopilación* IV: 12–9 and VI: 3–20; William B. Taylor, *Landlord and Peasant in Colonial Oaxaca* (Palo Alto: Stanford University Press, 1974) 46; Charles Gibson, *The Aztecs under Spanish Rule: A History of the Indians of the Valley of Mexico, 1519–1810* (Palo Alto: Stanford University Press, 1964) 274; White et al., *Land Title Study,* p. 223.

14. G. Emlen Hall, *Four Leagues of Pecos* (Albuquerque: University of New Mexico Press, 1984), pp. 26–30.

15. Jenkins, "Spanish Administration and the Tewa Indians," p. 26; Jenkins, "Taos Pueblo and Its Neighbors," pp. 85–114.

16. 1704 proceedings in a dispute over land between Ignacio Roybal and San Ildefonso Pueblo, beginning 18 September 1704, SANM I, 1339.

17. 1763 proceedings in land dispute between Spanish settlers and San Ildefonso Pueblo, beginning 4 February 1763, SANM I, 1351.

18. See generally G. Emlen Hall and David Weber, "Mexican Liberals and the Pueblo Indians, 1821–1829," *NMHR* 4 (January 1984): 5–32.

19. Hall and Weber, "Mexican Liberals," *NMHR* 4 (January 1984): 7–8; *Sunol v. Hepburn,* 1 Cal. (1853); see, e.g., decision of Jose Andres Sandoval, 30 June 1836 in Angostura settlers v. Pueblo of Santa Ana, Seligman Collection, University of New Mexico Special Collections.

20. Hall and Weber, "Spanish Liberals," *NMHR* 4 (January 1984): 21, nn. 64–65.

21. Hall, *Four Leagues of Pecos,* pp. 31–66.

22. See, e.g., "Indian Deeds: San Ildefonso Pueblo," file numbers 300.10-9-5, 8, 9, 12 and "Indian Deeds: Nambe Pueblo," file numbers 300.5-9-9, 9.1 in the records of the Pueblo Lands Board, Southern Pueblos Agency, Albuquerque.

23. SANM I, 1245 (Jemez, 1833); 1380 (Santo Domingo, 1844); 1169 (Picuris, 1845); 1381 (Isleta, 1845).

24. Governor to alcalde constitucional, 22 March 1832, MANM R. 14, Fr. 718.

25. John Baxter, *Spanish Irrigation in the Pojoaque and Tesuque Valleys During the Eighteenth and Early Nineteenth Centuries* (State Engineer's Office: Santa Fe, 1984), pp. 3–5, nn. 8–13.

26. Statement by Victor Garcia 20 April 1836, Book A-1, Santa Fe County Deeds, p. 56; Affidavit of Jesus Maria Ortiz, 5 June 1874, NMSG R. 22, R. 92, fr. 14–15.

27. 9 Stat. 922; Wilson to Pelham, 21 August 1854, "Misc.," R. 23, f.49 ff.

28. Annie H. Abel, *The Official Correspondence of James S. Calhoun* (Washington, D.C.: U.S. Government Printing Office, 1915); Hall, *Four Leagues of Pecos*, pp. 71–74.

29. De La O v. Pueblo of Acoma, 1 N.M. 226 (1857), gives the details of the initial formal incorporation.

30. Sec. 7, Ch. XIV, Act of 27 Feb. 1851, 9 Stat. 587.

31. Act of 22 July 1854, 10 Stat. 308; Hall, *Four Leagues*, pp. 73–79, nn. ch. 4 36–43; Annual Report of the Secretary of the Interior, 1856, 411–12, 513, 519–20.

32. Act of 22 December 1858; House Committee on Private Land Claims, 15 March 1870, 41st Congress, 2d. session, report 38; Senate report to accompany H.R. 195, Committee on Private Land Claims, 19 May 1860, 36th Congress, 1st session.

33. United States of America to various Pueblos, 1 November 1864, copies in custody of the Bureau of Land Management, Santa Fe, New Mexico.

34. See, e.g., the Town of Las Vegas grant and the Baca Float No. 1, in which Congress granted the claimed lands to the Town of Las Vegas and allowed the competing claimants from the C de Baca family to select alternative lands from the public domain. Compare the Anton Chico and the Preston Beck, Jr., grants, both of which Congress fully patented even though the two grants overlapped. For the judicial response, see *Tamelling v. Freehold & Immigration Co.*, 94 U.S. 644 (1876).

35. Section 37-1-21 and 22 NMSA 1978 first adopted in 1857.

36. Hall, *Four Leagues*, pp. 111–38.

37. See Reports of the Secretary of the Interior for 1872–1874, including annual reports from the surveyor general of New Mexico for each year. The 1872 Report lists as approved nine land claims including what became the Cuyamungue grant. (124) The 1873 Report lists as approved the Caja del Rio, the Juana Lopez, and the Juan Gabaldon grants, all of which lie in the Nambe-Pojoaque watershed and parts of each of which overlie already patented

Pueblo lands. (101) The 1874 Report lists as approved the Sierra Mosca, the Juan de Mestas, the Gaspar Ortiz, and the Roival [sic] and Pelaez grants (113), all of which lie in the same watershed.

38. *United States v. Joseph,* 94 U.S 614 (1876).

39. For the changes, see *United States v. Sandoval,* 13 U.S. 28 (1912); House Committee on Territories, Report 1025 on the Admission of Dakota, Montana, Washington, and New Mexico to the Union, 1888, 50th Congress, 1st Session (Government Printing Office, Washington, D.C.).

40. Act of March 3, 1891, 26 Stat. 854; Pueblo of Laguna, Claim no. 133 before the Court of Private Land Claims, testimony of Will Tipton in SCRA.

41. Hall, *Four Leagues,* pp. 221–23; Act of June 20, 1910, Ch. 310, 36 Stat. 557.

42. Testimony of San Ildefonso and Pojoaque leaders before Surveyor General of New Mexico 16 June 1856 and 28th June 1856 in 1856 *Report of the Secretary of the Interior,* 516–17.

43. Westphall, *Mercedes Reales,* pp. 113–14; Schedule of documents relating to grants of land, 1 August 1856, 413–32 in 1856 *Report of the Secretary of the Interior.*

44. Petition 5 January 1874 and decision 10 June 1874 with regard to the Jacona grant, report 92, NMSG R. 22, fr. 1, 18; J. J. Bowden, "Private Land Claims in the Southwest," 6 vols. (LLM thesis, Southern Methodist University) 3: 536.

45. NMPLC R. 36, fr. 1 ff. case 35, Town of Jacona grant.

46. See, e.g., Adolph Bandelier and Edgar L. Hewitt, Indians of the Rio Grande Valley 39; Horace J. Johnson to Commissioner of Indian Affairs 22 March 1920, NARG 75: 4018.308.2.

47. Robert W. Larson, *New Mexico's Quest for Statehood 1846–1912* (Albuquerque: University of New Mexico Press, 1968), pp. 253 ff.; see testimony of Francis C. Wilson in "Hearings before the Committee on Indian Affairs, United States Senate, 62d Congress, third session, on S. 6085, a bill to authorize the acceptance of trusts from the Pueblo Indians of New Mexico, 13 February 1913" (Washington, D.C., 1913); Act of June 20, 1910, ch. 310, 36 Stat. 557.

48. *United States v. Mares,* 14 N.M. 1 (1905) (construing act of Jan. 30, 1897, ch. 109, 29 Stat. 506); *United States v. Felipe Sandoval,* 198 F. Supp. 539 (1912); Hall, *Four Leagues,* pp. 201–3.

49. *United States v. Sandoval,* 13 U.S. 28 (1913); see *Mountain States Tel. & Tel. v. Pueblo of Santa Ana,* — U.S. — (1985); Leo Crane, *Desert Drums* (Boston: Little Brown & Co., 1928) 170–71.

50. Richard H. Frost, "Relations Between the Pueblo Indians and the Federal Government, 1910–1933, with Particular Reference to Water Rights" (Unpub. ms., Chicago: Center for the History of the American Indian, 1980) 117–24.

51. Frost, "Relations Between the Pueblo Indians and the Federal Government" 9–24; Hall, *Four Leagues,* pp. 219–20.

52. *United States v. Rupert Archuleta et al.,* filed April 10, 1920, USDC NM, FRCD; NARG 75: 018: 154; Frost, "Relations Between the Pueblo Indians and the Federal Government" 58–66 and nn. 181–86; Complaint, *United States v. Guy S. Exon et al.,* USDC NM FRCD.

53. Hall, *Four Leagues,* pp. 221–43; Lawrence Kelly, *The Assault on Assimilation, John Collier and the Origins of Indian Policy Reform* (Albuquerque: University of New Mexico Press, 1983), pp. 163–294.

54. Act of 7 June 1924, 43 Stat. 636; Hall, *Four Leagues,* op. cit.

55. Hall, *Four Leagues,* pp. 245–51; Frost, "Relations Between the Pueblos" 50–54, 81–88.

56. "Tesuque Pueblo: Report on Indian Titles Extinguished," 9 November 1925, SPA, Albuquerque; "San Ildefonso Pueblo: Report on Indian Titles Extinguished," 22 July 1929, SPA, Albuquerque: House Report 820 on H.B. 9071, 72d Congress, 1st Session (1932).

57. Senate Report 73, 73rd Congress, 1st Session, 15 May 1933; Senate Committee on Indian Affairs, Conditions of the Indians in the United States, v. 20, p. 10914 (1931).

58. "San Ildefonso Pueblo: Report on Indian Titles Extinguished" op. cit.; Hall, *Four Leagues,* pp. 268–69 and accompanying notes.

59. Hagerman to G. A. H. Fraser, 15 December 1925, Misc. SPA, Albuquerque; "San Ildefonso Pueblo: Report No. 2," 22 July 1929, p. 26, SPA, Albuquerque.

60. *State ex rel. Reynolds v. Aamodt et al.,* 537 F.2d 1102 (10th Cir. 1976).

61. *United States as the Guardian of the Nambe Pueblo v. David Herrera et al.,* No. 1720 USDC NM, per curiam opinion August 1928 in SPA, Albuquerque; *United States v. Wooten,* 147 F. 926 (8th Cir. 1930).

62. *United States v. Candelaria,* 271 U.S. 432 (1926); *United States v. Chavez,* 290 U.S. 357 (1933).

63. E. G. Ickes to Wheeler, 9 May 1933, NARG 48–018 pt. 22 and Frost, "Relations between the Federal Government and the Pueblos" 151–53; Armijo to Hagerman, 11 Jan. 1932, NARG 75, 013, pt. 30.

64. SCIUS (1932) v. 20, 11211–94 et seq.; H.R. 820, 72d Congress, 1st Session; *State ex rel. Reynolds v. Aamodt et al.,* op. cit.; 48 Stat. 108.

65. E. G. Frost, "Relations between the Federal Government and the Pueblos" 98–124 and accompanying notes.

66. See, e.g., Myra Ellen Jenkins, "Taos Pueblo and Its Neighbors, 1540–1847," *NMHR* 41 (April 1966): 101; Richard E. Greenleaf, "Land and Water in New Mexico, 1700–1821," *NMHR* 47 (April 1972): 104; Hall and David J. Weber, "Mexican Liberals and the Pueblo Indians, 1821–1829," *NMHR* 59 (January 1984): 1; Marc Simmons, "History of the Pueblos since 1821," in William C. Sturtevant, ed., *Handbook of North American Indians,* vol. 9, *Southwest,* Alfonso Ortiz, ed. (Washington: Smithsonian Institution, 1979); Lawrence Kelly, *The Assault on Assimilation* (Albuquerque: University of New Mexico Press, 1983); James A. Vlasich, "Transitions in Pueblo Agriculture, 1938–1948," *NMHR* 55 (January 1980): 1.

67. Ward Alan Minge, *Acoma; Pueblo in the Sky* (Albuquerque: University

of New Mexico Press, 1976); Joe S. Sando, *Nee Hemish: A History of Jemez Pueblo* (Albuquerque: University of New Mexico Press, 1982).

68. Section 72–11–1 NMSA 1958; *Mountain States Tel. & Tel. v. Santa Ana Pueblo,* supra.

69. *State ex rel. Reynolds v. Aamodt,* No. 6639 (D.N.M.); *State ex rel. Reynolds v. Aamodt,* 537 F.2d 1102 (10th Cir. 1976).

Cañones, New Mexico, with the top of Cerro Pedernal showing beyond the valley escarpment. George McCue photograph.

THREE

Hispanic Land Grants: Ecology and Subsistence

THREE

Hispanic Land Grants
Ecology and Subsistence in the Uplands of Northern New Mexico and Southern Colorado[1]

John R. Van Ness

Introduction

The true history of the Hispanic land grants of northern New Mexico and southern Colorado is to be found in the study off the people who received the grants and settled them. It is a chronicle of a rugged people who employed a community-based agro-pastoral system of subsistence to wrest a livelihood from a meager frontier environment. That they were able to accomplish this feat speaks both for fidelity to their cultural heritage and for adaptive ingenuity.

This essay, however, will focus more on the analysis of historical and physical patterns in man's relationship to the land than on particular people or Hispanic communities. Specifically, the goal is to show that this historical tradition cannot be understood without closely examining the unique upland environment and the adaptations of humans to it. The region's breathtaking beauty (a heightened awareness of which has been fostered for decades by legions of painters, writers, and photographers) belies its poverty of resources to support the farmers and ranchers of past generations as well as today. The stark contrasts of the broken landscape—high mountains, arid foothills and mesas, miniature green river valleys—and the crisp, clear high-altitude climate have been found stimulating and invigorating by the tourists, summer residents, and many others who come to the region to rest and relax or retire. However, the scant resources and rainfall as well as unpredictable sudden fluctuations in temperature, wind, and precipitation contributed to a life of considerable difficulty and uncertainty for the small subsistence farmer/rancher. The margin of security in this way of winning a livelihood has always been very slim at best.

Since modern urban eyes and sensibilities serve us very poorly when we attempt to understand the rural Hispanic traditions in this unique section of our United States, a fundamentally different frame of mind and body of understanding is required. To acquire this critical knowledge, a holistic anthropological approach will be employed here, with the use of an ecological framework, so that the Hispanic land grants settled in northern New Mexico and southern Colorado may be viewed in genuine human and environmental terms. It will be argued that no other approach to this subject can be wholly satisfactory, and that much of the unjust treatment which has been the experience of several generations of Hispanos under the United States government is in part attributable to gross ignorance on the part of legions of officials, attorneys, businessmen, and others. Regrettably, the majority of the scholars who have chronicled and analyzed this abysmal chapter in the history of the Southwest have also failed to understand the Hispanic cultural ecology.

The Plan of Attack

To explore the cultural ecology (an anthropological term to be defined in a few moments) of the upland Hispanic grants, one must gain an overview of the important environmental features of this diverse mountain region. Then, the sociocultural mechanisms employed by the Hispanic settlers for subsistence must be studied—settlement patterns, landholding systems, land use practices, and social organization for economic pursuits. To convey the nature of the Hispanic cultural ecology in the upland region most cogently, we will move from a general overview to a specific example, settlement of the Cañones microbasin in Rio Arriba County, near Abiquiu, New Mexico. The perspective gained in these investigations, then, will enable the writer to explore the changes brought with American sovereignty in the Southwest.

Ecology and Subsistence

At this juncture a few words should be said about the term *ecology,* for in popular usage it is often treated as though it were synonymous with *environment.* From the conventional usage in the biological sciences, there is widespread agreement that ecology deals with organisms in an environment and the relationships and processes that link organisms and place. When anthropologists borrowed the term *ecology* from the biologists they retained the same general sense of the term, while molding it somewhat to serve their own purposes.[2]

Unlike other organisms, generally speaking, "between the physical environment and human activity there is always a middle term, a collection of specific objectives and values, a body of knowledge and belief: in other words, a cultural pattern."[3] Thus, for treating human ecology anthropologists coined the term *cultural ecology.* In cultural ecology studies anthropologists have attempted to examine the environment as people are affected by it, use it to win a livelihood, seek to understand it, and modify it to serve their needs. For our purposes, the most important of the cultural ecology patterns are those that determine the way in which a society settles the land and the closely related social organization and technical knowledge employed in exploiting the natural resources to gain a livelihood.

Anthropologists have been particularly cognizant of the fact that making comparisons between societies in similar habitats or those in adjacent regions entailed the analysis of the complexities of the relationship between the environment and the technical and social devices for exploiting it.[4] Neither general similarities in habitat nor in modes of exploiting the environment can be taken for granted, especially when comparisons between different ethnic groups or societies are being attempted.

An Example of Uninformed Analysis

Perhaps a useful way to quickly reach the heart of this essay is to review a recent article which makes the error just mentioned. The article was written by Gary D. Libecap and George Alter and is titled "Agricultural Productivity, Partible Inheritance and the Demographic Response to Rural Poverty: An Examination of the Spanish Southwest."[5] The fallacious assumptions underlying this article are common to much of the literature devoted to economic development in the region. It argues that declining agricultural productivity in Hispanic northern New Mexico was the result of partible inheritance, which caused the equal division of farms among sons and daughters or other heirs and thus with each generation created even smaller farm plots. In time, plots became so small that they were uneconomic units for agricultural production.

The authors use Taos County as a unit of comparison with the larger Rocky Mountain region—including Colorado, Utah, Wyoming, Montana, and Idaho—where, in their view, the natural resources are very similar. The Rocky Mountain region is characterized by its mountainous landscape, short growing seasons, limited precipitation, and the production of irrigated crops and livestock. To gauge the impact of farm size on agricultural production, the authors utilized U.S. census data from 1850 to 1940, comparing the Taos County, New Mexico data with the larger mountain states area. The resulting table of comparison shows that from 1900 in Taos County, the improved acreage per farm was nearly static, averaging just over 20 acres, while generally in the mountain states, acreage per farm more than doubled, from 89 to 212 acres per farm in 1940. In the mountain states area, farm acreage increased largely through consolidation; however, this did not occur in Taos County. Thus, the authors conclude that partible inheritance, a cultural characteristic, coupled with a growing population created this unfortunate situation for agricultural life in Taos County.

On the surface, with no deeper examination of Taos County's environment and distinctive Hispanic cultural ecology, this argument makes very good sense. Indeed, partible inheritance created smaller agricultural units, and overpopulation in this meager environment became a problem. However, as will be demonstrated, closer analysis reveals that Libecap and Alter's conclusions are spurious because they compare the largely Anglo-American commercial farming of the mountain states area with the very different historic mode of subsistence farming and stock raising practiced by the Hispanic communities of Taos County. This Hispanic pattern, with local roots more than three hundred years old, persisted in slightly modified form until World War II. Further, they give too little attention to the particularities of the habitat. To begin this analysis, it is necessary to examine the upland environment of northern New Mexico and southern Colorado in some detail.

The Upland Environment[6]

In general, the history of the arid Southwest has been treated in the same conventional manner as that of the humid East, notwithstanding the fact that the four centuries of recorded history are only half-intelligible when divorced from the peculiarities of their climatic setting. While such neglect among historians is regrettable, it should be unconscionable among social scientists. Nonetheless, this generalization applies to the majority of social scientists as well. Chroniclers and interpreters of the human experiences in the American Southwest have seldom made more than a few perfunctory remarks, if any, regarding the environmental setting in which the human dramas they recount and analyze have occurred. Yet, the sequence of events and the direction of cultures has been drastically affected by the peculiar relief and climate of the Southwest. "The climate with its physical and psychic influence, the soil and its potentiality, the geologic structure of the country and its relations to the simplest problems of welfare are phenomena that must be reckoned with."[7]

The natural environment is clearly a crucial variable in the analysis of Hispanic settlement patterns, social organization, and subsistence in the region under discussion. Further, it is a particularly important factor in the development of the Hispanic land grant farming/ranching communities. Thus, this section will be devoted to a systematic outline of the upland environmental characteristics: topography, geology, soils, hydrology, flora, and fauna will be described and the impact of these factors on Hispanic occupation evaluated. To make this analysis as concrete as possible, then, a particular microbasin where Hispanic settlements developed, the Cañones region, will be treated in detail.

Physiography

North-central New Mexico and south-central Colorado are characterized by high mountains, wide plateaus, and narrow valleys. This part of the great barrier of mountains between the North American great plains on the east and Colorado Plateau, Great Basin, and Columbia Plateau on the west, is called the Rocky Mountain System.[8] As classified by Feeneman, this region falls into the southern Rocky Mountain province (see Map 4). This province is made up mainly of a lineal, north-south-oriented anticlinal range. The main crests are generally flanked by outward-dipping strata making hogback foothills. Within the southern Rocky Mountain province, two ranges—the Sangre de Cristo and the San Juan—are of particular concern. The Sangre

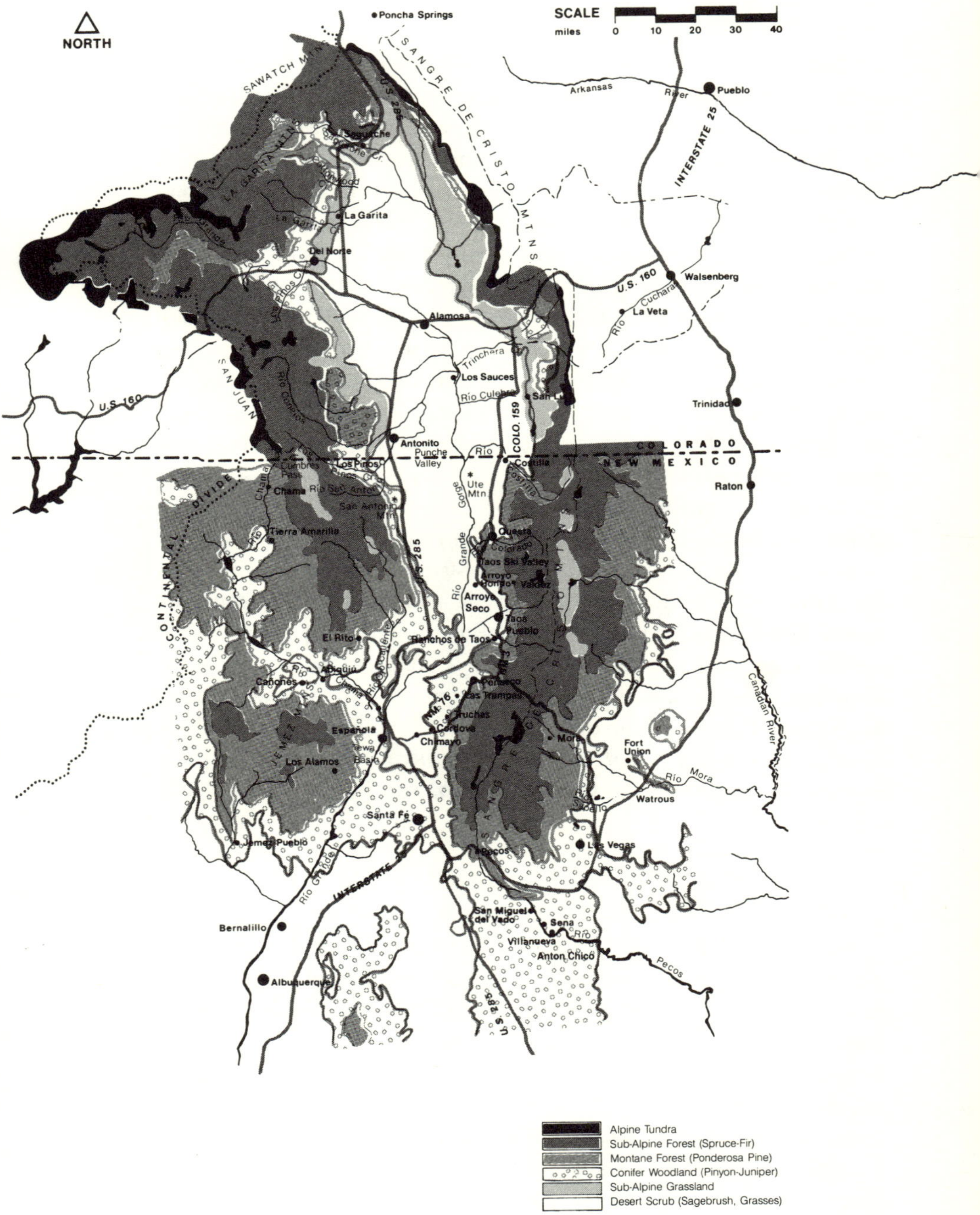

MAP 4. Physiographic map of southern Colorado and northern New Mexico.

de Cristo range extends from near Salida, Colorado on the Arkansas River southeastward for 140 miles to somewhat beyond Santa Fe, New Mexico and forms the eastern margin of north-central New Mexico. The San Juan Mountains to the west of the Rio Grande valley, in similar fashion, form the western margin of the region.

At the southern end of the San Juan range are the Jemez Mountains, a minor range. They form the very southern end of the western side of the southern Rockies. The Jemez range lies at the western margin of the Rio Grande depression and is broken by a number of faults which drop mountain blocks progressively downward to the east.[9] The Jemez range has been divided into a number of subranges and spurs locally known as the Tierra Amarilla, the Gallinas, the Nacimiento, and Valles mountains. These mountains are characterized by broadly rounded contours with elevated valleys between the ranges. The highest peaks have an altitude of just above 11,000 feet and are remnants of old crater rims.

Between the great plains uplift of the Sangre de Cristo Mountains to the east and the San Juan Mountains to the west lies a broad faulted belt. Within this rift zone a series of north-south-trending faults have produced not only the mountain ranges but also downfaulted basins. These structural basins, which actually begin with the San Luis Basin in Colorado extend through north-central New Mexico and reach as far south as the Palomas Basin near El Paso, Texas and are linked together by the Rio Grande. These basins are referred to collectively as the Rio Grande depression.

Soils

In general, four broad surface textural separations are found: loams, clay loams, sandy loams, and gravelly loams. Recent valley soils are entirely loam. Overall the profile is quite homogeneous, open, and well-aerated although variations in texture and profile do occur. The channels of major drainageways consist of sand and a fine gravel classified as river wash. The eroded bench lands of the valley consist of a shallow face of gravelly loam or gravelly, fine, sandy loam, and its subsoil is compact and quite impervious. The soil of the long, narrow ridges may be characterized as heavy loam or clay loam. Here the substratum varies from parent rock to a gravelly loam. The valley slopes are covered with a solid face of gravelly loam and the subsoil is more open than that of the bench lands. Thus, the valley sides have a better water-holding capacity and trees and grasses can grow much better. Mountainous lands are surfaced with shallow loam or rock. The soil is very shallow and about thirty percent of the mountain area is bare rock. Generally, vegetation is found only in soil-filled crevices or small depressions. Gully and sheet erosion is severe over the entire region, except for the recent valley soils and the mountain land. Also, a few areas evidence wind erosion.[10]

Hydrology

Water is the resource of greatest importance in this semiarid region. The character of the waters, big and little, is therefore of tremendous importance. The entire north-central New Mexico and southern Colorado region is drained by the Rio Grande and its tributaries. The larger tributaries head back into the mountains and are fed by springs and by the water from melting snow each spring in the high country. Normally, these streams maintain their flow throughout the year. In addition, there are numerous arroyos and dry washes which follow the large network of small canyons that cover the entire region. These watercourses flow intermittently following storms or periods of rapid melt-off in the high country; all too often, when flowing, the run-off is very rapid and the drainage in these watercourses is usually more of a detriment than an aid to the dry lowlands.[11]

Climate

As previously mentioned, this upland region is climatically a semiarid land of little rain. Yet, it is a region dramatically marked by wide variations in temperature and rainfall. Meteorological conditions throughout the region may be characterized in the following fashion: There is a high percentage of cloudless weather, a rare transparent atmosphere, rapid evaporation of what precipitation there is, very low humidity, and considerable wind, especially in the spring. Thus, vegetation dries up rather than decaying.

In the lower valleys, precipitation varies from about eight to ten inches, with very little in the form of snow. Precipitation is unequally distributed throughout the year. Heavy rainfall of a few hours to several days duration is often followed by months virtually devoid of moisture. Light snows and rain fall during January, February, and March. July and August are wet months, with much of the precipitation coming in torrential showers. Due to these precipitation patterns and the characteristics of soil and atmosphere, the effects of rainfall disappear rapidly. In the high mountains, precipitation ranges from twenty-four to thirty inches, with a considerable amount of winter snow. This zone is also characterized by more frequent and regular spring and summer rainfalls. Having made these generalizations, it must be emphasized that there are many local variations in precipitation and the effects of precipitation on the land. Variations are conditioned by microvariations in altitude, topography (for instance, the direction of slope), soils, and vegetation.[12] (These considerations will be given fuller attention under the heading of life zones.)

The range of temperature is also considerable in the upland region. Temperature varies daily, seasonally, and with changes in altitude. Nights are generally cool even in the summer. Except in the highest altitudes, the temperature rarely drops to zero. On the other hand, oppressive heat is unusual even in mid-summer due to the lack of humidity. Sultry, muggy days are unknown. To illustrate the variations in precipitation and temperature, one might compare the town of Española, a low spot in the region (5,600 feet), with the village of Chama at 7,804 feet (see Table 1).

Flora and Fauna

The upland region of north-central New Mexico and south-central Colorado possesses five different life zones, as classified by Bailey.[14] These zones are the Upper Sonoran, Transitional, Canadian, Hudsonian, and Arctic-Alpine. Of course, variations within the life zones occur locally and from year to year, depending on the weather. Also, zone boundaries are never sharply marked in nature except on steep slopes; rather, zones change gradually.

The *Upper Sonoran zone* encompasses most of the valleys and foothills of the upland region. Its lower border reaches down to 4,000 feet in some locations and the upper border varies from approximately 7,000

TABLE 1
Variations in Uplands Climate[13]

Daily Mean Temperature Range:	Española—69.2 to 33.5 degrees (Average 51.4 degrees) Chama—58.6 to 26.3 degrees (Average 42.8 degrees)
Mean Annual Precipitation:	Española—9.55 inches Chama—20.29 inches
Growing Season:	Española—151 days (May 9 to October 7) Chama—108 days (June 7 to September 24)

to 8,000 feet. This zone includes the bulk of the agricultural and grazing land in the region. However, dependable agriculture is not possible without irrigation. The climate of the upper Sonoran is mild without great extremes of heat or cold but the greater part of the zone in the upland region is extremely arid. The average rainfall is approximately ten inches; thus, the vegetation is sparse over large areas. This vegetation consists of desert shrubs, cacti, yuccas, and short grasses. The recent alluvial deposits of the valley bottoms are covered by grasslands, among the chief species are blue gramma grass, ring grass, and galleta. At certain seasons of the year these lands provide good grazing for livestock. In addition to grasses, other characteristic Upper Sonoran plants found in the valleys are cat's claw, salt brush, sage brush, white sage, rabbit brush, yucca, bear grass, and many species of cacti. The higher edges of the Upper Sonoran zone, including the bench lands and the old peneplain, are conspicuously less arid. Here grassland-woodland of juniper, piñon, sage, and more luxuriant spans of blue gramma grass are characteristic. Live oaks, sumacs, mountain mahogany, silk tassel, mescal, and several species of cactus are found. The most common mammals found in this zone are a variety of rats and mice, prairie dogs, large spotted ground squirrels, Texas jackrabbits, and cedarbelt cottontails.[15]

The *Transition zone* covers the middle slopes of the higher mountains and the upper slopes and tops of most of the lower ranges. This zone begins at 7,000 to 8,500 feet above sea level on northeast slopes and 8,000 to 9,500 feet on southwest slopes. It is characterized by large, open, grassy forests. The principal timber tree of the region, the yellow pine, is found in this zone. In addition, the forests include Douglas fir and various other pines, a variety of oak trees, willows, and Rocky Mountain birch. Shrubs include chokecherry, red currant, gooseberry, wild rose, and elderberry. The high valleys of this zone are covered with a variety of types of grasses. Characteristic mammals of the transition zone are mule deer, squirrels, several species of chipmunks, prairie dogs, a variety of wood rats, beavers, badgers, bobcats, porcupines, rabbits, mountain lions, bears, and mountain coyotes. This zone is valuable for seasonal grazing and permits some farming. Usually, sufficient rain occurs for dry farming of such crops as potatoes, grain, and some garden vegetables.[16]

The *Canadian zone* covers most of the higher parts of the Sangre de Cristo and the San Juan ranges. It extends from approximately 8,500 to 11,000 feet on cold slopes and from 9,500 to 12,000 feet on warm slopes. However, it may vary as much as a thousand feet according to local conditions. This zone is densely forested with spruce, balsam, and aspen. In the midst of an arid region, it is a humid zone, catching the maximum fall of rain and snow. During the summer there are frequent showers and, in the winter, large snow falls that are released to feed the mountain springs in late spring. Although no agriculture is possible here, the zone's water storage "is the fountainhead of the agricultural wealth of the surrounding region," to use Bailey's words. The major tree species found in the Canadian zone are blue spruce, Engelmann spruce, white fir, Rocky Mountain white pine, Douglas fir, and aspen. Mammals found in this zone include elk, mule deer, squirrels, several species of mice, snowshoe rabbits, Canadian lynxes, mountain red foxes, black bear, and several varieties of shrews.[17]

The *Hudsonian zone* and the *Arctic-Alpine zone* are found on peaks that reach near or above the timberline. These zones occur mainly along the Sangre de Cristo range, beginning at 11,000 to 12,000 feet on northeast slopes and 12,000 to 13,000 feet on southwest slopes. The Hudsonian is well marked by a stunted growth of gnarled and dwarf trees, mainly Engelmann spruce, corkbar fir, and foxtail pine. However, for a few months in the late summer there is good grazing for goats and sheep, the only domesticated livestock that adapt to these elevations. Mammals native to the Hudsonian zone include mountain sheep, Rocky Mountain woodchucks, conies, and shrews. The Arctic-Alpine zone caps the highest peaks along the Sangres. On the coldest slopes it begins at 12,000 feet and on the warmest slopes, about 13,000 feet. It is a treeless zone, marked by low and often matted vegetation of hardy alpine plants. It is covered with deep snow for eight or nine months of the year, thereby storing great quantities of moisture. Several species of Hudsonian mammals penetrate the Arctic-Alpine zone, especially during the brief summer. Because of the altitude and cold, the variety of flora and fauna is quite limited.[18]

In summary, the uplands of north-central New Mexico and south-central Colorado constitute a subalpine and alpine zone characterized by very rugged terrain. The region exhibits a distinct pattern of vertical biotic zonation resulting from altitudinal differences in temperature, precipitation, and pressure. The life zones range from the Upper Sonoran to the Arctic-Alpine. Arable land and water for irrigation are extremely limited resources, and they are found mainly in the valley of the Upper Sonoran zone. Under the best conditions, the region's environment is marginal for subsistence farming; farming on a commercial scale is truly a dubious enterprise. While the Rocky Mountain region as a whole is far from an ideal agricultural zone, Libecap and Alter fail to appreciate that northern New Mexico is an especially marginal area for agriculture. The majority of the land within the region is most adaptable to the seasonal grazing of livestock and the harvesting of wild foodstuffs.

The Cañones Microbasin

The Cañones drainage, one of the many small Upper Sonoran canyon-valley systems where human settlement has been possible, will serve as an example for this essay. The mouth of Cañones Creek reaches the Chama River two and one-half miles above the northwest end of the Chama valley, where the bottomland widened to form the Vega de Riaño. (In 1961 Abiquiu dam and reservoir were constructed here, so Cañones Creek now flows into the reservoir covering the vega.) The confluence of Cañones Creek and the Chama is approximately seven miles west-northwest of the mouth of Abiquiu Creek, and the site of the Hispanic village known by the same name.

From its headwaters in the Polvadera highlands, the Cañones drainage system flows approximately twenty miles northward to its outlet (see Map 5). Three other streams which have their origins in this high country, Polvadera Creek, Cañoncito Seco, and Chihuahueños Creek, merge with Cañones Creek before it reaches the Chama River.

Chihuahueños Creek originates to the east of Mesa del Medio and flows north and northeast approximately eighteen miles to its confluence with Cañones Creek, four miles south of the Cañones *placita* (small village). Cañoncito Seco rises at an elevation of 10,000 feet on the north side of the Santa Clara Mountains (part of the Valles range) east of Cañones Creek, and flows in a north-northeasterly direction approximately eleven miles to its confluence with Cañones Creek at a point two and one-half miles south of the placita. For the most part, Cañoncito Seco is dry below 8,500 feet, but there is spring near the point where it joins Cañones Creek. Polvadera Creek originates on the north side of the Santa Clara Mountains and flows north-northwesterly to its confluence with Cañones Creek at the Cañones placita.[19]

Together these creeks and their network of branches, along with the many associated arroyos and washes (which flow intermittently), delineate a small microbasin. This microbasin is about eight miles wide at the headwaters of the drainage system, narrowing as the watercourses converge in the Cañones valley. In all, this microbasin drainage system constitutes an area of approximately 70,000 acres, or about 110 square miles, 89 percent of which is now within the Santa Fe National Forest. The average yield of the drainage system to the area is 33 acre-feet of water per year. While the flow of the Cañones system is reduced from time to time, it may be characterized as one of the most dependable watercourses in the region. Thus, it lends itself well to extensive use for irrigation.

The elevation of the Cañones microbasin ranges from 6,058 feet at its northern limit to 11,232 feet on Polvadera Peak to the south. The basin is bordered on the west by Cerro Pedernal (9,862 feet), the most distinctive topographical feature of the area, and to the south of the Pedernal, the highlands locally known as the Sierra Valdez. On the east the Cañones basin is separated from the Abiquiu region by Cañones Mesa (7,559 feet) and to the southeast by Cerro Pelon (9,367 feet). The village of Cañones is situated at 6,500 feet.

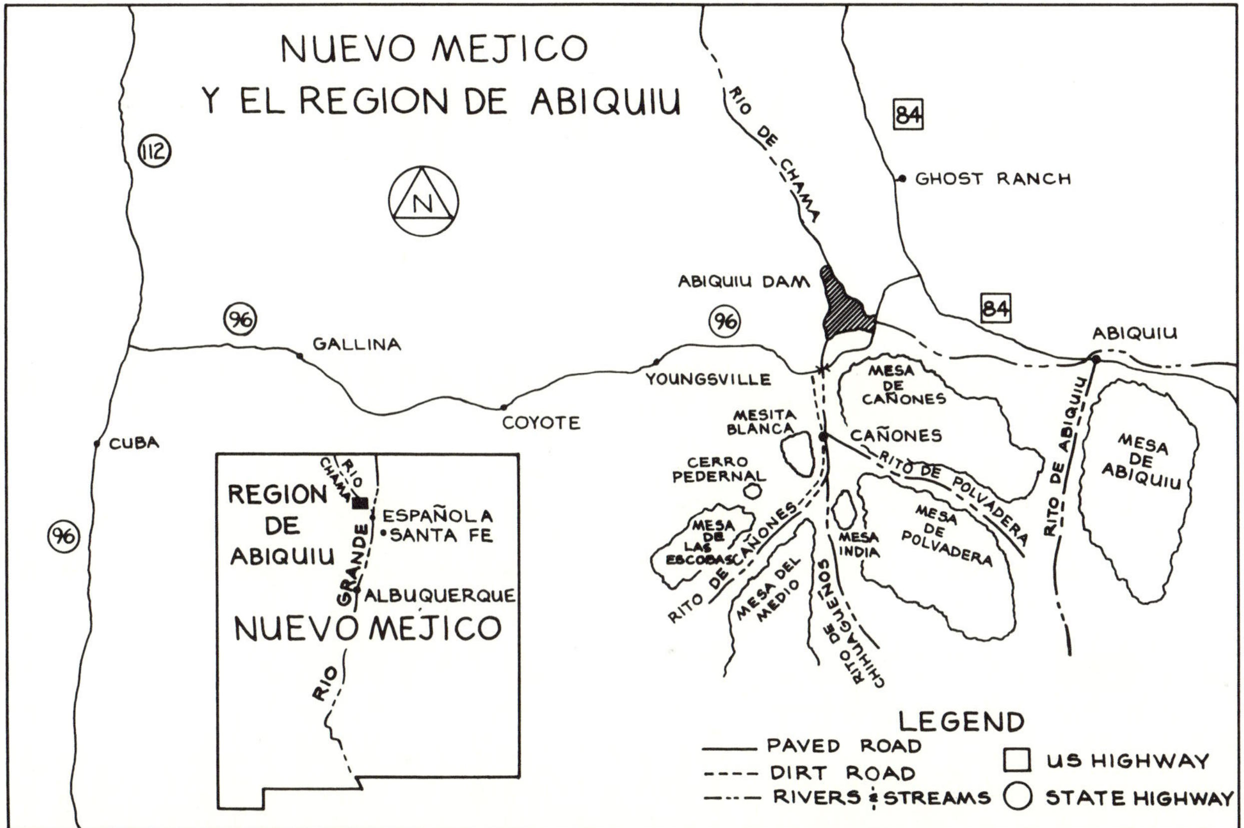

MAP 5. New Mexico and the Cañones region (from Paul Kutsche and John R. Van Ness, *Cañones: Values, Crisis, and Survival in a Northern New Mexico Village* (Albuquerque: University of New Mexico Press, 1981).

As the crow flies, the Cañones plaza is only a little over seven miles west and slightly south of Abiquiu. However, because of the local topography, access to Cañones by road or trail has always been difficult. Formerly, the traveler either went up and over Cañones Mesa or up the Chama from Abiquiu to Cañones Creek and then followed the road south along the Cañones valley to the village. Both routes were difficult before the advent of paved roads. Today the highway takes the traveler up the Chama valley, across the Abiquiu dam, and then approximately five miles south to Cañones via a gravel road. In wet weather this gravel road is frequently difficult to traverse.

The alluvial bottomland along the Cañones drainage is discontinuous and at no point extensive. From its mouth southward, the creek is flanked by narrow canyon for two miles. The valley then begins (see Map 6). From this point the bottomland is nearly one-half mile wide for approximately two additional miles until the confluence of the Polvadera Creek. Cañones plaza sits to the west on higher ground above the creek at this point. Upstream from where Polvadera Creek flows into Cañones Creek, it is separated by a knifelike ridge from the Cañones valley. Along the Polvadera, for approximately three-quarters of a mile, a small pocket of bottomland, locally called Cienaguitas (meaning a marshy place), occurs. Some three miles above Cienaguitas on the Polvadera there is also a small section of irrigable bottomland.

Cañones Creek itself flows through bottomland, which is approximately one-quarter of a mile in width, for a mile above the confluence of the Polvadera Creek. Then once again it becomes narrower as the creek enters Mogote Canyon. In the canyon one finds intermittent pockets of bottomland for another two miles.

In all, the alluvial bottomland in the microbasin suited for irrigation agriculture constitutes only slightly more than three hundred acres. The extremely limited amount of farmland is a salient feature of the microbasin, and characterizes many other valleys in the upland region. It is one of the principal environmental features that shaped the Hispanic cultural ecology which will be described.

Much of the lower section of the Cañones microbasin (roughly twenty thousand acres), which is within the boundaries of the old Hispanic Piedra Lumbre grant, consists of Upper Sonoran grass-shrub lands. The largest area with this variety of plant cover is northwest of the Cañones bottomland and is called La Joya de Pedregal. On the margins of the valley to the east, west, and south, sparse juniper-piñon wood-

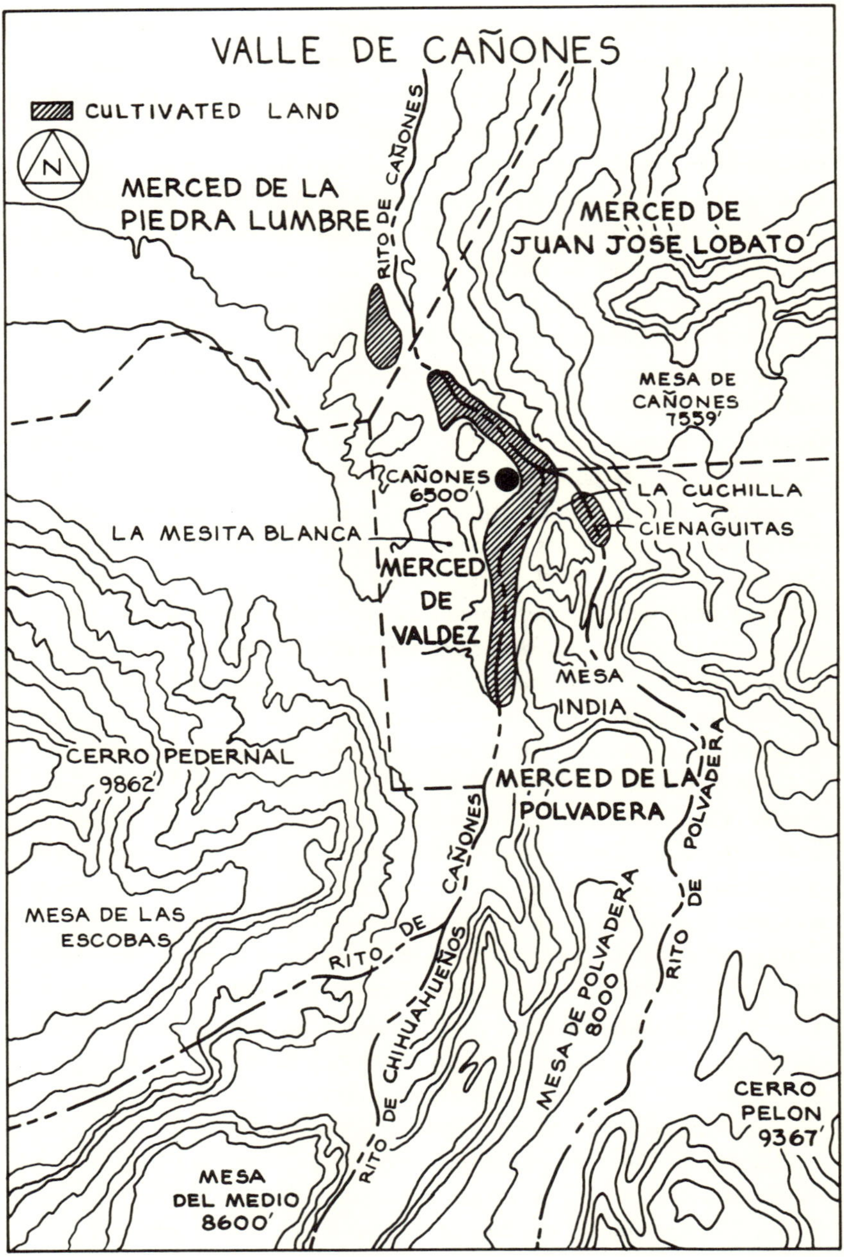

MAP 6. Topography of Cañones valley (from Kutsche and Van Ness, *Cañones*).

lands are found. This type of vegetation covers thirteen thousand acres of the microbasin's hills and low mesas. Its arid character contrasts strikingly with the green vegetation of the irrigated valley bottom.

In the higher elevations to the south, some thirty-two thousand acres are covered with transitional forests of pine and spruce of varying density. There are approximately one thousand acres of mountain chaparral located south of Cerro Pelon and north of Polvadera Peak. On the highest slope of Polvadera Peak there are three thousand five hundred acres of Canadian zone aspen forest.[20] The growing season, or average frost-free period, in the Cañones systems extends from 24 May to 26 September. No precise precipitation figures are available for the Cañones microbasin, but they fall within the range of those given for the larger region, that is, from eight to ten inches at the lowest elevation to twenty-four to thirty inches in the mountains.

In summary, the Cañones microbasin is typical of dozens found in this region. Year-round settlement was possible only in the Upper Sonoran valley. This environmental zone offered a very limited amount of irrigable farmland (no more than 5 percent of the basin's land area), winter and spring grazing land, timber for fuel and building, and, periodically, the nuts of the piñon tree. The Transition zone, at a higher altitude, permitted some dry farming of selected crops, allowed summer grazing, and provided some game. The highest elevations of the southern rim of the basin, characterized by Canadian flora and fauna, offered the residents a limited amount of summer grazing land, game animals, and the much needed water reserves stored in the annual snowpack. All of the microbasin's resources were necessary for the Hispanic settlers to win a livelihood; agriculture alone could not provide for subsistence. In terms of the frame of analysis employed by Libecap and Alter, successful commercial farming was surely impossible.

Hispanic Cultural Ecology

The nature of Hispanic cultural ecology in the uplands of northern New Mexico and southern Colorado, and its Old World historical roots, were first grasped and articulated by Peter van Dresser.[21] He wrote that the very rigidity and ruggedness of the upland terrain had much to do with its favorable circumstances for Hispanic settlement:

> In such an environment, the logic of topography and hydrology strongly

> determine the conditions of human life. Here the watershed is no mere geographer's abstraction but a microcosm to which social organization must specifically adapt itself. Its upper boundaries are usually steep and not conveniently crossed by roads; its drainage sump contains generally the only land suitable for settlement and attempts at cultivation; and all social and economic activities of necessity ebb and flow through it. Additionally, the control and management of the water collected and sharply concentrated by gravity here imposes on the community an incentive for collective action internally, and a collective external responsibility to water users on the lower reaches of the stream system which the watershed feeds. Finally, the considerable range in elevation and climatic zones usually embraced within such a microcosm results in a corresponding range of biotic resources which encourages a healthy degree of internal differentiation in economic activities.[22]

We have said that cultural ecology treats the interrelationship between human organisms and their biotic and physical environments. This is a dynamic processual relationship; it is not static. The environment we described above includes all factors biotic and abiotic, including other human populations. A useful new term that may now be introduced is *effective environment.* This refers to factors of the universe external to the human population that are directly or indirectly crucial to survival. In the upland regions, the effective environment must be described as extremely unpredictable. The most obvious unpredictable elements being precipitation and surface water run-off, which can exhibit disastrous fluctuations. Other variables of the effective environment in the uplands are the following:

1. *Solar energy,* essential to the growth of wild and domestic plant life. In broken canyon country the available solar energy varies drastically depending upon the orientation and slope of the land, location of precipices, and other topographic features.
2. *Soil characteristics and nutrients* in this region vary considerably from area to area. Areas abutting arroyos and gravel terraces are marginal because they are subject to flash floods that wash away topsoil and/or spread sterile sand and rock over the surface.
3. *Moisture,* as we have said, is exceedingly unpredictable and varies depending upon altitude and local topography. Even water for irrigation is unpredictable, and depends upon rain and snowfall at higher elevations. Also, should the spring melt be too rapid, the run-off descends on the valley bottoms with vicious force and great volume, preventing its practical use.

4. *Temperature* varies greatly due to altitude and local topography. For agricultural purposes the most important variable is the first and last day of frost each year.
5. *Wind* brings about rapid evaporation and frequently damages crops, but tends to be very localized.
6. *Insects and animals* cause damage to crops and grazing land, particuarly such insects as grasshoppers and such animals as rabbits, bears, and skunks.
7. *Other human societies,* such as the nomadic Indians, whose incursions were the scourge of the Hispanic settlements until the late nineteenth century. These raids and the destruction they caused occurred at irregular intervals and were also highly localized.

All of the above factors are systematically interconnected and have affected domesticated and wild plants and animals. Thus, demands on the Hispanic settlers in this region were considerable; successful farming and stock raising were uncertain even in the best times. The crucial societal factor that determined the margin for survival was population size and density. As population grew in this region of modest resources, more and more marginal land had to be used for both farming and grazing. As a result, the settlers became more vulnerable to the fluctuations in the effective environment and were more likely to encounter disaster. Perhaps the only environmental hazard ameliorated by population growth was the risk associated with nomadic Indian incursions. Larger villages were better able to defend themselves and thus more secure. The Hispanic population had to come to terms with the above environmental realities through the forms of social organization they employed, the available technology, and the knowledge that constituted their cultural heritage.

The Hispanic settlement, which began in the upland region of New Mexico at the very end of the sixteenth century, may be characterized as a largely self-sufficient population of farmer-soldiers. They settled the land principally through the provisions made by the Spanish Crown in New Spain for community land grants. Additionally, leading citizens frequently received larger grazing grants.

The small settlements that developed in the upland river valleys consisted of subsistence farmers and stock raisers. In this semiarid region stock raising usually predominated. Also, they supplemented their livelihood through trading—meats, hides, slaves, horses, and *punche* (a wild tobacco plant)—as well as hunting and harvesting wild food plants, seeds, and nuts. Like other populations on the far northern frontier of New Spain, these people carried a simplified or pared-down form of Hispanic culture, in which many elements of the indigenous Indian cultures had been incorporated. (These Hispanos have been most thoroughly studied by Oakah Jones.)[23] Their technology was very simple and fashioned largely from wood and other locally available materials. Few iron implements were available. This technology changed little over the centuries due to isolation and their impoverished existence. A principal technological system, and part of their Iberian heritage, was ditch-based irrigation agriculture.

The outstanding feature of the Hispanic response to the northern frontier region was the creation of an agro-pastoral tradition that joined plow agriculture and animal husbandry. The small corporate village community, which was the primary unit of rural social organization, landholding, and agro-pastoral production, organized and carried on this form of subsistence livelihood. (The general European, Iberian, and Latin American antecedents of these villages have been fully discussed by the author in a previous article.)[24]

These small corporate villages provided the organizational basis for production, control, and management of the two basic factors in production: land and water. At the core of this system was a complex of social relations that integrated the principles of individual and communal landholding and use for subsistence purposes. In addition to structuring and regulating economic life, the corporate village community provided for the greater part of all the individual's social and religious needs. As Rhoades and Thompson have demonstrated, such communities also function well to meet the subsistence needs of human existence in rugged alpine or upland environments, where a unique set of effective environmental characteristics creates a number of special problems for human exploitation.[25] Among technologically simple rural people, diversified agro-pastoral exploitation is most productive and is the only means by which population aggregations can be supported in such environments.

The genius of this system is the arrangement that permits the variable land forms, water, and other resources to be available for each family production unit. Farmers are able to have rights to tracts on various portions of the arable land and to various types of grazing land which provide for year-round maintenance of livestock. To achieve this end, the extensive grazing land at various mountain altitudes is made available on a communal basis; this serves everyone, not just a few farm families. With this landholding arrangement, vertical transhumance can be practiced; pasturage at higher altitudes can be utilized when it is available in the spring and summer, and grazing land at lower altitudes can be used during the cold months of the year when the highest altitudes are covered with snow and subject to extremely low temperatures.

The striking contrast between this Hispanic community-based subsistence economy and the Anglo-American commercial farm should now be evident. Thus, a second weakness in the Libecap and Alter argument is revealed. They should not have assumed a general similarity between the Hispanic and the Anglo-American modes of exploiting the environment. Simple comparisons cannot be made between these sharply contrasting rural economies.

Having outlined the parameters of the Hispanic cultural ecology in the uplands, it is now time to turn to a specific case, the settlement pattern developed in the Cañones region. The reader has been provided with a physical description of the Cañones microbasin, as well as the elements of the effect environment crucial to the Hispanic settlers. Armed with a basic understanding of Hispanic cultural ecology and the upland environment, the evolution of Hispanic settlement will become intelligible in a way that totally escapes the individual who is poorly informed regarding these factors. Further, knowledge of some of the details of this regional history will be crucial for comprehending the impact of land alienation after 1846 under the U.S. administration, which will be discussed at the conclusion of this essay.

Early Land Grants: The Settlement Pattern in the Cañones Region[26]

The Cañones microbasin had been well known to human inhabitants of the region since prehistoric times. This was due both to the Cerro Pedernal's important chert quarries and Cañones's location on a prehistoric Tewa Indian route to Navajo and Ute country. The route was protected by the prehistoric Tsiping Pueblo during the Classic period (A.D. 1000–1300). The Pueblo's ruins are located on a mesa above the valley.

Since this area was frequently traversed by Hispanic trading parties and military expeditions, its potential for pasturing livestock no doubt became well known. It is likely that herds occasionally were pushed out into this area as early as the 1720s, although no formal allotments of grazing lands were made until the next decade.

The first official allotment in the Cañones region was made by Governor Cruzat Gongora (1731–1736), who granted a square *league* (a league equals 2.6 miles) of grazing land to José de Riaño y Tagle in the Piedra Lumbre valley (see Map 7). The exact date for the grant is not part of the colonial record, and Riaño appears to have held the land only long enough to have his title confirmed under Spanish colonial law, probably only a short time beyond the four years required. Furthermore, it is doubtful if he ever personally occupied the tract, although he did have a log house and corrals constructed on the property where his herdsmen lived and tended his stock.[27] Nevertheless, Riaño's imprint on the land was an enduring one. Among the several names for the Cañones valley that persisted is Cañon de Riaño. The bottomland along the Rio Chama where it crosses the Piedra Lumbre, now covered by the Abiquiu reservoir, was called the Vega de Riaño.

Following the Riaño grant, the tract adjoining the Piedra Lumbre on the south was granted in 1740 for grazing purposes to three brothers, Captain Miguel Montoya, Juan Manuel Montoya, and Bernardo Baltazar Montoya. The petitioners, with their father, Antonio Montoya, were natives of New Mexico and residents of Abiquiu, where they held farmland. Recognizing that the natural boundaries of the Piedra Lumbre encompassed a much larger area than the square league granted Riaño, and that the mountain grazing lands to the south were also desirable, they requested all surplus land in the Piedra Lumbre as well as the contiguous highlands south to the Santa Clara Mountains. In their request, the Montoyas stated that the land they desired as located in the Valle de la Piedra Lumbre, bounded on the east by the lands of Geronimo Martín, on the west by the brow of the Piedra Lumbre, on the north by the lands of Don José Riaño, and on the south by the Santa Clara Mountains that extend to the canyon of the Piedra Lumbre.[28]

Near the date when the Montoyas received their grant, they made arrangements with José de Riaño to make use of his house and corrals on the Piedra Lumbre for their stock raising operation. It might be conjectured that they also acquired the use of Riaño's grazing land on the Piedra Lumbre at this time, since the two tracts made a natural unit for stock raising. (This unit permitted vertical transhumance; the

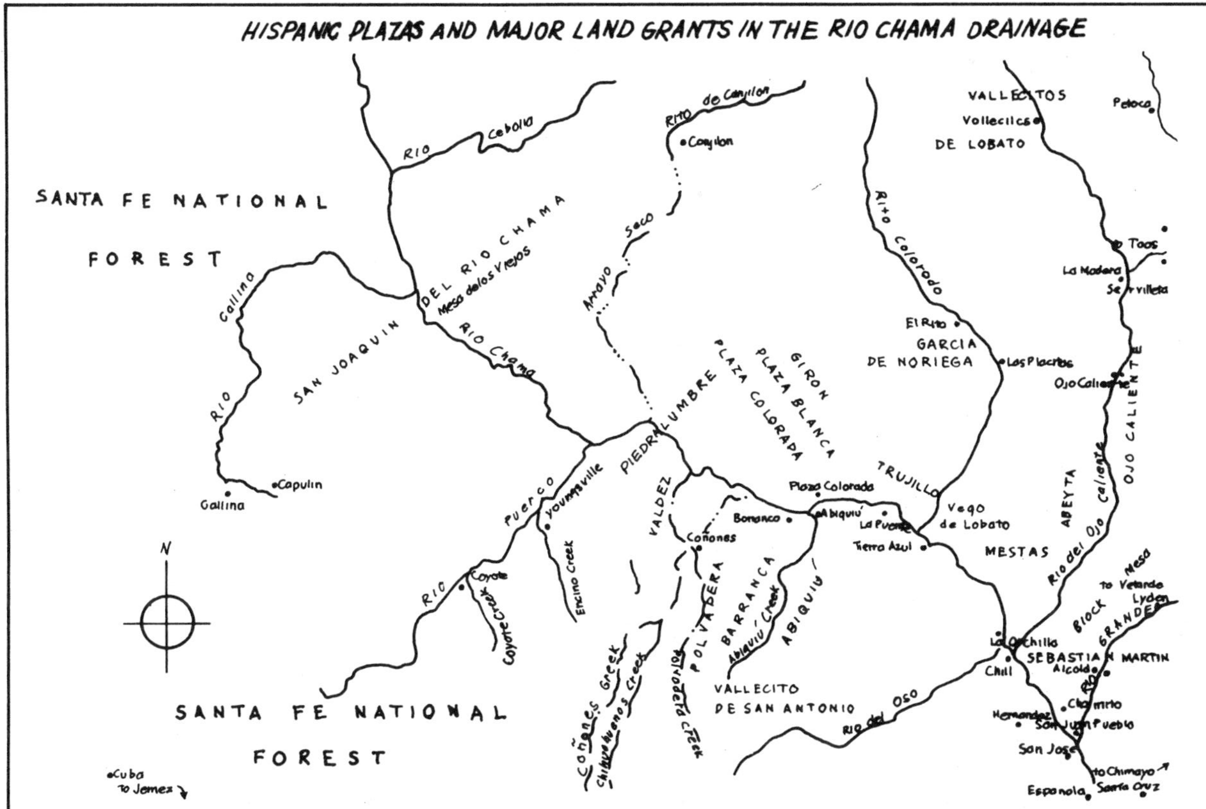

MAP 7. Hispanic plazas and major land grants in the Rio Chama drainage.

Piedra Lumbre could provide ample winter pasturage, with the Montoya tract to the south serving as mountain pasturage for the summer.) At any rate, shortly after Riaño's death Captain Antonio Montoya (the eldest member of the extended family) acquired Riaño's rights to the Piedra Lumbre valley from his widow, Maria Roybal.[29]

As with José de Riaño, the Montoyas' hold on the region proved to be short lived. As nearly as can be reckoned, the Montoyas used the grant until 1745. During this period they maintained a house in nearby Abiquiu, which was most likely their primary residence, as well as the *rancho* (small ranch) on the Piedra Lumbre. However, while herding sheep on the rancho during 1745 they were attacked by a band of Ute Indians. In this encounter Juan Manuel was killed and Miguel received "fourteen wounds." Miguel and three *genizaro* (Christianized Hispanized Indian) shepherds, who were also wounded, escaped and returned to Abiquiu. When his father, Antonio, and brother, Baltazar, died the following year, Miguel found himself alone with a large family nearly depleted of adult males. Still suffering from the consequence of his many wounds, Miguel was unable to support the family and decided to abandon the property at Abiquiu, perhaps leaving some of their genizaro servants behind to care for their land.[30] The Montoyas did not return to Abiquiu when it was resettled in 1750 following the Comanche raid of 1747, but instead thirteen genizaros settled on the Montoyas' property. The Montoya grant lands at Abiquiu were then used in 1754 to found the genizaro pueblo. Although apparently unused, the Montoya grants on the Piedra Lumbre and Polvadera were not subjected to *realengo* (royal forfeiture).

Nothing is known of the use of the Cañones region for a decade, until approximately 1760. At this time Pedro Martín Serrano secured the rights to use the Piedra Lumbre from a relative of Miguel Montoya and placed his livestock on the Piedra Lumbre and the highlands to the south, where they grazed for six years under this arrangement.[31] In 1766 he was able to purchase the Montoya rights and, to be secure in his tenure, he petitioned Governor Tomás Veléz Cachupín for a grant de novo covering all of the land within the same boundaries marked out for José de Riaño. To wit: "On the north, some red bluffs; on the east, a stoney hill; on the south, Cerro Pedernal; and on the west, the mesa adjoining the Cañon de la Piedra Lumbre."

In his request, Martín Serrano stated that the boundaries encompassed an area of approximately three leagues east to west and the same distance north to south. He also reported that he owned 480 head of cattle, 164 horses and mules, and 2,700 sheep.[32]

Coincident with the Piedra Lumbre grant to Pedro Martín Serrano, a grant was requested by his cousin, Juan Pablo Martín. This was for the tract to the south, previously granted in 1740 to the Montoyas. In Juan Pablo Martín's petition to Governor Veléz Cachupín, he stated that he had a small piece of land in the Abiquiu district but that it was curtailed for the establishment of the genizaro pueblo and was insufficient for the support of his large family. Moreover, he lacked pasture land for his livestock (listed as more than 100 cattle, 18 horses, and 400 head of small stock). For these reasons he requested a tract of unappropriated and unsettled land, commonly called La Polvadera, on which some patches were fit for cultivation and the balance for pasture. The boundaries of this tract were recited as:

> On the east, the straight road crossing the west boundary of the Pueblo de Santo Tomás de Abiquiu and running southward toward the Cerro Pelado; on the south, the head of the Polvadera Arroyo; on the west, the Arroyo de Cerro Pedernal; and on the north, the junction of the Pedernal and the Polvadera Arroyos.

These boundaries correspond closely with the Montoyas' grant on the Polvadera, although the Montoya boundaries encompassed somewhat more land to the west. The extent of the land requested approximated 1½ leagues east to west and three leagues north to south, according to Martín. Governor Veléz Cachupín approved the request and ordered the Alcalde Mayor de Santa Cruz to put him in possession.[33]

Immediately after the approval of the two new grants, a lengthy squabble erupted because of confusion caused by the earlier allotments in this region. Miguel Montoya and Santiago Montoya, residents of the town of Atrisco (in Rio Abajo or the Rio Grande valley south of Santa Fe) and the sons of the deceased Captain Miguel Montoya and Juan Manuel Montoya respectively, sent a formal complaint to Governor Veléz Cachupín in which they claimed that a great injustice had been done them and their younger brothers. They argued that the Piedra Lumbre and Polvadera still rightfully belonged to them, as their fathers' heirs. They claimed that their fathers had occupied the grants for at least the prescribed four years required to obtain rights in perpetuity and therefore the tracts should not have been given to the Martín-Serranos. They also suggested that if another grant of grazing land were offered them in the Rio Abajo region, they would be willing to give up their land rights in the Abiquiu district. Finally, in February 1767, after having the matter under consideration for six months, Governor Veléz Cachupín responded to the Montoyas' suggestion. He granted them a tract in the Rio Abajo region and reconfirmed the new Piedra Lumbre and Polvadera grants.[34]

Analysis of the Settlement Pattern and Adaptation on the Eighteenth-Century Land Grants

Spanish colonial laws regarding the distribution of Crown lands provided the framework within which land allotments were made and occupied in the Cañones region. However, it is clear that within this framework a number of modifications occurred to suit the special requirements of the region's environment and the adaptation to it by the Hispanic settlers.

The first grants in the Cañones microbasin were exclusively for the purpose of grazing livestock, as was the case throughout the Rio Chama region. These large allotments of land were generally made when intensive development of a region was not feasible, due to the low Hispanic population density and one particular element of the effective environment, marauding Indians. Some years would pass before the Cañones region would experience the development of year-round *plazas* (farming/ranching settlements).

An important consideration in awarding grants was the ability of petitioners to occupy and hold frontier lands against hostile Indians. To do this, they had to have adequate material resources and personnel at their disposal. The personnel might consist of members of kindred families and/or their servants. All adult males had to be willing to bear arms as well as perform the tasks of tilling the soil and caring for livestock. These special requirements were met by the Cañones region grantees. Riaño was able to retain shepherds in his service on the Piedra Lumbre. The Montoyas and Martín-Serranos marshaled the necessary manpower by pooling the resources of their large extended families, among whom were experienced militia leaders.

From the beginning, tenure rights (rights to hold and use land) to these grants were actually vested in the kindred families, represented by the elder male heads, in whose names the grants of land were made. The extended family units were the basic corporate, social, and economic units and constituted the nucleus from which plazas grew. Thus, in terms of the cultural ecology, they were the natural focus of land tenure rights as well.

Spanish colonial law set the amount of land to be included in a grant and the use to which land grants were to be put. However, in New Mexico the nature of the land, the forms of land usage, and the social setting strongly tempered the application of these regulations. Together the Piedra Lumbre and Polvadera grants totaled well over one hundred square miles, including the Cañones Creek and part of the Rio Puerco drainage systems. This is far more land than Spanish regulations sanctioned. However, since the grants were initially principally for seasonal grazing, and because of the environmental conditions, extremely large areas were required for pasturage. Moreover, here as elsewhere in New Mexico, historical records show that the pattern of landholding evolved as the region became more heavily occupied due to natural population growth and the movement of new settlers into a region. With the development of year-round settlements along the streams, regular subsistence farming began in conjunction with stock raising. With this intensification of land use, the extremely large grazing grants were frequenty divided into several smaller tracts to accommodate the needs of the new pattern of land utilization. Concomitantly, the land tenure rules changed to reflect multiple forms of use.

Another important fact in the cultural ecology is that from the beginning the Piedra Lumbre and Polvadera tracts were recognized as constituting a natural unit for exploitive purposes. Here one found irrigable farmland in the valley, Upper Sonoran rangeland on the Piedra Lumbre, and mountain forests and meadows in the Polvadera highlands. Thus, both the Montoyas and the Martín-Serranos acquired rights to the two tracts and used them through transhumant grazing practices as a single production unit. As occupation intensified, this pattern of land use in the microbasin continued.

A final factor that most likely exerted a special influence on the development of early occupation in the Cañones region was a motivation on the part of the grantees to carry on contraband trade with the Utes and Navajo, since trading was an important part of the subsistence system. Swadesh argues that the development of trading partnerships with the nomadic Indians made it possible to request grants in these outlying areas.[35] Since the area was traversed by a frequently used Indian trail to the north and northwest, the probability that such trade took place is very high. Unfortunately this illegal trade became part of the official record only when it was brought to the attention of the authorities. Although there is no mention of this activity in the foregoing account, it should be understood that it is a factor in the Hispanic adaptation of the region.

The Final Decades of the Eighteenth Century in the Abiquiu Jurisdiction

The records tell us very little of the Cañones region during the latter part of the century, and it must be concluded that its fortunes rose and fell as did those of the larger Abiquiu jurisdiction. Periods of peace and trading, followed by interludes of Indian hostilities, continued throughout the waning years of the eighteenth century. New settlements were founded as the result of a gradual population increase. However, there is no evidence that the Cañones region became more heavily populated during this period. Instead it remained essentially grazing land, dotted with small ranchos here and there along its watercourses. The Martín-Serranos, who seasonally worked the ranchos in the Cañones region, continued to maintain primary residences in the Chama valley in the vicinity of Abiquiu, namely at the plazas of Antonio, San Jose, and San Miguel.

Fray Dominguez reported in 1776 that farming was very limited because the settlers were kept in a continual state of terror due to the nomadic Indian threat. As a consequence, the farmers sowed their lands like transients, going to their fields and returning to the place where they could live in less fear.[36]

In spite of the threat of nomadic Indian hostilities, Dominguez found that trading with them had become firmly institutionalized at Abiquiu:

> Every year, between the end of October and the beginning of November, many heathens of the Ute nation come to the vicinity of this Pueblo. They come very well laden with good deerskins, and they celebrate their fair with them. This is held for the sole purpose of buying horses. If one is much to the taste and satisfaction of an Indian (the trial is a good race), he gives fifteen to twenty good deerskins for the horse; and if not, there is no purchase. They also sell deer or buffalo meat for maize or corn flour. Sometimes there are little captive heathen Indians (male or female) as with the Comanches, whom they resemble in the manner of selling them. They usually sell deerskins for *belduques*

> (long hunting knives) only, and they are given two of the latter for a good one of the former.[37]

Fray Dominguez also mentioned that the mission was in charge of the administration of Hispanic settlers, some of whom lived in ranchos scattered to the west and north, and some to the east in a small plaza. He stated that these settlers lived in a fashion that, to his way of thinking, was very sorry indeed, as he had detailed earlier in his account of the province. For example, in describing the Villa of Santa Fe he noted:

> in the final analysis it lacks everything. Its appearance is mournful because not only are the houses of earth, but they are not adorned by any artifice of brush or construction. To conclude, the Villa of Santa Fe (for the most part) consists of many small ranchos at various distances from one another, with no plan as to their location, for each owner built as he was able, wished to, or found convenient, now for the little farms they have there, now for the small herds of cattle which they keep in corrals of stakes, or else for other reasons.[38]

The Abiquiu settlers' lands began where those of the genizaros left off. Like the other settlers of the province, in their small irrigated fields they grew wheat, maize, legumes, green vegetables, melon, watermelon, and apricots, of which there were small orchards. Fray Dominguez noted that the Hispanos' fields yielded more and better crops because they worked more diligently than the genizaros.[39] For some reason, Fray Dominguez took no notice of the importance of the Abiquiu regions' animal husbandry, a livelihood that he generally overlooked in his travels throughout the province.

By the latter years of the 1780s, with the reduction of the Indian threat, the frontier settlements of New Mexico were becoming more prosperous and expanding. Thus began an era of peace, population growth, and increase in the livestock industry.

The growing prosperity is reflected in the 1789 census of the Abiquiu jurisdiction. The document shows that the population had reached 1,079, an increase of approximately thirty-five percent in a single decade.[40] This increase was due largely to the growth of the Hispanic *vecino* (citizen) population, because the genizaro population had not increased. The population of the genizaro Pueblo of Santo Tomás consisted of 55 households (177 individuals), and the vecinos residing in 8 surrounding plazas totaled 203 households (902 individuals).

By the turn of the century, a thriving heterogeneous population that was well equipped to extract a living from local natural and human resources in a variety of ways inhabited the Abiquiu region. This local adaptation was one of flexibility rather than narrow specialization. In 1798 the population of the Abiquiu district had reached 1,749.[41] With an expanding population and growing herds of livestock, new farms and grazing lands were needed. Thus, a new sequence of expansion of the frontier began, accompanied by the usual petitions to the Spanish Crown for additional land grants. With the opening of the nineteenth century, new settlements were founded and old ranchos reoccupied in the Cañones region.

Settlement of the Cañones Placita

Settlement of the Cañones placita took place in the context of a general expansion of the Abiquiu region's population, particularly to the north and west, at the opening of the nineteenth century. By 1808 the population had reached 1,938, including 122 genizaros and 1,816 Hispanos.[42] Lands northwest of Abiquiu saw the development of small farming settlements along the watercourses, accompanied by intensified use of the rangeland to graze the settlers' herds. As has been recounted, in spite of the grazing grants previously made in this region, pressure from the nomadic Indians had made use of these lands sporadic during the last decades of the eighteenth century.

Formal requests for the distribution of farmlands to the north and west of Abiquiu began in 1806, although clearing the land and breaking the soil appears to have preceded this date by a few years. A large number of the descendants of the early grantees in the region lived in the Abiquiu jurisdiction, among them sons, daughters, grandchildren, and even a number of great-grandchildren. Because partible inheritance was the rule, many of these descendants possessed long-standing usufructuary rights to run their stock on the Piedra Lumbre and Polvadera grazing land. It is only natural that these descendants regarded it as their prerogative to initiate the development of farmlands in the region encompassed by the old grants and beyond. Families drawn from this group, then, accompanied by others from the Abiquiu jurisdiction, led the way in this new sequence of frontier development. Thus, in terms of the Hispanic population involved, there was continuity from the first historical period to the one presently under discussion.

Of record in 1806 are a request for the revalidation of the Piedra

Lumbre grant and a petition for a grant of a tract along the Rio Chama to the west of the Piedra Lumbre. Early in the following year a petition was sent to Governor Joaquín Real Alencaster requesting that land be distributed in the Cañon de los Pedernales (the Cañones valley). Many settlers for these new communities were drawn from the plazas near Abiquiu. These plazas—San Jose de Barranco, San Antonio, and San Miguel—were predominantly populated by those related to the Martín-Serrano families, by descent or through marriage.

The request for the revalidation of the Piedra Lumbre grant was made by Mariano Martín, a grandson of Pedro Martín Serrano, on behalf of himself and a large number of the grantee's descendants. In his request Mariano presented the original grant document to the governor and stated that the land had been abandoned for a period of years due to wars with the nomadic Indians. On 10 August 1806, the governor issued a decree revalidating the grant and ordering the alcalde of Santa Cruz de la Cañada to give the petitioners possession of the land that belonged to them as a result of their ancient rights. In particular, the alcalde was directed to see that agricultural lands were fairly distributed.[43]

As nearly as can be ascertained, Mariano Martín's father was Santiago, the second son of Pedro Martín Serrano. Santiago Martín also had a son called Pedro Martín Serrano, no doubt named in honor of his grandfather. This grandson was married to María Manuela Sisneros, with whom he had four children.[44] In 1789 Juan Pablo (the grandson) was a resident of the Plaza de San Miguel, along with a number of other members of the Martín lineage. He died in the year 1806. Since this was the same year of the request for revalidation of the Piedra Lumbre grant, it seems likely that the request was at least partly prompted by Juan Pablo's death, as a way to sort out the rights of his heirs and all others who possessed rights to the grant. The revalidation request was also linked to the new grants made to the west and south of the Piedra Lumbre, as will be seen.

To the west of the Piedra Lumbre, Alferez Francisco Salazar petitioned in 1806 for a grant for himself, his two brothers, and twenty-eight needy citizens.[45] Under instructions from the governor, the alcalde of Santa Cruz examined the lands solicited and reported that the tract requested was unoccupied and situated one league from the last grant to the east (that of the Martíns). He stated that the tract contained about two leagues of arable lands in the Cañon del Rio Chama to accommodate the families and that enough land would remain for possible increases in the way of children and sons-in-law. Finally, on the north and south, one league from each side could be assigned for pastures. On these two sides no injury could result since there was neither a settlement nor a grant.

After receiving this favorable report, Governor Real Alencaster ordered the alcalde to place the colonists in possession, allocating to each an agricultural tract capable of being planted with three *cuartillas* (61.92 dry quarts) of wheat, three *almudes* (20.64 dry quarts) of corn, and another three *almudes* of beans. Thus, a tract totaled approximately ten acres. As principal settler, Francisco Salazar was to receive a double allotment. In addition, each family was to be given a lot for a small house and garden. For this purpose a town site was set aside and named San Joaquín del Rio de Chama. Finally, the boundary lines with adjoining lands were to be described, so that the rights to pastures and watering places could be clearly understood.

The third land grant in this region, one of central concern to this essay, was requested in 1807 by Juan Bautista Valdez and centered on the Cañones or Pedernales valley. Valdez requested a grant in this region for himself, his family, seven companions and, presumably, their families. This grant bordered the Piedra Lumbre on the north and the Polvadera on the east, and its agricultural lands were at first restricted to the cañon of the Pedernales. (Today this place is simply referred to as Cañones. In the old records it is also called the Cañon de Riaño and the Cañon de San Miguel.) In his petition, Valdez states that with prior permission of the alcalde, 2,000 varas, or about 1,800 yards (a vara is approximately 33 inches), of land had already been cleared in the canyon, presumably during the preceding year or earlier. Furthermore, no one was domiciled on this tract of land, so there would be no injuries to the water, woods, or pastures of any other parties. Appended to this request was a statement by Alcalde García de la Mora verifying that the facts set forth in the petition were true and recommending that the request be approved, since the petitioner had a large family and insufficient land on which to live. With the governor's approval, the alcalde proceeded to the Cañon de San Miguel and placed Juan Bautista Valdez and his companions (whose number had now grown to nine families) in possession. In doing so he cited the following boundaries: "on the east the river of the same cañon, which reaches the boundary of the Polvadera, on the west the mesa blanca, on the north the boundary of the Martins', and on the south the source of said river."[46]

The documents recording the Cañon de los Pedernales grant do not explicitly mention an allotment of woods and pasture land, leading to arguments nearly a century later that no such rights were accorded these settlers. However, the writer believes that formally allocating woods and pasture land may have been thought unnecessary, since the grant was made in the little valley which had been previously occupied by ranchos of the earlier Piedra Lumbre and Polvadera grantees. In addition, the grant coincided with a revalidation of the Piedra Lumbre grant, thereby once more linking the two tracts of land and their owners together as an ecological unit. It appears certain that this period of development was a cooperative venture by the group of interrelated families from the Chama valley who resettled the lands of the Piedra Lumbre and the northwestern reaches of the Polvadera. What is known about Juan Bautista Valdez, his family, and wider kinship ties lends considerable support to this line of argument.

By the time the Cañon de los Pedernales grant was made in 1807, Valdez was almost sixty years old with grown children, most of whom were married. Therefore, he headed a large extended family, as is mentioned in his petition. It is not surprising to find that many of the early owners of agricultural plots along Cañones Creek are closely linked to him by kinship ties. Kinship ties, particularly fraternal links, among his companion settlers are also apparent. These links are illustrated by the list of landholders other than Juan Bautista himself in about 1820 (see Table 2). Beginning at the south head of the canyon and moving northward, twenty-three tracts along the creek are enumerated. These total approximately 6,500 varas, or nearly four miles of creek frontage, and are held by nineteen different owners.[47]

In addition to farming, the new settlers of the Cañones placita owned a large number of livestock that they pastured in the mountains to the south and on the Piedra Lumbre to the north. Juan Bautista Valdez was reported to have owned 50 head of horses, about 200 head of cattle, over 1,000 head of sheep, and some goats and burros.[48] Thus, stock raising was a major subsistence industry of the Cañones settlers as it was with other settlers of the region.

By the year 1814, the population of the Cañones plaza had increased sufficiently that the settlers went to the alcalde, Pedro Ignacio Gallegos, presented their royal grant to him, and requested that their holdings

TABLE 2
Landholdings in the Cañones Valley Circa 1820*

Owner	*Amount of Land*	*Known Kinship Ties*
Sixto García	1,000 varas	father of R. García
Baltazar Quintana	1,000 varas	
Juan Antonio Velasquez	500 varas	
Diego Velasquez	200 varas	
Juan de Jesus Molina	100 varas	
Cristobal Molina	100 varas	
Juan Antonio Velasquez	50 varas	
Antonia Rosa Valdez	400 varas	daughter of JBV
Pedro Valdez	100 varas	grandson of JBV
Jose Ortega	90 varas	son-in-law of JBV
Jose Antonio Valdez	100 varas	son of JBV
Jose Ortega	310 varas	
Ramon García	40 varas	husband of JBV's granddaughter; son of S. García
Juan Salazar	100 varas	
Juan Cristobal Martín	50 varas	
Gregorio Martín	100 varas	
Jose Antonio Valdez	1,000 varas	
Pedro Trujillo	40 varas	
Vicente Gonzales	100 varas	
Jose Trujillo	90 varas	brother of F. Trujillo
Francisco Trujillo	1,500 varas	brother of J. Trujillo
Juan Trujillo	25 varas	
Francisco Vigil	20 varas	

(*from the head of the canyon northward, excluding tracts held by Juan Bautista Valdez)

be examined, with a view toward assigning them additional tracts, so that they might support their families more comfortably. The alcalde responded to their request and, on examining their present holdings, found them to be insufficient. To remedy this situation, additional allotments were made within the grant boundaries, and *hijuelas* (documents detailing the division or transfer of property) were issued on 5 July 1814 to each party.[49] As the leading elder citizen and principal settler, Juan Bautista Valdez requested that he be given a separate tract near the western edge of the grant, at the *paraje* (encampment) of the Encino. This tract was located along the Rito Encino (also called El Rito de Faustín), a tributary of the Rio Puerco, situated west of the Cerro Pedernal. The hijuela given to Valdez for this tract cites the following boundaries: "on the east a *mojonera* (land monument) which faces La Joya, on the west a small mountain at the Canada de los Corrales, on the north some rocks, and on the south the peaks of the mountains."[50] These boundaries place the tract at the southwestern corner of the Piedra Lumbre grant, where the modern community bears the unlikely name of Youngsville (thanks to the U.S. Postal Service).

As in the previous periods, Indian hostilities from time to time threatened the new frontier settlements of the nineteenth century. The period from 1806 to 1818 had been an interval of general peace on the northwestern frontier. In 1818, hostilities with the Navajo flared again. Throughout the winter and spring (1818–1819), Navajo war parties harassed the New Mexican frontier.

On 10 April 1819, Alcalde Pedro Ignacio Gallegos of Abiquiu reported to the governor that the settlers in the plazas of San Joaquín del Cañon del Rio de Chama and Cañones de Riaño had abandoned their homes because their forces were insufficient to curb the invasions of many Indians. The alcalde requested that the governor send a detachment of troops to be stationed at one of these localities so that the settlers might return to their homes to plant their fields. Governor Facundo Melgares responded immediately to the alcalde's communication, saying that the property holders of the canyons should return to their homes without fear and commence their planting, because the Navajos had asked for peace.[51]

There is considerable doubt whether Governor Melgares succeeded in reassuring the Cañones settlers. It is not known if they immediately returned to their homes. During the last years of the Melgares administration, the Navajo held the upper hand and were able to commit many successful raids along the New Mexican frontier. The records do show that Cañones had been reoccupied by 1824, for in that year a new group of settlers were given land at the Cañon de Riaño.

On 1 April 1824, the alcalde and the petitioners went to the canyon, accompanied by two witnesses, Lorenzo Molina and Francisco Valdez. Arriving at the Plaza de Riaño, the alcalde summoned the settlers to present themselves with the documents that would prove their ownership. José Miguel Valdez, the eldest son of Juan Bautista, stepped forward as a representative for the settlers, in place of his now-deceased father. The boundaries of the farmlands held by the Riaño or Cañones settlers were examined and at the upper boundary a permanent landmark was set. Above this point tracts useful for farming were assigned to the new settlers. The alcalde gave each individual 150 varas or more, according to the characteristics of the land.[52]

Thus, in the two decades following the grant made in the name of Juan Bautista Valdez a large number of settlers had come to hold farm tracts along the Cañones Creek drainage. In all, the landowners totaled 35 and indications are that the population of the Cañones placita had reached approximately 150.

In addition to those given possession of Cañones grant lands by the alcalde, the record shows that quite a number of farm tracts had changed hands through inheritance and sale. Land transfers continued throughout the remaining years of the Mexican administration, for which the documentation is quite limited. The overwhelming majority of these land transfers were among relatives. Custom dictated that grant lands should not be sold to anyone other than kinsmen. (This prohibition is understandable given the need for cooperative management and use of community irrigation systems, pastures, and woods.)

Since neither the Spanish or Mexican administrations had a comprehensive system for keeping public records of land transfers, it is impossible to know how many tracts of land changed hands during this period. Every indication is, however, that such transfers were quite numerous. The population in this frontier region was quite fluid and, as new areas were opened for settlement, members of some Cañones families moved on. During the Mexican administration, farmlands were opened up on the Rio Puerco and its tribuaries, Rito Encino and Coyote Creek. Since the western edges of the Pedernales grant and the Piedra Lumbre grant reached these streams, they were logical sites to attract the Cañones surplus population. In addition, new areas were opening to the north of Abiquiu. In 1824 Vallecitos de Lobato and Petaca, north of El Rito, were settled. In 1832 a large grant made on the upper Rio Chama at Tierra Amarilla also attracted settlers from the regions closer to Abiquiu. Therefore, while the continuity of the Cañones region's population from generation to generation is clear, it should also be recognized that new family names regularly appear among the residents.

Analysis of the Nineteenth-Century Settlement Pattern and Adaptation

The continuities in settlement policies from the previous century are evident during the last years of the Spanish colonial government and the Mexican Republic administration that spanned the years from 1821 to 1846. The Mexican government made few substantive changes in land policy. Because of population growth and a good deal of social leveling, made possible by the opportunities for economic and social advancement on the frontier, grants in this period favored more settlers of modest means.

By the beginning of the nineteenth century, even the older grazing grants in the Cañones region, the Piedra Lumbre and the Polvadera, were held in common tenure by a large number of individuals. This was due to the practice of partible inheritance and the frequency with which sons-in-law were fully incorporated into the expanded kin groups and acquired property rights. Such factors facilitated the communal use of grazing and woodlands, characteristic of the Hispanic adaptation to the uplands.

The ability of the settlers to occupy and hold the lands allotted them against hostile Indians remained an important consideration. Adult males continued in their dual role of militia men and farmers/ranchers. The greater size of grantee groups during this period made it somewhat easier to cope with the threat of Indian incursions, but occasional short periods of forced abandonment of their land continued throughout the decades of the Mexican Period and well into the initial years of the United States territorial administration.

The provisions of the Spanish colonial land laws continued to give form to the process of settling the New Mexico frontier lands; however, the nature of the land, the forms of land usage, and the social setting exerted a strong influence on the implementation of land allotments.

Since this period represented a new pattern of occupancy and land utilization, that is to say a different adaptation, in the Cañones region, it should be expected that the tenure arrangements were somewhat different, and this was indeed the case. The nineteenth-century grants definitely took the form of community grants. Whereas this was implicitly the case during the previous century when the Cañones region served as grazing land, it became explicit with the advent of settled plazas. The new residents took up both farming and stock raising on the grant lands of the vicinity, thereby establishing the pattern of cultural ecology embodied in the Hispanic community tradition.

From an ecological perspective, it can be observed that the unity of the Polvadera and Piedra Lumbre tracts continued to be recognized through their use to sustain the mixed agro-pastoral subsistence economy of the nineteenth-century settlers. The only modification of this pattern was a gradual process of subdivision as the region became more heavily populated.

The Mexican Republic and the Abiquiu Jurisdiction

In the brief period during which New Mexico was governed by the independent Mexican administration, one can see the steady growth of a way of life which had been developing for more than 200 years. Yet the seeds of change which were to eventually destroy that way of life may also be perceived. The most significant harbingers of change were the opening of new avenues of trade with the United States over the Santa Fe Trail, and the growth of the old trade route south to Chihuahua. In addition, Hispanic trappers began to penetrate the San Juan region northwest of Abiquiu, leading to contacts with New Mexicans in Rio Arriba.

New Mexico had seen a steady increase in the population and each generation was more clearly indigenous. The general census of 1827 showed that the Villa de Santa Cruz de la Cañada contained a total population of 19,537. Of this number, 3,557 individuals resided in the jurisdiction of Abiquiu. This census also showed that at Abiquiu fewer than 70 genizaros remained. Categorized by occupation, the Abiquiu population numbered 508 farmers, 301 day laborers, 48 craftsmen, 6 merchants, a priest, and a schoolteacher.[53]

The transition to the Mexican Republic period was scarcely felt politically in New Mexico. This distant province had steadily become more independent during the eighteenth and the beginning of the nineteenth centuries. An important change, however, was an end to the trade monopoly which Spain had enjoyed with its American colonies. Spain had formerly prohibited commerce between the colonies and other nations, and had greatly constrained private trading in general in New Mexico. With the beginning of the Mexican administration, these prohibitions were lifted and the opportunities for economic gain through trading of all sorts were much enhanced.

The old Spanish Trail had been pioneered in the eighteenth century by Hispanic trading expeditions to the San Juan country and westward to the Great Basin in search of animal pelts and slaves. Some traders spent as much as two, three, or four months in the country of the Utes before returning home.[54] This mobile, free, and adventurous lifestyle was quite attractive to many male Hispanos of the Abiquiu region, and led to much cultural exchange with the Utes and other nomadic bands.

As Alta California continued to develop, it became more and more desirable to open an overland trade route from New Mexico to this province. In the fall and winter of 1829–1830, a company of some sixty traders led by Antonio Armijo succeeded in reaching California and returning. This pack train, loaded with blankets and other trade items, left Abiquiu on 7 November 1829, and reached California at the end of January. There the merchandise was traded principally for mules to bring back to New Mexico, where the animals were much in demand for use in the thriving Santa Fe Trail trade to Missouri.[55]

As the gateway to California and the trapping country to the northwest, Abiquiu grew in importance. Abiquiu became the supply center where numerous expeditions were outfitted before heading west. Besides supplies and equipment, expeditions could also secure guides, interpreters, and whatever laborers might be needed for the trip.

During this period of expanding commerce, the Abiquiu region's exports included sheep, wool, dressed animal hides, Hispanic blankets, dried deer and buffalo meat, and piñon nuts. Access to new and distant markets spurred contraband trade in stolen horses and Indian captives. The resulting prosperity brought to the Abiquiu region provided the basis for an economic stratification that began during the latter years of the Mexican administration.[56]

The foregoing historical sketch serves to reveal that the Cañones region enjoyed a hundred-year-long period of Hispanic development before the onset of U.S. control in 1846. An evolution of the regional Hispanic subsistence economy occurred, which was strongly influenced by the pecularities of the environment and the special characteristics of the Hispanic technology and social organization for economic pursuits. Before taking up the changes brought with modernization, it will be profitable to examine the social organization and economy in the Cañones region more closely.

Social Organization for Subsistence Purposes in the Cañones Region

The Hispanic land grants of the nineteenth century clearly constituted community grants to provide for all subsistence needs. Each was made to a substantial number of families and was settled by establishing farming/ranching plazas. The provisions of the San Joaquín del Rio Chama grant follow the letter of colonial land grant law closely, for each family received a house lot, agricultural land, and rights to use communal grazing land and woodlands. In distributing land to these settlers, care was taken to see that each family received an adequate allotment to provide for its subsistence. While attention to the letter of the law was not so great in the revalidation of the Piedra Lumbre grant or the new Pedernales grant, the intent of the granting officials and the objectives of the petitioning settlers were the same as those of the San Joaquín grant.

These new plazas were significantly larger than comparable settlements established in the Rio Chama valley during the preceding century, and their populations grew rapidly. Their size afforded them significantly greater security against the nomadic Indian threat, so they were more stable. At the same time, their size necessitated more intensive use of the limited quantities of irrigable farmland. Thus considerable organized labor had to be devoted to developing all potential farm plots and a network of acequias to irrigate them. In a similar fashion, the sizeable herds of livestock needed to support the plaza required increased cooperation. In short, these plazas became well-organized communities and constituted the basic social and economic framework for Hispanic life in the region.

The setting in which the Cañones plaza developed provided an environment conducive to the emergence of a well-defined ecological unit. The topographic and hydrologic characteristics of Cañones define a relatively isolated microbasin with three distinct vertical life zones, as has been outlined earlier. These physical characteristics provided the natural resources on which the community was built. One senses that social and psychological boundaries are virtually written on the land as one traverses for the first time the Cañones valley-canyon system; the place seems a distinctive entity.

Residential Pattern

In the summer of 1967, when the writer first viewed Cañones, it looked much as it must have during the nineteenth century. Residential sites or farmsteads are conspicuous because of their bright splashes of green—trees, irrigated kitchen gardens, and small *vegas* (meadows). They contrast very sharply with the surrounding arid rust-brown slopes, hills, and mesas. The nucleus of the community is formed by the loose cluster of dwellings and associated farm buildings surrounding the *placita* (which in this context means a small open space). The settlement is located on a slight eminence west of the point where Cañones and Polvadera creeks meet. It is approximately four miles south of the confluence of Cañones Creek and the Abiquiu reservoir. There are twenty-three residences located here. This is approximately the number of residences found here in the past, for there are few abandoned houses or old house foundations and little obviously new construction. Housing has been improved by adding to or remodeling older structures. Unlike urbanites, the Cañoneros are not given to demolishing old structures and building anew from scratch.

The placita is an irregular open space located in the approximate center of the cluster of buildings (see Map 8). To the west fronting the placita is the Catholic church or chapel. Adjacent to the placita is the community corral. At one time a small cantina used to face the placita on the north side, but it has been closed for many years. The *morada* (the chapter house and chapel of the community's *cofradia,* or lay religious brotherhood) is located five hundred feet southwest of the placita and apart from most of the dwellings. Two small *tienditas* (stores) occupy one room each in private houses surrounding the placita. (These tiny stores came into existence in this century and have vanished since the author began his fieldwork in the community.) Also adjacent to the placita is a small structure that served as the first schoolhouse in Cañones. This school was built near the end of the nineteenth century. The *campo santo* (cemetery) is situated on the northwest edge of the settlement.

The community's dwellings surround the placita in a highly irregular fashion, seemingly without order. The topography, a desire to be near

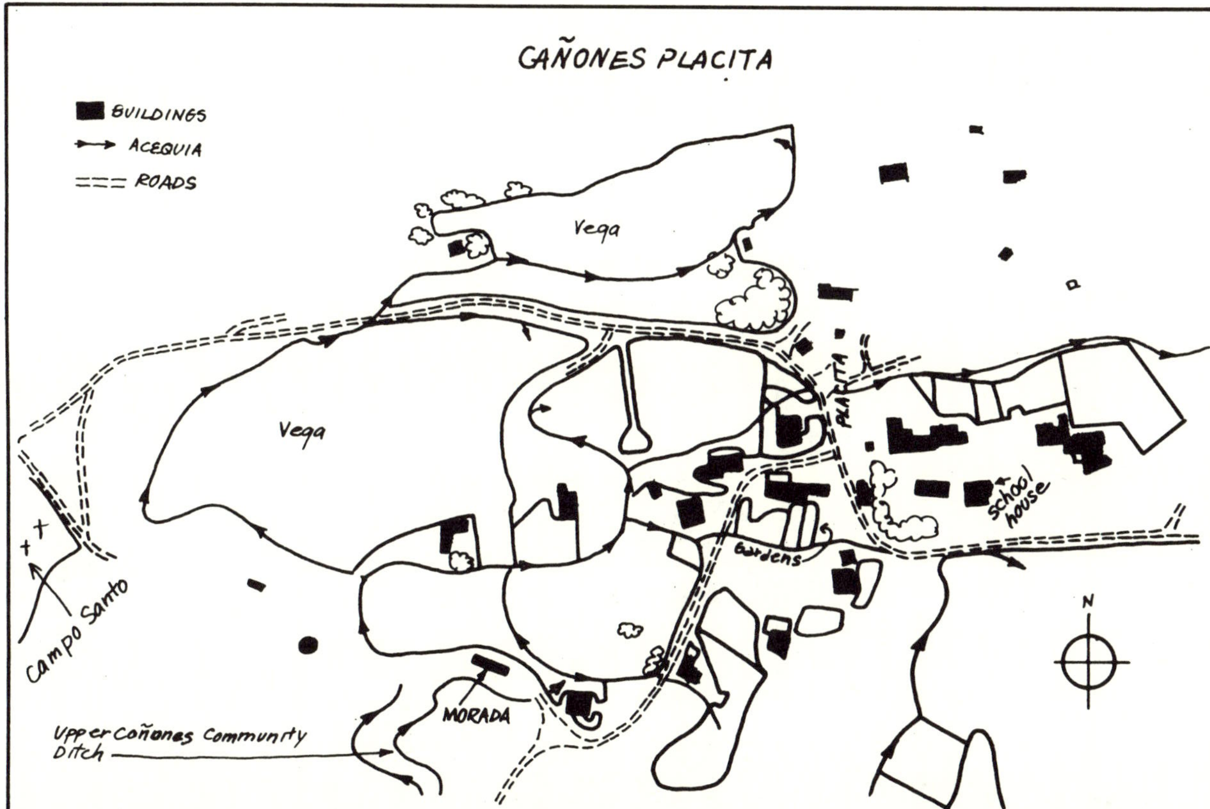

MAP 8. Cañones placita (drawn from State of New Mexico, Office of State Engineer, Cañones and Polvadera Creeks Hydrographic Survey 1973, Map Sheet #3).

close kinsmen, and convenience have clearly been the principal criteria in locating dwellings and their outbuildings. The outbuildings generally consist of a shed or small barn, a *soterraño* (a partially subterranean storeroom), a *horno* (an outdoor oven), sometimes a small corral, and a latrine (an innovation dating from about 1900). In the nineteenth century an additional auxiliary structure may have been a *torreon* (a small fortified defensive tower).

With one exception, all of the houses are constructed of adobe and contain three to five rooms. The one cement block house stands out for its uniqueness. In the 1970s, a dramatic transformation in housing began with the introduction of mobile homes. The adobe houses, many exhibitingg considerable age, have been altered somewhat in recent decades. The flat dirt roofs have been replaced by pitched tin roofs, which keep out the rain better. Windows and doors have been enlarged and new aluminum framed windows and sliding glass doors have been installed in some houses. Most outside walls have been cemented to create a more durable surface. Four or five of the dwellings are attached wall-to-wall to form the long "gallery" arrangement so common in the past century. The majority of the dwellings, however, are independent units one room deep and are rectangular or L-shaped, depending on the number of rooms.

In addition to the houses around the placita, there are three residences within view of it along the edge of the valley to the south and southeast. On the east side of the *cuchilla* (knife-like ridge) that separates the Cañones and Polvadera valleys are four dispersed farmsteads. This area is called *cieneguitas* (little marsh) by Cañoneros. In the lower valley, approximately a mile and a half below the placita, there is a small cluster of dwellings. These units house two year-round residents and three families from the placita who reside there during the summer. Finally, the lower valley also contains two independent farmsteads that are well removed from any other residences.

In the nineteenth century, and in this century until World War II, many households had summer homes up the valley from the placita. These secondary residences were smaller and of simpler construction, either *jacales* (made of vertical poles plastered with mud) or *fuertes* (structures made of notched horizontal logs, which were sometimes plastered with mud). Additional seasonal dwellings were constructed in the sierra to the south. These units were used to facilitate farming and herding respectively, and they reflect the diversified subsistence economy. The practice of using seasonal secondary residences has nearly died out, reflecting the general decline of subsistence farming and stock raising in the community.

In sum, the predominant form of farm settlement in Cañones is a nucleated pattern. Today the residents of all of the households, whatever their location, are regarded as members of the community and participate in community life. In the nineteenth century this pattern was somewhat more complex because of seasonal variations in residence. It was highly nucleated during the winter months and dispersed along the valley and into the sierra during the summer. In all, this settlement pattern stands in stark contrast to the predominant Anglo-American pattern of individual, dispersed farmsteads.

Farming

The foundation of the plaza's cultural ecology consists of the distribution of land and water rights and the means of using these resources. The irregular configuration of the valley and canyon bottoms is such that only small discontinuous pockets of land were available for farm plots. The largest of these pockets contains only slightly over one hundred acres. The second largest contains only about half that amount, and the average tract of arable land is approximately five acres. From the beginning, the farm plots in Cañones were quite small, and through the years they became even smaller as they were subdivided among heirs. Individual settlers typically held farm plots in several different locations along the valley. To the Anglo-American farmer, such fragmented landholding seems very undesirable, for it is not conducive to the application of modern, mechanized, commercial farming practices. However, to the Hispanic subsistence farmer, it was highly adaptive. This type of land distribution helped to insure that not all of the best land would be in the hands of a single farm family, a monopoly that otherwise could have easily occurred given the varied localized manifestations of the effective environment—soil characteristics, sunlight, moisture, and other variables. Also, dispersed farm plots afforded each farmer some protection against the ravages of insects, animals, and wind that might vary from year to year in a given field.

By the 1820s, approximately fifty separate farm plots had been created, and by the 1850s farmlands reportedly extended for nearly nine miles along the Cañones and Polvadera creeks.[57] Today the total land under irrigation is approximately 312 acres, consisting of 92 different tracts distributed among 50 different owners.[58] In the nineteenth century, and still today, contiguous farm plots were usually held by close kinsmen, and cooperative labor arrangements among kinsmen were fostered. Whatever the social ties between adjoining owners, gaining access to and farming the plots required a substantial amount of cooperation. Joint efforts ranged from breaking ground to irrigating, harvesting, and communal grazing of the plaza's livestock on the stubble left from the harvest.

During the nineteenth century farmers grew wheat, corn, beans, onions, garlic, squash, melons, and chile (although chile does not grow well at this altitude). Cultivation was carried out with a Mediterranean scratch plow or, sometimes, a digging stick and a hoe. In addition, small orchards of apricot, apple, and plum trees were grown. These crops, together with herds of sheep, goats, and cattle, provided the staples of the diet: beans, corn tortillas, chile, goat's milk, cheese, and meat. Chile was cooked in a sauce with onions, garlic, and small chunks of meat. The basic subsistence foods have changed little over the years, except that goats and sheep are now seldom raised. Today chile sauce, beans, and tortillas (now made with wheat flour) are offered at virtually every meal.

Since World War II, most of the residents of Cañones have been increasingly drawn to wage labor outside the community, so it is no longer feasible to practice full-time farming and stock raising. Furthermore, because the community has lost virtually all communal grazing land, more agricultural land must be devoted to growing fodder, and a large portion of the valley land must be used as year-round pasturage. At present 33.9 percent of the farmland is devoted to raising alfalfa for livestock, 42.8 percent is used as year-round pasture, 6 percent is planted in spring grain, 7.9 percent is planted in vegetables (kitchen gardens for the most part), and 7 percent is allowed to remain fallow.[59] In spite of this fact, today nearly half of the Cañones households obtain the greater part of their subsistence from their kitchen gardens and orchards, buying only sugar, coffee, flour, lard, baking soda, and potatoes. Many vegetables and fruits are canned and stored in the soterraño for the winter months.

Irrigation

The single most important aspect of the community's adaptation was, and remains, supplying water for domestic and agricultural purposes. A dependable supply of water is critical to the survival of any community in this semiarid climate. Constructing and maintaining an acequia or ditch irrigation system required many hands; thus, communal labor was imperative. Satisfactory distribution of the water required communal cooperation, for water use has always been regulated without centralized authority or official mechanisms for adjudication. Generally the distribution system worked well in Cañones because the streams in the drainage basin provided an abundant flow of water in all but the very driest years.

The acequia system in Cañones is complex because not all fields could be served by one ditch due to the geographical features previously described. The system grew gradually by accretion over time, but the major ditches certainly were first dug in the early decades of the community's development. At present there are seventeen acequias that serve fields located along the Cañones valley and Mogote canyon. Of these, thirteen ditches derive their water from diversions of Cañones Creek, three utilize water from natural springs, and the last originated on Chihuahueños Creek. The agricultural lands along the Polvadera valley are served by seven acequias, all of which were created by diverting Polvadera Creek. In all, then, there are twenty-four acequias. Fifteen of the acequias irrigate more than one tract and may serve more than one owner. There are seven major acequias of substantial antiquity that average one and a half miles in length (excluding laterals). These acequias serve the bulk of the farm tracts, numbering approximately seventy. Constructing and maintaining these ditches and *presas* (diversion dams) was no mean feat.

The acequias also provided the water power to operate the community's *molinos* (small gristmills). The principal creeks in the Cañones drainage system are capable of providing a sufficient volume of reliable water flow during the summer and autumn to successfully operate gristmills. This is an added blessing of the abundant water supply in the Cañones microbasin. Other plazas in the region are not so fortunate. Oral sources report that four molinos operated at Cañones, although probably not all of them functioned at the same time.

The Cañones system has worked basically through a series of informal water-sharing agreements among community residents. The major acequias have been informally governed by independent associations of users, each making their own rules. The associations elect a *mayordomo* (ditch boss) and, if the number of users is large enough, a board of commissioners as well. The duties of the officers, which devolve principally to the mayordomo in day-to-day business, are to organize the members for cleaning and other work on the *acequia madre* (main ditch) and to settle disputes between members involving damage to ditches by livestock and theft of water. Generally the acequia madre is cleaned each spring by a joint labor force. Each user must contribute a day or more of labor, depending on the number of days of water rights he owns, which in turn depends on the amount of land he irrigates from a given acequia. The lateral ditches are maintained by the individual users they serve.

The system of water distribution is simple in its ideal form. Use is computed on a regular cycle of days, depending on the number of users. Each user has a set number of days of water rights in this cycle, determined by his total acreage served by the system, even if this acreage is broken up into several parcels (which is more often the rule than the exception). Generally, the sequence of the cycle begins with the owners of the tracts nearest to the head of the acequia and follows down the ditch to its end. Landowners who have nothing more than a kitchen garden are accorded half-day rights, and may take water at any convenient time. Acequias serving the land close to and within the placita regularly reserve a portion of the water for these kitchen gardens.

In sum, this irrigation system has always been an integral part of farming in Cañones. It has served to integrate man, land, and water over time and space. That is, the system has clear-cut spatial and temporal dimensions. Together, these qualities of the acequia system have always contributed enormously to the maintenance of ecological boundaries that correspond physically to the geographical limits of the microbasin's drainage system. These physical boundaries assured the community of full control over its vital water supply. The effect of these dimensions of the acequia system on the movement of the Cañoneros in time and space have helped to create and maintain important psychological boundaries as well. The rhythm of life and the enduring attachments to this particular microbasin have become ingrained in the Cañoneros and illustrate a uniquely human aspect of this ecological system.

Stock Raising

While the discussion to this point has emphasized farming, it should be remembered that in the nineteenth century animal husbandry was the most important component of the subsistence economy. The distinctive characteristic of animal husbandry in Cañones, as elsewhere in the Hispanic uplands, was that it was integrated with plant production. It involved not merely a juxtaposition of the two types of production, but a genuine wedding, whereby one branch supported the other. Neither mode of production could have been carried on in the same fashion without the other. Livestock were not simply objects of production in this system, but they were also important factors in production. They served as draft animals, to trample the grain on the threshing floor, as beasts of burden to transport crops, and as producers of manure to fertilize fields. All of these functions were vital to the practice of agriculture. On the other side, farming provided winter fodder and stubble grazing for the livestock. Without these, the community's herd could not have been adequately maintained from year to year.

In addition, animal production in this agro-pastoral system differed significantly from commercial production of livestock. The basic goal of production was to increase the number of stock and the use of animal products—milk, meat, and wool—for local subsistence, not to fatten stock for the market. In this system the number of stock was not permitted to increase indefinitely, however, for herds could only be sustained with a workable ratio to available pasturage and the number of males in the community's households available to manage them. Herding competed for men's time with other production tasks.

The stock raised for food were, in order of their importance, sheep, goats, and cattle. During most of the nineteenth century, small stock outnumbered cattle by as much as twenty to one. In addition, horses, mules, and burros were kept as beasts of burden. By commercial standards the sizes of the community's herds were never large, probably never exceeding a few thousand. No reliable statistics exist for the holdings of the Cañones plaza during the nineteenth century. Judging from the general census figures for the Alcaldia de la Cañada during this period, the average household in Cañones probably owned about fifty to one hundred head of all kinds of stock.[60] The exceptions to this generalization were probably one or two prominent individuals, such as Juan Bautista Valdez, whose large extended household owned many more livestock than the average.

The plaza's livestock were cooperatively grazed in a patterned seasonal cycle on the valley lands, the surrounding Upper Sonoran grazing lands, and the mountain pastures. This seasonal cycle was one of vertical transhumance. It was integrated with the agricultural cycle, for the stock were moved away from the farm plots during the growing season. The cycle began at the end of April when the stock were driven up into the lower mountain pastures on the Mesa del Medio, the northwestern section of the Polvadera, and the Sierra Valdez. The stock were gradually pushed to higher altitudes as the summer season progressed and brought warmer temperatures and new stands of green vegetation to the highest reaches of the sierra. This sequence was reversed in the fall, as winter approached and the harvest had been completed. At this time all of the privately held farm plots were opened for communal grazing on the stubble. During the winter most of the small stock were penned in corrals during the night and driven out to the lower grazing land to the north of the community during the day. Draft animals wintered on the valley's fields. During the most severe weather the stock were maintained on fodder in the corrals.

The principal responsibility for herding the stock and milking the goats was given to the older boys and young men, under the supervision of the senior males. However, during the lambing season and when the sheep were sheared in the autumn, the hands of the entire male labor force were required.

From the foregoing description of the system of animal husbandry in Cañones, the logic of communal ownership of grazing land and its role in Hispanic cultural ecology becomes clear. The basic cultural principle that underlies this form of landholding and use comes from deeply rooted Iberian customs that were incorporated into the laws of the Indies and became commonplace in New Spain. This principle holds that no individual has the right to appropriate for himself and monopolize a part of the resources of nature that were produced without man's intervention. All individuals should be free to use such resources as their needs dictate. Thus, the Spanish Crown intended for all land or other resources—including pastures, woodlands, mountains, and waters—not specifically granted to individuals to be used in common.[61] Unimproved natural resources of these types that were granted to groups of settlers to found a community were expected to be used in common by all who resided in the community.

A second principle was that of accustomed range. This customary doctrine established that individual and community grazing rights to specific sections of the unallotted royal lands could be acquired through use.[62] These rights were solely usufructuary; that is, they were completely extinguished by failure to continue the established use of the land. According to this principle, communities such as Cañones could establish usufructuary rights to vacant or unimproved land not formally granted to them. Cañones, operating on the basis of these underlying premises, came to treat all of the unimproved land within the micro-basin as community property. As a corporate entity, the community of Cañones worked to protect its common land, keeping away strangers, avoiding encroachment by neighboring landowners, thwarting any attempts at private enclosure, and seeing that each community member's rights to use the common land were respected.

The practice of communal stubble grazing in Cañones also has venerable roots in Iberian tradition. It entails public grazing rights to private farmland for part of the year. This practice was of benefit to all community members. Animal droppings served to fertilize all fields. It also made for much more efficient use of available pasturage during the winter months, when it was most limited. The small fragmented farm plots did not lend themselves to private grazing. In addition, the general lack of fences made this an impractical alternative mode of grazing the stubble. In sum, all of the land used for grazing, public as well as private, was subject to control by the community.

The final important element in the Cañones system of animal husbandry was communal management of the stock. The stock had to be moved away from the agricultural fields at the same time each spring and could not return until the harvest was completed. Also, the movement of stock from pasture to pasture had to be coordinated to make the best use of all pasturage under the community's control. Since only a few *pastores* (shepherds) were needed to herd a large number of sheep and goats, it was most efficient to cooperate in rotating these duties among the young men, so that the rest of the males could devote their time to other tasks. Communal rights and responsibilities in raising livestock encompassed the system of landholding and use for grazing purposes, as well as the management of the stock. Together, they served to create a distinctive element of the Hispanic adaptation to the uplands.

Hunting and Trading

All male Cañoneros participated in hunting. This was and has remained an important subsistence activity. Rabbits, quail, partridges, wild turkeys, and mule deer were hunted on the common lands. In the past the Cañoneros sometimes organized hunting parties to travel further afield to hunt elk and buffalo. During most of the nineteenth century buffalo were quite important to New Mexicans. It is reported that as many as twelve thousand bulls were killed annually.[63] The bow and arrow were generally used for hunting; however, firearms became more common as the century progressed. When hunting parties returned home with large kills, they shared the meat among all the households in the community.

In conjunction with hunting expeditions, trading was carried on with the nomadic Indian bands. Trade items included salt, blankets, strips of iron for arrowheads, a type of hard bread made expressly for this trade, and dried fruit. Trading expeditions might last as long as three months and take the traders hundreds of miles from home.

These subsistence activities involved regular community cooperation. Not all of the adult males could be away from the plaza at one time, for their absence would have seriously jeopardized its safety. Furthermore, some regular household tasks required the males' strength, although the women, children, and elderly were perfectly capable of performing the bulk of the farming and ranching chores, and often did so when most of the men were away.

In sum, social organization for subsistence activities in Cañones illustrates the Hispanic pattern of corporate community-based agro-pastoral production in an upland microbasin. With this communal arrangement, the diverse land forms, water, and other resources were available for each extended family production unit. This technologically simple way of gaining a livelihood involved maintaining a relatively complex set of social relationships and an intricate, integrated way of exploiting the diverse environment. The totality of these social and economic factors can be understood as the unusual and distinctive Hispanic cultural ecology.

To return once again to the Libecap and Alter analysis, it can now be seen that to a significant extent, small dispersed fields enhanced the Hispanic community's adaptation to the environment. Further, the impact of land division among heirs was mitigated through cooperative farming by kinsmen. Most importantly, however, we see that farming cannot be considered alone, for stock raising was the most important component of the Hispanic economy. When discussing Hispanic farms, one must be cognizant of all the forms of land necessary to the economy—agricultural land, grazing land, and woodlands.

Modernization and Hispanic Cultural Ecology[64]

As was outlined above, the seeds of economic change in the uplands of northern New Mexico were planted during the brief Mexican administration, principally through the opening of trade with the United States and the resulting influx of foreign traders and trappers. With the American conquest in 1846, the process quickened. As van Dresser has described it, this modernization may be generally characterized as follows: (1) the expropriation of land and other natural resources from local resident ownership and their concentration for various forms of capitalistic exploitation; (2) as a consequence of this, localized economies are disrupted; (3) local exchange is monetized, replacing distribution of goods through barter or other customary arrangements sanctioned by family and community; and (4) the result is disintegration of traditional communities, their lifestyles, and, of course, their mode of livelihood.[65]

Perhaps the easiest way to grasp the nature of this change in the uplands region is to examine the contrasting patterns of traditional and modern land tenure as they affected the Hispanic cultural ecology in the uplands. The traditional system of land tenure in northern New Mexico and southern Colorado resulted, of course, from Spanish colonization. An important characteristic of the Spanish land grant system was that it was first and foremost a policy to encourage frontier settlement, not commercial land speculation. Thus, the provisions of the system took into account the total range of subsistence needs of the potential settlers. This included the number of settlers as well as the type and size of their herds of livestock. Provisions were made for ample farmland, grazing land, woodlands, and water. The size of the grant was ultimately determined by these subsistence considerations in relation to the character of the land to be settled.

As has been said, through the vehicle of the settlers' land grant, small communities of subsistence farmer-ranchers were established in virtually all of the microbasins in the uplands region. These grants were laid out in an irregular fashion by metes and bounds with the requirements of subsistence clearly in mind. The standard of living achieved fell short of abundance, but it was adequate. A very positive feature of this system was that the demands upon the natural resources were not extreme, so the Hispanos were able to establish a balance between man and environment approaching a state of equilibrium. Thus, a sustained yield adaptation prevailed, provided, of course, that excess population was able to move on to occupy new frontier lands.

Equilibrium was fostered by the complex community-based tenure system created by the land grant laws, as modified and adapted to meet local requirements. The genius of this system was that it combined individual and communal tenure rights in a fashion that permitted the community as a whole to maintain control over the exploitation of the environment, thereby avoiding the excesses that might have occurred with individual fee simple tenure. A special strength of this system was that all lands other than house lots and farm plots were held in common tenure with individual rights of usufruct. Thus, all members of the community had a strong vested interest in assuring a sustained yield from the communal lands.

The impact of modernization was limited at first under American rule, but accelerated sharply in the decades following the Civil War. One of the salient features of modernization was the new Anglo-American land tenure laws, which led legally and extralegally to expropriation of the bulk of the land (particularly common grazing land) from the village Hispanos and its concentration in the hands of the federal government and private commercial interests.

The essential features of the Anglo-American land tenure system imposed on the region may be outlined as follows. Frontier lands, when suitable, were distributed or sold in fee simple to individual farmers and ranchers so that they might establish commercial farms or ranches. The method for distributing lands was based upon the rectangular survey system. This involved the imposition on the land of a system of grids of uniform size, effected through the use of modern surveying and cartography. Precise documentation and recording of landownership and transfers were also part of this system. National standards were then developed, limiting the size of the land unit that an individual might acquire. (See Westphall for an extensive treatment of the distribution of the public domain in New Mexico.)[66]

The rectangular grid system of defining land units assumes that one unit will be essentially the same as the next; no allowance is made for regional topography, hydrology, or climate. Thus, the system was unsuitable for adapting man to the environments of the uplands. As has been shown, the uplands are characterized by great variations in land forms, altitude, climate, and vegetation, and valuable natural resources are distributed in a highly irregular fashion. Employing the grid system in such an environment results in grids with no surface water or arable land and others that contain arable land but none suitable for grazing or securing timber and firewood. Therefore, from an ecological perspective the superiority of the Hispanic system of land tenure for a subsistence economy is clear. Further, under the Anglo-American system the individual was free to exploit the environment as he saw fit, to realize the maximum profit. There were no immediate community restraints upon him, as there were among the village Hispanos, to be mindful of the continuing need to sustain the yield from the natural resources.

As Strickon has demonstrated in his study of the Euro-American ranching complex, the commercial rancher usually tended to overgraze the land because the larger his animal unit, the lower his production costs, and therefore the greater his potential for profit.[67] Also, low market prices often induced the rancher to keep his animals on the grass longer than was wise, while he awaited a more favorable price. The environmental costs of unrestrained commercial use of the fragile grazing lands of northern New Mexico and southern Colorado are apparent today.

In addition, the Hispanic mixed subsistence economy of northern New Mexico and southern Colorado was much better suited to effectively exploit the varied local environments and to sustain a modest population at an adequate level without causing permanent damage. In contrast, individual ownership of the rectangular units of the Anglo-American system presented many obstacles to effective land use due to the uneven distribution of resources. For instance, with individual ownership of rectangular grazing units came fences, the use of which enabled a few individuals to monopolize scarce sources of water, resulting in the breakdown of traditional patterns of grazing in the region.

It must be emphasized that much of north-central New Mexico and south-central Colorado were so thoroughly unsuited for the private Anglo-American system of land tenure and land economics that the system was never completely adopted. Also, due to the fact that this region was the stronghold of traditional Hispanic settlement, expropriation of the land occurred slowly, and then only after protracted legal proceedings. In fact, much of the mountain forest lands of the region, originally grant common lands, eventually came under federal control in the early decades of this century, and remain in that status today.

Nonetheless, the federal land has been turned to commercial use in an Anglo-American fashion, and economic benefits to local communities have been minimal. The mountain grazing land was fenced and grazing rights were allotted, usually through a fee permit system, more often than not to large-scale commercial ranchers. Similarly, timber cutting has been developed through commercial contracting on a large scale. A major percentage of the profits earned by these industries leaves the region and has no impact on the local economy. In spite of recent attention to "scientific" management by the federal government, the mountain lands suffer from a history of overuse by the commercial livestock and extractive industries. The history of economic change in the Cañones microbasin provides a concrete example of the patterns of change outlined above and will enable us to explore this theme in greater depth.

Land Alienation and Economic Change in Cañones

The principal factor that induced economic change in Cañones was the gradual alienation of the grant lands, particularly the common lands used for grazing, securing timber and firewood, and hunting. The events related to this process took place over several decades and involved many land transactions, lengthy and complex court proceedings, and a large number of individuals. Thus, it will be possible to summarize here only the sequence of major events for one of the grants, the Piedra Lumbre grant, whose history is similar to that of the others. (The history of the Polvadera grant adjudication and the Pedernales or

Juan Bautista Valdez grant were treated by the author in earlier publications.)[68] Of course, the territorial histories of each of the three land grants within the Cañones microbasin are interrelated in many important ways, as we have seen. These interrelationships will be discussed at the conclusion of the account of the Piedra Lumbre.

The Piedra Lumbre Grant

As with other Hispanic land grants in New Mexico and Colorado, the United States government took no initiative in assisting those possessing tenure rights to the Piedra Lumbre grant to have their rights officially recognized under American law. Rather, the government required the individuals and communities to initiate such private land claims as they wished to have tracts excluded from the United States public domain. The first petition to the U.S. surveyor general for confirmation of the Piedra Lumbre grant was not filed until 29 March 1872. This petition was made by Jose P. Gallegos, a resident of the grant and a representative of a number of local claimants. It was accompanied by the grant *testimonio* of 1766 (an official copy of the original grant documents, that had been delivered to the grantee as evidence of title).[69] Based principally upon the authenticity of the testimonio, Surveyor General James K. Proudfit decided that the Piedra Lumbre was a valid private grant. In 1877, a preliminary survey of the grant was conducted by the United States deputy surveyor; the grant was found to contain 48,336.12 acres. Proudfit recommended to Congress that the grant be confirmed to the heirs and assigns of the grantee, Pedro Martín Serrano, in spite of the fact that his office had done little or no historical investigation of the claim.[70] The communal character of the extensive grazing land on the grant, which had developed through many generations of use, received absolutely no notice. However, Congress did not act on Proudfit's recommendation. The claimants evidently lacked the necessary clout in Washington to gain congressional approval.

The Piedra Lumbre grant was still pending before Congress when the Court of Private Land Claims was created in 1891 to expedite the settlement of all Spanish and Mexican land claims. Consequently, on 19 August 1892, a new petition for confirmation was filed with the Court of Private Land Claims. This claim was submitted by an attorney, George Hill Howard, on behalf of sixteen individuals who resided on, or in the vicinity of, the grant. It argued that their rights were inherited from the grantee. As evidence of their rights, they submitted the testimonio of the grant revalidation that took place in 1806 in the name of Mariano Martín.[71] Once again the grant was treated as a private grant; no attempt was made to name as claimants all those residing in nearby communities who regularly used the Piedra Lumbre for grazing livestock.

In the twenty-nine years that had passed since confirmation of the Piedra Lumbre grant was first sought, representatives of the growing commercial interests in the territory had begun to work quietly to lay claim to the grant. The principal figures in this effort were General José María Chávez of Abiquiu, Ramon Salazar (a former priest at Abiquiu), and Thomas B. Catron, the most infamous of the land grant speculator/attorneys. Together they were able to make a rather simple claim to the grant. The grant was represented as a private grant to Pedro Martín Serrano and the testimonio of 1766 was presented as evidence of title. To legitimize their claims under the grantee, they simply concocted a greatly distorted and abbreviated genealogy. The grandson of the grantee, named Pedro Martín Serrano, was represented as the original grantee. Conveniently, the alleged grantee's four children had either moved to California, where they sold their interests to the speculators, or they had died leaving few or no heirs. The rights of the few resident descendants of the alleged grantee were also purchased by this group of speculators.[72] In this fashion Chavez, Salazar, and Catron attempted to establish the credibility of their claim to the entire grant. The other residents of the Piedra Lumbre grant proper and those who lived in the communities on its southern edge were treated as though they were squatters. General Chávez and his associates appointed the general's son, Francisco C. Chávez, as the resident agent on the grant. By the beginning of the 1890s, Francisco had taken up residence on the grant at the plaza of Rio Puerco and begun posting notices announcing that General Chávez and his associates were the owners of the grant. He offered to rent winter pasturage to local residents who wished to place their livestock on the grant. In addition, he began to rent the range to commercial stockmen from other areas. All other livestock discovered on the grant were run off.[73]

To support the above claims, Thomas Catron with his associates filed as cross-defendants in the Piedra Lumbre case before the Court of Private Land Claims. At the hearing, held on 25 August 1893, Catron skillfully managed to push aside the grant claims of the resident petitioners under the 1806 revalidation. On 30 August 1893, the court ruled that the grant was valid and confirmed it in its entirety to all heirs and legal assigns of Pedro Martín Serrano under the evidence of title found in the testimonio of 1766.[74] The court did not actually rule on the rights of the claimants under the original grantee; nonetheless, the decision was used by Catron to solidify his associates' claim to the grant.

The decision of the Court of Private Land Claims was followed by a suit in the District Court of Rio Arriba County to determine the rights of all parties who claimed an interest in the grant. Little or no attempt was made to assure representation for all parties who might claim adverse possession. It is highly unlikely that many of the grant residents, the so-called squatters, were even aware that this adjudication was in progress. Therefore, the final decree of the district court on 2 June 1894, awarded the fraction of thirty-seven fifty-fourths of the grant to Thomas Catron, José Patricio Chávez, and José María Chávez, and the remaining seventeen fifty-fourths of the land to Amado Chávez, Max Frost, and George Hill Howard (who had represented the interests of the claimants under Mariano Martín). The grant was partitioned into a northern third, deeded to the Howard claimants, and a southern two-thirds, which went to Catron and his associates. In sum, the commercial land speculators completely carried the day.

Subsequently, Catron acquired the right to act as the agent for the entire grant. Even though the final survey had not been completed nor the government patent issued, on 16 December 1896, he contracted with a San Francisco firm to purchase the entire grant for $72,800.[75] This sale eventually fell through, however.

The grant was officially surveyed in 1897, and a patent was issued 21 July 1902. This patent was forwarded to Claude Buckley, secretary-treasurer of the Chama Improvement Company, a company formed to plan the commercial development of the Piedra Lumbre.[76]

As the result of this travesty of justice, the Hispanic villagers on the southern edge of the grant were deprived of much of their winter grazing land. The survey of the south boundary of the Piedra Lumbre grant even cut off the lower portion of the Cañones valley, where the largest single tract of arable land is located (see Map 9). Since the turn of the century, skirmishes have continued over the loss of this land,

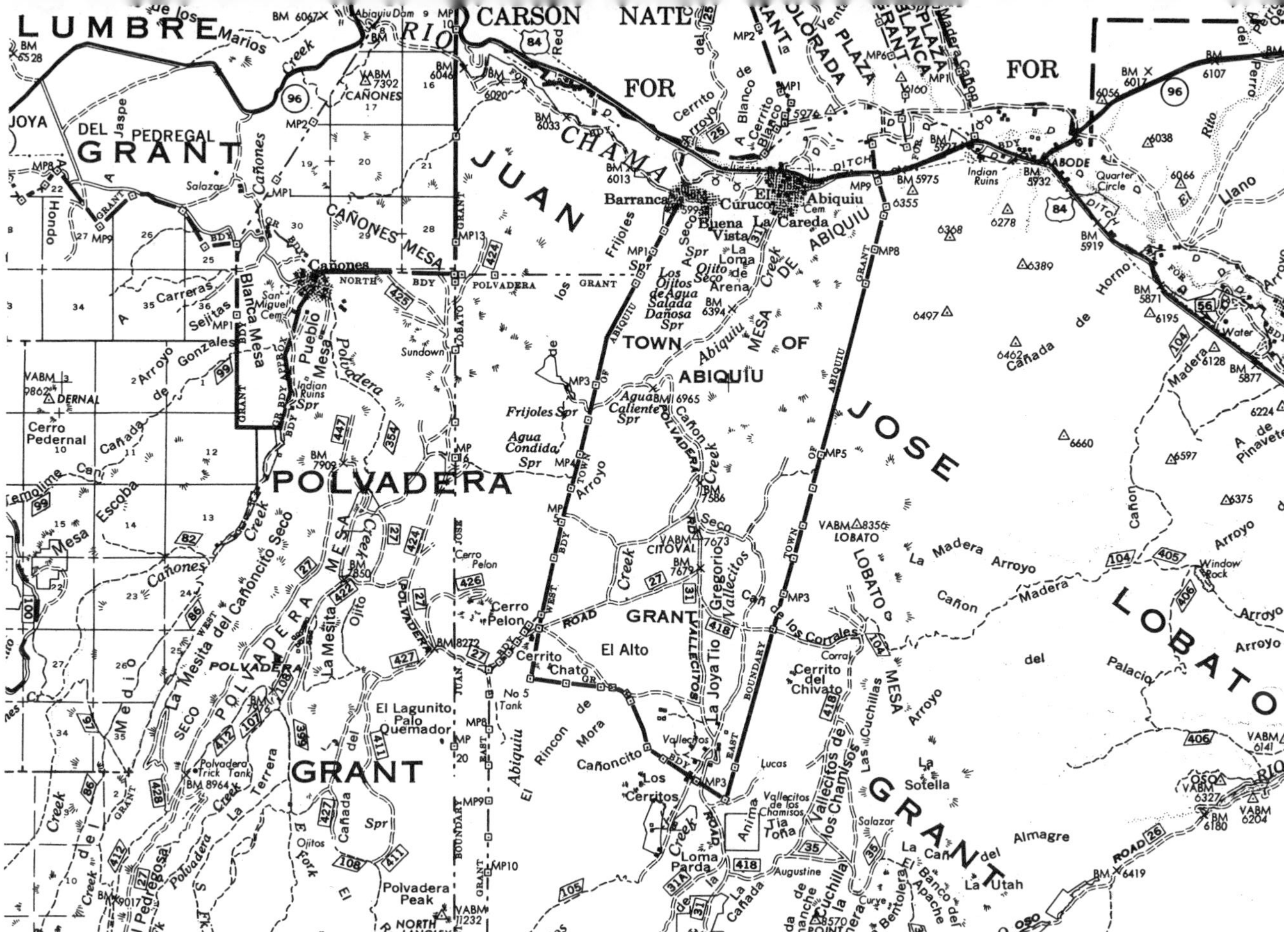

MAP 9. Hispanic land grants in the Cañones region.

even though the war was won long ago by those who represented the interests of the new economic order.

As late as 1920, court hearings were still being held regarding disputes over the boundaries of the grant and grazing rights claimed by the local Hispanos. At a hearing on 5 August 1920, Francisco C. Chávez, still the overseer of the grant, steadfastly asserted that none of the people in the local villages claimed ownership in the grant. Those who maintained residences within the grant and/or made use of the grant lands did so at his sufferance. He asserted that, legally, they were squatters encroaching on the grant lands. If he sometimes looked the other way and permitted these small farmers to make some use of a portion of the grant, he was merely performing a charitable act.

The long and complex period of litigation over the Cañones area grants ended with the sizeable Piedra Lumbre and Polvadera grants in the hands of land speculators, while only the Pedernales or Juan Bautista Valdez grant was confirmed to resident Hispanos. However, the Valdez grant was limited to a mere 1,468 acres of the land claimed, and was not patented as a community grant. The Cañoneros were denied the bulk of the Valdez grant common land to the south and west, as well as the sections of the Polvadera and Piedra Lumbre grants they had customarily used for grazing their livestock, gathering firewood, and other subsistence activities.

The Consequences of Land Alienation

The consequence of these legal decisions for the Cañoneros was that the natural watershed unit, the microbasin, that they had controlled and used for subsistence, was divided into three sections (see Map 9). Of course, the Cañoneros' portion (the confirmed Valdez grant lands) was by far the smallest, limited largely to the bottomland occupied by the village and its farm plots. They did not even receive all the irrigable bottomland in the microbasin, for portions fell within the Polvadera and Piedra Lumbre.

As ludicrous as it may seem, the west boundary of the Polvadera grant was surveyed so that it ran down the middle of Cañones Creek, passing through the nucleus of the placita itself. According to the Polvadera grant document of 1766, construed in its most literal fashion and ignoring the actual history of occupancy, this was the proper western boundary. Naturally the newly confirmed nonresident owners of the Polvadera grant favored this boundary, since they were interested in obtaining the largest possible acreage to enhance the grant's market value. Neither the Polvadera owners nor the government survey officials concerned themselves with the logic of Hispanic land use that had been developed in the watershed through more than a century of occupancy. Cañones Creek meanders through the narrow Mogote canyon in such a fashion that pockets of arable land are distributed in an irregular fashion, first on the east side of the creek and then on the west. Taking the grant boundaries as surveyed, some of the tracts fell into the Polvadera grant and others into the Juan Bautista Valdez grant. Since the tracts were generally little more than an acre or two in size, and the only access to the canyon was a road up the valley from Cañones, such a division of the land made no sense whatsoever. Of course, fixing the boundary so that it nearly bisected the Cañones placita itself made even less sense.

Attempts at commercial cattle and sheep ranching began in the Cañones region as early as the 1880s. However, rental of the grazing land to outside stockmen failed due to the rapid depletion of the grass caused by commercial grazing of large herds. The income from commercial exploitation of the Polvadera grant, for example, was never sufficient to pay the county taxes, let alone to realize a profit. Consequently, when the opportunity arose to sell the grant to the federal government in 1937, the owners hastened to do so.

As a result of this sale and the conversion of the former common lands of the Valdez grant to national forest, Cañones eventually came to be surrounded on three sides by land under the jurisdiction of the U.S. Forest Service. In all, this federal land constituted eighty-nine percent of the land in the Cañones microbasin. The advent of private ownership of the Piedra Lumbre grant to the north had likewise led to the exclusion of the Cañoneros from its grazing lands. Thus, the village found itself surrounded and hemmed into the small bottomland acreage of the microbasin. In spite of the Polvadera survey, villagers had also been able to retain possession of, if not legal title to, this portion of the valley.

Farming alone, however, had never been sufficient to maintain a viable subsistence economy. Animal husbandry, gathering, and hunting were also essential to the village's economy. As has been argued, agriculture and animal husbandry were wedded, to form a single system in the Hispanic cultural ecology. With the loss of communal grazing land the number of stock had to be greatly reduced. Without the manure regularly deposited on the farm plots, the fields became less fertile. In sum, the entire Hispanic system of adaptation broke down; the traditional cultural ecology no longer functioned.

The conservation measures instituted by the U.S. Forest Service since World War II brought about not only drastic reductions in the number of stock permitted to graze on the mountain lands, but also regulation of the types of stock allowed. Goats have been forbidden, allegedly because they are more destructive to the vegetation than cattle or sheep. Understandably, there are very few goats in the community today. This is most unfortunate, because goats provided a very important part of the Cañoneros' diet in milk and milk products. Cattle grazing has been encouraged over sheep grazing on the forest service lands; thus, the Cañoneros have become largely cattlemen. In all, federal regulation has caused the number of stock owned in the community to be reduced drastically. Many households own none at all, and the average stock-owner has only a few.

The elements of community social organization that were concerned with managing the communal lands and cooperative grazing of the community's livestock have largely disappeared. Small-scale stock raising has become principally an individual family enterprise. The U.S. Forest Service has organized cattlemen's associations, but the Cañoneros and residents of other local villages are not enthusiastic about participating in them.

The loss of the community's common grazing lands has required the Cañoneros to devote more and more of the limited irrigated valley land to pasturage and to raising fodder. This land pressure, coupled with the growth of outside wage labor, has spelled the end of subsistence farming, with the exception of kitchen gardens. Fields are now fenced and cooperative labor in farming and communal stubble grazing have disappeared. Nonetheless, there is still considerable community sentiment against the sale of private land to outsiders, particularly Anglos. In spite of this, a few such sales have occurred in recent years.

Communal use of the woodlands to gather firewood and to cut building timber has been terminated. Cañoneros may secure permits to collect fallen wood, but only at designated sites that are far removed from the microbasin. Thus, this element of the community's local subsistence base has also ceased to exist. Nonetheless, symbolically the microbasin is still broadly perceived of as the territorial basis of the community. The idiosyncrasies of the local geography are an inseparable part of the community's identity, and faint hope remains that somehow the common lands will eventually be restored.

One element of the community's resources—the irrigation system—has remained under local control and management. The state of New Mexico has theoretically exercised control over irrigation rights for years, but this was only in theory, for the first hydrological survey of the Cañones watershed and the basin's irrigation system was not carried out until 1973. The system has always been, and continues to be, under the informal corporate form of management described earlier in the essay. Indeed, in the last ten years the community has even found in possible to work in partnership with the State Engineer Office and the U.S. Soil Conservation Service to make capital improvements to the system. New concrete diversion dams and watergates have been built for several of the major acequias.

Legally and politically, Cañones remains an unincorporated rural hamlet. Thus, as an entity, the community lacks many of the rights and privileges it should enjoy. Its only salvation has been that most of the schemes for economic development of the surrounding lands have not been realized. Large-scale commercial ranching failed. Commercial logging has taken place, particularly on the Polvadera grant, but not on a large enough scale to overwhelm the community. To date, recreational use of the national forest land has been limited, so the influx of tourists and outsiders seeking summer residences has not been too large. However, there are fears that recreational land developers are about to descend on the region in force.

The limited grazing allowed under Forest Service permits, wage labor in logging operations on the federal land, and employment in other areas of the private sector of the region have not adequately compensated Cañoneros for the loss of their land. The Cañoneros, like the residents of the other isolated Hispanic communities of the uplands region, cling to the little land they have left and subsist on what wage labor can be found and on federal welfare programs. Unlike the central Rio Grande valley villages, they are too far from Los Alamos, Santa Fe, or Albuquerque to find adequate employment through daily commuting. By all conventional measures, this is one of the most economically depressed areas in the nation. Naturally there has been a long-term pattern of out-migration. Large numbers of upland villagers have moved to the urban centers of Santa Fe and Albuquerque, as well as to more distant cities in other states.

All of this adversity notwithstanding, Cañones has recently shown signs of beginning to rebuild its economy. In recent years, a community economic development project, El Proyecto, was organized. El Proyecto was incorporated as a nonprofit community organization and received financial support from an outside private foundation. The project sponsored the construction of a community social and recreational center and several cooperative farming ventures. Plans have been considered for improving the small amount of Valdez grant communal grazing land and a comprehensive land title clearance project. Surprisingly, the population of the plaza has begun to grow again, with several young families establishing new residences.

Summary and Conclusions

This essay has attempted to convey the complexity of the Hispanic adaptation to the uplands of northern New Mexico and southern Colorado. It has outlined the characteristics of the upland environment, particularly the critical elements of this environment for Hispanic adjustment, that we have termed the "effective environment." It has been demonstrated through a close examination of one small region of the uplands, the Cañones region, that the Hispanic settlers achieved a remarkable and distinctive adjustment to a very rugged frontier environment. This adaptation was characterized by a community-based agro-pastoral system of subsistence, a system that successfully sustained many small communities for generations.

The present argument has demonstrated that the issue addressed by Libecap and Alter, the cause of rural poverty in Taos County, New Mexico, is considerably more complex than those authors have implied. Indeed, the Hispanic settlers practiced partible inheritance—land was usually divided among children or other heirs. This frequently led to smaller tracts of farmland, yet the process of fragmentation of ownership was strongly counteracted by out-migration to settle new areas and by the cooperative nature of agricultural life. In practice, plots divided among siblings were frequently farmed jointly, so this did not result in smaller agricultural units. Further, the farm units in the Hispanic adaptation were always very small by Anglo-American commercial standards. Clearly, partible inheritance was not the principal cause of growing poverty in the Hispanic uplands during the early decades of this century. As this essay has demonstrated, the fundamental problem was the alienation and spoilation of the communal grazing areas and woodlands that were essential to the Hispanic cultural ecology. George I. Sanchez stated the facts very succinctly forty-seven years ago,

> The land of Taos is poor. Under the best of circumstances, the natural resources of the area will provide only a meager living to the tillers of the soil. In the past, the *Taoseno* supplemented the production of his subsistence farm by grazing small herds of sheep, cattle, or goats on the open range. That range is no longer open to him on terms that he can meet. Commercial livestock operators have acquired his land grants and compete with him for grazing leases and permits on public lands. Exorbitant fees, taxes, and forced sales have crowded him out of his former grazing domain. Overuse of surrounding range and forest lands have depreciated further its limited worth. Subdivision, through inheritance, has reduced its size. There is very little private work to be had, so he is forced into relief wage work, into seasonal labor, into destitution.[77]

The Hispanic system of subsistence agriculture and animal husbandry was fostered through a form of social organization and land tenure very different from that of the Anglo-American farmer, as we have seen. It should be understood that the Hispanic agricultural and pastoral regime could not easily be transformed into a commercial enterprise comparable to Anglo-American farming practices and agricultural economics. It is true that to a limited extent commercial farming has been undertaken in the uplands, notably in settlements along the Rio Grande. Apple orchards and chile growers have had some commercial success. However, students of the region all recognize that these commercial pursuits are economically marginal due to the difficulties presented by the environment, particularly the unpredictability of water supplies and the short growing season. (See Hamon for a discussion of commercial farms in Santa Cruz.)[78]

To fully understand the varied upland environments of northern New Mexico and southern Colorado and all of the efforts to conquer the land and win a livelihood from it, much more detailed research needs to be conducted. The range of diversity within specific regions and between different sections of the uplands, with respect to land use practices and economic activities, call for extensive study. The final section of this essay addresses the question of research methodology in the pursuit of this knowledge.

Methodology in Land Grant Research

Having conducted research on the Spanish and Mexican land grants in northern New Mexico and southern Colorado for twenty years, it may be useful to share my thoughts about research methodology. As an anthropologist, I have approached land grant research with a strategy that clearly reflects my disciplinary background. An important part of the theoretical underpinnings of this research methodology relies on an ecological perspective.

In undertaking a study of the Hispanic land grants and the communities that developed on the grants, one must first gain an understanding of Spanish and Mexican land tenure laws and the history of the Spanish and Mexican periods in New Mexico and the greater Southwest. Of particular concern is the organization of society and social and legal processes on the New Mexican frontier during the eighteenth and nineteenth centuries. This I endeavored to do, giving special attention to the relationship between the spatial distribution of the population through time and the patterns of landholding and use as molded by the granting of royal lands. The rights in land established through the land grant mechanism, along with the opportunities provided and restrictions imposed by the environment (given the society's technological kit for its utilization) are crucial factors to study. Further, a regional approach is recommended, rather than a focus on a single grant. It is important to view a grant in its geographical and environmental context as well as its historical and social parameters: the view, in other words, of cultural ecology.

An adequate study must encompass not only the ideal types of land tenure and use provided by the land grants, but also the actual practices adopted in particular instances, for custom was fully as important as the law. This can be accomplished only by making case studies of particular land grants and the settlement which developed on them. To succeed, a study must be carried out both in the field and in the archives, in order to gather all types of pertinent data. Merely studying the records of the surveyors general and the Court of Private Land Claims is inadequate, for these records do not provide the researcher with many types of information needed to adequately interpret land grant histories. To begin with, extensive and detailed information is needed on the local environment and the history of land use on each grant. Such information is quite limited, if present at all, in the legal records.

In initiating research on the land grants in the Cañones region, I gathered data on the environment, noting in particular its stable features, features that have been modified through time, and whether these modifications were due to natural or human causes. Other environmental data concerned the distribution of critical natural resources, such as water, and of land forms and their types as defined by the inhabitants for exploitive purposes. At the same time, agricultural practices and the animal husbandry of the local society were studied. Changes over time in technology, crops, and/or types of stock raising had to be systematically charted, giving special attention to the changes resulting from the arrival of Anglo-Americans in numbers during the territorial period. These data have a direct impact on the land tenure systems, because the Hispanic system is based on the use value of land and not on abstract notions of land as an economic commodity. Furthermore, changes in land tenure practices occur under changing conditions. If change occurs in the resource being exploited, the competition for its use, the nature of the products, their use, or in any combination of these factors, then alterations of land tenure practices are to be expected.[79]

The study of the changing environment of the Cañones region with regard to the way it has affected patterns of landholding and use proceeded through culling data gathered by the U.S. Geological Survey, the Soil Conservation Service, the New Mexico State Hydrological Survey Office, and the U.S. Forest Service over a considerable number of years (the earliest field data were gathered in 1859 and the most recent in 1973). Similarly, data on the history of human exploitation of the region have been drawn from the records of governmental agencies and from private documents.

To understand the workings of land tenure on the Hispanic grant lands, a study must be explicitly diachronic, because the changes in environment, landholding and use, transfer and inheritance of land, and human relationships can only be observed over a considerable time span. Thus, the approach of the ethnohistorian was adopted for the purposes of this research. All available documentary evidence pertaining to the three land grants in the Cañones microbasin was gathered. These documents include the records of the U.S. Private Land Claims, the papers of numerous attorneys who took part in the land grant litigation, Rio Arriba County tax records, relevant documents from the Spanish and Mexican Archives of New Mexico, U.S. Soil Conservation Service documents, the U.S. Census for the Territory of New Mexico, the private papers of land grant claimants, and historical maps.

In addition to the documentary data, full use has been made of field data collected from Cañoneros and other individuals in the region. I have attempted to work back and forth from the field to the archives as much as possible, as suggested by Lurie and Pitt.[80] This methodological approach has been very useful. For example, through the collection of oral history, it has been possible to corroborate some documented events and cast doubt upon others, as well compensate for some gaps and deficiencies in the public and private records. These gaps frequently concern informal practices of land transfer and use, which are not part of the public record.

Other field data derived from the common field notes of the Cañones community study have also been utilized (see Kutsche and Van Ness).[81] The lengthy village census and extensive genealogies have been especially useful. These data permit what William Fenton has termed "upstreaming," that is, enabling researchers to reconstruct historic patterns and processes by careful extrapolation from their knowledge of the contemporary society.[82] Because of the ethnocentric bias and partisan interests displayed in much of the reporting by territorial officials, which makes up the bulk of the documentary record, the collection and use of field data along with documentary data has been essential to this research. In addition, these kinds of data give one other information of great importance in understanding the land grants and traditional modes of exploitation associated with the grants. Landholding is not merely a dimension of social and political organization. People attach meanings to the land their place on it which are particularly important in nonindustrial rural societies. By and large, such information is totally absent from the official documentary land grant records.

The meaning attached to land is very significant in the Hispanic tradition, for it has a direct bearing on the way people organize themselves for economic activities. In this tradition, the concept of human community is based on place. *Pueblo* (town) means both a physical place on the surface of the earth and also the people who belong to that place.[83] Man, society, and geographical place are conceptually integrated in Hispanic thought. That is to say, to talk of people is to talk of where they live; to talk of a given land area is to talk of the people who reside there or who have resided there in the past; to talk of where people reside is to talk of the natural resources they call their own and from which they draw their sustenance. A brief illustration will serve to emphasize the importance of this observation for research purposes.

A persistent problem in land grant research has been the question of location and boundaries of many grants, for they do not conform to Anglo-American standards for legal description. When such questions are evaluated using the approach outlined here the so-called vague, inadequate, or primitive method of delineating land units and boundaries in the Hispanic system becomes comprehensible. In fact, casting such aspersion on the Hispanic practices is shown to represent an ethnocentric bias rather than fact. For example, to describe the boundaries of a given tract of land as, bounded on the east by the land of the Garcias, on the south by the Sierra Valdez, on the west by the acequia of the Lovatos, and on the north by the Rito Grande, is adequate and makes perfectly good sense if we recognize that this system of reckoning is based upon the conceptual merging of three sets of criteria, the physical features of a given region of the earth's surface, the people who reside there, and the social arrangements and methods of exploiting the land. Of course, if one is ignorant of the local geography, the local residents, and how the land was used, such a description is incomprehensible. This is to say, the perspective gained from an ecological approach may be useful.

The research strategy outlined in this brief discussion has its limitations. One of the most obvious drawbacks is that by gathering such a variety of detailed information about each grant, one runs the risk of becoming so inundated with a large number of seemingly unrelated facts that making sense of it all becomes an impossibility. The genealogical information alone is enough to overwhelm a researcher. I have attempted to overcome this problem in the following manner. All of the data for each grant studied have been organized on five-by-eight note cards and cross-filed by significant categories of information. These categories include names of individuals residing on the grants and genealogical connections between these grant residents and others holding rights in the grants; names of plazas, ranchos, plots of agriculture land, pastures, trails, and roads located within the grant lands throughout their histories; records of land use—residential, agricultural, and pastoral; records of land transfers through inheritances and sales; tax records; names and activities of attorneys, local merchants, and stockmen, and land speculators associated with the grants; and court proceedings. The data have also been organized chronologically wherever possible. This system of indexing is helpful, but hardly an ideal scheme for quickly retrieving information and seeing interrelationships among the various types of data. Today's technology argues that this data should be computerized, which would solve many problems in working with such varied and detailed information.

A second major drawback of this research methodology is that it requires a very considerable amount of time to complete a study of a single grant, not to mention the expense incurred in supporting a researcher in the field and at the archives for an extended period of time. A related problem is that the methodology demands that a researcher acquire the skills and knowledge to gather and analyze a wide variety of data, ranging from legal records to hydrological data to genealogies. A possible solution to this problem would be to organize research teams made up of specialists from each of the requisite disciplines and local community members who have been trained to assist with the research.

Drawbacks to this approach to land grant research notwithstanding, it has many virtues. Its greatest virtue is that it places at the center of the investigation the people who settled the grant lands, their descendants and later settlers who worked the grant lands to win their livelihood and made them their home. To the writer's way of thinking, one should not study the Spanish and Mexican land grants without proper attention to the living Hispanic people who are the cultural heirs of this remarkable tradition.

Notes

Abbreviations

NMLG: Papers of the Surveyors General and the Court of Private Land Claims, indexed in *A Guide to the Microfilm of Papers Relating to New Mexico Land Grants,* ed. James Diaz (Albuquerque: University of New Mexico Press, 1960). The New Mexico State Records Center and Archives has microfilmed these documents; the following notes indicate the microfilm reel (r), case (c), and frame (f) for documents cited.

NMSEO: New Mexico State Engineers Office

SANM: Spanish Archives of New Mexico (Santa Fe: New Mexico State Records Center and Archives), indexed and described by Ralph Emerson Twitchell, *Spanish Archives of New Mexico* (Cedar Rapids, IA: The Torch Press, 1914), Volume I: Wills and Land Transfers, Volume II: Judicial and Military Documents.

SCS: United States Soil Conservation Service

USDA: United States Department of Agriculture

1. I am most appreciative of the help of Marianne L. Stoller and Christine M. Van Ness who read the manuscript and offered suggestions. I also benefited greatly from the editorial eye of Charles L. Briggs. Finally, I gratefully acknowledge the word-processing assistance of Helen Eash and Jeri Ruser.
2. Robert McC. Netting, *Cultural Ecology* (Menlo Park, CA: Cummings Publishing Co., 1977), p. 1.
3. C. Daryll Forde, *Habitat, Economy and Society* (New York: E. P. Dutton and Co., 1963), p. 463.
4. Netting, *Cultural Ecology,* p. 4.
5. *Explorations in Economic History* 19 (1982), pp. 184–200.
6. This section is drawn from John R. Van Ness, *Hispanos in Northern New Mexico: The Development of Corporate Community and Multicommunity* (Philadelphia, PA: Ph.D. diss., University of Pennsylvania, 1979), Chapter 3.
7. Edgar L. Hewett and Bertha P. Dutton, eds., *The Pueblo Indian World* (Albuquerque: University of New Mexico Press, 1945), p. 21.
8. Nevin M. Feeneman, *Physiography of the Western United States* (New York: McGraw-Hill Co., 1931), p. 92.
9. William De. Thornbury, *Regional Geomorphology of the United States* (New York: John Wiley and Sons, 1965), p. 92.
10. USDA, *Land Management Plan for Northern New Mexico Grant Lands Project* (Santa Fe: Soil Conservation Service, 1941), pp. 5–6.
11. USDA, *Tewa Basin Study,* Vol. 3 (Albuquerque, Soil Conservation Service, 1939), p. 4.
12. Hewett and Dutton, eds., *The Pueblo Indian World;* USDA, *Tewa Basin Study.*
13. Margaret Meaders, "The Economy of Rio Arriba County," *New Mexico Business* (Reprint, 1965), p. 4.
14. Vernon Bailey, "Life Zone and Crop Zones of New Mexico," *North American Fauna,* No. 35 (Washington, DC: USDA, Bureau of Biological Survey, 1913).
15. Bailey, "Life Zone and Crop Zones of New Mexico," pp. 25–28.

16. Bailey, "Life Zone and Crop Zones of New Mexico," pp. 41–46.

17. Bailey, "Life Zone and Crop Zones of New Mexico," pp. 46–49.

18. Bailey, "Life Zone and Crop Zones of New Mexico," pp. 50–53.

19. NMSEO, "Rio Chama Hydrographic Survey Report: Cañones and Polvadera Creeks Section," Vol. 4 (Santa Fe, Unpublished Report, 1974); SCS, "Cañones Creek Watershed," Unpublished Field Notes, Rio Chama–Otowi Sub-basin (Albuquerque, 1965).

20. SCS, "Cañones Creek Watershed."

21. Peter van Dresser, "The Bio-economic Community: Reflections on a Development Philosophy for a Semi-arid Environment," in *Indian and Spanish-American Adjustments to Arid and Semi-arid Environments,* ed. Clark S. Knowlton (Lubbock: Texas Technical Press, 1964), pp. 53–74; Peter van Dresser, *A Landscape for Humans* (Albuquerque: Biotechnic Press, 1972).

22. Van Dresser, "The Bio-economic Community: Reflections on a Development Philosophy for a Semi-arid Environment," pp. 64–65.

23. Oakah L. Jones, *Los Paisanos: Spanish Settlers on the Northern Frontier of New Spain* (Norman: University of Oklahoma Press, 1979).

24. John R. Van Ness, "Hispanic Village Organization in Northern New Mexico: Corporate Community Structure in Historical and Comparative Perspective," in *The Survival of Spanish American Villages,* ed. Paul Kutsche (Colorado Springs: The Colorado College, 1979).

25. Robert E. Rhoades and Stephen I. Thompson, "Adaptive Strategies in Alpine Environments: Beyond Ecological Particularism," *American Ethnologist* 2 (1975): 535–51.

26. This historical account of the development of the Cañones region is a summary of portions of Van Ness, *Hispanos in Northern New Mexico: The Development of Corporate Community and Multi-community,* Chapters 7, 8. Some of this chronicle has previously appeared in John R. Van Ness, "The Polvadera Grant: Hispanic Settlement in the Cañones Region," in *Spanish Colonial Frontier Research,* ed. Henry F. Dobyns (Albuquerque: Center for Anthropological Studies, 1980); John R. Van Ness, "The Juan Bautista Valdez Grant: Was It a Community Land Grant?" in *Spanish and Mexican Land Grants in New Mexico and Colorado,* ed. John R. and Christine M. Van Ness (Manhattan, KS: The Sunflower University Press, 1980).

27. NMLG, f. 20, c. 73, f. 11–18.

28. SANM I, 571.

29. SANM I, 963.

30. SANM I, 571.

31. NMLG, r. 20, c. 73, f. 11–18; SANM I, 870.

32. NMLG, r. 20, c. 73, f. 11–18.

33. SANM I, 568.

34. SANM I, 571.

35. Frances Leon Swadesh, *Los Primeros Pobladores: Hispanic Americans of the Ute Frontiers* (Notre Dame, IN: University of Notre Dame Press, 1974).

36. Eleanor B. Adams and Fray Angelico Chavez, *The Missions of New Mexico, 1776* (Albuquerque: University of New Mexico Press, 1956).

37. Adams and Chavez, *The Missions of New Mexico, 1776,* pp. 252–53.
38. Adams and Chavez, *The Missions of New Mexico, 1776,* pp. 39–40.
39. Adams and Chavez, *The Missions of New Mexico, 1776,* pp. 41, 126.
40. Alfred B. Thomas, trans. and ed., *Forgotten Frontiers* (Norman: University of Oklahoma Press, 1932); Pinart Collection, Spanish Colonial Documents Relating to New Mexico, in *Bancroft Collection* (Berkeley, CA: Bancroft Library).
41. Swadesh, *Los Primeros Pobladores: Hispanic Americans of the Ute Frontier,* p. 46.
42. SANM I, 1191.
43. NMLG, r. 35, c. 30, f. 19–20.
44. Papers of Thomas B. Catron in Coronado Room, University of New Mexico Library (Albuquerque: University of New Mexico), box 3, folder 1.
45. NMLG, r. 20, c. 71.
46. NMLG, r. 20, c. 113, f. 1–4.
47. NMLG, r. 50, c. 179, f. 41–43.
48. NMLG, r. 50, c. 179, f. 39.
49. NMLG, r. 50, c. 179, f. 22–24; r. 18, c. 55, f. 2.
50. NMLG, r. 18, c. 55, f. 2.
51. SANM II, 1282.
52. SANM I, 387.
53. Bailey H. Carroll and J. Villasana Haggard, ed. and trans., *Three New Mexico Chronicles,* Quivira Society, no. 11 (Albuquerque: University of New Mexico Press, 1942); Father Stanley (Crocchiola), *The Abiquiu Story* (Private Publication, no date), 13.
54. Joseph J. Hill, "The Old Spanish Trail," *Hispanic American Historical Review* 4 (1921): 444–49.
55. LeRoy R. Hafen, "Armijo's Journal of 1829–30: The Beginning of Trade Between New Mexico and California," *Colorado Magazine* 27 (1950): 120–31; Hill, "The Old Spanish Trail," pp. 464–66.
56. Swadesh, *Los Primeros Pobladores: Hispanic Americans of the Ute Frontiers,* pp. 59–61.
57. NMLG, r. 23, c. 113, f. 37–42.
58. NMSEO, "Rio Chama Hydrographic Survey Report: Cañones and Polvadera Creeks Section."
59. NMSEO, "Rio Chama Hydrographic Survey Report: Cañones and Polvadera Creeks Section," p. 7.
60. Carroll and Haggard, *Three New Mexico Chronicles,* 43; United States Bureau of Census, *Territory of New Mexico, Household Census and Census of Agriculture,* 8th Census (1860), 9th Census (1870) (Santa Fe: New Mexico State Records Center and Archives).
61. David E. Vassberg, "The *Tierra Baldias:* Community Property and Public Lands in 16th Century Castile," *Agricultural History* 48 (1974): 384.
62. William H. Dusenbury, *The Mexican Mesta: The Administration of Ranching in Colonial Mexico* (Urbana, IL: University of Illinois Press, 1963), p. 72.
63. Caroll and Haggard, *Three New Mexico Chronicles,* p. 102.

64. This section is a modified and abbreviated version of an earlier publication, John R. Van Ness, "Modernization, Land Tenure, and Ecology: The Costs of Change in Northern New Mexico," *Papers in Anthropology* 13 (University of Oklahoma, 1976).

65. Van Dresser, *A Landscape for Humans,* p. 32.

66. Victor Westphall, *The Public Domain in New Mexico 1854–1891* (Albuquerque: University of New Mexico Press, 1965).

67. Arnold Strickon, "The Euro-American Ranching Complex," in *Man, Culture and Animals,* ed. Anthony Leeds and Andrew P. Vayda (Washington, DC: American Association for the Advancement of Science, 1965).

68. Van Ness, "The Polvadera Grant: Hispanic Settlement in the Cañones Region"; Van Ness, "The Juan Bautista Valdez Grant: Was It a Community Grant?"

69. NMLG, r. 20, c. 73, f. 7–8.

70. NMLG, r. 20, c. 73, f. 29–30.

71. NMLG, r. 35, c. 30, f. 1–7.

72. NMLG, r. 35, c. 30, f. 112–50.

73. The L. Bradford Prince Papers (Santa Fe: New Mexico State Records Center and Archives).

74. NMLG, r. 35, c. 30, f. 109–11.

75. The Papers of Thomas B. Catron, box 3, folder 1.

76. NMLG, r. 35, c. 30, f. 163–67.

77. George I. Sanchez, *Forgotten People: A Study of New Mexicans* (Albuquerque: University of New Mexico Press, 1940), pp. 69–70.

78. Peter G. Hamon, "The Landholding System of Santa Cruz," in *Papers in Anthropology* 11 (University of Oklahoma, 1970).

79. Robert McC. Netting, "What Alpine Peasants Have in Common: Observations on Communal Tenture in a Swiss Village" (Paper read at the Annual Meeting of the American Anthropological Association, November 29, 1973, New Orleans).

80. Nancy O. Lurie, "Ethnohistory: An Ethnological Point of View," *Ethnohistory* 8 (1961): 78–92; David C. Pitt, *Using Historical Sources in Anthropology and Sociology* (New York: Holt, Rinehart and Winston, Inc., 1972).

81. Paul Kutsche and John R. Van Ness, *Cañones: Values, Crisis, and Survival in a Northern New Mexico Village* (Albuquerque: University of New Mexico Press, 1981).

82. William N. Fenton, "Ethnohistory and Its Problems," *Ethnohistory* 9 (1962): 1–23.

83. Julian A. Pitt-Rivers, *People of the Sierra* (Chicago, IL: University of Chicago Press, 1971).

Lawrence and Grandpa Gurule. Kathryn Nelson photograph.

FOUR

Getting Both Sides of the Story

FOUR

Getting Both Sides of the Story
Oral History in Land Grant Research and Litigation

Charles L. Briggs

Although orally transmitted accounts formed the original basis of historical research, the modern discipline of history arose in the wake of the conquest of the oral by the written word. Having lost their status as respected repositories of knowledge and tradition, orally transmitted forms—folktales, myths, folksongs, and oral traditions—came to be seen as mere curiosities. In keeping with this belief, oral history is commonly thought to lack historical validity. Although this view has become less prevalent during the last decade, our understanding of the nature of oral testimony and its potential as an historical resource is still poorly developed.

This view permeates the literature on the Spanish and Mexican land grants of New Mexico and Colorado. Scholars, attorneys, and judges have often made highly disparaging remarks about oral testimony, rejecting it out of hand as inconsistent, misleading, and inaccurate. To cite a recent example, Westphall, who has written extensively and persuasively on land grants,[1] begins his study of Thomas Benton Catron by dismissing the value of oral sources:

> This present book is an attempt to evaluate Catron's life and his era *objectively.* The prevailing *oral stories* have been subjected to *factual research,* and the interpretations given herein have been based on *verifiable evidence.* Because the nefarious nature heretofore attributed to the man is not generally borne out in the recorded evidence, *much of the oral tradition has of necessity been discarded here.*[2]

Works such as Swadesh's *Los primeros pobladores*[3] suggest that not all researchers have dismissed oral sources. The point remains, however, that land grant studies have seldom profited from systematic use of documentary evidence and oral history. This is all the more striking in view of the fact that the settlement of land grant communities in New Mexico and southern Colorado forms a part of Latin American history, a field in which awareness of the value of oral tradition has deep roots.[4]

My purpose in this article is to demonstrate that oral history is a rich source of reliable historical information. The problems that have been found in the use of oral sources are quite real; practitioners would be foolish to draw on oral history without taking its limitations into account. The notorious inconsistencies and inaccuracies are, however, not *inherent* in oral historical sources: they are *introduced* by practitioners through the use of poor techniques of collection and interpretation.

Oral history is plagued by two basic types of methodological distortion. First, students of history, sociology, anthropology, and other disciplines sometimes supplement their research by collecting oral histories. Work in their own disciplines is often informed by formal study, awareness of acceptable research techniques, and painstaking thoroughness. Many investigators seem to think that, in contrast, the collection of oral history involves no special preparation and no consideration of technique—you simply ask the questions.

Oral historians themselves are often guilty of the second type of distortion. Oral history emerges in interviews. Interviews are human encounters, involving the participation of at least two people. The motives that bring both interviewer and respondent to the meeting are often as different as their social, cultural, and educational backgrounds. Every bit of information derived from oral sources is surrounded by a unique context. Unfortunately, most practitioners treat the interviewee's responses as "facts" which can be immediately extracted from this context and placed alongside other "facts." More often than not, this leads the researcher to draw a conclusion from the respondent's statement that differs from that attached to it by the respondent. Thus, taking oral history out of the context in which it was first articulated and incorporating it into another context, such as a historical study or a legal brief, demands a great deal of sensitivity to the differences between the two types of contexts.

The purpose of this article is to provide researchers, particularly those interested in land grants, with the tools to avoid both kinds of distortion. I will begin by introducing the discipline of oral history and the techniques which have been developed in it. I will then show

how oral history methods can be used in land grant research by presenting an oral history of the Pueblo Quemado land grant which surrounds Córdova, New Mexico (see Maps 1 and 2). The picture of the grant and community that emerges from oral sources will be contrasted with the documentary record. In accounting for the differences between these two views, I will discuss the nature of oral historical consciousness in Hispanic New Mexico. The essay will conclude with an assessment of the value of oral sources for the study of land grant history and its growing importance as a resource in defending the land rights of Hispano and Native American communities.

Oral History: Discipline and Practice

Historical research has involved an oral historical component since classical antiquity. It is only during the past fifty years, however, that scholars trained in history, sociology, anthropology, folklore, library science, and other fields have joined forces with lay oral historians in creating a discipline of oral history. American oral historians have formed an association (Oral History Association), which sponsors an annual meeting and a journal (*The Oral History Review*). Another major journal, the *International Journal of Oral History,* has also appeared.

This organizational growth has been accompanied by a tremendous increase in the quantity and variety of publications in the field. The literature initially consisted primarily of articles that focused on the recollections of members of a particular community, organization, occupational, or political group, or the like. The last two decades have witnessed the publication of practical manuals that tell, step-by-step, how to conduct oral historical research and how to create an archive.[5] A number of works also grapple with questions regarding the nature of oral history and its theoretical underpinnings.[6] An anthology covering a wide range of topics in oral history has recently become available.[7]

One of the most significant developments in the field emerged during the 1960s and 1970s. Oral history came to be recognized as a powerful tool for bringing groups into the historical record which have traditionally been overlooked through historians' preoccupation with great men. Oral histories of blacks and other ethnic groups, women, and the working class began to fill many of the gaps left by standard documentary sources. Alex Haley's *Roots*[8] and Studs Terkel's *Hard Times*[9] were extremely successful in bringing oral history's potential to the attention of a broad audience.

Oral History and Oral Tradition: Definitions

The term *oral history* is used in both broad and narrow senses. In general terms, oral history refers to the recording of individuals' recollections of past events and eras. Collecting oral history thus involves discussions, generally in an interview format, in which a researcher poses questions designed to elicit historically relevant information. Oral history is also used in a more restricted sense to refer to the reconstruction of events that lie within the interviewee's firsthand experience. This definition thus excludes legends and other materials that are transmitted from generation to generation, since a narrator's knowledge is also derived from verbal sources. The terms *oral tradition* and *oral testimony* are often used in pointing to the latter class of information, particularly as it is passed on in narrative form.[10] Oral history and oral tradition are both important sources of information on the history of land grants in New Mexico and Colorado.

It is also important to distinguish between oral historical research and the casual collection of historical reminiscences. As in any field, the collection of accurate and useful oral historical material involves acquiring training, forethought, and sensitivity in conducting the interviewing, as well as patience and thoroughness in transcribing the tapes and analyzing their historical significance. Collecting oral history is not difficult, and advanced training in a specialized program is not indispensable. As in any other pursuit, however, one cannot expect to produce good, reliable results until the basic methodological principles have been acquired and put into practice.

Basic Concepts and Methods of Oral Historical Research

Project Design. The task of collecting oral historical information on a particular land grant is best begun by thinking carefully about what is to be learned. Information which will stand up in court and/or inform a sound history of a particular grant must be *systematically* organized, and it must thoroughly address the important questions. Adequately covering a given topic involves figuring out the focus and scope of the research. What geographic area is to be covered? Will the subject of the investigation be the history of an area, a single grant, or part of a grant (e.g., the settlement or the common lands)? What is the time frame—the grant's entire history, the turn of the century, or another distinct period?

In making these decisions, two things need to be borne in mind. First, it would be good to know everything about a particular settlement or grant; if the researcher tries to learn everything at once, however, she or he will likely give up in face of the magnitude of the task. It is thus important to figure out which issues are of the greatest importance to achieve the purpose of the study. If one's goal is to collect oral history for use in resolving a court case, it is probably best to concentrate on the places and the eras that are likely to be most crucial in the courtroom. For example, if the original granting papers are missing, oral history may be needed to determine the circumstances surrounding the initial settlement.

A second concern is time and money. It is of no use to anyone to create a research plan so unrealistic that it will never be completed. Fortunately, oral historical research is inexpensive, involving mainly tape, a tape recorder and a typewriter, with perhaps some travel costs. A museum, college or university, or a governmental agency may be able to assist with recording equipment and tape. For a small project, the most important question at this point is how much time can be devoted to the project. This is particularly important in view of the fact that it nearly always takes a great deal longer to complete a research project than is anticipated.

Be Prepared. Once the researcher has a clear idea of the scope of the research, the next step is to familiarize oneself with the grant or community. Adequate preparation leads to better interviews, more thorough research, and a better chance of completing the project in a reasonable amount of time. It is also a way to demonstrate respect for potential interviewees, showing them that the researcher takes the subject seriously and is not going to waste their time.

The first thing to do is to find out what information has already been collected on the subject. Oral historians are the first to point out that oral sources are best used in conjunction with all other available and historically relevant materials, including written documents.[11] It is a waste of time—both the collector's and the interviewees'—simply to duplicate past research.

As has been noted in previous chapters, the State Records Center and Archives, the Special Collections of the University of New Mexico Library, the History Library of the Museum of New Mexico, and other institutions hold documents pertaining to all of the land grants in New Mexico and southern Colorado. A great deal of oral history on land grants is contained in the testimony taken by the surveyor general and the Court of Private Land Claims; these are contained in the files for each grant in the above locations. Books, articles, theses, and unpublished manuscripts may present previous findings and are likely to be available.

Oral historical and folkloric studies may be available as well; many of the original materials for these studies are housed in the J. D. Robb Archive of Southwestern Music in the Fine Arts Library of the University of New Mexico.[12] Folklore and oral history were collected for many communities by the workers of the New Mexico Federal Writers' Project (1936–1939) and the Work Projects Administration Writers' Program (1939–1943); copies of most of the work are available in the State Records Center and Archives and in the History Library of the Museum of New Mexico.[13] The state historian, whose office is in the State Records Center and Archives in Santa Fe, can provide assistance on both the planning of oral history projects and on the resources that are available throughout the state.

If the oral historian does not come from the community to be studied, it is equally important to spend some time there before beginning the first interview. This will help in establishing rapport, a relationship of trust between researcher and interviewee. The experiences of Native American and Hispanic communities with outsiders who arrive in search of land grant histories have not always been positive. People have a right to get to know potential researchers and to ascertain their motives before answering any questions. Such initial contact is similarly crucial to the ultimate success of the project. Careful observation can help reveal who can appropriately ask what questions to whom in what settings and how people ordinarily discuss oral historical themes. This can help prevent unproductive interviews that occur when the research cannot connect with the ways interviewees think of and talk about their own history. I have presented techniques for conducting this type of preliminary research in another publication.[14]

A third preparatory step is to practice interviewing. Unless the researcher is an experienced interviewer, it is best to try a few short interviews with friends or family. The most important thing is to learn how to formulate questions which are clear, interesting, and open-ended. The researcher should avoid the tendency to try to demonstrate her or his own expertise in each query: the interviewee is the expert. If the interviews are recorded, the novice interviewer can then listen to the tape to discover possible areas for improvement.[15]

Getting the right recording equipment and becoming thoroughly familiar with it are also crucial steps. A great deal can be learned without using a tape recorder, but a tape recording and a transcript provide much more information than a summary of what was said. As I will argue below, in order to assess the historical value of an interview, it is necessary to look both at what is said and how it is said. Further, researchers and courts of law are likely to place more weight on an interview if the original recording is available and can be quoted verbatim.[16]

In choosing a tape recorder, the most important considerations are cost, recording quality, and unobtrusiveness. Fortunately, relatively inexpensive cassette tape recorders provide a recording which is of sufficient quality for all projects that are not geared toward radio or television broadcast.[17] Good tape is an excellent investment; cheap tape is harder to transcribe and easier to snarl or break. Whatever equipment is chosen, it is essential to obtain it far enough in advance to become expert in its use before the first interview.

Oral History Interviewing. Once the researcher is ready to begin interviewing, the first thing to do is to locate appropriate interviewees. In Hispano communities, the elders are charged with the task of passing oral history and folklore along to their juniors (see below). They tend to feel most comfortable in the role of teaching about past events, and they are most likely to have been around when the events in question took place or to have heard their own grandparents' accounts. This does not mean, however, that one should interview only the "most knowledgable" members of the community. The breadth and reliability of the information will be greatly enhanced by the inclusion of as great a variety of interviewees—older and middle-aged, female and male, rich and poor, etc.—as possible. It is particularly important to get both sides of major disputes.

Since it is extremely important to conduct the interviewing in the native language, linguistic competence is one of the central criteria for matching interviewer and interviewee. Elderly Hispanos and Native

Americans may not be able to express themselves fully in English. They should be allowed, in any case, to convey the information in their own terms. This is particularly important in that, as I noted above, both what they say and how they say it is meaningful. If the researcher is not fluent in Spanish or the appropriate Native American language, practice on her/his part and collaboration with native residents of the grant or community are crucial. Even if the researcher is a native of the community, it might be wise to work with a member of another family or a person of the opposite sex to ensure that all sides have been covered.[18]

In conducting the interview, the most important thing to remember is that interviews are human encounters and not simply formal channels for transmitting information.[19] The respondent should be accorded respect and sensitive treatment in exchange for her or his willingness to assist the interviewer. The least appropriate thing to do is to bully the interviewee. In addition to damaging rapport, such tactics will deprive the researcher of the opportunity to learn about potential, undiscovered topics. Too many questions or too much concern with staying on the track similarly thwart the ability of interviewees to convey the range and the richness of their recollections. If some of the researcher's questions are neglected in the process, it is possible to return to them toward the end of the interview.

It is very helpful to review each interview before conducting another. This enables the researcher to see how she or he can improve on recording and interviewing techniques. It also assists the interviewer in determining whether further interviews with the same person are necessary and, if so, what topics should be covered. If this exercise is performed consistently, it will be easier to keep an overall sense of the progress of the research project.

Archiving, Indexing, and Transcribing. The steps outlined above yield a number of tapes containing historical information of great potential value. The question becomes what to do with these tapes. One facet of this issue should be addressed even before the interviewing begins. Protecting the rights of interviewees is essential; this involves demonstrating that the collector has obtained the permission of each participant for legitimate use of the materials. It is thus standard procedure to obtain a signed release which authorizes the researcher to deposit tapes and transcripts in an archive and to use the interview in publications and presentations.[20]

Obtaining a release may present special problems, however, in the study of New Mexico land grants. Both Hispanic and Native American communities have suffered at the hands of persons who have come in and asked owners to sign legal documents; many individuals will accordingly be reluctant to sign anything. This is less likely to be a problem if the researcher has spent time in the community and familiarized the residents with the study and its objectives. If a reluctance to sign threatens to abort a potentially valuable interview, the researcher can simply obtain oral permission before proceeding with the interview. A transcript can later be given to the interviewee, along with an explanation of how the researcher plans to use the materials. If the information is sensitive, the interviewee can request that it be withheld from public use for a given period of time or until after the interviewee's death.

There are a number of important reasons to deposit the original interview tape or a copy in an archive. A good archive will preserve the tape in such a way that the recording will never be lost through accidental erasure, breakage, snarling, or print through. Having a safe copy can prevent the loss of the whole collection due to fire or theft. It is also worthwhile to make a spare working copy in order to avoid erasing or snarling the original. Depositing the tapes in an archive also ensures that the interviewee's community and descendants will have access to the materials.[21]

In terms of processing the tapes, the ideal is to have all of them transcribed accurately and available in typescript. Unfortunately, transcription is time consuming and, if undertaken by a professional transcriber, quite costly; it takes between about six and fifteen hours to transcribe a single hour of tape, depending on the skill of the transcriber, his or her control of the language, the quality of the recording, and the clarity of the speech. Full transcription is thus a goal achieved by few researchers. A less ambitious technique is to provide an index of the topics covered in each tape. Regardless of the constraints, the goal is the same: to preserve historical information as accurately and as securely as possible for use by community residents and researchers.

An Oral History of Córdova and the Pueblo Quemado Grant

I argued at the beginning of this chapter that the use of oral history has been plagued by two fundamental problems. First, historians, sociologists, anthropologists, and other researchers who occasionally draw on oral materials often fail to apply the same care and thoroughness in the collection and analysis of oral history as they do in their work with more "traditional" sources. The preceding section addressed this problem by sketching the techniques developed by oral historians to obtain historically interesting and accurate information.

Second, I have suggested that many of the inaccuracies and inconsistencies which lead scholars to reject oral history actually emerge from a lack of understanding of the nature of oral history and the way it differs from other types of sources. My goal is to show how researchers can avoid these kinds of errors and thereby gain a great deal more historical insight from oral materials. If I were to advance this argument in the abstract, however, the reader would be forced to choose between accepting it on faith and rejecting it out of hand. Such an approach would also fail to provide readers with an idea of the sorts of information that residents of land grant communities have preserved through their oral traditions.

This section will accordingly focus on the history of a single grant—the Pueblo Quemado grant of Córdova, New Mexico (see Map 1). I will describe the history of the community as it emerges, first from the oral history and traditions of the current residents[22] and second, from written documents. A comparison of these two bodies of information will enable me to suggest some of the relative strengths and weaknesses of the two types of sources. The subsequent section will discuss the impact of this comparison on our understanding of the nature of oral history. I will also present a technique for collecting and analyzing oral materials which is informed by these insights.

The Period of Initial Settlement

The contemporary residents of Córdova are quite concerned with the history of their community; they have preserved a host of oral traditions. Although Córdovans are most concerned with the last century and a half, a number of traditions focus on the early history of the community. The Tanoan (Pueblo) Indians who lived on the mesa northwest of Córdova are called the Huachines. They are said to have been forced from their homes by nomadic tribes prior to the founding of Córdova. The people who subsequently settled the area were of another race, the Españoles. They are distinguished from the contemporary residents, who refer to themselves as Mexicanos, or as members of La Raza. The settlement was named El Pueblo Quemado (the burned town) after the abandoned pueblo. The name was shortened to Quemado in the nineteenth century, and it was changed to Córdova when the post office was opened in 1900.

The settlers' initial concerns were twofold. First, they required a subsistence base. Many of their needs were met by the produce of their gardens in the Quemado valley. Hunters also took to the surrounding hills and mountains in pursuit of game. One aspect of the first century of the settlement's history stands out in these descriptions: the Córdovans were all quite poor, and life was hard. One characteristic, however, is said to have made life relatively pleasant during this period—all work was undertaken as a communal enterprise. Individuals assumed roles as tillers of the soil, hunters, guards, and so forth in accordance with the needs of the settlement as a whole. Each family received an equal portion of the produce and game. One essential characteristic distinguishes this mode of gaining a livelihood from contemporary work relationships—money. "They didn't pay them anything, they just helped." This cooperative arrangement is held to be absent today: "Now there is no one who would help out anyone else. 'If you want me to work, pay me,' they tell you."

The Españoles' second concern was defense. The settlement did not consist of isolated ranchos; rather, the houses formed a single plaza of roughly rectangular shape, with one thick adobe wall abutting another. The *viejitos* (elders) often note that *podía uno caminar por las soteas pa' toda la plaza* (a person could walk on the roofs around the entire plaza), the two *puertas de la plaza* (plaza gates) providing the only interruptions. Windows were high and small, and doors to the individual houses opened into the plaza enclosure.

Bands of Utes, Comanches, or Apaches would fall upon Córdova from the mesa above the plaza. Lookouts were posted at each of the two *torreones* (circular guard towers), and their cry of alarm would bring Córdovans from the fields and, if they could make it, from the nearby hills. Some elders say that the residents would fight from inside the houses, shooting their firearms and bows and arrows through the windows, while others maintain that the defense was mounted from the rooftops, with the women throwing stones and the men firing from that vantage point. A number of the Españoles were particularly good fighters, and the most valiant are still commemorated in legend. The

Indios (Indians) were, however, both determined and *muy tiradores con la flecha* (good marksmen with bows and arrows), and they killed many men and either killed or captured numerous women and children.

The Rise of Pedro Córdova

Life in the community during the initial period contrasted sharply with that of the succeeding era. The transition between the two periods is signaled by the ascendance of Pedro Córdova, a resident who came to own nearly all of the land and livestock in the community. *Más antes, aquí estaba un hombre muy riquote; era como un rey* (somewhat earlier, there was a truly rich man here; he was like a king). Pedro Córdova is said to have owned land in Santa Cruz, Chimayo, Las Joyas, El Llano de los Quemadeños, Las Truchas, Las Trampas, and as far away as Peñasco. Córdova was able to gain such an economic hold over Córdova and surrounding communities due to the dire poverty of the inhabitants and because he was *inteligente,* meaning that he had an innate, God-given talent for amassing material possessions.

Having no resources of their own, the remainder of the community members worked for Córdova. The men tended his crops and flocks, the women worked in his large household under the supervision of his wife, Ramona, and the children carried water to the house. Just as Córdova was "like a king," the workers were "like slaves," since they had no resources of their own. His household also contained a number of Indians, captured or ransomed from nomadic tribes. Pedro Córdova assigned *mayordomos* (foremen) to oversee the workers. The laborers were recompensed with a portion of the crops and meat; special allocations were made when a wedding, baptism, or other special occasion was celebrated.

The "reign" of Don Pedro was a time of relative abundance. He sold grain for food and seed to nearby farmers, and his cattle and sheep were driven as far away as Taos for sale or barter. His trading caravans likewise headed south in ox-driven carts to Juarez and Chihuahua, and they would return with gold, silver, and luxury items. Since nearly all of his needs were provided for by his flocks and fields or through trade, Córdova merely placed the gold and silver that he acquired into *ollas* (jars) and hid them. He was a good *rico* (very rich person), however, because he also used his wealth to sponsor community events, such as casting a bell for the local chapel, and the celebrations which follow the completion of such projects.[23] It is precisely his *caridad* (charity) and generosity which is believed to have made this period so fertile.

Pedro Córdova died after eating fruit which had been accidentally contaminated with poison. In passing, he took his treasure with him, so to speak, since he never told anyone of its whereabouts. This event brings out the irony that is evident in the way Córdovans characterize Pedro Córdova. He was a good rico in that he recognized that the fruit of his flocks and fields were both individual and community resources; thus, he accepted an obligation to meet the needs of his fellow villagers. This system served, however, to impoverish the majority of the residents and to render them dependent upon Córdova. His sudden death and the loss of his treasure is thus associated with the negative side of his role in the community.

Córdovans still occasionally look for the treasure; only one person is believed to have ever found any of it, however, and that was a small cache.[24] As a result, Córdova's widow and children were left with only his land and cattle; their fortune was hardly comparable to that of Pedro Córdova.

The Death of "Bygone Days"

No individual came to enjoy Pedro Córdova's level of wealth and influence during the period from Córdova's death until 1916. Although a few individuals, including several of Córdova's sons and their descendants, were somewhat better off than the remainder of the Córdovans, there were no true ricos: "all of the people were poor." The individuals who did amass any surpluses did so in terms of wealth on the hoof—livestock. The well-to-do of this period were the stockmen who kept large flocks of sheep. Most of the ranchers obtained their sheep *al partido* (on shares), renting them from Frank Bond of Española in return for a given number of pounds of wool per sheep per year. They summered their sheep in the surrounding uplands, not just on the slopes near Córdova. The sons of the *borregueros* (sheep ranchers) were charged with tending the herds, but many stockmen found it necessary to hire a few of their neighbors as well, particularly during lambing and shearing seasons.

Like the preceding period, this era was a good one. Cooperation prevailed. Although the houses and garden plots were privately owned during the growing season, help was available for planting, harvesting, and the like. A large group of people would harvest one person's fields, then those of the neighbor, and so on. The people also operated in accordance with the principle of charity in their daily lives, helping out those who were in need. An orphan or imbecile would be cared for by the community as a whole, not just by relatives.[25]

The people were strong, because they ate the good food of the land: *atole* (blue cornmeal gruel), beans, wheat, and vegetables. Their herds and the wild game of the uplands provided meat. The sheep brought a double harvest—first the wool and then the lambs. There was little cash in circulation, but nearly all of the Córdovans' requirements were met through agriculture and pastoralism, the production of handicrafts, and barter. This prosperity emanated, as it had before, from a combination of very hard work and faith in God, especially as expressed in the extension of caridad as well as in wakes and feast days for the saints.

The wake for Saint Isidore, the patron saint of New Mexican farmers, provides a striking example of the way in which religion, social structure, and subsistence patterns were closely associated in community-wide celebrations. On 14 May, the eve of the feast day, the people took Saint Isidore's image out of the chapel and carried it in procession across the community and up to the upland dry farms at Las Joyas. Here an all-night vigil began; hymns dedicated to Saint Isidore and prayers soliciting his intercession with God to ensure bountiful crops alternated with the praying of the rosary. The service was interrupted only by a communal meal, taken at midnight. Next morning, as the first rays of light struck the face of the image, a procession formed once again. In descending from the mountain, the people carried the image through each field, both at Las Joyas and in the Quemado valley. The wake thus articulated the people's belief that each individual must cooperate, both with God and with neighbors, in securing a bountiful harvest.[26]

The end of this era was signaled by an event that transpired during the lifetime of most of the contemporary elders of the community. They emphasize that *antes estaba todo libre* (in bygone days, everything was open). This refers to rights to the uplands between the villages and the high peaks. Unlike the farms in the valley, all members of the community had free access to the uplands for hunting and fishing, cutting timber and fuel wood, grazing, etc. The residents of the surrounding communities recognized the Córdovans' rights to the area between Córdova and the Truchas Peaks.

Pero entonces pusieron la floresta, y se acabó todo (but then they put in the national forest, and it all came to an end). Córdovans still recall the meetings, called by the U.S. Forest Service, where it was announced that they would no longer be allowed to graze their goats and sheep in the uplands above Córdova. "They allowed us to graze a few head of cattle on the forest," it is said, "but it was the goats and the sheep that sustained the people." The Córdovans continued to plant their fields, but the produce of these small fields had never been sufficient to sustain the population. Limited arable land and a semiarid environment necessitated a complex and multifaceted mode of subsistence; goats and sheep played an important role in this balance. (See chapter 3 in this volume by Van Ness.)

The demise of the pastoral component of the economy also undermined agricultural production in another way. The elders often note that the land became less fertile at about this time. The situation is related to the breakdown of cooperative labor patterns that resulted from the need to leave the community in search of a job. It also reflects the breakdown of the cycle of feast days and other rituals which solicited the help of God and the saints in the process of securing a livelihood. Saint Isidore's image, for example, was no longer taken out to bless the fields. The elders have also put their fingers on an important ecological process as well—the loss of the herds left the farmers without a source of fertilizer. The U.S. government denied a valid land claim and restricted access to traditional community lands. The result was a deathblow to the villagers' way of life.

The men found it necessary to travel to other states to obtain jobs; such employment included *el traque* (section gangs), *las papas* (potato picking) and other farmwork, *la borrega* (sheepherding), and *las minas* (mines and smelters). These jobs took them to Colorado, Utah, Wyoming, and elsewhere. They would often plant their fields before they left and return home for the harvest; the remainder of the work fell on the shoulders of those who were left behind.

Pero, cuando vino la Depresión, se acabó todo eso (but when the Depression came, all of this came to an end). President Franklin D. Roosevelt is regarded as a culture hero: "I hope that President Roosevelt is in heaven, because if it hadn't been for him, all of the people [meaning Mexicanos] would have starved." The Depression years are remembered as having been "very, very hard on the people." Relief was provided by jobs *en La Loma* (on the hill), meaning Los Alamos. In turning to daily wage labor, however, the young turned away from the land. The displacement of the subsistence economy, the prevalence of wage labor, commercialization and a large influx of Anglo-Americans into the region have wrought deep changes in the fabric of communities such as Córdova. As the elders put it, *ya se acabó todo* (everything has ended).

Archival Evidence on Córdova and the Pueblo Quemado Grant

As I noted above, oral historians hardly recommend that oral sources be used exclusively, at least when other types of documentation exist. Fortunately, a number of repositories contain information on Córdova. The Spanish, Mexican, and U.S. territorial archives of New Mexico provide a wide range of civil records bearing on population, landownership, defense, civil and criminal cases, trade, and many other topics. The Archives of the Archiocese of Santa Fe lists baptisms, marriages, and burials, in addition to such documents as licenses for churches, lists of tithes given, censuses, and visitations by ecclesiastical officials. The Córdova Family Papers contain records of land transfers, wills, etc., mainly from the nineteenth century, for this local family. The records of the surveyors general of New Mexico and the Court of Private Land Claims provide essential information on the Pueblo Quemado grant and surrounding grants and how they fared in the United States legal system. All of these sources are available in the State Records Center and Archives, Santa Fe.

More land grant material is available in the Catron, Reeve, and other papers in the Special Collections of the University of New Mexico's General Library (Albuquerque). The County Clerk's Office in the famed County Courthouse of Rio Arriba County in Tierra Amarilla[27] has virtually untapped records of wills, land transfers, and other legal records. A number of public and private institutions house specialized archives which contain information on Córdova. The U.S. Forest Service, for example, houses records in Española, Santa Fe, Albuquerque, and Washington, D.C., which pertain to the grazing of livestock on forest lands. It is fortunate that such a wealth of archival sources exists for studying the history of Córdova. As was the case with the oral historical evidence, however, the abundance of material forces me to confine my discussion to key documents.

Initial Settlement, Circa 1730–1830

Unfortunately, the documents that record the exact date of the community's settlement have not come to light. The Pueblo Quemado is mentioned as constituting the northern boundary of the Santo Domingo de Cundiyo grant in 1743.[28] A grant of land in the Cundiyo area in 1725 (later revoked) does not refer to Córdova, suggesting that settlement probably took place between 1725 and 1743.[29] The absence of the settlers' original petition for the Pueblo Quemado grant, the alcalde's endorsement, the governor's reply, and the alcalde's report on his placement of the settlers in possession of the land has greatly hampered Córdovans' attempts to document their land rights (see below).

Córdova and similar outlying communities were settled as buffers against incursions by nomadic tribes. Native Americans did not normally greet this expansionism passively, however, and they launched numerous attempts to push back the Hispanos and their allies. A document dated 1748 requests permission for the residents of three villages, including Pueblo Quemado,[30] to withdraw into "more populated areas in which most of the petitioners have houses and land." The residents of Pueblo Quemado petitioned the governor again the following year. The petition notes that the settlers were then living in neighboring Chimayo. They recount their flight from Pueblo Quemado, where they had resided previously for "many years," noting that the governor had granted them permission to flee the settlment. In view of a shortage of land and water in Chimayo, they request permission

> to go to and plant our fields, such that only the men and the older boys would ascend all together and collectively [*todos juntos y en común*], some to do the planting and those who are not involved in cultivation to watch from the peaks.

The signatures on this document provide the first listing of the citizens of Pueblo Quemado. In granting the petition, Governor Codallo y Rabal admonishes them to proceed *bien unidos y armados* (well united and armed).

These documents on the community's early history are supplemented by land conveyances and similar records. The land conveyances show that plots of land around the settlement and in the Quemado valley below it were privately owned as early as 1746.[31] They were often laid out in terms of the number of varas (one vara is approximately thirty-three inches) of river or ditch frontage. Nevertheless, maintaining these land rights was contingent upon cultivating the land; abandoned fields were subject to redistribution. By the late eighteenth century, Córdovans had expanded their holdings to include dry farms in the uplands above the community. For example, a 1790 transfer relates to a dwelling and a rancho located "in the place which is called La Jolla [The Jewel] on the Rio en Medio."[32]

The community was described in the following way by Fray Francisco Atanasio Domínguez during his visitation of the missions of New Mexico in 1776:[33]

> Quemado, a league above Chimayo and in the same direction, is about three leagues from the aforesaid villa [Santa Cruz de la Cañada]. This large settlement is so near the foot of the Sierra Madre that it lies in one of its cañadas. This runs about half a league from north to south, and its width offers very good level sites of farmland. These are planted on either side of a pretty good river with a rapid current and very clear, delicious water that runs from north to south until it joins the one that flows to La Cañada in an appropriate place. The settlers of Quemado use its river for irrigation and harvest well and abundantly from their good lands. There is no fruit. The fish in the river, small trout.

Domínguez reported that Quemado's population included 52 families and a total of 220 inhabitants.[34] He also noted that the community lacked a church at that time. In 1832, however, the residents promised to construct a public chapel dedicated to their patron, Saint Anthony. Bishop Zubiria of Durango confirmed the licensing on 17 April of that year, and the chapel was probably completed shortly thereafter.[35]

The Rise of Pedro Córdova, 1830–1858

Pablo Córdova, one of the petitioners of 1749, baptized a son, Santiago Celedonio Córdova, on 12 December 1756.[36] Celedón married Juliana Martín on 18 November 1783.[37] Córdova and Martín were solid, if not extraordinarily wealthy, citizens of the day. Pedro Córdova was their son. Since an ecclesiastical census of 1822 lists his age as twenty-eight,[38] Pedro Córdova must have been born in 1794. He married Ramona Mondragón, also a native of Córdova, in 1817, and they had ten children.[39]

Pedro Córdova did not possess great wealth or exercise a high degree of influence in the area prior to the 1830s. He was listed as a member of the local militia in 1806. He lacked a firearm, lance, and even a horse, his equipment being limited to a bow and twenty-five arrows.[40] The situation had changed drastically, however, by 1838. Córdova received permits in 1838, 1844, and 1845, for transporting goods to and from provinces to the south, including Chihuahua, Durango, Zacatecas, and Lagos. He took eight to ten wagons out of New Mexico, and these were loaded primarily with wool and woven goods, such as blankets, serapes, pants, linen, and cloth.[41] Although such an inventory was not unusual for traders of the time, it certainly indicates that Córdova was much better off than his neighbors.

By far the most fascinating documents pertaining to Pedro Córdova are the papers relating to his estate.[42] There is no will, but the administrators of his estate compiled a detailed inventory of his "goods, furniture, property, and money" following his death in 1858. Córdova's agricultural holdings were simply phenomenal. He owned 1,948 varas of land in Córdova. Given the fact that less land had been cleared and cultivated than at present, this constituted more than half of the available agricultural land. Córdova also owned 1,296 varas in Las Truchas (see Map 1), 700 varas on the *llano* (plain) east of Córdova, 250 varas on the Río de en Medio, 475 in Cundiyo, 503 in Chimayo, and 308 in the region's administrative center, Santa Cruz de la Cañada. In addition, the house in which Córdova lived with his wife and four of his children had thirteen rooms; this is quite a large house for the time. He also owned another house in Córdova, seven houses in Truchas, one on the Río de en Medio, two in Cundiyo, and one in Chimayo.

Córdova also possessed many other goods, such as firearms, images of the saints, a mill, and a *mielero* used for making molasses, that must have served as community resources. A large percentage of his other goods were similarly loaned out to Córdovans and others, although it is unlikely that any fee was charged for this use. Pedro Córdova's storehouses contained 100 sacks of corn, 150 fanegas of wheat, and 8 fanegas of peas. (A *fanega* measured between 1.5 and 2.5 bushels, depending upon the locality.)[43] A total of 57 persons owed Córdova 158 fanegas and 16 *almores* (double handfuls) of wheat, 10 fanegas of corn, and 80.5 fanegas and 40 almores of grain, probably also wheat, valued at $278.25. Córdova's livestock holdings boasted 40 teams of oxen, 29 head of cattle, 20 mules and donkeys, 7 horses, 80 goats, and 6 pigs; these were valued at $1,506. The debts owed to Córdova in livestock totaled $872, and these included 322 goats, 37 head of cattle, 5 mules and donkeys, and 3 horses.

By far the largest percentage of Córdova's wealth, 35.27 percent, took the form of debts owed the estate by 103 persons. The amounts ranged from as little as $1.50 to $534, the average debt being $31.65. These entries are followed by a category for "money which the *peones* must pay with their service or labor to the estate." The five *peones,* all adult males, owed between $37 and $121.

A sense of the magnitude of Córdova's holdings relative to those of his contemporaries can be gained through comparison with other estates. Since very few residents of Córdova or other communities recorded wills or had estate papers filed after their deaths, it seems safe to assume that such persons were among the wealthier inhabitants. José Antonio Córdova, a resident of neighboring Truchas, died intestate in 1853, leaving $375.50 in possessions.[44] Hilario Trujillo died in the San Buenaventura plaza of Chimayo in 1860, leaving an estate valued at $263.20.[45] Perhaps the best comparison can be made with José Antonio Vigil in neighboring Cundiyo. Vigil, who was famous throughout the area for his cunning as a soldier,[46] amassed most of the property in Cundiyo. At the time of his death in 1861, Vigil's landholdings consisted of 979 varas of land in Cundiyo, a five-room house, and eighty-eight fruit trees, and his estate was valued at $1,682.63.[47] Although Vigil was hardly a pauper, his wealth did not begin to compare to Córdova's 5,480 varas of land in six communities and thirteen houses in an estate valued at $9,243.88. In local terms, Pedro Córdova was indeed "like a king."

Turn-of-the-Century Córdova

Records for the years following Pedro Córdova's death suggest that a few individuals, such as his son, Antonio Guadalupe, possessed greater wealth and influence than other Córdovans. No one, however, ever assumed a position which rivaled that of Pedro Córdova. Documents from the last half of the nineteenth century also point to a gradual increase in the size of the population, which reached 246 in 1900.[48] Archival sources for this era similarly reveal two trends in the region that would have a profound impact on the community.

First, after Native American resistance was quelled, the population, particularly its Anglo-American component, rose substantially. New Mexico also became linked by rail to major markets to the east and west in 1878–1880. These factors fostered a growing commercialization of production in the area. Commercialization contributed to a growing displacement of handicraft production by mass-produced goods throughout the region, including Mexicano villages. As both the demand for consumer goods and their availability increased, small mercantile stores sprang up nearly everywhere.

Within the community, Calletano Córdova ran both a general merchandise store and a bar in Córdova in 1885–1886.[49] Matías Córdova operated both a bar and store from 1891 through at least 1895.[50] Matías was the oldest son of Pedro Córdova's most financially successful offspring, Antonio Guadalupe. The latter served as one of the administrators for the estates of his father, his mother, and José Antonio Vigil of Cundiyo, among others. He also acted as a local justice of the peace, the alcalde, and a member of the Rio Arriba County Grand Jury.[51] Antonio Guadalupe was literate, and he emphasized the importance of education for his children. Matías also drew on these skills in operating the bar and store, in securing the position of the first postmaster in the community in 1900, and as a schoolteacher, a justice of the peace, and a probate judge for Rio Arriba County.[52]

These facts point to an increasing level of contact between Córdovans and Anglo-Americans in the economic and political realms. This intercourse was fostered by a few individuals, such as Antonio Guadalupe Córdova and his son Matías, who were particularly adept in gaining the skills needed to succeed in the new political-economic order. The tradition was carried on in this century by Matías's son Emilio.

Other Córdovans used a different strategy in adapting to the commercial economy. Sheep had always been kept by Córdovans, although their role in subsistence was secondary to that of goats. The availability of livestock breeds more suited to commercial ranching and transport to eastern and midwestern markets by rail expanded the commercial potential of sheep ranching. One Córdovan amassed a substantial herd of his own. Five other ranchers rented sheep *al partido* (on shares) from Frank Bond of the G. W. Bond and Bro. and Bond & Nohl Companies in Española.[53] The appeal of this contractual arrangement was the possibility of using the wool to pay the rental on the sheep, to pay one's bill at the Bond store, and perhaps retain a modest cash profit, while retaining the lambs for consumption.

Sheep contracts and other materials in the Bond Papers[54] indicate that this system provided Bond with a great deal of control over the Mexicano ranchers' operations. Other sources document the economic precariousness of the sheep industry, particularly when sheep were rented on shares.[55] Bond noted in 1915 that two pounds of wool per sheep per year was "no rent at all," and he changed the fee to twenty (and later twenty-two) lambs per one hundred ewes per year.[56] This brought to an end the ranchers' ability to participate simultaneously in two economic systems—raising lambs for subsistence and wool for profit.

The demise of the Córdovan sheep ranching industry was also caused by a much more devastating event—the loss of free access to the uplands above the community. Here the vast array of documents pertaining to Córdova were of little assistance in obtaining legal title to the lands that, along with the irrigated plots, had formed the backbone of the residents' subsistence. No petition for confirmation of the Pueblo Quemado grant was ever filed with the Office of the Surveyor General of New Mexico. Since the Córdovans' access to the uplands between the community and the Truchas Peaks was recognized by the residents of the surrounding villages and had never been challenged, they were quite unlikely to have known that legal action might be necessary to prevent expropriation.

The notorious Thomas Benton Catron and his partner Charles Coons petitioned the Court of Private Land Claims for confirmation of the grant in 1893. Unfortunately, the community could not produce papers relating to the settlers' original petition, the governor's approval and the alcalde's approval. Although grants with even poorer documentation had been confirmed, the court rejected the petition in 1893, and Catron and Coons did not contest the decision or pursue the case.[57] The Quemado valley, including the house and garden plots and the nearby fields, were then included in the survey of the adjoining Nuestra Señora del Rosario, San Fernando y Santiago grant in 1895.[58] Córdovans thus gained title to these lands as claimants under the latter grant, and no efforts were made to deny them their rights to valley lands or homesites.

Such was not the case, unfortunately, with respect to the uplands. Córdovans, along with the residents of neighboring communities, had always depended on the area between the village (at 6,900 feet of elevation) and the Truchas Peaks (13,102 feet) for firewood, timber, hunting, and fishing grounds. Produce from the small farm plots in the valley had never sufficed to feed the entire population; goats and sheep had always formed a vital part of community subsistence. The uplands also provided the only lands available to Córdovans for summer sheep grazing. This area became part of the Pecos River Forest Reserve on 11 January 1892.[59] Although some grazing restrictions were imposed, enforcement was initially nonexistent, and Córdovans were not even aware of changes in administrative jurisdiction and regulatory policy.

Once the uplands were incorporated into the newly created Santa Fe National Forest in 1915, however, a series of changes in grazing regulations severely restricted the local Mexicanos' access to this area.[60] These restrictions eventually deprived Córdovans of nearly all of the subsistence that they had derived from raising goats and sheep. Residents were thus forced to find work in the railroad and sheep camps, the mines, and the farms of New Mexico, Colorado, Utah, Wyoming, Montana, and elsewhere in order to survive.

Comparing the Oral and Archival Accounts

An initial, striking observation about the oral historical and archival sources on Córdova is that *there are remarkably few discrepancies of fact between the two sources of evidence.* Only a handful of discrepancies emerged in the course of years of archival and oral historical research. One elder contended, for instance, that Pedro Córdova was "from the outside," i.e., not born in Córdova or the surrounding communities. Other oral accounts did not support this contention.

Some apparent discrepancies are more complex. A number of elders claimed that *antes, todo estaba libre.* This notion of openness was extended to the irrigated fields in the Quemado valley, suggesting that they were not privately owned prior to this century. Documents from as early as the mid-eighteenth century indicate that private ownership was common. Underlying this seeming contradiction is a complex system of land tenure. (See chapter 3 by Van Ness.) The documents themselves suggest that individuals might have lost rights to their fields if they failed to cultivate them.[61] Similarly, private ownership applied only between the spring plowing and the fall harvest. The few existing fences had to be removed once the crops were in, and the fields became a collective livestock pasture until spring.

Statements such as *antes, todo estaba libre* thus sought to contrast the fee-simple tenure system with the complex system of land tenure, particularly its collective forms, of the past. In sum, apparent inconsistencies or discrepancies often disappear in the face of a more adequate understanding of their historical and cultural context, and of the speaker's intended meaning.

Having made a case for the compatibility of oral historical and archival materials, I actually see the two as quite different and as requiring different modes of interpretation. Even though their historical content may be analogous, they are put together for different reasons and in different ways. These points of divergence are most apparent with respect to the emphases given by the two kinds of sources and the style in which the historical information is conveyed. The point is that the interpretation of oral history and its comparison with archival sources can result in gross distortion if these two types of differences are not borne in mind.

Structure and Meaning in Written Documents

A fundamental contrast between written documents and oral historical accounts is that the former focus on the *details* with respect to the official (governmental or ecclesiastical) status of events, whereas the latter are concerned with the *meaning* of these events for the participants and the present generation. With regard to the documents, their orientation is expressed in a simultaneous concern with two facets of what has happened or is happening. First, the document must record the civil or ecclesiastical categories of persons and the types of formal transactions used to legitimize the event. Since only certain officials could legally authorize a wedding or the establishment of a new community, the document has to demonstrate that the appropriate officials were present. A great deal can hang on whether the event in question was a burial or a baptism or the donation, sale, exchange, or theft of a plot of land. Second, officials, the participants, and their descendants will want to know exactly *who* got married or gained a plot of land and, in the latter case, how much land was involved and where it is located. In subsequent years, such facts as precisely when, where, and how the event took place and who witnessed it may determine the outcome of trials or inquiries that draw on the document as evidence.

For example, a common type of document pertaining to Córdova during the Spanish and subsequent periods was the land conveyance. The structure and content of these papers followed a standardized format. The place and the date of execution were generally presented first. This information was followed by the name, title, and jurisdiction of the presiding official and the names of the parties who appeared before him. Next came a description of the object of the transaction, including a statement of the type of property conveyed (e.g., two parcels of land, a farm-ranch, or a piece of land with a house), the price paid, the size of the property, its boundaries, and generally a statement to the effect that all rights of entrance and exit were simultaneously transferred. These facts were followed by the seller's assurance that the goods received constitute a fair price, and that neither the seller nor any of the seller's heirs will ever make adverse claim.

Documents generally concluded with a statement by the local *teniente alcalde* or other official which restated his name and title and asserted that the necessary legal procedures had been met in the execution of the papers. Two *testigos de asistencia* (witnesses in attendance) were listed, followed by the signatures or rubrics of the official, the witnesses, and, in most cases, the seller(s). One of the witnesses generally signed on behalf of those who could not do so for themselves.

Such documents focus on the transactions themselves or, more precisely, the way these transactions relate to officially accepted categories of legal procedure. They are largely unconcerned with the motives behind such events. One cannot learn from the documents whether love, greed, or necessity lay behind the marriage, or poverty behind the land sale. The documents are even less concerned with the meaning that these transactions will hold henceforth for the participants and their descendants. Obviously, the documents are written at a given time, and they are not meant to be updated.

This characteristic of the archival record is frequently cited by opponents of oral history as evidence of the greater reliability of written sources. True, this does make documents better guides *in general* to the details of past events. (Many examples could be offered, however, in which oral testimony has revealed that crucial information has been falsified or entirely left out of written documents.) Nevertheless, history, particularly social history, does not deal with behavioral detail alone. As White and others have shown,[62] even those who profess interest exclusively in the concrete details of events must deal (if covertly) with questions of meaning and motives as well.

Such issues are precisely the purview of oral history. It is thus a particularly good source of information on the dimensions of events that are not recorded in written documents. Oral history frequently treats events, processes, and ideas that are not directly related to civil or ecclesiastical procedures; the basis of selection is rather continuing relevance of the past for the present. Otherwise, given the limitations of human memory, the carriers of oral tradition would not continue to remember and recount them. This is especially the case with what Vansina refers to as "oral traditions,"[63] accounts of past events that were handed down in traditional form to the narrator, rather than eyewitness accounts. Oral traditions are recounted because they continue to be of interest to the community or society, not to one individual or family alone. This is not to say that written documents have no relevance for the present or that researchers who work with archival sources are not concerned with questions of meaning. Social historians focus on precisely such issues. The point is rather that civil and ecclesiastical documents on the one hand and oral historical discourse on the other are oriented toward contrastive communicative goals.

Mucho más antes

These divergent foci of interest and ways of presenting oral and written historical content produce complementary accounts of the same events. With regard to the initial century of Córdova's history, documents such as those of 1748 and 1749 provide us with a good record of when the community was founded, even if the exact date of initial settlement has not come to light. The documentary record establishes the number of settlers and their names, along with the fact that they owned land in the neighboring settlement of Chimayo. The petition of 1749 provides a glimpse of the collective character of the community and its division of labor.

Oral accounts, on the other hand, are mute on such details. Dates are, in fact, not part of the oral historical record. Córdovans do not organize their historical discourse chronologically, punctuating it by years, decades, and centuries. Rather it is grouped into three periods: (1) *Antes* (bygone days) is used in a general sense to refer to the community's pre-1916 past as a whole and, in a more specific sense, to refer to the era of the present elders' grandparents, roughly 1880–1920; (2) *Más antes* (earlier bygone days) is the time of the elders' grandparents' grandparents, and is most closely associated with the "reign" of Pedro Córdova, extending from about 1830 to 1880; and (3) *Mucho más antes* (much earlier in bygone days), on the other hand, lacks a specific generational referent. It is identified with the initial era of the settlement's history, roughly 1730 to 1830.

Grasping the place of a given event within one of these historical periods is the focus of oral history. Trying to elicit specific dates in the course of oral historical discussions is inappropriate, because it misconstrues what "the talk of bygone days" is all about. Such a request is likely to force an elder to guess at a date or plead ignorance. Mexicanos obviously can think in terms of chronology, and accounts of events that occurred in this century are peppered with exact dates. This, however, is simply not the way that oral history is structured.

The oral record's strength lies rather in interpreting the *character* of life in the past. For example, in discussing *mucho más antes,* the elders expand the principle of working collectively and sharing the labor into a vivid sketch of economic and social relations. They talk about how the people worked the land and prepared the harvest prior to the advent of gristmills or before horse-drawn wagons were common. The construction of the homes, the plaza, the *puertas de la plaza,* are all recounted in terms of their contribution to the defensive posture of the community. The elders will, for instance, describe in detail the two guard towers; these do not appear in the documents or photographs relating to the community. The elders also recount the manner in which the early Córdovans defended themselves against the Navajos, Utes, and Comanches.

Más antes

During the *más antes* period, the documents date Pedro Córdova's rise to power. They provide details regarding his ancestors and descendants. The written records enable the historian to compare the extent of Córdova's wealth to that of ricos in neighboring communities. The detailed inventory of his estate not only reveals what and how much he owned, but it also provides a good inventory of the material culture of a Mexicano village of the mid-nineteenth century. Dates are absent in the oral record; neither does it provide a record of Córdova's ancestors, and it yields only the broadest of comparisons between Córdova's wealth and that of other ricos.

Oral testimony, in contrast, provides a great deal of information on the organization of Córdova's household, and the way he ran his agricultural and pastoral production. The relations that Pedro and Ramona enjoyed with their fellow Córdovans are treated in some depth, and the special relationship which Pedro Córdova enjoyed vis-à-vis visiting dignitaries is neatly captured.[64] The oral record provides a glimpse of the cultural values underlying this pattern, a topic not easily researched in the archives. Oral history also includes detailed sketches of a number of important events, such as Pedro and Ramona's sponsorship of the casting and christening of the bell (which still hangs in the local chapel), and of the circumstances surrounding Pedro's death, circumstances that left little documentary trail.

Antes

Both archival and oral sources are plentiful for the *antes* period. Documents point to the rising importance of commercial sheep ranching and the other ways in which mercantile capitalism was incorporated into village life (e.g., stores and bars). Written sources treating New Mexican and wider economic patterns and the Bond sheep operations assist the researcher in understanding the broader social and economic forces that shaped these events. With regard to the Pueblo Quemado grant, the documents reveal the legal procedures that led to the rejection of the Córdovans' claim, the Forest Service policies that restricted access to the uplands, and the types of employment sought by the men to cope with the resulting economic disaster.

From the perspective of the documentary record, the rise and fall of commercial sheep ranching had few lasting effects on the community. The oral record reveals, however, that the industry's impact on social relations and cultural values was profound. Participation in the commercial sheep ranching industry constituted the Córdovans' first step in learning capitalist economics.[65] With respect to land tenure, legal actions that took place outside the community are not described in the oral record. What is available is in-depth information on who planted what crops in which areas, where the grazing and firewood lands lay, what landmarks provided boundaries between the commons of neighboring communities, and so forth. These facts are, of course, of tremendous importance for the documentation of custom and usage; accordingly, they constitute an important source of evidence for litigating land claims. Oral history also reveals how Córdovans first sensed that they had lost control over the commons and the way they reacted to the grazing restrictions.

Mexicano Oral History: La Platica de los Viejitos de Antes

I have argued that both archival and oral historical sources constitute valid and complementary sources of historical information, provided that their respective strengths and weaknesses are recognized. This contention has been supported by pointing out contrasts in historical content. Another crucial distinction between oral and documentary sources lies in the realm of form, or how the facts are conveyed in the two kinds of sources. Unfortunately, most writers who use oral historical information are unaware of how critical it is to take both the form and context of oral historical data into account in interpreting its historical significance.

Historians are quick to take the neophyte to task for a naive reading of the archival evidence. Researchers must learn techniques for interpreting written sources as well as a host of details regarding the period in question (paleography, categories of officials, official actions, documents, and administrative districts, to name a few) if they are to avoid misinterpretation and to learn as much as possible from each document. Unfortunately, few professional or lay historians realize that using oral history involves mastering a similarly complex, if quite different, set of skills for collecting and interpreting testimony. It is particularly important to understand the communicative and social patterns that shape oral historical discourse and inform its interpretation. What, in the Mexicano case, must one know to avoid distorting the meaning of oral historical evidence?

Settings for Discussions of "Bygone Days"

Los ancianos or *los viejitos,* women and men of about seventy years of age and over, are the legitimate carriers of traditional knowledge in Mexicano society. The oldest members of the community have the right and the duty to preserve and transmit "the talk of the elders of bygone days," and they are the only individuals who can draw freely on proverbs, scriptural allusions, jokes, oral history, and numerous types of narratives in doing so. Exhibiting respect for one's elders is a central cultural value, and conversation is one of the main contexts in which this ideal is realized. A respectful younger speaker will always yield the floor to an older person, will never contradict his or her senior, and will not become angry if contradicted by an elder. The elders thus do much of the talking, especially when two or more of them are present.

"The talk of the elders of bygone days" emerges in three principal social situations. First, elders who are highly skilled in performing these traditions enter into exchanges of oral historical vignettes, proverbs, and anecdotes. These are true virtuoso performances. The elderly participants are experts in presenting these forms of speech; the young and inexperienced may listen, but they keep their distance. The talk is presented in an abbreviated fashion with subtle, implicit allusions. These rhetorical duels are reminiscent of the highly elaborate competitions that took place between troubadours in the nineteenth century.

A second context consists of informal discussions of the past among individuals who are roughly thirty to sixty years of age. The subject is generally the more recent past; the historical content is presented as the personal recollection of the speaker (e.g., *yo no tenía más que como diez años cuando* ["I was only about ten years old when"]). Such exchanges of stories are viewed as recreational, rather than competitive or pedagogical.

The third and most common setting for such presentations is pedagogical discourse. Here an elder or elders engage one or more younger persons in a dialogue about the past. The object is to inculcate the basic moral values that underlie the actions of "the elders of bygone days" in their descendants to such a degree that these values come to be reflected in the thought and actions of succeeding generations.

Three moral themes predominate. First, selfish or egoistic behavior should give way to actions that are in accordance with the needs of the group as a whole. The second is the principle of religiosity, which also fosters the suppression of individualistic desires by promoting dedication to God's will. Finally, it is important to be knowledgeable about the natural environment and to provide for one's needs, if possible, by working the land.

Common settings for pedagogical discussions are informal gatherings in living rooms or kitchens; elders also frequently launch into pedagogical discourse when passing a notable local landmark during a walk or a trip into town. These conversations are generally initiated by the elder, although younger persons' questions regarding some facet of the past can serve as an entrée into a lengthy exposition. Elders have much more control over what will be discussed and how the conversation will proceed. Nevertheless, pedagogical discourse revolves around dialogue. The elders often check to see if the meaning of what they have said is clear by ending a statement with *¿ves?* (you see?), *¿sabes cómo te digo?* (do you know what I'm telling you?), or *¿verdad?* (right?). Similarly, the "student" is free to ask the elder to repeat or elaborate on what has been said. Younger persons use questions (e.g., *¿verdad?* or *¿sí?* [really?]) or such exclamations as *sí* (yes) and um hum to signal comprehension of the "lesson."

The Structure of "Talk About the Past"

The manner in which "the talk of the elders of bygone days" is presented reflects the manner in which rhetorical skill is evaluated in Mexicano society. This process is neatly encapsulated in the phrase *traer el sentido* (to convey the sense or meaning). Skill in getting the meaning across involves two complex sets of subskills.

First, the best pedagogues can draw upon a wide range of spoken and musical genres. In presenting oral traditions, accuracy, breadth of knowledge, and the ability to recount interesting details are esteemed. The critical skill is the ability to draw upon "the talk of the elders of bygone days" to find the oral historical vignette or other form that best applies to the situation at hand. The object is to convey the manner in which this body of traditional wisdom illuminates the problems of contemporary society. This involves finding a speech form to match the social context and the predominant topic of the conversation.

A second factor entails the development of a heightened pragmatic sense. Having selected just the right story or proverb, the pedagogue will shape the way it is spoken to fit the current social interaction. The text can be highly abbreviated or greatly elaborated; similarly, information to assist listeners in comprehending the meaning—background material, illustrative examples, and the application to the current circumstances—can either be explained or left implicit. The basic rule is to state overtly only what you think your listeners do not know;

restating the obvious constitutes an insult to the rhetorical competence of the audience. The best performances are accomplished without faltering and are accompanied by appropriate gesticulation, body movement, facial expressions, and verbal style. A good speaker thus makes the listeners aware, explicitly or implicitly, of the relevance of the remarks to the present situation. Such individuals subtly manipulate both linguistic forms and aspects of the social situation to lend compelling force to their words.

The notion of *traer el sentido* succinctly points to the dual nature of Mexicano oral history. The elders' words provide compelling portraits of the persons, places, and events of the past and of the values that underlie them. Teaching "the talk of the elders of bygone days" also demonstrates the meaning that the past holds for the current generation. Linking one's words to the current situation renders them perceptive readings of particular social interactions. Oral history thus stands with one foot in a people's past and the other in its most immediate present. Each recounting of a traditional genre links these two domains. Mexicano oral history is thus inconsistent by nature, since elders must vary the form and content of traditions if they are to present them effectively.

¿Lo Agarraste? *On Becoming a Good Listener*

This portrait of oral history raises anew the troublesome question of the historical validity of oral sources. "This is all very well and good," the critics may argue, "but I am not interested in the way oral history is presented or its meaning for present generations. All I really want to know is what happened in the past." Does this juxtaposition of past and present render oral history an unreliable source of historical information?

It is indeed possible to examine oral historical testimony for its historical content, i.e., to isolate the "facts" from the influence of the situation in which they were presented. This can only be done, however, by a close examination of the social interaction itself. The point is that the meaning of the words themselves are affected by the components of, as linguists call it, the *speech event*. To cite simple examples, the words "what a beautiful day!" are not meant to be taken at face value if it is raining outside. Similarly, an upward turn of the eyes or a facetious tone of voice can indicate that an expression such as "John is *so* intelligent" is not to be interpreted literally. The processes are much more subtle when it comes to oral history. The fact remains, however, that the meaning of any one component of a speech event depends on the way it relates to the other components.

A Model of the Oral Historical Interview

Fortunately, sorting out the relationship between the various components of a speech event is not as daunting a task as it may first appear. It requires only a good idea as to what is transpiring in a given conversation and a means of making sense of it. A simple model of communication can assist the researcher in deciphering the meaning of oral historical testimony.[66] The discussion which follows is not intended as an exhaustive statement of what can happen in such an interview; it is presented to aid the reader in identifying the central components of oral historical discourse and in understanding the role of each component in determining the meaning of what is said. (The model is represented in Figure 4.1.)

First, oral testimony is presented by someone to someone else. Given the central role of the elders in preserving and presenting Mexicano oral history, the primary participants in such an encounter have been labeled *elder(s)* and *oral historian*. The identity of these parties shapes what is said. Elders differ significantly in how much of "the talk of the elders of bygone days" they have mastered and in the skill with which they present it. Similarly, not everyone is equally interested in every topic, so some elders concentrate, for example, on the early eras of their community's history, while others concentrate on the turn of the century.

The identity of the oral historian is crucial as well. A native of the community will obtain a different range of material than a person who has just entered from the outside, especially if the outsider is an Anglo-American. The oral historian's fluency in New Mexican Spanish and in Mexicano culture will have a profound impact on what she or he collects. This is not to say that Anglo-Americans who speak another dialect of Spanish will be unable to obtain worthwhile testimony. They will, however, have to take into account the manner in which their background affects the nature of the material that they collect. The point is that the outsider's participation in and interpretation of the

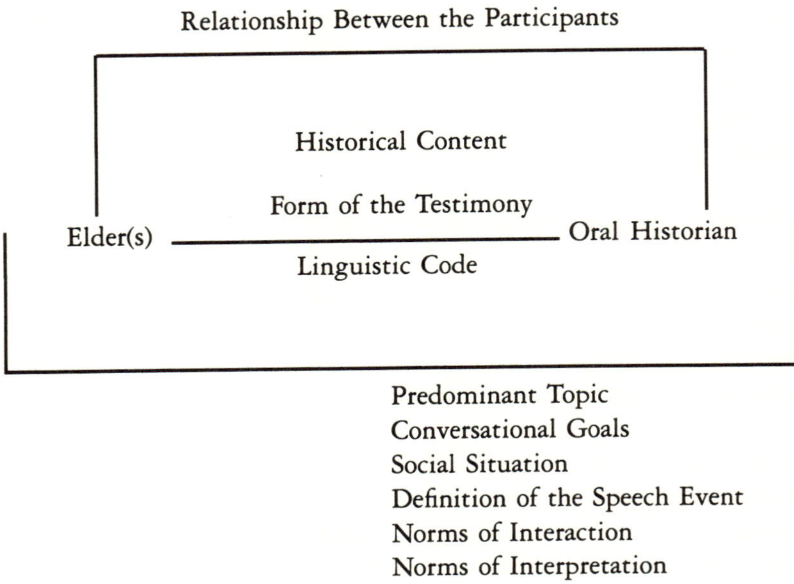

FIGURE 4.1. Speech Event Model of the Oral History Interview.

dialogue is not informed by an insider's understanding of the language and culture. The *relationship between the participants* will also affect the character and content of the dialogue. The tenor of the discussion is likely to be quite different in cases where interviewer and interviewee are strangers, as opposed to situations in which they are relatives or close friends.

Four components of the discourse are particularly pertinent. The *historical content* corresponds to the historical information conveyed by the words in their common usage. The *form of the testimony* also has an important bearing on the meaning of what is said. A passage may be framed as a direct quote from "the elders of bygone days" or as a reflection of the direct experience of the elder. The same historical content can be conveyed in ordinary language or as a proverb, a scriptural allusion, or a narrative. The manner in which the material is conveyed provides crucial clues as to the elder's sense of the way it should be interpreted, i.e., as literally true, possibly true, or representing the general sense of a situation but not its details.

The oral historian will also want to note the way a given statement relates to the *predominant topic* of that section of the conversation. Does the material form the focus of the dialogue at that point, or is it used to comment on a broader subject? As I have noted elsewhere, it is sometimes difficult to identify the broader topic to which individual statements relate, and this can lead to misunderstanding among the participants.[67]

Considerations of the *linguistic code* pertain initially to the language in which the oral history is collected. Testimony given in English will hardly be equivalent to that which would have been given in Spanish, and the use of a translator (e.g., in courtroom proceedings) raises special difficulties. (This paper assumes that both the elder[s] and the oral historian are fluent in Spanish.) If the oral historian uses standard rather than New Mexican Spanish, this will also affect what is said. Practitioners should be sensitive to the possibility that a given word or phrase may bear a special association in a particular community or when used in "the talk of the elders of bygone days."

Conversational goals present a particular problem in collecting oral history. This factor is especially critical when the oral historian's and the other participants' reasons for entering into the dialogue are different. Given the discrepancy between the roles of interviewee and interviewer, this gap will always be present to some degree. If the researcher is not aware of this issue, she or he will overlook a crucial feature of the manner in which the elder is connecting the past with the conversational context; the lack of awareness is likely to lead to misunderstanding with respect to the meaning of what is said. Researchers would benefit from keeping this in mind during interviews. I have found that my attempts to collect oral history have met with the least success when I failed to realize that the elder(s) and I had very different goals for the conversation. My questions seemed irrelevant to them, and their responses did not address the topics I had in mind. Given the importance of respect and the need for sensitivity, two factors inherent in the interview situation, the burden of accommodation lies much more heavily on the side of the "pupil."

The *social situation* of a conversation consists of the aspects of time, place, participants, and predominant activity associated with the interaction. A question may elicit quite different responses when it is posed during the course of a walk through the community, a town meeting, or in the elder's living room. The form and content of oral historical testimony given in court contrasts markedly with that given in the elder's own home. The presence of other participants, such as other elders or the speaker's grandchildren, also has an important influence. Historical vignettes are sometimes presented in response to news reports on the local Spanish-language radio station or to the behavior of a recalcitrant youth. The connection between the two is, however, frequently implicit; the oral historian will thus need to decipher such associations in order to make sense of the historical information which they occasion.

The nature of the verbal exchange in which the oral history is collected is the *definition of the speech event.* This factor is important for two reasons. The same social situation generally includes a variety of speech events. In some types of speech events, such as pedagogical discussions, the oral historical material may occupy center stage. Historical vignettes also appear, however, in such contexts as political debates, analyses of contemporary events, and warning of impending danger; here their role is likely to be less focal. References to the past are also incorporated into performances of jokes, proverbs, and legends. The verbal context will determine in large measure the importance the elder attaches to the historical information. Second, participants are not always in agreement as to what kind of event is taking place. This is often the case in interviews. While the oral historian may view the conversation as a means of recording historical content, the elder may view it as pedagogy or entertainment.

All of the above components, the identity of the elder and oral historian, their relationship and their respective conversational goals, the form and the historical content of the testimony, its predominant topic and linguistic code, the social situation, and the definition of the speech event, are crucial for two reasons. First, from the perspective of collecting the material, they determine the *norms of interaction.* These are the normative patterns concerning who has the right to choose what will be discussed and how, what topics will be avoided, who can participate in the conversation, and what range of speech forms (e.g., jokes, stories, etc.) may be used. Would-be oral historians who, through either ignorance or insensitivity, violate these norms are not likely to obtain extensive, useful accounts.

Second, these components also evoke *norms of interpretation.* Features of form, content, and social situation signal the listener as to how to take what is said, i.e., as serious, humorous, metaphorical, or facetious. Many of the inconsistencies and inaccuracies attributed to oral testimony are created by the inability of the researcher to discern these differences.

What does one have, then, once all these factors have been evaluated for a particular segment of oral testimony? I am hardly suggesting that the ultimate goal of this sort of analysis is the identification of each component of the speech event. The task is rather to put them all together into a picture of what was being said in the interview. The purpose of the model is to identify the ways in which the meaning of the testimony is shaped by the relations between the sum total of its various components. This bears on the task of the oral historian in two ways.

First, I have tried to argue that many of the inconsistencies and inaccuracies attributed to oral testimony are introduced by the analyst, not the interviewee. The most important single means of introducing distortion is the attempt to interpret the historical significance of a given statement about the past without first ascertaining the overall meaning of the surrounding testimony. Unless we know what the person was trying to get across, how can we grasp the meaning of a part of that whole?

Second, having interpreted the meaning of the exchange, how are we to convey the historical significance of a given body of material to the reader? Once we have gone to the trouble to interpret the interview materials in context, the last thing we should do is to return to business as usual—viewing the historical content in isolation. Rather, the best approach is to place the historical content within the broader meaning conveyed by the interviewee. For example, an interviewee may emphasize that the land in Las Joyas and the Quemado valley was individually owned when the question asks for a list of the interviewee's father's holdings. In commenting on the importance of agriculture or cooperative labor in "bygone days," however, the same individual may stress the way farmers shared the tasks of harvesting and threshing. If only the bald statements themselves are presented to the reader, the testimony will appear contradictory. A simple statement of the context in which each remark was offered would be sufficient to resolve the apparent controversy. In other words, distortion will creep into the testimony at the last possible moment if the process of grasping the place of a given fact in the flow of discourse is not carried through into the final stage of the investigation.

The Growing Importance of Oral History

I have tried to show that many of the old criticisms of oral history can be overcome once researchers gain sensitivity to the nature of oral materials and acquire adequate procedures for their collection and analysis. Developing a better sense of how oral historical research can best be conducted is particularly important at present in view of the fact that oral history is gaining increasing acceptance. The popularity of such works as *Roots* and *Hard Times* helped bring oral history into the public eye. The Southwest is quite rich in local history, and this has led many residents to interview their relatives and neighbors. Native Americans and Hispanos have become increasingly convinced that the local residents themselves must take an active role in documenting the oral history of their communities.

Scholars also accept the validity of oral history to a much greater extent than was the case even a few years ago. Anthropologists are presently interested in historical questions, and more of them have become familiar with oral historical techniques. Historians have long been skeptical of research that is not based on documents written at or near the time of the events in question. In the past few years, however, oral history has become a promising new field within the discipline, and many more historians now supplement contemporaneous written accounts with interviews. Oral history has provided an especially powerful tool for researchers interested in the history of minorities, labor organizations, women, and other groups that have been overlooked in traditional historical writing.[68]

Oral History in the Courtroom

Oral history has seen a particularly striking growth in the past several years in the field of law. Lawyers and judges who, until recently, rejected oral historical testimony have come to believe that it constitutes necessary evidence in certain types of cases. One of the biggest advances in this regard has been a liberalization of the types of evidence that are admissible in the courtroom.[69]

As Teitelbaum has noted,[70] the two issues which have been most problematic in the use of oral history in land-related litigation are *materiality* or relevance and the legal *reliability of evidence.* In litigation, the fact that a given statement bears on the question at hand is not sufficient to render it material. Rather, the determination of materiality is based on the applicable substantive law and rules of procedure. Legal materiality is thus basically external to the specifics of a given case. The point is that evidence must bear directly on the legal questions deciding the case. Otherwise, not only will it be excluded from consideration in ruling on the case, but it cannot be brought into the case at all. The materiality of a given line of evidence is also affected by previous cases. Once the Supreme Court has decided that an aspect of a given situation has no legal consequences, then evidence bearing on this aspect for a similar case will be barred forever from consideration in future cases of this type.

The question of reliability is of particular importance to the use of oral history in the courtroom. Both the federal judicial system and individual states have bodies of law called *Rules of Evidence.*[71] One of the fundamental principles of such legal canons is the judicial system's preference for testimony given in court. If statements about a given set of events are made in this context, the witnesses can be cross-examined in order to ascertain their personal character, the degree to which they are acquainted with the events, and the accuracy of their memory. If the testimony is taken out of court or if the witnesses are reporting on the statements of another person, then the truth of the original account cannot be verified through cross-examination. This is the famous hearsay rule. As is the case with immaterial information, evidence which falls under the hearsay rule cannot be presented in the courtroom.

The problem is, of course, that many of the events which provide crucial evidence on land grants occurred prior to the lifetime of the current residents. Fortunately, a number of exceptions to the hearsay rule have been established, and their scope has been widened in recent years. Two exceptions provide central avenues for introducing oral historical evidence in litigation. The first, called the reputation exception, pertains to statements known and believed by the community as a whole. Their validity is not based on a single communication made out of court. In order to satisfy the conditions for this exception, the statements must pertain to "the boundaries of or customs affecting lands" or to events of "general history" important to the community.[72] It must also be shown that these beliefs within the community existed prior to the controversy which gave rise to the litigation.

The legal reasoning behind this exception lends itself well to the conception of oral history advanced in this paper. As Teitelbaum notes,[73]

> The special reliability attributed to reputation evidence rests on the assumption that the view of the entire community will be rounded; that it reflects a sifting of facts and events and acts as a check on the perception of any single person regarding the circumstance or event.

I have argued that oral history is a social product; both form and content are shaped by the community's views of who can legitimately say what to whom in which circumstances and, most importantly, what such statements mean. Careful research on the speech events in which oral historical material is conveyed thus provides precisely the sort of information needed to show that a given body of testimony reflects community reputation. The fact that "talking about the past" is an ongoing and central social process within the community provides a basis for demonstrating that the traditions in question did not arise simply in response to a particular court case.

The speech patterns which embrace oral historical discourse do complicate the process in one important way. "Talk about the past" generally emerges either in discussions between peers, generally elders, or in the process of teaching younger persons. In either case, the carriers of historical information control the flow of talk. In the courtroom, however, the right to talk is strictly controlled by legal professionals, and statements are generally provided in response to questions posed by these professionals. In other words, speech patterns required for testifying on the oral history of one's community contrast sharply with those of other contexts in which elders discuss the past. Finding themselves in a foreign environment, forced to speak in English or to use a translator, and having lost control over the situation, the carriers of oral historical information face tremendous handicaps in trying to present their information in a convincing manner.

There are two principal ways to get around this difficulty. Attorneys who are experienced in land grant litigation, such as Santiago Chávez and Malcolm Ebright, have experimented with the introduction of videotaped segments of testimony from elders in the courtroom. Here the attorney or someone else obtains the testimony in the elders' homes. The problem with this approach is that the judge may either refuse to admit the evidence or accord it less weight, due to the fact that the witnesses cannot be cross-examined. Otherwise, an oral historian may testify to the fact that the evidence is reputational within the community. This can raise legal issues with respect to the ability of a nonresident to testify on community reputation and with respect to whether or not the reputation predated the controversy.

Another legal avenue is open for justifying the testimony of an oral historian, native or nonresident. Expert testimony can be offered by a person who has the appropriate professional qualifications and has conducted research in the community.[74] This approach has been used extensively in Native American lands cases, both in the Southwest and elsewhere in the United States and Canada. Here the validity of the evidence rests on the professional opinion of the expert as derived from a variety of sources. In other words, the testimony cannot simply repeat statements made by community members. Expert witnesses must be able to show that their research is guided by discovery and verification procedures that are accepted in their field.

This discussion underlines the importance of several points that were made earlier with respect to oral historical methodology. To testify as an expert witness, a researcher must base conclusions on various types of evidence. I argued above that oral historical research should be undertaken in conjunction with other types of research. In the case of work on the history of land grant communities, archival materials provide a crucial complement. The testimony of an expert witness who can show that the written documents and the oral history both point to the same facts, each in their own historical language, is more likely to be admissible and convincing.

I also noted at the beginning of the chapter that persons who wish to collect oral history often fail to prepare themselves by acquiring competence in oral historical methodology. The lack of proper training and of in-depth, systematic research is likely to jeopardize the success of the project in the courtroom just as it would the success of a published work. In expert witness testimony, both the credentials of the expert and the adequacy of her or his methodology will be on trial along with the quality of the evidence itself. In both cases, superficial, methodologically unsound research is probably worse than no research at all. Historians and social scientists who are skeptical of the validity of oral history are likely to become firmer in their rejection of the field when confronted with shoddy work. The courtroom is even more closely ruled by precedent; if the expert distorts oral history in the courtroom and the resulting inaccuracies are revealed, this makes it that much harder for attorneys and oral historians to introduce oral testimony in similar cases in the future.

Oral History and Cultural Survival

By way of conclusion, I would like to return to the starting point. I noted that it was once common for scholars, attorneys, judges, and others to reject oral history out of hand. This position is usually justified through assertions that oral historical evidence is inaccurate. Oral historical research is indeed vulnerable to distortion and inaccuracy, as is true of research in any field. I devoted a good deal of the discussion to trying to show that serious problems of this nature are not intrinsic to oral testimony; rather, they pose a threat when the practitioner fails to grasp the nature of oral historical discourse. I then presented a conceptual and methodological framework designed to avoid such pitfalls and to show researchers how they can best appreciate the historical insights that emerge from oral data.

The rejection of oral history is not a theoretical and methodological question alone, however, but one that has profound political implications. Oral history is people's history. It is rooted in contemporary communities, and "talk about the past" continues to be one of the central ways in which residents exhibit their identity as a community. I have tried to show that the historical accuracy of oral testimony is not compromised by its responsiveness to the rhythms of daily life. The meeting of past and present in oral historical discourse produces a continual reexamination of the meaning of the past, not a distortion of its historical content. For example, the data I collected in Córdova between 1972 and the present differ only in a few details from what Córdovans told Lorin Brown about their past nearly half a century ago.[75]

With regard to the land grants of New Mexico and Colorado, oral history provides a particularly good source of evidence on precisely those facets of the past that are vital to the future of the communities. Malcolm Ebright's chapter stressed the importance of custom and of common lands in the establishment and validation of land grants under Spain and Mexico. Establishing the legitimacy of customary law and common lands is presently crucial in defending the land rights of Hispanos. Oral testimony provides detailed evidence regarding the use of common lands and the nature of customary law. In many cases, it is not only the best evidence on these points, it is the only evidence.

Finally, oral testimony is the only body of evidence over which the community exercises control. Córdovans can hardly choose the researchers who consult the Pueblo Quemado files in the State Records Center and Archives. It is up to the residents to decide, however, whether or not they want to share their community's history, as they can tell it, with an outsider. Participating in such research gives the people a chance to learn the investigator's motives and to attempt to convey the meaning which the past holds for the contemporary community. In other words, it is very difficult to collect oral history without hearing the community's side of the story.

Oral history is one area in which the outsider is always at a disadvantage. Growing up in a community provides one with a wealth of information on geography, place names, genealogy, and social dynamics in a framework for oral historical discourse. It also affords a command of the nuances of the language and dialect of the community rarely acquired by newcomers. Similarly, native members of the community are *expected* to participate in performances of oral history, while strangers generally gain access to such presentations only after they have become integrated into the community. In sum, the argument for trained native oral historians over outsiders is very strong.

This is not to say, however, that nonnatives cannot conduct good oral historical research. It does mean that members of the community are in a particularly advantageous position, if they are properly trained. Local residents must familiarize themselves with oral historical methodology if they want to be able to place the materials in a form that is accessible to the larger society, either through publication or in court. The native can, however, complement this second frame of reference with an insider's sense of the community and its language. Thus, there exists a great need for workshops and training programs in libraries, community colleges, and other institutions which can provide training in oral historical methodology.

In short, *oral history is power.* It is a resource controlled by the community and most accessible to local residents, and it plays a crucial role in the community's self-definition. Oral history can also be a powerful tool that residents can use in defending their land and way of life. To claim that oral history is unreliable, that it does not deserve a central role in research and litigation, is more than an intellectual posture. Rather, it robs local communities of one of their most important weapons. Collecting oral histories and developing programs that assist local communities in documenting their histories thus provide crucial means of resisting the destruction caused by land loss in Native American and Hispano communities.

Notes

1. Victor Westphall, *The Public Domain in New Mexico, 1854–1891* (Albuquerque: University of New Mexico Press, 1965) and *Mercedes Reales: Hispanic Land Grants of the Upper Río Grande Region* (Albuquerque: University of New Mexico Press, 1983).

2. Victor Westphall, *Thomas Benton Catron and His Era* (Tucson: University of Arizona Press, 1973), p. ix; emphasis added.

3. Frances Leon Swadesh, *Los primeros pobladores: Hispanc Americans of the Ute Frontier* (Notre Dame, Ind.: University of Notre Dame Press, 1974).

4. See for example Arthur J. O. Anderson, Frances Berdan, and James Lockhart, eds., *Beyond the Codices: The Nahua View of Colonial Mexico* (Berkeley: University of California Press, 1976) and Nathan Wachtel, *Vision of the Vanquished: The Spanish Conquest of Peru Through Indian Eyes,* Ben and Sian Reynolds, trans. (B and N Imports, 1977).

5. See for example Cullom Davis, Kathryn Back, and Kay MacLean, *Oral History: From Tape to Type* (Chicago: American Library Assocation, 1977); Edward D. Ives, *The Tape-Recorded Interview: A Manual for Field Workers in Folklore and Oral History* (Knoxville: University of Tennessee Press, 1974); Thad Sitton, George L. Mehaffy, and O. L. Davis, Jr., *Oral History: A Guide for Teachers (and Others)* (Austin: University of Texas Press, 1983).

6. See for example Barbara Allen and Lynwood Montell, *From Memory to History: Using Oral Sources in Local Historical Research* (Nashville, Tenn.: American Association for State and Local History, 1981); James Hoopes, *Oral History: An Introduction for Students* (Chapel Hill: The University of North Carolina Press, 1979); Paul Thompson, *The Voice of the Past: Oral History* (Oxford: Oxford University Press, 1978).

7. David K. Dunaway and Willa K. Baum, *Oral History: An Interdisciplinary Anthology* (Nashville, Tenn.: American Association for State and Local History, 1984).

8. Alex Haley, *Roots* (New York: Doubleday, 1976).

9. Studs Terkel, *Hard Times: An Oral History of the Great Depression* (New York: Pantheon, 1970).

10. See Jan Vansina, *Oral Tradition: A Study in Historical Methodology,* H. M. Wright, trans. (Chicago: Aldine Publishing Company, 1965) and Marco Lunghi, *Oralita e Transmisione in Africa Nera* (Milano).

11. This point has been made, for example, by William L. Lang and Laurie

K. Mercier, "Getting It Down Right: Oral History's Reliability in Local History Research," *Oral History Review* 12 (1984): 82; Thompson, *Voice of the Past,* pp. 91–137, 210–26; Allen and Montell, *Memory to History,* pp. 1, 14–19, 83–87.

12. A major collection of Native American oral history is contained in the Doris Duke Collection in the Special Collections of the University of New Mexico Library. Hispano oral history from the Las Vegas, New Mexico, area is available in the Carnegie Library, Las Vegas.

13. See Gilberto Benito Córdova, *Bibliography of Unpublished Materials Pertaining to Hispanic Culture in the New Mexico WPA Writers' Files* (Santa Fe: New Mexico State Department of Education, 1972); Lorin W. Brown with Charles L. Briggs and Marta Weigle, *Hispano Folklife of New Mexico: The Lorin W. Brown Federal Writers' Project Manuscripts* (Albuquerque: University of New Mexico Press, 1978); Marta Weigle, ed., *New Mexicans in Cameo and Camera: New Deal Documentation of Twentieth-Century Lives* (Albuquerque: University of New Mexico Press, 1985).

14. See Charles L. Briggs, *Learning How to Ask: A Sociolinguistic Appraisal of the Role of the Interview in Social Science Research* (Cambridge: Cambridge University Press, 1986), Chapter 5.

15. A number of manuals have suggestions regarding which types of questions are good or bad. See for example Davis et al., *Oral History,* pp. 20–22, 27–33; Ives, *Tape-Recorded Interview,* pp. 66–70.

16. The use of audio-video vs. audio recording is more complex. Videotaping enables others to see the setting in which the interview occurred as well as the way in which the interviewee's gestures and facial expressions may change or add to the meaning of the words themselves. On the other hand, video cameras are much more intrusive than compact tape recorders, and they are much more likely to make the respondent stiff and self-conscious.

17. See David Dunaway, "Radio and the Public Use of Oral History," in Dunaway and Baum, *Oral History,* pp. 333–46.

18. See Land and Mercier, "Getting It Down Right," pp. 85–86.

19. On the interactional nature of interviews, see Barbara Allen, "Recreating the Past: The Narrator's Perspective in Oral History," *Oral History Review* 12 (1984): 1–12; Briggs, *Learning How to Ask;* Lewis Anthony Dexter, *Elite and Specialized Interviewing* (Evanston, Ill.: Northwestern University Press, 1970); Charles W. Joyner, "Oral History as Communicative Event," *Oral History Review* 7 (1979): 47–52; Allen and Montell, *From Memory to History;* E. Culpepper Clark, Michael J. Hyde, and Eva M. McMahan, "Communicating in the Oral History Interview: Investigating Problems of Interpreting Oral Data," *International Journal of Oral History* 1 (1980): 28–40.

20. Most oral history manuals contain sample release forms; see for example Davis et al., *Oral History,* pp. 11–16; Ives, *Tape-Recorded Interview,* pp. 51, 84–85, 111–14.

21. There are no set rules regarding where you should deposit the tapes. Obviously, they are more likely to be of use to the local community and area historians if the archive is as close as possible to the research site. A local

library or college may thus be ideal. It is also important to make sure that the facility has the experience and the equipment to take good care of the recordings and that they will insure their accessibility to the general public. The depositor is generally required to sign a release with the institution, and some of these concerns can be put in writing.

22. I have conducted research in Córdova between 1972 and the present. Tape recordings have been made of interviews, informal discussions, public meetings, and other types of discourse. Funding has been provided by the International Folk Art Foundation, the National Institute of Mental Health, the National Science Foundation, and the Faculty Research Committee of Vassar College. The writing of this chapter was aided by an Andrew W. Mellon Faculty Fellowship at Harvard University in the Committee on Degrees in Folklore and Mythology.

23. See Brown et al., *Hispano Folklife,* pp. 101–5.

24. See Brown et al., *Hispano Folklife,* pp. 105–9; Charles L. Briggs, "Treasure Tales and Pedagogical Discourse in *Mexicano* New Mexico," *Journal of American Folklore* 98 (1985): 287–314.

25. See Brown et al., *Hispano Folklife,* pp. 120–24.

26. Lorin W. Brown wrote a description of Saint Isidore day in Córdova which was published anonymously as "Fiestas in New Mexico," *El Palacio* 48 (1941): 239–42; also see Charles L. Briggs, "A Conversation with St. Isidore: Teachings of the Elders," in Marta Weigle with Claudia Larcombe and Samuel Larcombe, eds., *Hispanic Arts and Ethnohistory in the Southwest: New Papers Inspired by the Work of E. Boyd* (Albuquerque: University of New Mexico Press, 1983), pp. 104–15.

27. The allusion here is to the fact that the courthouse was the location of the "raid" by Reis López Tijerina and other members of La Alianza Federal de Mercedes. See the chapter by Rosenbaum and Larson.

28. Spanish Archives of New Mexico I (hereafter abbreviated as SANM I), No. 211, New Mexico State Records Center and Archives, Santa Fe.

29. SANM I, No. 1041.

30. SANM I, No. 28. Frances Leon Swadesh, *Los Primeros Pobladores: Hispanic Americans of the Ute Frontier* (Notre Dame, Ind.: University of Notre Dame Press, 1974), pp. 34–35, appears to argue that the petition of 1748 refers, inter alia, to a Pueblo Quemado which is located to the west of the Rio Grande in the Río del Oso. Myra Ellen Jenkins, "Documentation Concerning Settlement of Pueblo Quemado (Córdova)" (ms. on file in the State Records Center and Archives, Santa Fe, 1974), contrastively asserts that the reference is to the Pueblo Quemado near Chimayo. Since both of these Pueblo Quemados lay within the alcaldía mayor (district) of Santa Cruz, the document could refer to either. I follow Jenkins in her interpretation for two reasons. First, the petition of 1749 (see below in text) by the residents of the eastern Pueblo Quemado (Córdova) clearly alludes to a request by the citizens for permission to abandon their lands during the previous year. By all indications, this reference is to the 1748 document. Second, Swadesh does not list cor-

responding documentation for the return of the settlers of the western Pueblo Quemado in the succeeding years.

31. SANM I, No. 40. The document, whch is dated 1767, refers to a land donation of 1746.

32. Córdova Family Papers (hereafter CFP), 10 April 1790, State Records Center and Archives, Santa Fe.

33. Eleanor B. Adams and Fray Angélico Chávez, eds., *The Missions of New Mexico, 1776* (Albuquerque: University of New Mexico Press, 1956), p. 83.

34. Adams and Chávez, *Missions of New Mexico,* p. 84.

35. Archives of the Archdiocese of Santa Fe (hereafter AASF), *Patentes,* Reel 55, Frames 222–23, 230, State Records Center and Archives, Santa Fe.

36. AASF, Santa Cruz Parish, Baptisms, 12 December 1756.

37. AASF, Santa Cruz Parish, Marriages, 18 November 1783. Celedón Córdova and Juliana Martín had at least nine children, all born in Quemado. Celedón owned a fair-sized farm-ranch, a holding that extended on both sides of the Río Quemado; see CFP, 23 November 1803. His status as a respected citizen is suggested by his position as the *testigo de asistencia* of the local *alcalde de barrio.*

38. AASF, *Patentes,* Reel 54, Frame 560.

39. AASF, Santa Cruz Parish, Marriages, 15 April 1817; see the baptismal records for 1820–1844.

40. SANM II, Reel 16, Frame 169, dated 18 June 1806.

41. Mexican Archives of New Mexico, *Hacienda, Aduana, facturas, guías,* and *tornaguías* for 1838, 1844, and 1845, State Records Center and Archives, Santa Fe. It is quite likely that Córdova made the trip in other years and that the records have been lost.

42. Rio Arriba County Clerk's Office (hereafter RACCO), *Libro de Testamentos, Etc.,* 1852–1862, Record Book No. 1, Rio Arriba County Courthouse, Tierra Amarilla, New Mexico, pp. 295–307.

43. See Marc Simmons, *Spanish Government in New Mexico* (Albuquerque: University of New Mexico Press, 1968), p. 221.

44. RACCO, *Testamentos,* pp. 53–57.

45. Ibid., pp. 359–62.

46. Brown et al., *Hispano Folklife,* pp. 46–48.

47. RACCO, *Testamentos,* pp. 384–94. Vigil did own 170 varas of land and part of a house in Santa Cruz de la Cañada, but these were an inheritance of his late wife which had been placed in Vigil's custody; p. 388.

48. Twelfth Federal Census, 1900, New Mexico, Vol. 5, Rio Arriba County, Precinct No. 6, State Records Center and Archives, Santa Fe.

49. Territorial Archives of New Mexico (hereafter TANM), Reel 51, Frame 106, State Records Center and Archives, Santa Fe. It is quite likely that Calletano Córdova operated these businesses before and after these dates, since the records of retail outlets appear to be incomplete.

50. TANM, Reel 51, Frames 115, 121, 132; and Rio Arriba County Records, Applications for Licenses, 1884–1925, State Records Center and Archives, Santa Fe.

51. RACCO, record books numbered 1 and 5 and Rio Arriba and Taos County Court, Journal, Civil and Criminal, entry for 14 September 1863; see also Frank Driver Reeve Papers, Archive No. 158, Box No. 31, Folder No. 1, dated 24 March 1856.

52. Córdova Family Papers, 8 July 1868 and Court of Private Land Claims, Case No. 212 both in the State Records Center and Archives, Santa Fe; Jerome Finister, Personal Communication, 1971, provided a listing of the early postmasters of Córdova.

53. Frank H. Grubbs, "Frank Bond: Gentleman Sheepherder of Northern New Mexico, 1883–1915," *New Mexico Historical Review* 35 (1960): 169–99, 293–308, 36 (1961): 138–58, 230–43, 274–345, 37 (1962): 43–71.

54. Frank Bond Papers, Special Collections, General Library, University of New Mexico, Albuquerque.

55. See U.S. Soil Conservation Service, *Tenant Herding in the Cuba Valley* (Regional Bulletin No. 37, Conservation Economics Series No. 10; Albuquerque: Soil Conservation Service, 1937); Marta Weigle, ed., *Hispanic Villages of Northern New Mexico: A Reprint of Volume II of the 1935 Tewa Basin Study, with Supplementary Materials* (Santa Fe: Lightning Tree, 1975).

56. Grubbs, "Frank Bond," vol. 35, p. 300.

57. Court of Private Land Claims, Case No. 212, State Records Center and Archives, Santa Fe.

58. Court of Private Land Claims, Case No. 28; Office of the Surveyor General, File 227, State Records Center and Archives, Santa Fe.

59. A copy of the presidential proclamation which created the Reserve is on file in the office of the forest supervisor, Santa Fe National Forest, Santa Fe.

60. See U.S. Forest Service, *The Western Range* (74th Congress, 2nd Section, Document No. 199; Washington: Government Printing Office, 1936); David "A" Gillio, *Santa Fe National Forest Area: An Historical Perspective for Management* (Cultural Resources Report No. 30; Albuquerque: USDA Forest Service, Southwestern Region, 1979); E. Louise Peffer, *The Closing of the Public Domain: Disposal and Reservation Policies,* 1900–1950 (Stanford, Cal.: Stanford University Press, 1951); Paul H. Roberts, *Hoof Prints on Forest Ranges: The Early Years of National Forest Range Administration* (San Antonio: Tex.: Naylor, 1963). See also the so-called "Use Books" of the U.S. Forest Service, e.g., *The Use of the National Forest Reserves: Regulations* (Washington: Government Printing Office, 1905). This information is also based upon correspondence and conversations with officials of the Santa Fe National Forest and research in the History Section of the Forest Service, U.S. Department of Agriculture, Washington.

61. Suaso Family Papers, 18–29 April 1826, State Records Center and Archives, Santa Fe.

62. See Hayden White, *Metahistory: The Historical Imagination in Nineteenth-Century Europe* (Baltimore: Johns Hopkins University Press, 1973) and *Tropics of Discourse: Essays in Cultural Criticism* (Baltimore: Johns Hopkins University

Press, 1978); see also Hans-Georg Gadamer, *Truth and Method* (New York: Crossroad, 1975).

63. Vansina, *Oral Tradition,* pp. 19–20.

64. See Brown et al., *Hispano Folklife,* pp. 99–105.

65. Charles L. Briggs, "*Mexicano* Sheep Ranchers in Northern New Mexico, 1880–1920: Cultural Dimensions of the Capitalization of Production," unpublished manuscript.

66. This model is based upon frameworks for the analysis of communicative events which were developed by Roman Jakobson, "Concluding Statement: Linguistics and Poetics," in Thomas A. Sebeok, *Style in Language* (Cambridge, Mass.: M.I.T. Press, 1960), pp. 350–77 and Dell Hymes, "Introduction: Toward Ethnographies of Communication," in John J. Gumperz and Dell Hymes, eds., *The Ethnography of Communication, American Anthropologist* 66 (1964): 1–34; "Models of the Interaction of Language and Social Life," in John J. Gumperz and Dell Hymes, eds., *Directions in Sociolinguistics: The Ethnography of Communication* (New York: Holt, Rinehart, and Winston, 1972), pp. 38–71. See Joyner, "Oral History as a Communicative Event."

67. "Questions for the Ethnographer: A Critical Examination of the Role of the Interview in Fieldwork," *Semiotica* 46 (1983): 233–61.

68. Thompson, *Oral History,* makes a particularly strong case for the importance of oral history in historical research.

69. See Joseph M. McLaughlin, *Practical Trial Evidence* (New York: Practising Law Institute, 1977).

70. Lee E. Teitelbaum, "Law and Oral History" (Paper presented in a Symposium on Land, Law, and Oral History at the Annual Meeting of the American Society for Ethnohistory, Albuquerque, New Mexico, 5 November 1983). I am greatly indebted to Professor Teitelbaum for allowing me to draw extensively on his insights into the relationship between oral history and the law. The symposium, which was funded by the New Mexico Humanities Council, consisted of a series of formal papers, a panel discussion, and a workshop; a videotape of the entire symposium is available in the Special Collections of the University of New Mexico General Library. My understanding of the legal dimensions of these issues has also benefited from conversations with William C. Briggs.

71. *Rules of Evidence for United States Court and Magistrates, 28 USCS Appendix* (United States Code Service, Lawyers Edition; Rochester: Lawyers Co-operative, and San Francisco: Bancroft-Whitney, 1975); *Cumulative Supplement, Rules of Evidence for United States Courts and Magistrates* (United States Code Service, Lawyers Edition; Rochester: Lawyers Co-operative and San Francisco: Bancroft-Whitney, 1985).

72. *Rules of Evidence,* Rule 803(21), p. 112.

73. Teitelbaum, "Law and Oral History," p. 9.

74. *Rules of Evidence,* Article VII, Rules 701–6.

75. Brown, *Hispano Folklife.*

Cundiyo, New Mexico. Ernest Knee photograph. Courtesy of Andrew Smith Gallery, Santa Fe.

FIVE

Mexicano Resistance to the Expropriation of Grant Lands in New Mexico

FIVE

Mexicano Resistance to the Expropriation of Grant Lands in New Mexico

Robert J. Rosenbaum and Robert W. Larson

The well-publicized attack on the Rio Arriba County Courthouse at Tierra Amarilla served notice that the Mexicanos of northern New Mexico were not only still angry about the expropriation of their lands by Anglos, they were prepared to act. The raid took most Anglos by surprise and their reactions ranged from shocked outrage to bemused condescension: "The poor jerkoff thinks he's Moses come again," was how one reporter described Alianza leader Reies Tijerina.[1]

Traditionally, Anglos looked upon Mexicanos as a quaint, backward folk characterized by their docility, fatalism, and charming propensity for procrastination. New Mexico was "the land of *poco tiempo,*" according to Charles F. Lummis, and subsequent writers have consistently echoed Lummis's nineteenth-century observation. Native New Mexicans were supposed to be grateful for the opportunities made possible by aggressive Anglo development, and if Mexicanos did not enjoy an equal share of the proceeds that resulted it was because of flaws in their cultural heritage—Mexican and Indian—or weaknesses that stemmed from their mongrelized genetic lineage. In the minds of most Anglos, an armed uprising by these humble and childlike people was tantamount to a crime against nature.

Longtime Anglo residents of northern New Mexico knew better: they had been sued, harassed, and attacked by Mexicanos for the better part of the century. But Tijerina's Alianza Federal de Mercedes looked as though it might transform resistance from sporadic violence and discrete legal actions into a concerted movement that could challenge private landholders and the U.S. Forest Service alike. Consequently, many knowledgeable Anglos in the state joined the chorus that denounced the raiders as unwitting dupes bewitched by the rantings of a Communist-backed outside agitator.

The reaction to the courthouse raid is typical of the way Anglos have responded to expressions of discontent in New Mexico since 1848. It is also typical of the responses by dominant groups everywhere to the mutinous rumblings of the subjugated. Those in power living close to the situation rarely publicize friction or report conflict because such revelations might frighten investment or, even worse, might raise troubling questions about the legitimacy of their dominance. Those more distant from the subordinated area enjoy the complacency of insulation, and the secure belief that all is as it should be and everything is going well. When confronted by dramatic evidence to the contrary, their usual response is to look for an insidious outside influence to explain the deviation from the normal and good.

Blaming unrest on the outside agitators—the "our niggers are happy" posture—is condescension of the highest magnitude for it assumes that the people in question are inferior, have no understanding of their collective self-interest, and are unable to act on their own behalf. Applying the explanation to the Mexicanos of New Mexico is just as erroneous as applying it to black people in Selma, Alabama. The historical record is far from complete, but it is clear on this point: Mexicanos have resisted Anglo encroachment in New Mexico for almost a century and a half.

Mexicanos resisted the expropriation of their lands in ways unique to the New Mexico situation. Their resistance, nonetheless, is a part of the Mexicano resistance against Anglo domination across the Southwest. It is also a part of the ethnic pride and cultural nationalism movement of recent decades, forming a major position in the debate between melting pot homogeneity and cultural pluralism as a primary American national characteristic.

Indeed, New Mexico provides a striking example of cultural diversity in a nation that prides itself on being the great melting pot of the world. Whether the national self-image is correct or not, the bilingual tradition of this southwestern state is one of the countless examples of the cultural distinctiveness found among the Mexicanos of this region. This diversity predates the Chicano movements and has profoundly influenced them in the Southwest and throughout the rest of the country.

Mexicano resistance also falls squarely within the timeless and global tradition of popular rebellion. As part of a worldwide phenomenon, it bears upon issues of conquest and colonization, imperialism and development, insurgency and civil disorder, nationalism and cultural pluralism, resistance and revolution and, unhappily, the rising tide of international terrorism.

The Scholarly Study of Popular Resistance

Resistance to oppression is as old as oppression. The study of popular resistance—peasant or primitive rebellions, as they are often called—is, however, a relatively recent development. "History is written by winners," goes the adage, and therein lies one explanation for the lack of attention given to unsuccessful resisters. Whether consciously or unconsciously, winners rarely expose anything that might undermine their ascendancy.

The history of scholarship also helps account for the comparative lack of attention given to popular and folk movements in literature about revolution. Inspired by democratic theory and democratic revolutions, further spurred by Marxism and Marxist revolutions, scholars interested in political and social upheavals have concentrated their efforts on revolutionary movements. Two criteria seem to stand out as determinants of importance: the presence of an organizing ideology; and the potency of the revolt—potency defined as the degree to which the established regime is threatened. Successful revolutions are the most potent and, therefore, the most important. They have received treatment in works like Robert Palmer's *The Age of Democratic Revolution,* Hannah Arendt's *On Revolution,* or Crane Brinton's *The Anatomy of Revolution.*

By this definition, peasant or primitive rebellions are not important. They possess no discernible ideologies—at least no "forward-looking" democratic or Marxist ones—and they have not toppled regimes. Only since World War II have historians, political scientists, anthropologists, and sociologists produced a body of literature that examines urban riots, industrial sabotage, social banditry, agrarian uprisings, and strikes as authentic and serious attempts to right perceived wrongs. But the literature dealing with popular resistance is sparse and embryonic when compared to that addressing the history and theory of revolutions. Literature that deals with popular resistance in the United States has just begun.[2]

Studies about violence in the United States abound, for it is accepted that Americans have a long history of violence. Studies about politics are even more numerous, since political participation is a fundamental tenet of American social theory and the history of that participation has received, and continues to receive, a great deal of deserved attention. But since most violence in the United States appears to have been aimed at so-called deviant groups or private corporations, or has been attributed to mindless frustration or psychotic terrorism, scholars have rarely connected violence to political resistance. Most violent attacks of this nature do not appear to present viable threats to our government institutions. In a like manner, those who study political participation tend to concentrate on elections or pressure group activities, manifestations of the types of action taken by those who are willing to work within the system. Rarely do such scholars make a serious attempt to connect violence to such legitimate political efforts.

In some ways the scant attention paid to popular rebellions in the United States is appropriate. The country has never experienced a social revolution or a serious attempt at one. Whether this is due to its geographical size, the diversity of concerns and interests among its population, or a social elasticity made possible by the country's abundance and made conceivable by democratic theory, the fact remains that this nation has exhibited a remarkable stability. And what has been true for the country as a whole has been true for New Mexico: geography, diversity, and opportunity have all mitigated against a large-scale and widespread organization among Mexicanos capable of threatening the hold that the United States has exercised in this region.

All of this seems reasonable and proper. But, as the urban riots that convulsed American cities during the mid-sixties made clear, a great deal of violence throughout the history of the United States was political. It represented an attempt, however ill-conceived or unsuccessful, to correct a problem that threatened a particular community. The Mexicano community in the Southwest was a conquered people whose conquerors wrought sweeping changes that meant great hardship for a majority of *los hombres pobres* (the poor people). Moreover, los pobres Mexicanos resisted the most destructive manifestations of the Anglo domination whenever those manifestations were clearly apparent. The history of that quaint backwater called New Mexico—the Land of Enchantment—lies fully within at least one mainstream of contemporary social scholarship.

The History of the Problem

The courthouse raid which confounded many Anglo presumptions about New Mexico's population spurred some students of the state's history to wonder whether anything similar had happened before. The answer, of course, is yes.

A systematic rereading of the histories of New Mexico by those attuned to recognizing the clues of Mexicano resistance reveals a number of incidents that date back to the series of uprisings at Mora, Santa Cruz, Las Vegas, and El Brazito that followed the Taos Revolt of January 1847. They include skirmishing in Colfax County, masked nightriders in San Miguel County during the nineteenth century, and the alleged activities of the mysterious La Mano Negra in northern New Mexico during the 1920s and 1930s.

Most of these episodes, however, are usually mentioned in passing, as mere asides to the primary thrust of the historian's narrative. A handful of historians have begun to probe more deeply, but their results are as yet incomplete. Some studies deal explicitly with specific movements to resist Anglo expropriation of land. But Mexicano resistance to such appropriation and, indeed, Mexicano resistance to any forms of Anglo-American sovereignty, awaits the publication of exhaustive monographs before it can be described through well-founded generalizations.

There are reasons for this dearth. One has to do with the major focus of Chicano scholarship to date. Chicano historians tend to stress topics such as immigration, labor, discrimination, and political and social activism. Another reason has to do with the difficulty of effectively researching resistance movements, a problem we shall discuss in a later section. At this point in our study, however, we propose to sketch what is known about Mexicano resistance to land expropriation and follow this with some very tentative suggestions about the general characteristics and trends of this ongoing resistance. For convenience, we have divided our chronology into the territorial and statehood periods and the types of resistance into violent and political (political meaning nonviolent) categories.

The Territorial Context

From the vantage point of the late twentieth century, the three decades after William Becknell's arrival in Santa Fe in 1821 appear to follow an inevitable progression toward the Anglo-American acquisition of New Mexico. And the apparent inexorable process of Americanization that accompanied it brought a major threat to Mexicano occupancy of their territorial lands. Yet what in hindsight appears inevitable seemed far from predetermined for those who lived at the time. In the matter of land, the certainty of Anglo expropriation seemed even less pronounced than did American sovereignty over the former Mexican province. In truth, the completeness of that expropriation remains in doubt today.

The Treaty of Guadalupe Hidalgo, which concluded the conquest, provided for the recognition of all property rights valid under the laws of Mexico, as Malcolm Ebright's essay in this volume describes admirably. New Mexico was enhanced by the territory's relative lack of natural bounty: the lack of attractive resources allowed the treaty provisions to have some actual impact. Although the United States conquered New Mexico and imposed its political institutions and economic systems, the territory did not experience the massive inundation of Anglo migrants that the gold rush caused in California. And Mexicano unrest did not provoke the wrath of a police force like the Texas Rangers or the strong presence of the U.S. Army, as was the case along the southern border of Texas. The United States conquered the province of New Mexico in 1846, but Anglo-American ascendancy in that state came through a slow process of attrition that, even after more than a century, is far from complete.

Attrition, although snail-like, has been made quite effective through Anglo expropriation of Mexicano land. Three stages of expropriation, with their approximate time periods, can be perceived as follows during the territorial years: (1) documentation and patenting (1850–70); (2) confrontation and chicanery (1870–92); and (3) litigation and legislating (1892 to present).

The presentation of documents, the initiation and the prosecution of law suits, and the use of coercion, confrontation, and fraud were, to be sure, constant factors in the long history of New Mexico's tangled land situation. But we regard the stages listed above as fair characterizations of the *dominant approach that Anglos adopted* during each particular time period. Moreover, they represent the primary ways Anglo speculators dealt with the land's Spanish-speaking occupants, los hombres pobres.

During the era of documentation, the first stage, those concerned about land and conversant with the appropriate procedures to acquire it, devoted their energies to obtaining patents that recognized the legality of Spanish and Mexican land grants. Others dealt with the problems attendant in translating a metes-and-bounds system, in which use and custom were the principal determinants of land tenure, into a system emphasizing precise measurement. Land, in the latter system, is first of all a commodity, and the map is a primary arbiter of ownership.[3] Suffice to say, it was a difficult exercise even for honest men with good intentions, traits not common among New Mexico land speculators. Even so, during the documentation era, territorial magnates, or those who aspired to such distinction, legally petitioned the U.S. Surveyor General of New Mexico for approval of their land claims. And, if they were unsuccessful, they presented their case before Congress in hopes of obtaining a patent.

Most Mexicanos were not affected by the machinations of land speculators in Santa Fe and Washington; they managed to ignore the fact of American sovereignty and carry on their day-to-day activites as usual. A significant manifestation of this business-as-usual attitude was an almost century-long migration of Mexicanos outward from the colonial population centers along the upper Rio Grande and its tributaries.

Migration began as early as the eighteenth century. In need of buffering settlements to protect the center of the remote province, Spanish governors of New Mexico offered land in the form of community grants to groups willing to move to the frontier. The plan enjoyed marginal success for much of the century as plazas were established, abandoned for a decade or more, and then resettled. But, as the eighteenth century gave way to the nineteenth, some settlements began to take permanent root. First along the Chama north and west of Española, then amid the foothills of the Sangre de Cristos east of Santa Fe and Taos, and even to the south and southeast in what would later become Doña Ana and Lincoln counties, Mexicanos moved outward in what geographer D. W. Meinig has called a "spontaneous folk migration."[4]

This significant migration accelerated during the Mexican period, usually because of the exceptionally generous land grants made by the government. After the United States acquired the territory, these migration patterns continued, usually without official sanctions, until at least the 1890s. Thus, while land speculators and cooperative ricos devoted themselves to the political and bureaucratic intricacies of the new American regime, los pobres continued to migrate to and settle on lands in search of improving circumstances for themselves and their children.

After the Civil War, the Mexicano frontiersmen began to face competition as Anglo migration to New Mexico became an increasingly important factor. Soldiers with Carleton's California Column took their discharges in the territory and stayed there to seek their fortunes.[5] Westering Texas cattlemen moved onto the eastern plains to take advantage of the growing markets provided by the needs of the U.S. Army and those of the government's new wards on the Indian reservations established in the territory. The discovery of gold brought Anglo prospectors and miners to New Mexico's mountains.

Aggressive speculators like Stephen B. Elkins and Thomas B. Catron of the Santa Fe Ring also arrived; they were among a band of ambitious Anglos determined to make successful financial and political careers in the territory. And, with a number of land grants patented, or looking as though they soon would be patented, large land and cattle companies began to claim huge tracts of territorial land and exert pressure on the Mexicano residents. This interaction between native migrants and Anglo investors moved the question of landownership from the realm of documentation and patenting to the world of confrontation and chicanery.

It must be remembered, however, that nothing in New Mexico breaks into neat categories. As political scientist Jack E. Holmes observed in *Politics in New Mexico,* "New Mexico's several cultural areas move in discrete orbits and in different directions in their response to forces common to them all."[6] A historian who shall remain nameless once exploded, "New Mexico politics is a can of worms." Thus, while confrontation and chicanery characterized the last three decades of the nineteenth-century land controversy, the competing factions involved did not divide neatly along Anglo-Mexicano lines. Rather, rancher, homesteader, speculator, rico, and pobre all united and fragmented and united again in a kaleidoscope of alliances.

There were, however, some fundamental orientations for each of these competing groups that help to bring a bit of order out of the chaos. Anglo speculators, for example, wanted Spanish and Mexican land grants recognized by the United States government, and they wanted the largest amount of acreage that friendly land surveyors and sympathetic legal interpretations would allow.

They also wanted the lands in question removed from the public domain; no matter how creatively a speculator might deal with the

General Land Office, he could not acquire anything like the size of the land tracts that would be made available through the legal recognition of a Spanish or Mexican land grant.

Problems with land titles could be handled with relative ease in the case of propriety grants like the Maxwell, but they would prove more difficult in the case of community grants. In the latter cases, the speculators were confronted with a difficult paradox: They wanted the grants recognized as legitimate, but to profit from them they had to invalidate the claims of the occupants whose presence had provided justification for the land grant in the first place.

Two of the least odious solutions to this dilemma involved partitioning. First, a lawyer might take his fee in land for obtaining the title for the occupants of a community grant and then claim the land he received as one undivided, privately held tract. Second, a speculator might purchase the interests in a community grant from a number of grant residents or heirs and then claim his acquisitions on the grant as a separate tract of land, undivided and owned solely by him. Either approach removed a great amount of the common land from common use. They were both clear violations of the intent of a community grant under Spanish or Mexican practice and brought about the virtual destruction of the economic utility of the grant for most residents.[7]

Ranchers, homesteaders, and miners took a different approach. They opposed the speculators and the land and cattle companies that claimed large estates, not out of sympathy for los pobres, but because they regarded the land as public domain and open to preemption and settlement just like other parts of the American frontier.

Ricos and the upwardly mobile native politicos in New Mexico tried to stay afloat in these turbulent waters by taking advantage of all opportunities as they appeared. For some, this tack involved nothing beyond personal aggrandizement. For many, however, it meant coming to terms with and adjusting to the new order.

As for los pobres, they just wanted to live as they had always lived. Even so, friction between those competing for land in New Mexico began to increase dramatically during the 1870s. Often this friction erupted into violence; various coalitions were pitted against each other only to fragment and reappear with equally bizarre realignments. But as pressure and friction mounted, los pobres increasingly recognized the tangible new threats to their land and to their way of life. They began to take steps to cope with these dangers. Moreover, they were remarkably successful when fighting on their own lands. But when Anglo speculators moved the struggle from confrontation on the land to manipulation in the courts and in the legislature, los pobres did not fare well.

Violent Resistance in Territorial New Mexico

Violent resistance occurs when a people accept violence as a possible and desirable course of action. It often results when a threat is perceived as being sufficiently severe to warrant a violent response or when it is widely believed that such violence will succeed. Violence had long been a fact of life for Mexicanos in the territory. Its occurrence was not necessarily frequent, nor was it usually regarded as the preferred option, but it had nonetheless been an important part of the life of many pobres. Violent confrontation could arise from disputes between individuals, out of family feuds, or as a response to Indian attacks. Perhaps coping with Indian attack provides the most relevant example of how los pobres had historically dealt with threats to the security of their land. Provisions for Indian defense were a major part of the requirements for maintaining a community grant. Settlers on New Mexico's expanding frontier were expected to, and became accustomed to, making their own decisions about such protection as well as other serious matters of survival.

Loss of land was indeed a matter of survival. The loss, or threat of loss, could come in the form of company agents demanding rent, Anglo cowboys trying to drive Mexicano flocks and herds from their grazing lands, or land grabbers fencing common land and thus blocking vital access to pasture and water. All were threats, all were tangible, and all were visible manifestations of a serious problem.

History had taught Mexicanos that violence could solve problems and might be the only solution to the problems created by Anglo intruders, especially violent intruders with a "Remember the Alamo" mentality. Looking at the situation through the filter of their experience made violent resistance seem like a sound idea to many of los pobres. Mexicanos were in the numerical majority; the threats involved their own land, a terrain they knew well. It seemed that the intruders—fence builders, agents, or cowboys—could be removed by violence or the threat of violence. The historical record shows that these assessments were correct. Anglos usually lost when there was a direct confrontation between Anglos and Mexicanos over control of land.

Published research to date indicates that those regions that witnessed violent resistance were located on the periphery of population centers on the upper Rio Grande. They were the arenas where Mexicano frontiersman and Anglo migrant met. These points of encounter collectively formed something of an arc along roughly three-quarters of the territory's border. The arc began in Rio Arriba country northwest of Santa Fe, broke a bit when it reached the Rio Grande, and resumed on the eastern slope of the Sangre de Cristos beyond Taos, continuing southward through the San Miguel country to Lincoln County.

Mexicano settlement and Anglo intrusion in this arc varied somewhat from region to region. In northwestern New Mexico, for example, settlement, though sparse, dated from the eighteenth century. Initiated through community grants, it expanded into southern Colorado and the Four Corners region. Anglo encroachment in the area initially came in the form of land speculators like Thomas B. Catron and corporations like the Rio Arriba Land and Cattle Company. Farther to the west, where Mexicanos had settled without benefit of grant, ranchers and homesteaders took up the public domain and competed with los pobres for land and water.[8]

Mexicano settlement in the northeast began later and with less formality. The dominant grant was the Maxwell. Awarded to Charles Beaubien and Guadalupe Miranda by Governor Manuel Armijo, the grant passed to Lucien B. Maxwell and eventually to wealthy Dutch investors who ultimately gained title to a tract in excess of two million acres.[9]

To the south, in the San Miguel region, Mexicano settlement was almost as old as that in the Rio Arriba country. It, too, was initiated by community land grants, and by the 1870s it had become the most populous region on the territory's periphery. Anglos made their presence felt relatively late in the century. They did so, as far as los pobres were concerned, when they constructed fences on the common lands of the grants.[10] Mexicano settlement in the southern and southeastern portions of the territory was sparse, recent, and informal; Anglo encroachment there took the form of westering Texas cattlemen, Army regulars, and Indian agency employees.[11]

When resistance came, it came in a variety of forms. The first, and the one that set the tone for all the others, took the form of *long-term skirmishing.* Long-term skirmishing is a community, or community-sanctioned, activity. It ought not be confused with social banditry wherein bandits attack the oppressors—conquerors, government agents and agencies, or even banks—and then retreat to be fed or hidden by their people. Skirmishing, on the other hand, is carried out by the residents of a particular area, *in* their area, and is aimed at specific threats to the common good. In this sense, skirmishing and coordinated rebellions—about which we will talk when we discuss San Miguel County—are extensions of the internal politics of communities. The degree of formal decision making and the degree of unanimity vary, of course, from community to community and from incident to incident within a particular community. But violence of the skirmishing sort is political because it results from attempts by communities to deal with problems that threaten the common welfare.

In Lincoln County, skirmishing began in the late 1860s and early 1870s when discharged soldiers, Texas cattlemen, active Army men, and Indian agents moved into the area and began to compete with resident Mexicanos for grazing land and water supplies of the region. The competition was for the economic and political control of land not granted by either Spain or Mexico. Recently settled, with comparatively little in the way of formal social and political institutions, and populated by aggressive settlers eager to maximize their own positions, it was an area ripe for violent turmoil.

The Anglo phase of this continuing turmoil reached sufficient proportions to go down in American mythology as the Lincoln County War. The Anglo myth centers around such legendary characters as John Chisum, Alexander McSween, and Billy the Kid; the part played by Mexicanos, especially Juan Patron and his followers, is omitted. Almost completely forgotten are the two decades of struggle between Anglos and Mexicanos that preceded and followed the legendary gun battles of the Lincoln struggle. Some elements of this prolonged conflict involved racism in its most virulent form (Phillip J. Rasch's article, "The Horrell War," chronicles one episode of violence inspired by race hatred),[12] and some conflicts revolved around water rights (see Phillip J. Rasch's "The Tularosa Ditch War" for a good account of this type of confrontation).[13] Another kind of struggle that was particularly prevalent during the 1880s can be couched in terms of another Western myth: cattlemen versus sheepherders.

Nevertheless, the fundamental issue in these struggles was land, and not just *who* could use the land but also *how* land would be owned. Although Spain and Mexico had not made grants in southeastern New Mexico, Mexicanos occupied and used land in traditional ways: they established plazas, constructed acequias, allotted fields, and grazed the vast grasslands in common. Anglos developed the informal custom of range as a way to apply the concept of private ownership to open-range ranching on the public domain. Cattlemen would homestead or purchase their ranch headquarters and obtain rights to water from streams or springs in a general area, then by consensus the range of each was thought to be the grazing land served by their water.

Lincoln County was the setting for long-term skirmishing lasting more than two decades. It was a struggle for both possession of resources and the ways they were to be used. Mexicanos scored some notable victories by defeating the Horrell clan and driving it from the territory, by deflecting the attack on the Tularosa acequia, and by grazing large flocks of sheep on the public domain well into the 1880s. Gradually, however, political control in Santa Fe and the southeastern counties shifted to Anglos, and the flow of newcomers from Texas earned the area the sobriquet "Little Texas." And Mexicanos lost.[14]

The Rio Arriba country in the northwest corner of the territory also witnessed long-term skirmishing. In this region that had been settled primarily by Mexicanos with community grants, encroachment began in the form of land speculators and politicians like Thomas Catron or Thomas Burns, and land and cattle companies like the Carlisle Cattle Company or the Rio Arriba Land and Cattle Company (both of which were owned by Englishmen). Lumbering, mining, and the Denver and Rio Grande Railroad added to the Anglo presence and potential for friction, but the primary and continual basis for conflict revolved around the use of common lands.[15]

Speculators tried to acquire title to community grants by purchasing or otherwise obtaining the interests of the original grantees and their heirs. If a speculator failed to get hold of all the extant interests, far and away the usual case, he would argue for the consolidation of his fractional interest—the undivided privately held tract ploy—and bring suit to have the grant partitioned. Speculators were not averse to selling their alleged grant interests to cattle companies well before the question of title had been settled. The report of an English land and cattle company officer to his fellow directors in London gives a glimpse of how the system worked:

> The point of greatest difficulty is to decide what to do with our Western land. Chaves in the middle is a troublesome neighbor; they envy us the Chama Canon, and in the partition have been allowed a footing, by which they can give us some trouble, by encroachment. The best plan seems to be crowd them out as much as possible. The partition does not preclude our herding cattle on their land, or they on ours, only each side has the right of driving the other's cattle back. . . . It is apparent, therefore, that the side which keeps the larger herd wins.[16]

The push-pull struggle for grazing land accounted for most of the friction between Anglo and Mexicano in the Rio Arriba region throughout most of the nineteenth century. And, in truth, the fact that Anglos were becoming active in the area, and the fact that, bit by bit, significant chunks of Mexicano land were being alienated before the law, did not affect the Mexicanos very much. They held a great numerical superiority in the region. They made up the juries in Tierra Amarilla. And, for the most part, they were still able to graze on the pasture land as they had in the past. Anglo and Mexicano engaged in comparatively low-key jousting along the banks of the Chama and its tributaries until well into the twentieth century.

This was not the case, however, farther to the northwest. Life in the area around Farmington moved at a faster tempo and with greater heat. The Four Corners area, like Lincoln County, was a frontier in which both Anglo and Mexicano were recent arrivals. Shooting wars between cattlemen and sheepmen—i.e., Anglo and Mexicano—occurred ever more frequently as the nineteenth century drew to a close. Anglos enjoyed a numerical parity in the northwest and chafed under the Mexicano county government seated at Tierra Amarilla. They solved this problem by successfully petitioning the territorial legislature to create San Juan County out of the western portion of Rio Arriba County and then instituting the practice of prohibiting Mexicanos from serving on juries there on the grounds that they were Penitentes.[17]

Our discussion thus far has addressed skirmishing in southeastern and northwestern New Mexico. These two areas of high violent activity during the territorial years had no direct connection with land grants. We have included these areas for two reasons: first, Mexicano resistance to the expropriation of grant lands is part and parcel of Mexicano resistance to Anglo encroachment in New Mexico as a whole, and second, the fundamental issue at stake in the southeast and the northwest was land—albeit land not formally granted by Spain and Mexico, but land which Mexicanos sought to use in traditional ways and which Anglos wanted to own in large private estates. And, as the comparative quiet of the Rio Arriba country during the territorial years illustrates, Mexicano resistance was touched off by actual, tangible interference in day-to-day land use. Two areas of the territory on the eastern slope of the Sangre de Cristo Mountains supported movements of violent resistance that arose directly from encroachment on grant land.

The Beaubien-Miranda or Maxwell land grant was awarded to Charles Beaubien and Guadalupe Miranda by Governor Manuel Armijo in 1841. Mexicanos migrated to the area, east from Taos and north from San Miguel, throughout the remainder of the century, taking up homesites along the Cimarron, Ponil, and Vermejo rivers and their tributaries. Lucien Maxwell, Charles Beaubien's son-in-law, was the only one connected with the original grantees to take an active interest in the grant, and he was more concerned with his ranching and mercantile interests than with exerting landlordship over Mexicano subsistence farmers, and he was uncertain as to the actual boundaries of the grant in any event. He was determined to become sole owner of the grant, however, and achieved his ambition by 1867.[18]

Gold was discovered high in the mountains claimed by Maxwell in 1866. The discovery brought a rush of Anglos. The miners were followed quickly by homesteaders and Texas cattlemen. Maxwell changed his casual attitudes toward rents and boundaries as the influx threatened his claim to the vast estate. According to one longtime resident, Maxwell did not claim the Moreno Valley or Ute Creek or "any such damn thing . . . [until] after gold was discovered there."[19] The population increase, and the reasons for it, attracted investors and, on 5 September 1870, Maxwell sold the estate, an estimated 2 million acres, to a group of Englishmen for $1.5 million.[20]

The Maxwell Land Grant and Railway Company began to pressure grant residents almost immediately. And they did so even though the size of their grant was still very much up in the air. Maxwell had cheerfully sold them title to 2,000,000 acres, but Columbus Delano, the incumbent Secretary of the Interior, interpreted Mexican law as limiting the grant to only 97,600 acres. A welter of legal maneuvers and bureaucratic inconstancy followed and lasted well into the ensuing decade; it is masterfully depicted in Jim B. Pearson's *The Maxwell Land Grant*. Undeterred by the cloud over the title, the company tried to exact rents or to force the occupants to purchase their holdings.

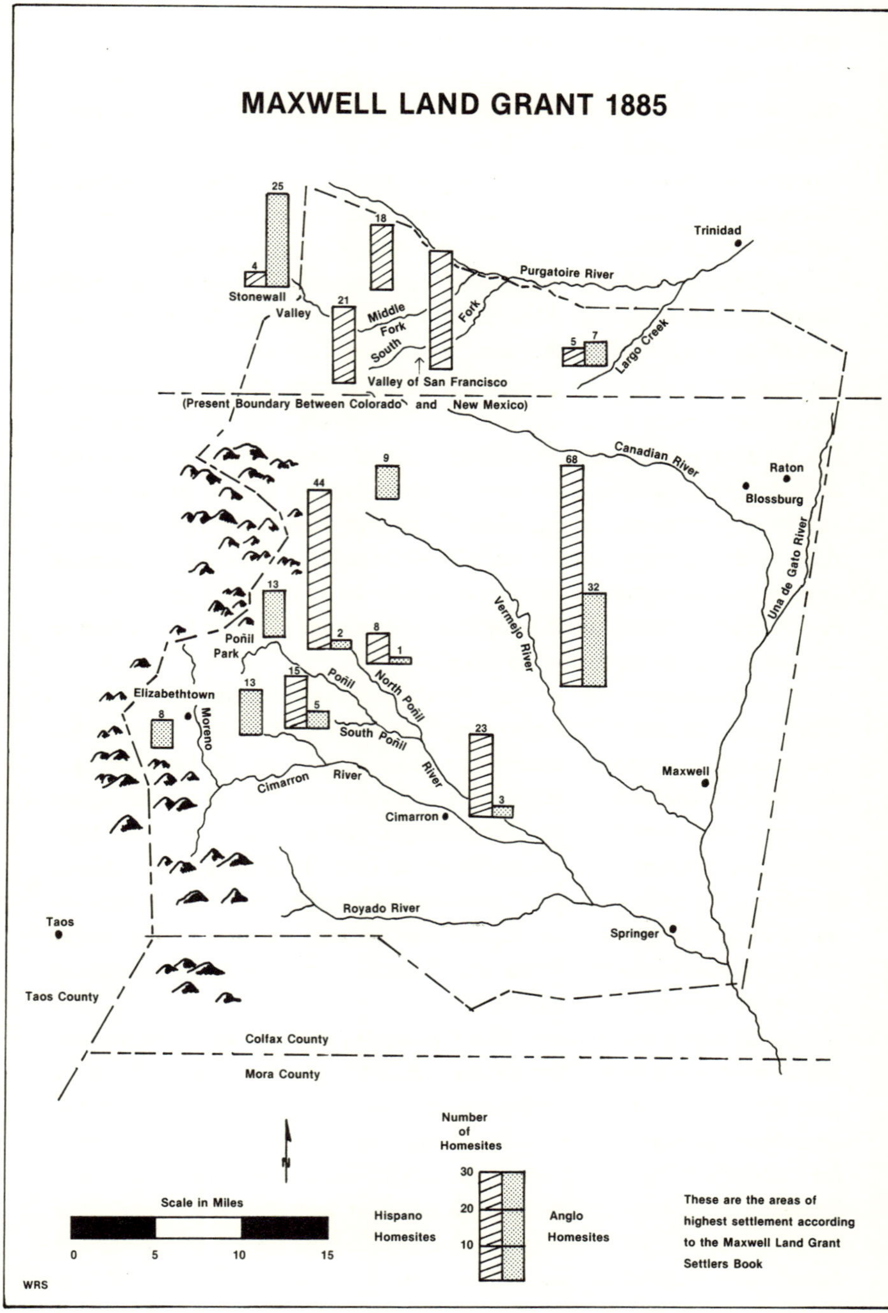

MAP 10. Maxwell land grant, 1885.

The grant residents resisted. During the turbulent decade of the 1870s, Anglo miners, homesteaders, and ranchers fought in the courts, in the legislatures, and with firearms against the corporate claimants. Mexicanos, however, remained aloof from the fray, a posture they maintained for the most straightforward of reasons: the company was not bothering them. Mining towns, mining claims, large ranches, and lumber mills were the most visible and pressing challenges to the Maxwell Land Grant and Railway Company's assertion of ownership.[21]

But things had changed by the turn of the decade. The company solved its financial problems and Dutch bondholders held control. The company was well on its way to clearing title. Company officials, accordingly, increased the pressure on residents to recognize the legitimacy of the company's ownership, using principally the carrot of inexpensive short-term leases and the stock of ejectment suits.

The Anglo dimensions of resistance have been much better covered than those offered by Mexicanos. The volume authored by Pearson has already been mentioned. To it should be added William A. Keleher's *The Maxwell Land Grant,* and Morris F. Taylor's *O. P. McMains and the Maxwell Land Grant Company,* a study of the most vocal company foe.[22] Such careful attention has not been paid to native resisters.

Yet many Mexicanos resisted in a number of ways. On occasion they joined with Anglos and rode in common cause. More often they rode with their friends to forestall the more visible threats posed by *los estranjeros* (outsiders) in their immediate neighborhoods. Company agents must have been surprised. Those who rode into the valleys of the Ponil, Cimarron, and Vermejo rivers in order to count the number of Mexicano farms and to attempt to persuade Mexicanos to sign short-term leases were met with silence, noncooperation, and drawn guns. Warning shots fired from ambush were a frequent occurrence and, occasionally these shots did more than warn. Throughout the 1880s, the company also increased the number of ranches it operated directly. These were ranches that the grant owners had purchased from defeated Anglos or had started from scratch. But as the company tried to bring the Mexicano residents into line, company-owned ranches suffered. Fences were cut; haystacks, barns, and out buildings were put to torch; livestock was stolen, killed, or maimed; and cowboys were fired upon, wounded, and sometimes even killed.[23]

These were not incidents of random violence or cases of isolated individuals frustrated beyond their breaking point (although a few might justly fall into one or the other of these categories). The vast majority of these incidents came about as the result of discussions and decisions carried out by groups of friends organized in *juntas* (meetings) and operating in their immediate locales. In rare instances, as many as 150 people might participate. They would plan resistance on a larger than neighborhood scale or agree to ride en masse against a company target. But the norm, by far, was for friends and neighbors to protect that portion of the earth in which they carried out their day-to-day activities.[24]

Mexicanos rode with Anglos a few times during the early part of the decade, but in most cases Mexicano resistance remained separate from, although parallel to, Anglo anti-grant activity. In fact, Anglo resistance was dead for all practical purposes by 1890, while Mexicano raids of resistance did not reach their peak until the summer of 1891. Company manager M. P. Pels regarded Mexicano resistance as severe enough to warrant using hand grenades to repel attacks. He decided against this course, however, because the last thing he wanted to do was to provoke "this uneducated class" into forming an even more effective combination. Pels adopted instead a policy of divide and conquer. He began to persuade Mexicanos to sign leases for twenty-five percent of their crops, a procedure more in accordance "with the customs of the Mexicans."[25] Patience brought slow results and, by 1899, acknowledgment of company title was virtually unanimous.

Both Mexicano residents and the Maxwell company had waged a true war of attrition. Mexicanos used raids to remove threats to their immediate neighborhoods and to hike the price of landownership above what the company was willing to pay. For his part, Pels recognized that acknowledgment of company title was more important than immediate profit, so he modified the company's position of insistence on cash payments from Mexicanos and the harsh threat of ejectment for those who did not pay to a kind of *partido* system, the traditional Mexicano grazing practice whereby the shepherd received a share of the lamb crop. The patience of Pels and his Dutch stockholders had brought victory.

One of the reasons Pels opted for patience was his fear of an effective combination of Mexicanos who would operate out of the Sangre de Cristos. And one of the reasons he feared such a combination was that at the height of Mexicano resistance on the Maxwell grant there occurred, a scant one hundred miles to the south in San Miguel County,

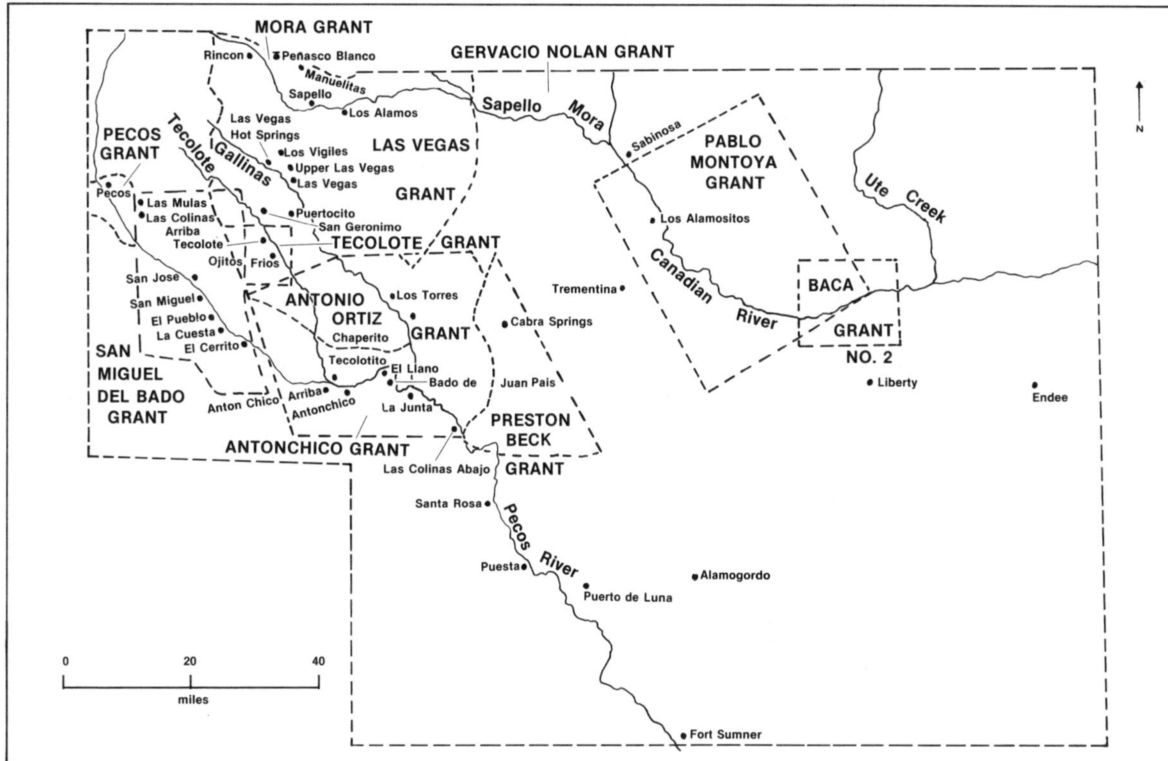

MAP 11. San Miguel County, New Mexico, 1890.

an example of how effectively the "uneducated class" of Mexicanos could combine and take decisive action.

Las Gorras Blancas, as the San Miguel combination of the uneducated class was called, struck at least seventy-eight times between April 1889, and September 1890. Their most frequent targets were the barbed wire fences that both Anglos and ricos were erecting to enclose large sections of the common land in the county, but they were also burning houses, barns, out buildings, railroad bridges, and sawmills. Las Gorras Blancas were armed resisters willing to use their weapons. They also knew the value of publicity and demonstrated their savvy by posting broadsides in the county seat of Las Vegas to promulgate their positions.[26]

The San Miguel region had been settled early in the nineteenth century; community grants were dominant from the beginning. There were fourteen major grants in the general area, of which six were community grants. Four of these—The San Miguel del Bado, the Antonchico, the Las Vegas, and the Tecolote—together encompassed more than 1,100,000 acres and they were virtually contiguous. It was on these grants that most of the controversial fencing occurred and it was from these grants that most of the night-riding Las Gorras Blancas came.[27]

Las Gorras Blancas were sufficiently numerous and unified and were drawn from a sufficiently widespread geographical area to have their effort termed a full-fledged coordinated rebellion. To this extent Las Gorras Blancas were unique in nineteenth-century New Mexico. They were also remarkably successful. By the end of the summer of 1890 no fences enclosed the common lands in the San Miguel country and none were being constructed.

A number of factors came together to produce at least a temporary victory for Las Gorras Blancas. Foremost among these was the overwhelming numerical superiority of Mexicanos in the population. A conservative estimate puts the ratio of Mexicano to Anglo in San Miguel at greater than five to one. Of almost equal importance in their success were the age and interconnections of the Mexicano communities. The oldest plazas had witnessed three generations come and go, and the newer ones had been settled by surplus population from the older. Thus, important kinship ties and long-standing relationships bound the natives of this region together. The coalition was enhanced by the mobility of a grazing economy.

The complexity and cohesion of the Mexicano society in San Miguel's countryside contrasted sharply with the differences that existed within the Anglo community. At the time, Las Vegas rivaled Albuquerque and Santa Fe as New Mexico's leading city. In the tradition of nineteenth-century boosterism, the city's Anglo merchants and politicians were often at odds with the large Anglo-owned cattle companies who threatened to enclose the surrounding common land for their own exclusive use. Las Vegas's city fathers worried about these cattle companies because one of the threatened grants, the Las Vegas grant, had been patented by Congress to the town of Las Vegas. This congressional act raised the happy possibility that the town's municipal government could control development on the grant's common land. Anglo homesteaders, small ranchers, and railroad workers opposed enclosure by large land and cattle companies, too. Their opposition, however, stemmed more from the conviction that the land in question was public domain and, therefore, available for preemption, rather than from any sympathy for the plight of los hombres pobres or an understanding of, or belief in the integrity of, community land grants.

The final element in the political chemistry of San Miguel County was a coterie of young, ambitious Mexicano businessmen and politicos who supported Las Gorras Blancas. They gave public support to the justice of the night-riders' position, and private support in more active ways, because these raiders were a force that could advance the businessmen's interests.

The combination of these elements, mercurial as some of them may have been, produced, by 1890, a widespread popular sympathy for Las Gorras Blancas. They were especially admired for their success in inhibiting the economic and political domination of the county by eastern- or foreign-owned land and cattle companies. An embarrassed Governor L. B. Prince tried to explain popular support for the Gorras to the Secretary of the Interior:

> half the population of Las Vegas, including the best citizens, sympathize with fence-cutting on the Las Vegas Grant, and this prevents that strong public sentiment which we ought to have as an aid in suppressing these outrages.[28]

The history of its settlement and a particular concatenation of factors provided the San Miguel region with an almost perfect setting for a coordinated rebellion. There was even an Anglo-American vehicle to coordinate the county's growing discontent. That vehicle was the Knights of Labor or Los Caballeros de Labor. It exerted its influence largely through the person of the Knight's district organizer, Juan Jose Herrera, who appears to have played a role similar to that of Primo Tapia as described in Paul Friedrich's *Agrarian Revolt in a Mexican Village.*[29] Herrera received his commission as an organizer in 1887, and his tireless efforts over the next three years brought about a proliferation of local assemblies. Emphasizing the anti-monopoly and anti-landgrabbing positions of the union as a national organization, Herrera used the local assemblies to link the angry Mexicanos living on the threatened grants. He even added such common labor issues of the day as discriminatory wage rates and political corruption to the fundamental concerns of the natives of San Miguel.

It is unlikely that there was a one hundred percent correlation in the membership of Los Caballeros de Labor and Las Gorras Blancas. Nevertheless, the observations of hostile critics at that time and current oral tradition insist that there was.[30] It is more probable, however, that Herrera, and his brothers Pablo and Nicanor, secretly recruited Las Gorras Blancas from the membership of the union's local assemblies. In some San Miguel locales there could have been a virtual duplication of Knights and night-riders. In others the correlation undoubtedly was not as great.

Herrera coordinated, but he did not create. Mexicanos knew, indeed had already defined, the fundamental issue that confronted them, and they were skilled in the basic tactics needed to cope with it. Herrera merely provided a better means of communication and cooperation among the resisters. He was also able to focus a Mexicano discontent over wages and politics that had never before been articulated. Moreover, he suggested to his embattled friends and neighbors the effectiveness of public demonstrations and the necessity of posting *proclamaciones* (in all probability he provided the printing press). Perhaps most important of all was the optimism he provided them in the form of his link with the natives' most powerful labor organization, the Knights of Labor. Even so, he did not teach los hombres pobres how to resist; he did not have to.

Herrera was from San Miguel County. Before becoming a leader, he had traveled throughout the Rocky Mountain West, joining the Knights of Labor at some point in his wanderings. His roots in the county were of primary importance in allowing him to organize as effectively as he did. The combination of his personal connections in San Miguel and his experience in the outside world helped him to bridge the gap between embattled farmers and grazers in the countryside and the young liberal politicos of Las Vegas. As a result of his success, he was able to bring about the most significant linkage between widespread popular discontent and conventional politics that New Mexico would witness during the entire territorial period.[31]

Politics: The Territorial Years

In September 1890, Las Vegas witnessed the birth of a new political party: El Partido del Pueblo Unido. The name was not new; a "People's Party" was organized by the San Miguel Anglo Knights of Labor in 1888. Indeed, it was common practice in the territory to give the name "People's Party" to new political coalitions. But El Partido del Pueblo stands above the run-of-the-mill people's parties because it emerged as an effort to channel the energies unleashed by Las Gorras Blancas, and because it eventually allied itself with the national People's Party soon to emerge from the Ocala Convention.[32]

The new coalition would give life to that old expression "politics makes strange bedfellows." Former Republican sheriff and *jefe politico* Lorenzo Lopez was there; involved in a growing feud with his brother-in-law, Eugenio Romero, Lopez saw in the new organization a chance to wrest political control of the county from his comfortably entrenched in-law. Anglo Democrats and Anglo Knights of Labor joined, viewing the party as the only local alternative to the Republicans. Some of them also saw the new party as a vehicle to give expression to the kind of anti-monopoly sentiment that would soon coalesce nationally around the Populists. Also prominent in the rolls of the new party were young, ambitious Mexicano politicos and businessmen whose political orientations were definitely liberal or progressive for the time.

Despite the heterogeneous nature of the new party's participants, El Partido del Pueblo Unido won the 1890 election, using a campaign that emphasized anti-landgrabbing and anti-monopoly themes. The precinct returns show that Mexicano voters knew whom and what they were voting for: only a handful of the sixty-three precincts show enough consistency of totals for each slate to raise suspicions of bossism, while most of them have enough variation to indicate that Mexicano voters were fully capable of making distinctions based upon the issues and relative merits of individual candidates. Los hombres pobres did not participate in the party councils or conventions, but the county election returns for 1890 (and later for 1892) make it clear that they were perfectly able to make electoral choices based upon their collective self-interest when the issues were cast in those terms—a rare happening during the territorial years.[33]

The territorial legislature passed two laws relating to land grants during the 1891 session. The first was an act to incorporate land grants. It called for the election of a board of trustees to administer the grant, its members to be drawn from legitimate grant residents. The second was a fence law introduced by Nestor Montoya from San Miguel's large legislative delegation. It provided that a "good title to lands" should be the touchstone for fencing. Moreover, Montoya's law made the destruction of fences where there was "good title" a felony. It also made the construction of fences without "title in fee simple" a felony.[34]

In San Miguel, activities aimed at resisting expropriation of grant lands revolved around movements either to incorporate grants under the new territorial statute or to file claims for them before the newly created U.S. Court of Private Land Claims. The history of the Las Vegas and San Miguel del Bado grants illustrates the pitfalls that los pobres encountered with each approach.

In the summer of 1891, District Judge James O'Brien elated many by ruling that there was a ten-year limitation law that gave all Mexicano residents of the Las Vegas grant clear title to their holdings. O'Brien's decision initiated a determined attempt to incorporate the grant; El Partido del Pueblo enthusiastically identified with it and soon dominated the proceedings. But internal differences brought it all to naught.

The problem was a serious three-way split over definitions of grant ownership. As Congress had originally patented it as the Town of Las Vegas grant, many Anglo entrepreneurs, progressive Mexicanos, and old-line jefes wanted control of the land to reside within the city limits where the municipal government could administer its development. More radical Anglos, soon to bolt from El Partido del Pueblo and join the nationally affiliated Populists, wanted the unoccupied land thrown open to homesteading. Los hombres pobres, and those most closely affiliated with them in party councils (people such as Juan Jose Herrera), wanted the board elected by residents from the entire grant. They also wanted the traditional practices on community land grants preserved as much as possible. The issue was not successfully resolved. The impasse and the tensions associated with it increased until the party fragmented, bringing about a complete reshuffling of political alignments by the election of 1894.[35]

A group of Anglos from San Miguel journeyed to Washington D.C. in 1895 and presented their case before the District Court in the nation's capital. Their suit was successful in that the court ruled that the town of Las Vegas did have jurisdiction over the grant. The Department of the Interior, unhappy with the decision, appealed it to the Supreme Court and lost. Reluctantly, Interior Secretary C. N. Bliss directed that the patent be issued to the town upon completion of an official survey. Such a survey was concluded in 1900, but another problem arose: Las Vegas was not an incorporated muncipality. This difficulty, too, was overcome; the territorial legislature and judiciary in a combined move vested control of the grant with an Anglo-dominated board appointed by the territorial district court. For all intents and purposes, the Las Vegas grant was in the hands of land speculators by 1902, and its common lands were disposed of in the name of progress.

The U.S. Court of Private Land Claims proved no kinder to community grant owners. The residents of the San Miguel del Bado grant applied to the court for confirmation as a community grant. The court ruled in their favor in 1894 and confirmed some 315,000 acres, the entire amount of the grant. U.S. Attorney Mathew G. Reynolds appealed, arguing that "a large amount of these three hundred thousand acres [have] never been used, or occupied beneficially by anybody."[36] The Supreme Court concurred with Reynolds and, in 1897, ordered that only those lands on the grant actually occupied should be confirmed, an area characterized by one observer as nothing but house lots and garden plots. Employing this criterion, only 5,024 acres were recognized, the balance of the grant being declared public domain. One result of this action was the destruction of the grant's viability for almost all its Mexicano residents. As Richard Bradfrute has observed in *The Court of Private Land Claims,* the San Miguel del Bado case established a precedent: the court could remove all unoccupied land (that is, land held in common) from its community grant confirmations.[37]

Not all community grants suffered the fate of the San Miguel and Las Vegas grants. The Antonchico grant, for example, was both patented by Congress and incorporated under territorial statute. An elected board of trustees was given the responsibility to administer it, an arrangement that still exists even though the grant is only one-third the size of its original patent. Nevertheless the history of the San Miguel and Las Vegas grants illustrates the problems Mexicanos encountered when their struggle for survival shifted from the familiar terrain of their grant to distant courts of law.

El Partido del Pueblo Unido stands out as the most clear-cut attempt to develop a political movement with the legitimate grievances of the Mexicanos as a primary motive. But the brevity of its life overshadowed its original successes. Organized to take advantage of the fierce energy unleashed by Las Gorras Blancas, its leaders used a rhetoric that spoke of uniting all Mexicanos in the territory and throughout the Southwest. They would organize an army of voters that would bring to poor Mexicanos the full privileges and benefits of American citizenship. Yet the party survived only four years in San Miguel.

The reasons for its surprisingly short life are several. The leadership of the party was divided in both composition and motive. The old-line jefes merely wanted to maintain their traditional activities and roles. Anglo radicals were concerned with a number of burning issues in which the preservation of the community land grants did not figure at all, and the young politicos were striving to gain leading positions in the world of liberal capitalism. Los pobres, the source of the party's electoral strength, cared little about such populistic issues as free silver, education, or a more equitable form of "progress"; they just wanted to keep their common land. When the movement became political, politicos took over, and Las Gorras Blancas watched with well-founded cynicism as matters turned to business as usual after only four short years. El Partido del Pueblo Unido was brought down as much by the diverse backgrounds and goals of the county's Mexicanos as by the effectiveness of Anglo opposition.

Other political activity germane to the land grant question included petitions to the territorial governor or other involved officials in order to obtain redress of grievances. Often the most active defenders of los pobres were those federally appointed officials who happened to be reformers. Governor Edmund G. Ross is a prime example, as the message accompanying his 1887 veto of a bill to regulate practices in cases of torts demonstrates. According to Ross, the purpose of the act was to "revolutionize the rules of evidence" regarding question of title to community land grants by placing the burden of proof on the defendant. This meant that a land speculator could claim a land grant virtually at will, confident that most community grant residents possessed neither the knowledge of the law nor the funds necessary to challenge his claim. The bill, Ross concluded, was a "cunningly devised scheme of robbery as directed mainly to the eviction of the occupants of this class of land grants."[38] Los pobres were fortunate to have Ross as their governor, for there were precious few watchdogs to guard their interests during the territorial period.

Violence: The Modern Era

Violence has continued to be a major part of Mexicano resistance into the twentieth century. Indeed, much of the recent resistance has direct connections with the bitter struggles of the preceding century. For example, Las Gorras Blancas, masked, mounted, and some one hundred strong, rode through the village of Antonchico in 1903 en route to cutting a fence that enclosed prime grazing lands atop a nearby mesa. Still at it in 1927, Las Gorras Blancas attacked the fences on the adjacent Preston Beck grant, an assault that was met by machine gun fire.[39]

In east-central New Mexico, the legacy of Las Gorras Blancas lived well into the new century. In the Rio Arriba country to the northwest, Anglo claimants to large landed estates exerted far more pressure on the everyday functions of Mexicanos than they ever had before. Native Rio Arriba residents responded with the traditional forms of violence: fence cutting, barn and haystack burning, cattle maiming, firing shots to warn intruders, and arranging ambushes. And there is some intriguing evidence that from the late twenties to the mid-thirties a shadowy organization known as La Mano Negra coordinated and executed a large number of these attacks.

La Mano Negra has been described variously as an anarchist society modeled after the Andalusian group of the same name and imported to New Mexico by recent Spanish immigrants, a bootlegging ring organized in response to Colorado's prohibition law of 1916, and a gang that controlled all of northern New Mexico's criminal activity.[40] Unfortunately, there are few known published materials that deal with La Mano Negra. But there are enough references to this alleged group to warrant an exhaustive investigation. Certainly, there is nothing inherently far-fetched about the possible existence of La Mano Negra. We know that violent attacks were directed against large landowners, that bootlegging was a significant economic activity, and that robbery and other crimes occurred with relatively high frequency. We also know that Mexicanos are quite adept at organizing around issues which directly affect their well-being.

It is not implausible, therefore, that an organization like La Mano Negra existed in Rio Arriba County during the second quarter of the twentieth century. Moreover, if it did exist, its mode of resistance would come closer than any of the groups in New Mexico to Eric Hobsbawm's social bandit model of rebellion. It was an organization whose activities were defined by the state as criminal; los pobres would have regarded them as such *if they had been committed against them,* but they generally applauded the actions as attacks against outsiders and oppressors.[41]

La Mano Negra aside, it is clear that fence cutting, burnings, and warning shots were a way of life (an inescapably present, if infrequent, fact of existence in rural Rio Arriba). As Richard Gardner observed, "countless marauding apparitions throng the folk memory of Rio Arriba, some with names, some known only by the name of the family or families involved."[42] It is in light of this legacy of long-term skirmishing that the courthouse raid at Tierra Amarilla must be viewed.

The story of the actual raid, its aftermath, and the general context in which it took place has been told often enough not to be repeated. The volumes by Peter Nabokov, Patricia Bell Blawis, and especially Richard Gardner deal with it very well. There are, however, two points about the raid that need emphasis: it was *not* an aberration of the Mexicano experience, and it *does* give evidence of a significant shift in the nature of Mexicano resistance.

The first point, that the courthouse raid was not an aberration, is absolutely fundamental. It is especially important because Tijerina—the leader of the Alianza and the person with whom the general public today links the land issue—is from Texas. To dismiss the raid as the work of an outside agitator and the aberrant behavior of a handful of misguided fools in the emotional thrall of a charismatic madman is to dismiss the issue. Indeed, by extension, it is to dismiss the severity of the overall land problem still facing Mexicanos. More importantly, it downgrades the people themselves; it somehow makes them less worthy, less human, in much the same way that the so-called gook syndrome allowed U.S. combat troops during World War II and the Vietnam War to downgrade peoples from the underdeveloped areas of the world. It is the same line of reasoning employed in the South during the civil rights turmoil of the late fifties and early sixties, i.e., that the violence there was a product of northern agitators because "our niggers are happy."

Anglos in the Rio Arriba country had known for decades that "their Meskins" were not happy. Furthermore, they knew why—land. People distant from the smoldering brushfires of long-term skirmishing may have been dumbfounded by the dramatic raid. Those closer to the situation knew better. Indeed many of them may have been happy to blame Tijerina for all the problems facing the people of Rio Arriba County. He was the one person who could transform their long-term discontent into a major upheaval. But violent attack was a fundamental, normal, basic, and understandable part of Mexicano life. This does not necessarily mean that it was frequent. It is normal for one company to sue another as a means to right a wrong, but this does not mean that a company must frequently be sued to be normal. What it does mean is this: Tijerina could get people to attack the courthouse because they knew how to do it and doing it made sense to them.

The second important point about the courthouse raid was the shift it symbolized in the thinking and perceptions of the Mexicanos of Rio Arriba County. As far as we can ascertain from our own research, the courthouse raid was the first time that violence was employed as a key element in a much larger strategy. All previous instances of violence had a measure of directness about them; they were attacks on the more visible and tangible causes of a situation, whether they involved problems pertaining to fences, livestock, buildings, or evil individuals. In the past, violence was a part of a world view that said, if offending objects or recalcitrant people were removed, problems could be solved and life could be returned to a proper balance. No one was under the illusion that raiding the courthouse at Tierra Amarilla in the hopes of capturing District Attorney Alfonso Sanchez was going to bring about a return of lands once held in common on the Tierra Amarilla grant. The raid was part of a larger strategy involving political action, action which antedates, significantly enough, the organization of Tijerina's Alianza.

Politics: The Modern Era

The nonviolent, or political, activity aimed at resistance to the expropriation (or in recent years, repossession) of grant lands appears to have evolved slowly among los pobres of New Mexico. It was the result of a gradual awareness that the law and the law courts could help them, too. It was an evolutionary change spurred on by increasing Anglo pressure on the lands held in common for many generations.

The pressures exerted on Mexicano grant residents varied from place to place. In the San Miguel country, for example, opportunities for wage labor offset the livestock reduction occasioned by the loss of the common lands. Consequently, the economic effects of land expropriation were not fully felt until the Great Depression. Similarly, Mexicanos were not barred from using common grazing land that had been transferred to the Forest Service until that agency began to favor the large (read Anglo) ranchers over small grazers in its permit policy.

The process of expropriation, like the growth of a cancer, was a slow and invisible one. In fact its progress was sometimes so advanced as to make its eventual discovery almost meaningless. William deBuys offers a lively case study of how this insidious process could work. His "Fractions of Justice: A Legal and Social History of Las Trampas Grant, N.M." describes a convolution three decades in the making that ultimately delivered the Las Trampas grant to the Carson National Forest. The tale begins with the greed of a Mexicano grant resident. With a smattering of knowledge about Anglo law, he began a process that proceeded through the requisite double-handful of lawyers and officials, men lacking even in Falstaff's claim to indifferent honesty. The process resulted in the bankruptcy of an Anglo lumber company before culminating in federal possession of the land tract. The irony of the Las Trampas case is that Juan Bautista Ortega, the grant resident who realized what was going on some fifteen years after the plot's inception and who organized the unsuccessful legal battle to resist the process, is now remembererd in the oral tradition of the area as the traitor who sold the grant.[43]

Successful maneuvering in Anglo courts did not necessarily guarantee eternal tranquility for the Mexicaños. Incorporating under the laws of New Mexico and the United States was one of the best methods available to a community grant for thwarting encroachment from the private sector or curbing the appetite of the federal government. But corporations, including incorporated land grants, must pay taxes (or hire good tax lawyers) and many of these patented and incorporated community grants soon ran afoul of the tax laws. Their problem was twofold. First, a grant was assessed as an entity—house lots, garden plots, and common land included—so that grant residents had to raise the needed amount in concert. Second, cash, the only acceptable form of payment, was usually a scarce commodity. Grants whose internal political structures were sufficiently resilient and whose residents had sufficient liquidity could meet these challenges and survive. Those without sufficient cooperative will or ready cash lost their common lands to tax sales.[44]

Law suits and participation in electoral politics (both overt and clandestine) provided other avenues for resistance. In the Rio Arriba country shortly after statehood, for example, the Abiquiu Corporation was formed to protect the interests of the grant residents from land loss. After four decades, the title machinations of speculators like Thomas Catron and T. D. Burns finally began to impinge on the traditional use of grazing land. Moreover, the federal government operating through the Carson National Forest curtailed usage even further in subsequent decades. For half a century, the Abiquiu Corporation, under various titles, channeled the efforts of its members into law suits against Anglo land claimants and into political support for friendly state and county candidates. The suits and the political activity, it must be remembered, occurred simultaneously with the violent resistance offered by La Mano Negra and its related combinations.

During the fifty years prior to Reies López Tijerina's arrival in northern New Mexico, Mexicanos were becoming increasingly aware of the threat posed by Anglo encroachment. With this awareness came a concomitant comprehension of the tactics needed for combat in an arena characterized by Anglo domination. But this comprehension was nascent. Lawsuits were brought in the name of individuals over control of specific land tracts. Politicos, of course, had many more issues to deal with than just land grant policy. And violence was still directed at such specific manifestations of Anglo encroachment as fences, haystacks, buildings, and livestock. More significant, however, Mexicanos of northern New Mexico were losing ground.

Tijerina based La Alianza on his conception of legal precedent and diplomatic procedure. Most important, he addressed the question of community land grants in a general rather than specific way. Tijerina and La Alianza, therefore, signaled a significantly different tack for resistance to land expropriation than that pursued by Las Gorras Blancas or the battle-hardened Mexicanos of the Rio Arriba country. As the San Miguel experience of the late nineteenth century demonstrates, los pobres did not perceive the boundaries and constituent elements of the actual arena in which their fate would be decided. Those native politicians who did understand all the complexities were neither interested in including los pobres in their councils nor concerned with making the integrity of the community land grants a *sine qua non* of their programs.

La Alianza was a major conceptual change, then, for the following reasons: los pobres were central to the movement; the courts, politics, and publicity were the principal means used in its battle; it sought alliances with other disenfranchised groups across the nation; and *violence was used for its symbolic effect,* not as a direct solution. Restoring or preserving community grants constituted the core of the movement's program. But social issues, such as employment, health, and education, were truly integrated elements of the Alianza platform not just a veneer added to attract support, such as Las Gorras Blancas tried to do through *La Platforma.* The campaign of La Alianza, in short, marked the first time that those involved in resistance to the expropriation of land grants in New Mexico recognized the true scope and dimensions of the arena in which it had to do battle.

La Alianza ultimately foundered on a number of elements, not the least of which were the unfavorable aftermath of the raid and Tijerina's subsequent imprisonment. The central issue, furthermore, failed to attract significant support from those Mexicanos who were neither grant residents nor grant heirs, simply because they could not partake in the fruits of possible victory. And for many the idea of community land grants, with its agrarian simplicity, was nothing but a romantic anachronism.

The Nature of Resistance

Resistance to the expropriation of grant lands is marked by its short-term successes and long-term failures. The reason for these mixed results is clear: Mexicanos have been good at fighting what they can see and comprehend and, like everybody else, ineffectual in combating attacks launched from outside their conceptual framework. Moreover, in fighting the bewildering challenge to their lands, New Mexico grant residents went through almost the same kind of processes experienced by colonized peoples the world over. And they responded in many of the same ways. But in New Mexico, the slow, tentative nature of Anglo America's gains through attrition worked to keep resistance even more isolated and confined than is generally the case when traditional societies are threatened by more modern ones. As historian Eric Hobsbawm has observed, peasants (or their agrarian equivalents in New Mexico) have only two frames of reference for action: the universe, which consists of everything they have ever heard about or conceived of, and their locality, the simple, practical world bounded by the limits of their actual activities.[45] Neither conceptualization makes for effective action against a modern opponent.

This circumscription was so pronounced in New Mexico that, prior to Tijerina, the coordination of Las Gorras Blancas represented the greatest degree of unity attained. Nowhere did it approach the commonality of focus achieved in a *jacquerie,* let alone possess any driving ideological force. The particular isolation of Mexicano enclaves and the lack of communication between them, when coupled with the diverse and fragmented pattern of Anglo encroachment and expropriation (it was very rare that significant numbers of Mexicano communities faced the same threat at the same time), accounts for the extreme localism of much of the native resistance. The geographic shift from territorial periphery to the Rio Arriba area only underscores this localism.

Localism was compounded by the nature of the community land grant issue itself. Legitimate residents resisted expropriation to retain *their* rights to *their* land, not for an abstract principle of civil government or social organization.[46] This exclusivity had a limiting effect much like that found in the fermentation of alcohol. Just as yeast in that process produces alcohol, so does a sense of belonging, such as that which united grant residents into concerted action, have the same effect. But just when enough alcohol is produced to kill the yeast and stop fermentation, so did the exclusivity of grant residency place a crippling limit on the number of people involved in any particular resistance movement. La Alianza redefined the issue enough to increase the number of resisters by an exponential factor, but not enough to stop the automatic cut-off point which results from such exclusivity.

New Mexico grant residents who resisted were (and are) a rural, self-sufficient people engaged in a straightforward economy founded on subsistence agriculture. They were confronted by emissaries from a powerful, modern nation-state bent on replacing the local economic system with one grounded on a market-oriented capitalism. Mexicanos fought back, using controlled, limited violence directed against offending and sometimes "evil" people. They were determined to drive los estranjeros from their world. No bloody riots or indiscriminate massacres appear in the chronicle of Mexicano resistance in New Mexico. Such absence underscores that these were patient, reasonable people from a traditional face-to-face world, who only wanted to put that world right again. It remains to be seen what their future course will be.

Sources and Methodology

As mentioned at the outset, research on Mexicano resistance to Anglo expropriation has just begun. The body of literature is neither mature nor voluminous enough to have gone through revisionistic cycles or to have fueled heated debates between schools of interpretation. More is needed. Resistance was carried out by los pobres and they left few written records. Such a dearth means that anyone interested in researching resistance must use a multiplicity of sources in conjunction with a carefully devised methodology to approximate or understand what happened and why.

It is our belief that the first element in any effective methodology directed at grasping the "whys" and "wherefores" of resistance is attitudinal. Simply stated, the proper attitude begins with a belief that resistance was not only possible but in many instances probable. Added to such a predisposition is a sensitivity to the range and variety of forms resistance can take. Finally, there must be a conviction that resistance does not have to be successful to be significant. Investigators of the history of native resistance in New Mexico or the resistance of oppressed people anywhere must put aside the strong cultural bias toward "significance."

Very little of New Mexico's historical literature deals expressly with native resistance. Published works on the subject tend to concentrate on either Las Gorras Blancas or La Alianza. Those that deal with Las Gorras include Andrew Bancroft Schlesinger's "Las Gorras Blancas, 1889–1891,"[47] Robert J. Rosenbaum's "*'Por las masas de los hombres pobres':* Las Gorras Blancas of San Miguel County, 1889–1890,"[48] and Robert W. Larson's "The White Caps of New Mexico: A Study of Ethnic Militancy in the Southwest."[49] Studies of La Alianza include Peter Nabakov's *Tijerina and the Courthouse Raid,*[50] Patricia Bell Blawis's *Tijerina and the Land Grants: Mexican Americans in Struggle for Their*

Heritage,[51] Frances L. Swadesh's "The Alianza Movement in New Mexico,"[52] and Richard Gardner's *Grito! Reies Tijerina and the New Mexico Land Grant War of 1967.*[53] The last work in the list is the most contextually complete—both historically and culturally—but in many ways the most frustrating because of Gardner's lack of documentation. Also relevant are Larson's *New Mexico Populism: A Study of Radical Protest in a Western Territory,*[54] which discusses El Partido del Pueblo Unido of San Miguel County at some length, and Rosenbaum's *Mexicano Resistance in the Southwest: "The Sacred Right of Self-Preservation,"*[55] which addresses several New Mexico resistance movements, along with several in Texas and California, during the nineteenth and early twentieth centuries.

Other published works that impinge on the issue of resistance include the growing body of land grant studies—exemplified by the series of which this study is a part—discussed elsewhere in this volume. Traditional New Mexico histories such as Howard R. Lamar's *The Far Southwest, 1846–1912: A Territorial History,*[56] Warren Beck's *New Mexico: A History of Four Centuries,*[57] or Lynn I. Perrigo's *The American Southwest: Its Peoples and Cultures*[58] ought to be reread in light of the attitude discussed earlier, for if the reader is properly sensitized, the indications of rumblings and discontent among the people will jump from the pages of these narratives.

Looking for clues of discontent, conflict, and resistance with antennae properly adjusted is an essential part of the methodology necessary to research native resistance effectively. In our view, such proper adjustment involves an understanding of the culture of the grant residents and some notion about the nature and causes of popular rebellions. Studies that we found useful in this regard include Olen C. Leonard's *The Role of the Land Grant in the Social Organization and Social Processes of a Spanish-American Village in New Mexico,*[59] Paul Kutsche's and John R. Van Ness's *Cañones: Values, Crisis, and Survival in a Northern New Mexico Village,*[60] and Frances L. Swadesh's *Los Primeros Pobladores: Hispanic Americans of the Ute Frontier.*[61] For analyses of popular rebellions, we recommend Eric Hobsbawm's *Social Bandits and Primitive Rebels,*[62] Eric Wolf's *Peasant Wars of the Twentieth Century,*[63] and Ted Robert Gurr's *Why Men Rebel.*[64]

Also we think we are justified in saying that historians of resistance should have some familiarity with the concept of culture. Our reason is simple: to understand why people did what they did, it is necessary to have some grasp of how they perceived a situation and what they conceived to be desirable and possible courses of action. We favor the concept of culture articulated by Clifford Geertz: "Culture consists of the socially established structures of meaning in terms of which people do such things as signal conspiracies and join them or perceive insults and answer them."[65] To comprehend such motivations, one needs some understanding of what the people under study thought were possible and desirable causes of action. Thus, we recommend using the concept of culture. We hasten to recommend it, however, as an *approach* to understanding a past event not as an explanation for it. We also warn against using the cultural concept to pit one culture against another in a hierarchy of superiority. Moreover, we emphasize in the strongest possible terms that using the concept of culture to approach the past should in no way preclude an economic, technological, or any other kind of causal analysis.

Armed with a proper attitude, an understanding of Mexicano culture, and some sense of the nature of popular rebellion, the researcher is ready to examine the documentary record. Newspapers, particularly from the Spanish-language press, are excellent sources for locating discontent: although not published by los pobres, many of the native newspapers report fights, slights, injustices, and tensions left uncovered by their English counterparts. The correspondence of Anglo politicians like Thomas B. Catron and his ilk are also helpful. These letters and personal memos reveal a great deal about how expectant political bosses attempted to woo Mexicano voters and, if the efforts were successful, how to maintain loyalty. A study of their strenuous efforts can also illuminate much about Mexicano village social structure. Helpful, too, are the papers of land grant companies, such as the Maxwell, and those from the Bureau of Land Management, particularly the transcripts of testimony involving particular land tracts. Court records can also provide insights into the perceptions and actions of Mexicano grant residents.

These traditional archival sources can yield reflections of Mexicano activity and motives, reflections that will sometimes appear without warning after painstaking and exhaustive research. Rarely does a collection contain a holding as conveniently organized as the "White Cap Folder" in the L. B. Prince Papers of the New Mexico State Records Center and Archives. Although the viewpoint found in this folder is strongly Anglo, its arrangement and content can save much time. Usually such research must proceed unguided, using randomly gathered scraps of information arranged and rearranged until some outline of the shape of things begins to form. The exercise is not unlike that of the O'Henry heroine in "The Gift of the Magi" who assessed her appearance by moving back and forth past the narrow pier-glass by the front door and added the fragmentary images to make a whole reflection. Statistical data, too, can add insights into the nature of Mexicano communities. And, of course, federal census returns, the returns from special censuses, election returns, and the rolls of the county tax assessors can provide invaluable contextual information.

Folklore—stories, poems, and especially ballads—offer contextual evidence about the values of the Mexicanos and their perceptions about the human condition. These can often provide a balance to the demographic profiles drawn from statistics. And the human element brings us to what we regard as the most important approach in the research of Mexicano resistance in New Mexico: oral history.

Charles Briggs's essay in this volume, "Getting Both Sides of the Story," is an excellent discussion about oral history that is focused specifically on the questions of how to incorporate oral history into land grant research. We will confine our comments to seconding Briggs's point about the need for preparation. In our experience, extensive preparation in secondary literature, archival sources, and existing oral history collections are prerequisites of the oral history approach. And we find it difficult to imagine effective research into Mexicano resistance that does not incorporate oral history.

Further Research

Since research into the resistance offered against Anglo expropriation of land grants is in its infancy, only the most visible and glamorous movements for protection and reacquisition have received published scrutiny. Unfortunately, these leave more unanswered than they explain. Moreover, next to nothing is known about the dynamics of the undramatic, bedrock type of resistance, such as the long-standing efforts to preserve cultural tradition.

The most obvious need is to fill the gap in the historical record. We know that Anglo speculators and Mexicano opportunists manipulated grant documents and amassed fractional interests in grants in all parts of New Mexico where Spanish or Mexican governors had awarded tracts.

Surely native residents were not totally oblivious to these machinations, especially when they appeared as tangible changes or ejectment suits. Resulting conflicts reported in the press, however minor, might provide invaluable information about resistance. So too might the selection of a particular grant and the study of it from the ground up. In other words, the researcher should begin with the grant residents and then move upward through the reams of paperwork necessitated by litigation.

Court cases, particularly suits brought by grant residents, also await their chroniclers and analysts. A history of the Abiquiu Corporation from its inception would provide an exceedingly valuable insight into resistance through litigation. Similarly, careful studies of the relationships between land grant problems, election campaigns, and legislative maneuverings are sorely needed. Intuition, conventional wisdom, and casual conversation may have some causal connections, but just what they are and how they work have yet to be explained.

The way grant residents organized to resist represents yet another blank page. A history of La Mano Negra would provide a fascinating New Mexico view of resistance founded on Hobsbawm's theory of social banditry, if indeed La Mano Negra really did exist. But at a more basic level, we have hardly established a foundation. We know neither the structure nor the internal dynamics of resisting communities; nor do we know about the relationships, if any, that might have existed between such organizations and the other societal groups from the community. Conventional wisdom, for example, frequently connects Las Gorras Blancas with the Penitentes, particularly in northwestern San Miguel County. We have no supporting evidence to make such a connection. Further research, particularly the kind that uses the technique of oral history, might well establish one. Penitentes aside, the social and organizational structure of Mexicano resistance falls into the category of unexplored territory.

Equally uncharted is the whole question of what constitutes resistance. Thus far we have identified as modes of resistance violence, electoral politics, and legal action. A fourth possibility is orderly retreat—what Gustav L. Seligmann, Jr. terms "withdrawal."[66] Retreat simply involves a distancing by native inhabitants from the encroaching estranjeros in order to protect and sustain their cultural values. The growth of the Penitentes after 1870—after the Anglo-American conquest and the arrival of Archbishop Lamy and his French priests—has been cited as evidence of withdrawal by some native New Mexicans.

To what extent was this duplicated in other facets of traditional Mexicano life, including the use of land?

We end where we started. The history of Mexicano resistance to the expropriation of grant lands remains to be written. When it is, it will tell us a great deal about colonization, culture conflict, and exploitation. It will also reveal the fascinating possibilities and potentialities of pluralistic societies such as the one that has provided New Mexico with such diversity.

Notes

1. Quoted in Richard Gardner, *Grito! Reies Tijerina and the New Mexico Land Grant War of 1967* (New York: Harper, Colophon Books, 1971), p. 9.

2. An exception are the historical monographs and articles that deal with celebrated strikes, such as the Pullman or Homestead strikes. Such studies, which are really quite numerous, do not analyze these turbulent events in any broad historical context which would relate them to movements of popular resistance elsewhere in the world and, consequently, have not served as seminal works for the development of a literature of popular resistance.

3. Two of the most recent are John R. Van Ness, "Introduction," in *Spanish and Mexican Land Grants in New Mexico and Colorado,* ed. John R. and Christine M. Van Ness (Manhattan, Kansas: Sunflower University Press, 1980), especially pp. 8–10 which concisely describe the major characteristics in each system of land tenure; and Victor Westphall, *Mercedes Reales: Hispanic Land Grants of the Upper Rio Grande Region* (Albuquerque: University of New Mexico Press, 1983).

4. D. W. Meinig, *Southwest: Three Peoples in Geographic Change, 1600–1970* (New York: Oxford University Press, 1971), p. 27.

5. An important new account about the activities of the Californians is Darlis A. Miller's *The California Column in New Mexico* (Albuquerque: University of New Mexico Press, 1982).

6. Jack E. Holmes, *Politics in New Mexico* (Albuquerque: University of New Mexico Press, 1967), p. 61.

7. Malcolm Ebright, *The Tierra Amarilla Grant: A History of Chicanery* (Santa Fe: Center for Land Grant Studies, 1980); Robert J. Rosenbaum, *Mexicano Resistance in the Southwest: The Sacred Right of Self-Preservation* (Austin: University of Texas Press, 1981), pp. 93–98, 202–3. See also pp. 21–22 and 45 for discussions about the partitioning of land grants.

8. Frances L. Swadesh, *Los Primeros Pobladores: Hispanic Americans of the Ute Frontier* (Notre Dame: University of Notre Dame Press, 1974); Ebright, *Tierra Amarilla Grant;* Robert J. Torrez, "El Bornes: La Tierra Amarilla and T. D. Burns," *New Mexico Historical Review* 56 (April 1981): 161–75; Roxanne Dunbar Ortiz, *Roots of Resistance: Land Tenure in New Mexico* (Los Angeles:

Chicano Studies Research Center Publications, University of California at Los Angeles and the American Indian Studies Center, 1980); Meinig, *Southwest.*

9. Jim B. Pearson, *The Maxwell Land Grant* (Norman: University of Oklahoma Press, 1961); William A. Keleher, *The Maxwell Land Grant: A New Mexico Item* (Albuquerque: University of New Mexico Press, 1984), Introduction by John R. Van Ness; Lawrence Murphy, "Master of the Cimarron-Maxwell," *NMHR* 55 (January 1980): 269–96.

10. Rosenbaum, *Mexicano Resistance,* pp. 112–18, 207–9.

11. Ibid., pp. 90–93, 201–3.

12. Phillip J. Rasch, "The Horrell War," *NMHR* 31 (July 1956): 223–31.

13. Phillip J. Rasch, "The Tularosa Ditch War," *NMHR* 47 (April 1972): 185–202.

14. Rosenbaum, *Mexicano Resistance,* pp. 93–98, 202–3.

15. Ebright, *Tierra Amarilla.*

16. S. E. Illingsworth, *Report on the Rio Arriba Land and Cattle Company, Limited,* signed 10 August 1887, Beinecke Collection of Western Americana, Beinecke Rare Book Library, Yale University.

17. Swadesh, *Los Primeros Pobladores,* p. 91. The specter of the "satanic" Penitentes and their alleged hold over juries was one frequently raised by frustrated Anglos. See also Rosenbaum, *Mexicano Resistance,* p. 7. The best treatment of the Penitentes is Marta Weigle's *Brothers of Light, Brothers of Blood: The Penitentes of the Southwest* (Albuquerque: University of New Mexico Press, 1976).

18. Pearson, *The Maxwell Land Grant.*

19. Testimony of William Brownell, 12 June 1878, in Bureau of Land Management, Santa Fe, *Papers Relating to Land Grants in the Office of the Surveyor General of New Mexico* (microfilm publication of the University of New Mexico Library, Albuquerque, 1955–1957), Reel 14.

20. Pearson, *Maxwell Land Grant,* pp. 52–53.

21. Rosenbaum, *Mexicano Resistance,* pp. 74–78, 197–98.

22. Morris F. Taylor, *O. P. McMains and the Maxwell Land Grant Conflict* (Tucson: University of Arizona Press, 1979).

23. Rosenbaum, *Mexicano Resistance,* pp. 83–90, 198–201.

24. Ibid., pp. 87–88.

25. M. P. Pels, "Report of the Board of Trustees," August 1890, Maxwell Land Grant Collection, University of New Mexico Library, Albuquerque.

26. Rosenbaum, *Mexicano Resistance,* pp. 99–110, 166–68, and 203–7.

27. Ibid., pp. 100, 112–18, 162–65, and 207–9.

28. L. B. Prince to Interior Secretary John Noble, August 20, 1890, L. B. Prince Papers, New Mexico State Record Center and Archives.

29. Paul Friedrich, *Agrarian Revolt in a Mexican Village* (Englewood Cliffs, New Jersey: Prentice-Hall, 1970).

30. Interviews with H. H. Mondragon, Miguel Gonzales, and Manuel Lucero, Antonchico grant, 15, 18 February 1972. For other insights regarding the relationship between the two groups, see Larson, "The Knights of Labor

and Native Protest in New Mexico," in *Labor in New Mexico: Unions, Strikes, and Social History since 1881,* ed. Robert Kern (Albuquerque: University of New Mexico Press, 1983), pp. 31–52.

31. The coauthors have a dispute of some ten years' standing over how much importance to ascribe to Herrera. Larson sees him as the central figure without whom there would have been no White Caps; Rosenbaum, while conceding the importance of the role he played, sees Herrera as being as much influenced by events as controlling them. Both Larson and Rosenbaum agree, however, that the Knights of Labor served as the vehicle for organization and communication among the White Caps.

32. Robert W. Larson, *New Mexico Populism: A Study of Radical Protest in a Western Territory* (Boulder: Colorado Associated University Press, 1974), pp. 30–47; Rosenbaum, *Mexicano Resistance,* pp. 125–39.

33. Rosenbaum, *Mexicano Resistance,* pp. 169–79.

34. *La Voz del Pueblo* (Las Vegas), 7, 14 March 1891.

35. Rosenbaum, *Mexicano Resistance,* pp. 137–39.

36. Ibid., and Clark S. Knowlton, "The Town of Las Vegas Community Land Grant: An Anglo-American Coup d'Etat," in Van Ness ed., *Spanish and Mexican Land Grants,* pp. 12–21.

37. Richard Wells Bradfute, *The Court of Private Land Claims: The Adjudication of Spanish and Mexican Land Grant Titles, 1891–1904* (Albuquerque: University of New Mexico Press, 1975), p. 114.

38. Edmund G. Ross, "Special Message," 28 February 1887, Interior Department, *Territory of New Mexico,* Reel 8.

39. Interviews with H. H. Mondragon and Miguel Gonzales, 18 February 1972.

40. Swadesh, *Los Primeros Pobladores,* identifies the Andalusian connection; Gardner, *Grito!,* the bootlegging origin, and Molly Bradford Martin in her paean to her husband—*Bill Martin, American* (Caldwell, Idaho: The Caxton Printers Ltd., 1959)—accords them control of organized crime in northern New Mexico.

41. Eric Hobsbawm, *Primitive Rebels and Social Bandits* (New York: The Free Press, 1959).

42. Gardner, *Grito!,* p. 76.

43. William deBuys, "Fractions of Justice: A Legal and Social History of Las Trampas Grant, N.M.," *NMHR* 56 (January 1981): 71–97.

44. Soil Conservation Service, Section of Human Surveys, Region Eight, "Notes on Community-Owned Land Grants in New Mexico," August 1937.

45. Hobsbawm, "Peasants and Politics," *Peasant Studies News Letter,* summary by T. J. Byers and C. A. Curwen, 1:3 (July 1972): 109–14.

46. This sense of exclusivity was brought home to Rosenbaum in an interview with Doña Pedro Lucero on the Antonchico grant (15 February 1972). Doña Lucero explained that she had no rights to the community grant even though she had lived on it for more than forty years because she was not an heir of an original grantee. Her children, however, did have such an interest through her husband and their father's legacy.

47. *Journal of Mexican-American History* (Spring 1971).

48. *Chicano: Evolution of a People* (Calvert, Rosaldo, and Selegmann, eds.; Minneapolis: Winston Press, 1973).

49. *Pacific Historical Review* 44 (May 1975): 171–85.

50. (Albuquerque: University of New Mexico Press, 1967, 1970).

51. (New York: International Publishers, 1971).

52. In *The Underside of American History,* Vol. 2, ed. Thomas R. Frazier (New York: Harcourt, Brace, Jovanovich, 1971).

53. (New York: Harper Colophon Books, 1971).

54. (Boulder: Colorado Associated University Press, 1974).

55. (Austin: University of Texas Press, 1981).

56. (New Haven: Yale University Press, 1966).

57. (Norman: University of Oklahoma Press, 1962).

58. (New York: Holt, Rinehart, and Winston, 1971).

59. (Albuquerque: Calvin Horn, 1970; first published in 1943).

60. (Albuquerque: University of New Mexico Press, 1981).

61. (Notre Dame: University of Notre Dame Press, 1974).

62. (New York: Free Press, 1959).

63. (New York: Harper and Row, 1969).

64. (Princeton: Princeton University Press, 1970).

65. Clifford Geertz, *The Interpretation of Cultures* (New York: Basic Books, 1973), 12–13.

66. Gustav L. Seligmann, Jr., "Withdrawal" (Paper delivered before the Southwestern Historical Assocation at Houston, Texas, on 3 April 1980).

Valdez, New Mexico. Ernest Knee photograph. Courtesy of Andrew Smith Gallery, Santa Fe.

SIX

Land, Water, and Ethnic Identity in Taos

SIX

Land, Water, and Ethnic Identity in Taos*

Sylvia Rodríguez

I. Introduction

Control over land and water remains the primary bone of contention in the relations among Indian, Hispano, and Anglo populations in northern New Mexico. This multifaceted set of issues has evolved out of a historical context of successive conquest, land expropriation, and sociopolitical domination by one ethnic group over another, a regional background captured by Spicer's phrase "cycles of conquest." For Hispanos alone among Mexican Americans, land remains an immediate and volatile issue rooted in everyday life. This state of affairs dates from the Treaty of Guadalupe Hidalgo, the political event that engendered the social category of *Mexican American* and signaled land expropriation for most Mexicanos outside the Hispano "homeland" region.[1] Despite the devastating land losses they suffered, Hispanos were nevertheless the only Mexicanos within the ceded territory who managed to stay on their land in significant numbers.

This essay will focus upon the contemporary case of Taos to demonstrate that essentially the same historic process of expropriation described by Knowlton, Ebright, and other land grant scholars continues today, in modified and more sophisticated form, while rural Hispanos resist their final extirpation and cling to their shrinking land base around land grant villages and their offshoot settlements.[2] During the past two decades, as Anglo in-migration and real-estate speculation have accelerated, Hispano resistance to further encroachment upon

*This essay is based upon research conducted with grants from the Wenner-Gren Foundation and the American Philosophical Society.

limited resources has intensified and become increasingly self-conscious. Evidence for this includes the emergence of popular protest against certain resort developments since 1970, and the concurrent public articulation of specific tracts of land and water as both essential to and symbolic of Hispano cultural survival. It is the central argument of this essay that the ongoing process of expropriation and its recent acceleration have, in concert with various local, regional, and macro-social factors, intensified rural Hispano resistance to further usurpation and displacement, and stimulated the crystallization of land as a symbol of Hispano cultural survival and social self-determination.

These reactions represent, I propose, strategies of ethnic boundary maintenance. They also form part of the ongoing historical process of enclavement and persistence of Hispanos as a self-identified people. The crucial element in the origin and persistence of a self-identified people is, according to Spicer, their opposition to surrounding dominant social and political forces.[3] Their proletarianization, urbanization, and variable assimilation notwithstanding, Hispanos today and at previous points in their post-American history (that is, after 1847) have in various ways expressed opposition to Anglo encroachment and domination. They continue to exhibit other features of a persistent people, including their own language, endogamy, the notion of a stable, inherited cultural tradition, a sense of shared identity, meanings, and history, and, finally, of a homeland.[4] The latter is of particular concern to the present discussion. The ways and degrees to which Hispanos have exhibited these characteristics can be seen to have fluctuated over time, with the critical events in their becoming a minority having been, of course, conquest and land expropriation, from which the population's steady proletarianization inevitably followed.[5]

While the major portion of this essay consists of historical and ethnographic narrative about Taos, the introductory and concluding sections attempt to place the descriptive material within a specific theoretical and methodological framework. The overall inquiry out of which this essay comes seeks to explore the nature of and interaction between ethnicity and stratification, under conditions of tourism development and competition for limited essential resources. The following pages present a case study of one particular manifestation of this problem. Its conceptual focus is the relationship between ethnicity and land or territory, in Taos in particular and the Rio Arriba in general. This introductory section explains the ideas which organize the historical-empirical account that will follow. The reader not especially interested in the theoretical apparatus behind the descriptive account of Taos may prefer to proceed directly to the historical and ethnographic sections, and then return to the introduction, and go on to the conclusion afterward. While theory is ultimately necessary to an understanding of Taos and is therefore included here, it may be taken up either before or after looking at the empirical situation.

Theoretical Framework

Basic to my approach is Barth's ecological model of ethnic boundary maintenance, which sees ethnic identity as reactive to intergroup contact, rather than as simply a creature of primordial isolation. In Barth's view, ethnic groups occupy ecological niches by means of their sociocultural adaptations.[6] Intergroup relations are or become competitive over access to and control of essential resources. Competition intensifies according to degree of niche "overlap," or demand for and use of the same resources within the same territory. The focus in Barth's approach is less upon the continuity of cultural tradition, and more upon the maintenance of ethnic boundaries or differentiation between groups. Boundaries, or the complex means by which ethnic difference is maintained, represent strategies for exercising claims over essential resources. Boundary maintenance through time is the essential feature of ethnic persistence, whereas specific cultural content changes more or less continuously. In a very practical sense, this perspective frees the investigator from the barren task of trying to measure or even explain cultural persistence or assimilation by means of culture trait inventories. Situational emphasis upon ethnic identity as a competitive strategy also allows for focus at the individual level, where boundaries may often be crossed at will.

To anyone acquainted with the perennial struggle over land and water in the Rio Arriba, it is readily apparent how a competitive model is applicable to interethnic—not to mention intraethnic—relations there. Indian-Hispano-Anglo relations have been determined by what can be described as chronologically successive niche overlaps by distinct populations, bearing distinct patterns of ecological adaptation and socioeconomic domination. The case of Taos will be examined here to show how this is so in one particular instance, which nevertheless is embedded in and influenced by a larger, extralocal context. Ethnographic focus will be upon the niche occupation and sociopolitical position of Hispanos via-à-vis other groups through time, with particular attention to Hispano-Anglo relations in the contemporary period. This involves looking at Taos explicitly as a changing, circumscribed situation, and, implicitly, as inseparable from an inclusive, in fact global, sociopolitical process.

Ethnic Boundaries

A bit more should be said about the concept of ethnic boundary. Anthropologists use the term to refer to the complex of rules and markers by which people identify and are identified as members of one or another ethnic group. Externally obvious ethnic markers can include language, phenotype, dress, and style, while more "subjective" ones include values, sensibilities, and manner, as well as implicit rules for identifying the ethnicity of others or of asserting one's own. Spicer offers an operational definition of ethnic boundaries as "those situations in which the sense of identity receives some kind of expression and where individuals align themselves in some manner as members of one ethnic group or another."[7] The operation of ethnic boundaries in face-to-face social interaction in Taos as elsewhere in the region is today no less important than it was 100 or 300 years ago, although to be sure the cultures "contained within" these boundaries have undergone radical transformation. Conceptual focus upon boundary maintenance rather than specific content allows us to account for the seemingly paradoxical coincidence of culture change with the persistence of ethnic difference.

Niche

The relationship between boundary and niche can also change over time, although theoretically at least, they coincide in "equilibrium."[8] The niche is both an adaptation and a

> cluster of environmental parameters which any species (or in this case ethnic group) may use . . . or overcome in order to survive. . . . The parameters of the niche, the various resource garnering abilities of the competing populations, and the carrying capacity of that portion of the environment utilized determine the relative proportions of the populations at equilibrium, and whether there can be an equilibrium.[9]

Niche theory is applicable to ethnic relations only at a local, microsocial level, and must be embedded in a larger theory of world political economy. Nevertheless it nicely captures the historical relations among Pueblo, Hispano, and Anglo populations in the Taos valley, where the three still occupy overlapping yet recognizably distinct ecological niches. The documentary record of Indian-Hispano relations is one of unending dispute over arable tracts of land in the Rio Pueblo and adjacent watersheds.[10] The political significance and intensity of this struggle were transformed by Americanization. The precise correspondences between cultural adaptation, ethnicity, and differential territory and resource control have therefore undergone profound changes during the past 400 years.

Originally of course, the Indians occupied the optimal farming, hunting, and defensible vantage point in the Taos valley, which, remarkably and through unrelenting effort, they have managed to retain. Hispanic Taos was first settled around—or radiated outward from—Taos Pueblo, in ever-widening circles as the population grew. It gradually consolidated around the central town of Don Fernando de Taos, becoming during the nineteenth century a system of fifteen interdependent but individual settlements, almost all of which encroached upon use areas claimed by the Pueblo. Today these settlements are each struggling to protect their traditionally differentiated spheres of local land and water control, as always in competition or cooperation with one another, but also against the town's urban spread, and a corresponding escalation of Anglo in-migration and ubiquitous real estate development.

The core elements in the Hispano niche have been occupation of contiguous village farmland and associated water rights ownership and management, and a numerical majority that still enables them to dominate the local political structure, which centers on town and county governments and the school system. Both Indian and Hispano attachments to a land base are rooted in their traditional subsistence economies. Attachment to a land base remains intrinsic to the ethnic self-identities of both groups, even though neither subsists any longer by agriculture, pastoralism, or hunting. The self-conscious ethnic symbolization of the subsistence base has been fueled, in the case of both Indians and Hispanos, by its progressive loss, and it represents an effort to forestall or reverse this relentless process.

Taos is of interest because it is both representative and atypical. On the one hand, it has much in common with the rest of the Rio Arriba and with the Southwest as a whole. On the other, its long-standing commercial importance has made it peculiar. Its interethnic, historic, and geographic "uniqueness," which the town markets as a tourist attraction, represents a distinctive configuration of features Taos shares with the Southwest in general. These include aridity, socioeconomic stratification along ethnic lines, and an ethnic boundary system that exhibits the characteristics identified by Spicer for the region: differential boundary awareness among dominant and subdominant groups, boundary fluidity, the reservation, and linguistic pluralism.[11] The first of these refers to the fact that the members of a dominant social stratum and ethnic group tend to be less aware of ethnic boundaries than members of a subordinated ethnic group. This has many implications for face-to-face ethnic relations, and is a major feature of Taos social life. Unidirectional boundary fluidity refers to the fact that individuals can cross ethnic boundaries, but the direction in which they assimilate tends to be "upward" along the stratification scale. The remainder of Spicer's characteristics, the reservation and linguistic pluralism, are self-explanatory. The salience of all four of these features in Taos will become clear in the narrative part of this paper.

Ethnicity and Class

Before describing Taos further, a word must be said about the relation between ethnicity and class. While interethnic competition over limited resources is a constant theme in local history, land, water, and other resource conflicts have never been exclusively interethnic matters. Conflict over resources occurs also within ethnic groups, along family and factional lines, within and between communities, and along the class lines which cross-cut community and ethnic boundaries. Indeed, instances in which class shapes or overrides ethnic interest are of particular significance in New Mexico history, as they are today. Modern examples include the regular operation of the Hispanic elite aligned with the ruling Anglo elite, or Anglo farmers and environmentalists who join in protest against resort development. That class and ethnic cleavages can both coincide and cross-cut each other is one of the complexities of the situation not adequately captured by a simple one-to-one boundary-niche model of local interethnic relations. While it is not the purpose of this essay to describe or analyze the interaction between ethnicity and class in Taos, the problem is mentioned because it is central to any kind of theoretical understanding of ethnic or race relations there or elsewhere in the Rio Arriba. I mention it also to avoid the implication that conflict over resources in the region is simply interethnic. (Nor, for that matter, do I mean to suggest that all conflict between members of different ethnic groups is necessarily over resources. Rather, I am addressing the implicitly understood ethnohistorical context of niche overlap within which intergroup relations are acted out and interpreted.) As shall be seen, the controversies described in the sections on modern Taos are as much between classes as ethnic groups.

It is therefore significant that they are commonly perceived and somewhat ambivalently regarded as interethnic conflicts, even though "on the ground," nearly everyone acknowledges the importance of class in determining peoples' choices about such matters. Beyond the most basic and obvious issue of threatened community resource domains, several other factors contribute to why the recent grassroots protests are commonly understood as ethnic conflicts and mobilizations. To begin with, the incidence of territoriality and distinct linguistic and cultural traditions tends to enhance the prospects for ethnic mobilization in any given situation. The primary ascriptive nature of ethnicity typically makes it a readier and more appealing basis than class for political mobilization in a plural or multiethnic setting.[12] Additional factors at play include the persistence of socioeconomic stratification along ethnic lines, the influence of tourism, and certain post-1960 regional and national influences. The latter two, the influences of tourism and regional and national trends or events upon local ethnic mobilization, are of particular interest to this discussion.

To recapitulate then, this paper deals with the modern symbolic identification of Hispano ethnic-cultural persistence with specific tracts of land and water in the Taos area. It pursues the obvious comparison between the emergence of Hispano ethnic land symbolism and the well-known Blue Lake case of the Taos Indians, in which the town watershed came over a period of several decades to symbolize the cultural survival of Taos Pueblo. Both Indian and Hispano ethnic land symbolizations are considered in terms of their extralocal ethnopolitical settings and significance, but my discussion will focus upon their immediate context of an evolving tourism economy.

The Significance of Taos

Taos's historic importance stems mostly from its long having been an interethnic trade center, and in this century, a focal point for tourism development and urban growth. It has also been the locus of significant interethnic violence, having served as the starting point for the Pueblo Revolt of 1680, and the site of Mexicano-Indian revolt against American occupation in 1847. Perhaps its most outstanding feature today is the effect that tourism, as the primary economic base other than federal subsidy and one molybdenum mine, exerts upon the local system of interethnic relations.

From its earliest beginnings, tourism in Taos marketed ethnicity and the natural environment, a combination that has fostered, in addition to heightened ethnic self-consciousness and the proliferation of ethnic symbolism in general, the emergence of ethnic land symbolism among Hispanos as well as Indians. Both Hispano and Indian land symbolisms link the issue of cultural survival to the preservation of a traditional land base, but they differ in other respects. Their dissimilarities are as much the result of distinctive political, economic, and legal circumstances as reflections of primordial social or cultural differences between the two groups.

Hispano ethnic land symbolism has developed within the context of continuous land loss and concomitant Anglo, federal, and apparent Indian land gain. It grows out of a very different set of legal and political conditions from those facing the Taos Indians. The American Indian "sacred land concept" originates in aboriginal animism, but today it is also a response to federal status and the reservation. The spiritual potency of Native American sacred natural areas stands in poignant contrast to actual Indian powerlessness over most reservation land and water. Pueblos differ from most reservations in that their "leagues" are held in fee simple title, and do not belong to the federal government.[13] Nevertheless, at Taos Pueblo as on other reservations, Indians are territorially segregated and directly subject to federal control, as is the administration of at least part of their land. The institutionalization of group identity, including the imposition of a colonial administrative apparatus, is more total for reservation Indians than for any other ethnic minority in this country. Yet the symbolic import of an Indian sacred land concept and the notion of Indian landownership, however ambiguously realized, are made concrete by actual geographic and associated social boundaries within Taos County. The local interpretation—or mystification—of this segregated arrangement has been for the most part unconsciously shaped by the needs and dictates of tourism.

The "Tri-Ethnic Trap" Revisited

John Bodine laid the cornerstone for the study of interethnic relations in Taos by placing the sixty-four-year legal battle for Blue Lake between Taos Pueblo and the federal government within the context of Taos's bohemian ethos of selective ethnophilia or the tri-ethnic trap.[14] The tri-ethnic trap is a situation in which Hispanos, unable to advance beyond clear-cut secondary economic status and faced with the steady and irrevocable loss of their traditional land base, must abide by a tourism-engendered Anglo glorification of Indian culture, as well as the federal protection and even restoration of Indian lands, sometimes at the expense of Hispano ownership. Conditions in Taos in the early 1980s represent a recognizable progression of what Bodine described in 1968, modified by the supercession of luxury recreational over ethnic-cultural tourism.[15] Taos has undergone two phases of tourism development in this century, the first being roughly between the two world wars, and the second extending from the 1960s to the early 1980s. The Blue Lake case preceded the first boom and lasted into the early part of the second, but its character and significance were shaped by the former. In his unpublished dissertation, Bodine showed how over a period of several decades Taos Pueblo came *publicly* and *legally* to define Blue Lake as "sacred," under the pressure of particular legal, political, social, and cultural circumstances.[16] The Blue Lake victory in 1970 enhanced a climate of already heightened ethnic self-consciousness, and served to reinforce the idea of a mystical connection between territory and indigenous population.

The most fundamental contrasts between Pueblo Indian and Hispano cases of enclavement derive from the differences in their respective political and legal positions vis-à-vis the state. Trust status has meant, among other things, that Indians cannot alienate their land and do not pay taxes on it, and that legal defense of their land, water, and other tribal claims is the responsibilty of the federal government, not infrequently in litigation against itself. Ironically, the immunities this nonetheless disastrously dependent status confers serve to preclude some of the very ways in which Hispanos have lost their land. Mexicanos were supposedly incorporated into the American state as regular citizens with full rights and privileges. The history of Mexican Americans, who have subsequently constituted the major source of cheap labor throughout the Southwest, shows otherwise. Like Mexican Americans elsewhere, Hispanos were proletarianized by means of dispossession. Because of the aridity and isolation of New Mexico, Mexicano land loss has been slower there than it was in California or Texas. In Taos their land loss has nevertheless been more or less continuous. Today the land tenure situation of Taos Pueblo appears, at least superficially, far more favorable in comparison to that of rural and semi-rural Hispanos in the area, whose farmland is being expropriated at an escalating rate by the luxury tourism real-estate boom.

The Stolen Homeland

The idea of a stolen homeland was invoked and dramatized in 1967 by Reies López Tijerina, the leader of La Alianza Federal de los Pueblos Libres, which attracted international attention to the long-buried land grant issue in New Mexico. Founded originally as La Alianza Federal de Mercedes in the early 1960s, the organization, comprised of landless Hispano poor and small ranchers and village farmers, sought to bring the matter of massive land grant loss to world attention as a violation of the Treaty of Guadalupe Hidalgo. Several years of protest activity finally culminated in the famous Tierra Amarilla courthouse raid, in which Tijerina and a score of armed Alianza followers wounded three men and kidnapped a deputy sheriff and a news reporter, setting off an intensive, five-day manhunt, and virtual military occupation of northern Rio Arriba County.[17] If the Alianza failed to restore the lost land grants, it nevertheless proclaimed Hispano existence to the outside world and inspired legal and scholarly interest in land grant history. Tijerina's contribution was to resurrect the land grant issue and link it to contemporary conditions. This galvanized Hispano-Chicano ethnopolitical awareness and changed the way in which isolated individuals would think of their personal disputes over land and water. It placed the individual problem within a larger, collective, historically defined context and gave voice to a deep, widespread, but still largely unarticulated sense of injury and outrage.

It would be difficult to measure Tijerina's impact on Hispanos in

Taos alone, where out-migration has linked rural families to the urban barrios of the Southwest, and where individual responses vary according to class, age, education, urban-rural orientation, and numerous other social factors. In Taos as elsewhere, Tijerina's impact was as much symbolic as political. Today, his enormous symbolic impact outlives his political effectiveness. Despite—or perhaps partly by means of—anomalous personal characteristics (evangelist, itinerant, Tejano), he managed to strike a chord among rural Hispanos that continues to resonate in the north even today, while their land base continues to diminish. For Chicanos in the cities, the Alianza helped to locate the homeland *mythos* of Aztlan in the geopolitical present.[18] For Hispanos in the Rio Arriba, it finally gave a name to what had happened to them as a people. Along with the California farmworkers' strike, the emergence of the Raza Unida party in Crystal City, Texas, the Crusade for Justice in Denver, and the Chicano student movement, the Tierra Amarilla courthouse raid and its aftermath became a milestone in the national process of Chicano ethnopolitical mobilization. These and instances of ethnic mobilization involving other minorities either preceded or roughly coincided with the emergence of Hispano-Chicano protest activity in Taos in the early 1970s, which at least initially took its inspiration from the spirit of the times.

Ethnic Symbolism and Tourism

The emergence of an explicit Hispano land symbolism in Taos since 1970 will be described in the final narrative sections of this paper. It will be shown to be the product of the history described in preceding sections, operating in concert with contemporary conditions, including the recent influence of extralocal Chicano ethnopolitical mobilizations. Hispano ethnic land symbolization in Taos was prefigured by the Indian example and conditioned by the type of tourism development that accompanied it. But it has been precipitated largely by the luxury tourism development generated by the ski industry. The following account will show how both Indian and Hispano cases of ethnic land symbolization have been profoundly affected by tourism, although in different ways, and at different stages of tourism development. As distinct yet comparable examples of ethnic mobilization they might seem to correspond, at first glance, to what MacCannell calls "reconstructed" and "constructed" ethnicity. The term "constructed ethnicity" refers to the self-conscious efforts of contemporary ethnopolitical activists and to "the various ethnic identities which emerged via opposition and assimilation during the colonial phase of Western history and in the new 'internal colonies.'" "Reconstructed ethnicity" on the other hand, refers to "the kinds of ethnic identities which have emerged from the pressures of tourism," it being understood that "tourism promotes the restoration, preservation, and fictional recreation of ethnic attributes."[19] In either case ethnicity is the product of a distinct pattern of colonial or post-colonial (that is asymmetrical and exploitative) intergroup relations: an explicitly political one in which the "inferior group defines itself in opposition to or the antithesis of the values of the dominant group," and a "touristic" situation in which a structurally "superior group associates itself with an inferior group" and where the latter engages in the "maintenance and preservation of ethnic forms for the entertainment of ethnically different [and structurally superior] others."[20]

Even before MacCannell and others made tourism a field of study, Bodine recognized that tourism and the art colony had deeply affected the ethnic strategy and self-image of Taos Pueblo. Certainly Taos ethnic identity is at least partly a reconstructed product in MacCannell's sense, just as the Pueblo itself has become *museumized.*[21] Yet the Pueblo's struggle to maintain its claim on the Rio Pueblo watershed and adjacent areas long antedates the advent of tourism, even though its means for doing so have now become inseparable from tourism's influence. Tourism and federal dependency became the twentieth-century political-economic context within which Taos Pueblo's ethnic boundary maintenance strategies have evolved. In a sense tourism, or a peculiar combination of ethnic-cultural tourism and federal dependency, has become a crucial component of the modern Pueblo niche. This will be elaborated upon later. The point to be made here is that both Taos Indian and Hispano ethnicity, including their respective symbolizations of land, are the products of construction as well as reconstruction, albeit in different ways. Neither represents a pure type, if such exists. They are rooted in a pre-United States history of political asymmetry and mutual niche overlap. Their respective modern characters share common elements in, yet also reflect differences between, the two groups' political, economic, and social situations.

Roadside poster in Valdez condominium dispute. Courtesy of Sylvia Rodríguez.

The Content and Structure of This Essay

In the text that follows, Part 2, about half of the main text, is a history of Taos, divided into three sections. The first part includes a description of the area's geographical and hydrological layout, and an overview of Taos's development from 1540 to 1847. It is followed by two sections on modern history from Americanization to the present. These focus primarily upon the two phases of tourism development in this century and their distinguishable impacts on local ethnicity and ethnic relations.

The second half of the main text, or Part 3, is an ethnographic account of a grassroots protest movement against condominium development by the village of Valdez, which occurred in 1981–1982. Because it is based upon ethnographic research involving participant

The Valdez float in the Taos Fiestas. Courtesy of Sylvia Rodríguez.

observation, this section, on the Valdez "condo war," reads more vividly than what precedes it. Yet its content is fully understandable only within the context of the former, that is, when viewed against the backdrop of the past 20, 100, and indeed, 400 years. The Valdez case is the most recent and dramatic example of protest activity that has emerged in Taos since 1970. It illustrates the contemporary situation of intensifying competition over limited land and water. It reveals conflict between ethnic groups, between classes, between urban and rural orientations, and between different economic interests. The case reveals the complex ways in which all these factors overlap and interact in modern Taos, and by extension, elsewhere in the Rio Arriba. At the same time, it signals a new phase in an old, yet ongoing process—the emergence, evolution, construction, and reconstruction of Hispanos as a self-identified people. Thus these four central sections, of different lengths and styles, together ground and inform the argument explained above. All this is summarized and put into theoretical perspective once

A marcher displays the "Blood of Valdez" banner. Courtesy of Sylvia Rodríguez.

The Valdez protest march to Gilson Motor Company. Courtesy of Sylvia Rodríguez.

again in the conclusion, which is followed by recommendations for further research.

Methodology

The research upon which this essay is based involved twenty-one months of ethnographic fieldwork in Taos from 1981–1983, undertaken to investigate interethnic relations and social change since 1930. The project was designed originally to investigate the seemingly paradoxical observation that, since World War II, despite economic development and the growth of Anglo, Indian, and especially Hispano middle classes in Taos, and despite increased contact, intermarriage, and cultural commonalities among the three groups, the boundaries between them persist and appear to be maintained and protected with increasing self-consciousness, if not intensity. Drawing upon conceptual frameworks offered by Barth and by Spicer, my approach posited a correlation among

Tijerina addresses the Valdez rally.

the following: increase in demographic pressure and demand upon the limited resource of water in Taos's arid, geographically circumscribed and seemingly isolated environment; interethnic and intraethnic social diversification; and the intensification of ethnic boundaries.

The project is essentially a community study, which seeks to investigate and describe contemporary Taos while also reconstructing its recent past. Thus both ethnographic and historical (or *synchronic* and *diachronic*) methods have been used. Ethnographic methods include participant observation in multiple settings, and both extensive and intensive interviews with a broad selection of area residents. Questionnaires concerning local water quality and quantity were distributed selectively in rural areas. Participant observation has encompassed a wide range of interethnic and intraethnic (primarily Hispano) social, civil, civic, ritual, and other events, activities, and occasions, including all regular and most special local governmental meetings of all types, as well as many hours of grassroots and partisan political meetings and activities in the town and surrounding communities. Local archival research has consisted of examining the county tax rolls for settlements within the municipal district from 1931–1980, and a detailed review of Taos newspapers for the same period. The tax rolls yield data on changing landownership and comparative wealth during the past fifty years, while the newspaper review has served to guide and inform much of the interview process, and to aid in the reconstruction of recent town history. Adjunct documentary research has entailed compilation of the available physiographic, demographic, economic, and other social data on Taos, as well as a more-or-less comprehensive review of the literature on Taos, which I classify under the three general headings of scholarly, policy-oriented, and promotional, listed in order from least to most abundant.

One factor which should be mentioned is that the investigator is a native of Taos. My native bias is partly an applied one that seeks to understand Taos as thoroughly, accurately, and "objectively" as possible, in order to help change it, or at the very least to cast new light on what seems a stringently unequal and, from the standpoint of Hispano land tenure, a worsening situation. Like most members of the post-1965 generation of Chicano and other minority scholars as well as some nonminority scholars who study minorities in the United States, I do not subscribe to the assimilationist bias or alleged political detachment which previous generations of social scientists simply (and rather naively) took for granted. Only time and further study will show the extent to which my description and analysis prove accurate or useful.

The long-range goal of the project is a community study of Taos that centers upon a description and analysis of ethnic—particularly Hispano-Anglo—relations during the middle and late twentieth century. But the project represents, one hopes, only the first stage in a continuing program of research that will eventually involve cooperative interdisciplinary efforts to investigate both past and present social phenomena and conditions in Taos County, ultimately for the purpose of comparison with other counties in the state, as well as with other regions, both within and outside the Southwest. A comparative perspective and understanding of diverse systems or situations of structural inequality seems one prerequisite to knowing how to transform them into more egalitarian relations. It is within this larger conceptual framework that the present essay, on the land-water issue and its ethnic meaning in northern New Mexico, is presented.

II. The History of Taos

Geographic Overview

Taos is a collectivity of villages, consisting of an aboriginal Tiwa pueblo and approximately (depending on how you count them) fifteen Hispanic settlements which crystallized around it during the eighteenth and early nineteenth centuries. The complex is located in a shallow basin on the eastern edge of a high (approximately 7,000 feet) arid plain, at a point just before where the land rises precipitously into the Sangre de Cristo range. These mountains run north-south through Taos County, paralleling the deep cut (approximately 650 feet) of the Rio Grande gorge through the western altiplano. Water for the town (Don Fernando de Taos) and surrounding communities comes from ground water and eight mountain streams that descend via forested canyons and run through settled, irrigated valleys, and down arroyos into the gorge. These streams are, from south to north: the Rio Grande del Rancho (formed by two tributaries); Rio Chiquito; Rio Fernando; Rio Pueblo; Rio Lucero; Arroyo Seco; Rio Hondo; and San Cristobal. The settlements, scattered inside a twenty-mile radius along the upper and lower portions of each of these watersheds, include, from south to north: Llano Quemado, Ranchos, Talpa, Los Cordovas, Cordillera, Ranchitos (Lower and Upper), Don Fernando de Taos, Cañon, San Geronimo de Taos or Taos Pueblo, El Prado, Las Colonias, Arroyo Seco, Des Montes, Valdez, Arroyo Hondo, and San Cristobal. The major portion of arable, habitable land in Taos County is located inside this basin within a relatively narrow central strip or valley, bordered on the east by the mountains, and on the west by the sageland desert. Officially designated the municipal district, this area today contains roughly sixty-five percent of the county population. Taos is connected to the nearest metropolitan areas of Denver, approximately 300 miles to the north, and Albuquerque, about 150 miles to the south, by Highway 3, which runs right through the town. Highway 64 runs east-northwest through Taos, linking it to Raton and the Texas-Oklahoma Panhandle to the east, and to Tierra Amarilla and Farmington to the west. Penetrated by only these two highways and surrounded by mountains and high desert, the Taos valley creates a predominant (for many, alluring) impression of lofty geographical circumscription and isolation (see Map 12).

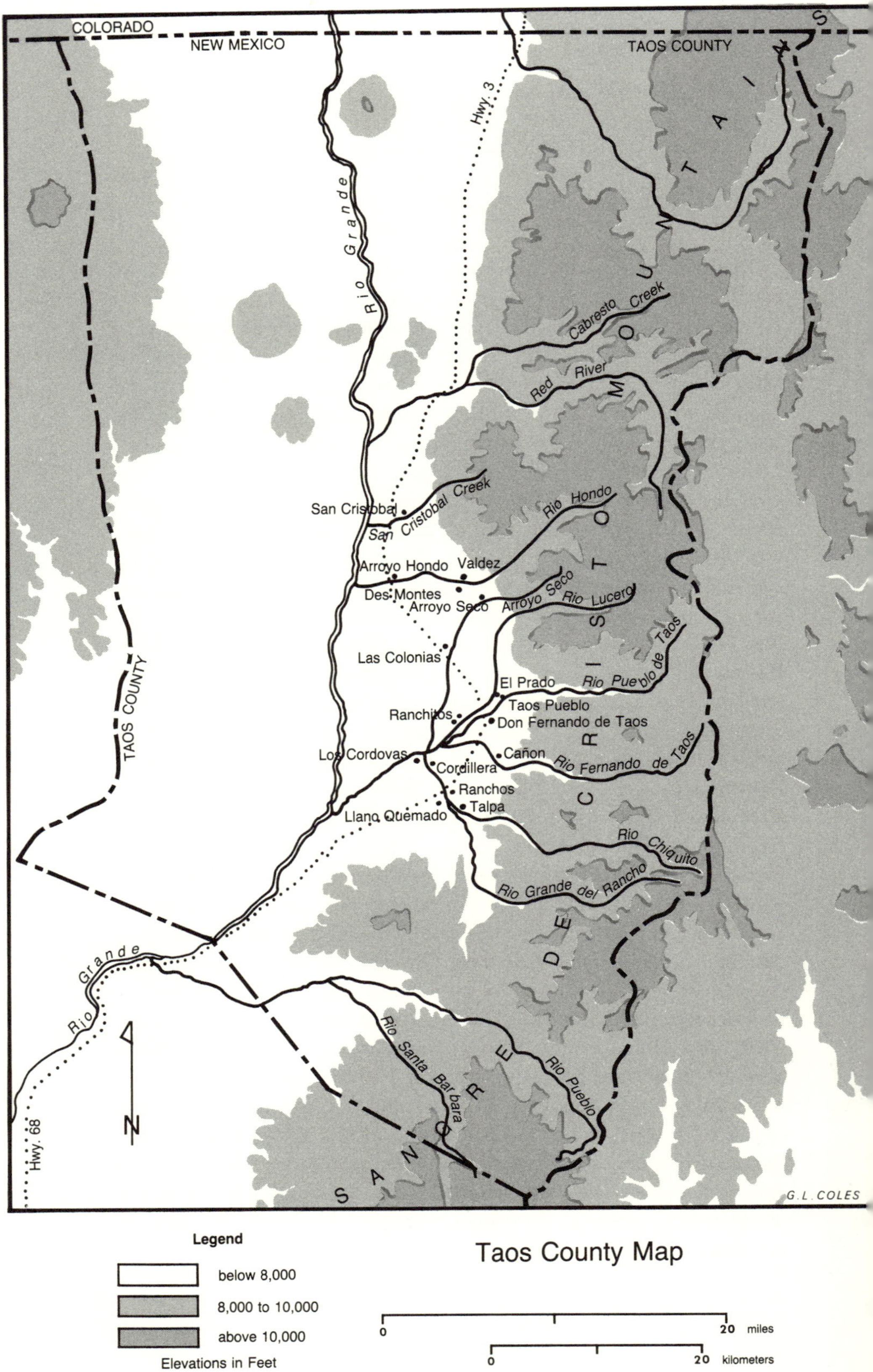

MAP 12. Taos County.

Human settlement in the Taos valley dates from about A.D. 1000–1200, although it was not until around 1350 that the present Pueblo area became the site of a major population center, following the abandonment of one to the south near Pot Creek on the Rio Grande del Rancho, which feeds the present-day Ranchos-Talpa-Llano Quemado area.[22]

1540–1847

Founded on the banks of the upper Rio Pueblo, Taos Pueblo occupies the best farming, hunting, and defensible vantage point in the valley. Its location at the base of Taos mountain gives easy access to rich mountain resources, including the river itself, as well as to fertile flatlands and meadows lying immediately west and south. The village and upland behind it afford commanding views of the entire Taos valley, and offer avenues for quick retreat into mountain canyons. The Pueblo was nearly 200 years old when Coronado's lieutenant Alvarado first saw it in 1540, and reported it to be the largest and most populous of the Indian villages he visited.[23] Northernmost of the eastern Pueblos, Taos shows signs of greater Plains culture contact[24] and reliance upon hunting than do its mostly Tewa neighbors to the south along the Rio Grande, and was undoubtedly an important point of contact between the two regions even in aboriginal times. Oñate assigned the Taos people their first mission in 1598, in the name of San Geronimo. Within another fifteen years the Pueblo had embarked upon its long career of resistance against European domination and encroachment.[25]

By the middle of the seventeenth century, Hispanic settlers were moving into the valley and occupying lands on at least two royal grants made to the south (on the Rio Grande del Rancho) and immediate west (on the Rio Lucero) of the Pueblo. Some seventy settlers and two priests were killed in the area during the Pueblo Revolt in 1680, which was planned from the kivas at Taos because of its strategic remoteness from Spanish headquarters in Santa Fe. Settlers reentered the valley with de Vargas's "bloodless reconquest," which the Taos people actively resisted until 1696. Thereafter, except for disastrous participation in the 1847 Taos revolt against American occupation, their overt resistance would assume increasingly litigious form.

The Land Grants. It was during the early to middle 1700s that

Hispanic settlers began to establish a foothold in the Taos valley. While the *casas reales* (government buildings) were housed at the Pueblo itself, the settlers lived scattered in *ranchos* (subsistence farms) around the valley. From three to five royal grants were made to individuals during this period, although only two of them were continuously occupied, after being sold by their original grantees. These included the Cristobal de la Serna, made in 1710 and revalidated in 1715, which lies south of the Pueblo and town and encompasses the Ranchos-Talpa-Llano Quemado area, and evidently corresponded to the prerevolt Duran y Chavez grant. The other was the Francisca Antonia de Gijosa grant, made in 1715. The grant lies to the west of La Serna, and contains the settlements of Los Cordovas, Cordillera, and Ranchitos. A third, on the site of the old Lucero de Godoy grant west of the Pueblo along the Rio Lucero, was issued in 1716 to Antonio Martinez of Sonora, who evidently never occupied it.[26] This grant would later contain El Prado, Las Colonias, Des Montes, and part of Arroyo Seco. Yet another, the Antoine Leroux grant, made in 1742, would overlap onto the Martinez grant, as well as onto the Pueblo league. Arroyo Seco would lie partly within this contested zone.[27] In 1730 the Pueblo filed the first of many complaints against trespassers grazing livestock along the Rio Lucero. The Spanish governor upheld the Pueblo claim and set a precedent, to be honored mainly in principle, for future decisions about this much disputed area.[28] Litigation over Hispano encroachments along the Rio Lucero has continued late into the twentieth century.

Hispano or mestizo population growth was held in check during much of the eighteenth century by generally harsh conditions, including devastating Comanche raids into the area. Despite whatever tensions persisted between them, the raiding eventually caused the settlers and Indians to pull together for purposes of mutual defense, and so while settlers maintained their fields and livestock on ranches around the valley, they lived inside the Pueblo walls, at least during the 1770s. Dominguez reported 306 non-Indian settlers living in the western portion of the heavily fortified Pueblo in 1776, while a plaza was under construciton in Las Trampas or Ranchos. The first permanently inhabited settlements seem to have been in the general Ranchos area, along the lower Rio Grande del Rancho watershed. By the 1790s the Comanche threat had subsided and various parts of the valley were being permanently resettled. In another decade the smallpox vaccination would reach the area,[29] and a population explosion was underway.

The earliest enumeration of distinct plazas for the Taos area is from 1796, the same year the town, or Don Fernando, grant was made. The account reported a non-Indian population of 774, and named six placitas, identifiable as present-day Taos, Ranchos, Upper Ranchitos, Lower Ranchitos, either Cañon or El Prado, and probably Los Cordovas.[30] The original town grant was made to sixty-three families, whose number was expanded in 1797 by two additional acts of possession.[31] The grant, including the plaza and numerous houses, overlapped onto the Pueblo league, a fact which would later result in drawn-out litigation and give the Pueblo a lingering claim over all town streets and alleys. Water from the Rio Pueblo, to which the Pueblo has first priority, would be used to irrigate lands in the town area including La Loma (now a barrio), Ranchitos, and part of Cañon. By this time, the Pueblo had begun to buy back lands north of the El Prado-Los Estiercoles area from the heirs of a Los Luceros (or Leroux) grant claimant (Sebastian Martin), whom it had first charged with trespassing nearly sixty-five years earlier. This area, part of the Lucero-Leroux-Martinez overlap, would later be known as the Tenorio tract, which the Pueblo would purchase yet again in 1818.[32]

A population explosion overtook the Taos valley around the turn of the century. Between 1794 and 1811 the non-Indian population more than doubled from 628 to 1274.[33] This resulted in the spread of existing settlements and the establishment of new ones, giving rise to Talpa and Llano Quemado in the Ranchos area, and Cordillera, above Los Cordovas to the northwest, near where six of the central valley streams drain into the Rio Grande.[34] In 1815 the Arroyo Seco, Arroyo Hondo, and San Cristobal grants were made in watersheds north of Don Fernando and the Rio Lucero, to mostly landless families from the town area. San Antonio or present-day Valdez, originally the upper placita of Arroyo Hondo, became a separate extension of that grant in 1823. The settlement of Las Colonias and Des Montes in the middle and lower Hondo-Seco drainages must also have taken place during this general period. By 1818, the Pueblo had engaged in litigation for nearly a century, and filed suit against settler-trespassers in at least Don Fernando, Ranchos, and El Prado, and had twice purchased the Tenorio tract. It would soon join with its old adversary El Prado in complaint against Arroyo Seco's upstream encroachment on the Rio Lucero, a problem that would remain volatile for many years. Population growth thus intensified the already constant pressures on the

Pueblo's league boundaries, as well as on all other arable lands and surface waters in the Taos valley. The fundamental patterns of intercommunity alliance and competition over land and water that persist today were thereby established during the early nineteenth century and, in some cases, much earlier.

Multicommunity. It was therefore during the latter eighteenth and early nineteenth centuries that Taos crystallized into a collectivity or system of differentiated, interdependent settlements, radiating outward from the Pueblo and early centers of Ranchos and Taos. This process took place more or less concurrently with the community's evolution into a lively trade and agricultural center. Some of the settlements, including most of the early six as well as La Loma, Arroyo Hondo, and San Antonio, were originally laid out as placitas. Others, like Cordillera and Des Montes, seem to have coalesced out of clusters or strings of dispersed ranchos at a point where there were no longer any vacant lands to which Taos or Ranchos or any other settlement could export their burgeoning populations. As Snow has argued for the Rio Arriba in general, the critical factor in precipitating this crystallization of distinct community boundaries was population pressure against local carrying capacity, or limited land with water.[35]

By the Mexican period, each of these settlements had become an individuated, bounded community organized around its own acequias and chapel and/or morada, and embedded in a nexus of kinship and reciprocal patterns of cooperation, exchange, and competition with its neighbors in the same or adjacent watersheds. As the components individuated, so did the whole take form. This pattern of intervillage growth and connectedness has been identified in other parts of the Rio Arriba by Van Ness who, following Reina and Aguilera, calls it a "multicommunity," with parallels in the Peten and southwestern Spain.[36] And like elsewhere in the Rio Arriba as well as other parts of highland Latin America, each village tended to acquire its own distinct character or personality. Community of origin, a person's *patria chica,* would become an important factor in defining individual social identity. Strong identification with one's community is found in Taos even today, where some settlements and their natives still have nicknames, and where old intercommunity rivalries and alliances over surface waters persevere under conditions of accelerating urbanization.

Commerce. Taos was the northern terminus of the trade route from Chihuahua and had become the site of an annual trade fair by the middle of the eighteenth century. Just as the Pueblo had been a contact point between northeastern and southern influences in pre-Hispanic times, Don Fernando soon became a kind of boom town at the edge of two frontiers. Taos was stratified by class as well as by race from its earliest frontier days. Its history as a community is largely the record of how these two forms or systems of stratification and inequality have interacted, interpenetrated, and evolved, under conditions of universal competition for land and water on the one hand, and progressive capitalist penetration and development on the other. There are different views as to when mercantile capitalism began to penetrate and transform the agro-pastoral-trade economy of the Rio Arriba. Most historians have assumed this took place during the Mexican period, after the area was opened to American trade across the Santa Fe trail. Other scholars claim the process began earlier. For example, Gutierrez has argued that it began in the 1770s, causing far-reaching social change, manifested in increasingly individualistic marriage practices and ideology and in overall transformation from a caste to a class society.[37] This might have helped to accommodate a rather swift American takeover of the local economy during the Mexican period.[38]

In any case, Taos evidently boomed during the Mexican period, when it became well-known to mountain men for its whiskey, wheat, and women, and as a rendezvous and port-of-entry. In addition to abundant wheat for sustenance and raw whiskey for inspiration, Taos supplied Mexicano labor for the construction of Bent's Fort,[39] a portent of future trends for a growing sector of landless laborers. A number of French and Anglo trapper-traders settled in Taos and married Hispanas from propertied families. Some branched out as merchants and land grant entrepreneurs, becoming recipients of such examples of Armijo's largesse as the Sangre de Cristo and Beaubien-Miranda or Maxwell grants. By American conquest these men, among them the Bents, Beaubien, St. Vrain, Lee, and Carson were well established in their roles as pillars of the new order.

After 1846 American conquest cut off Mexicano-Hispano domination by usurping the local subsistence economy and expropriating most of its land base. Hispanos were ultimately transformed from an internally stratified yet sociopolitically dominant majority into an impoverished ethnic underclass, with a small upper stratum of broker-entrepreneurs who aligned with the ruling Anglos. Overt resistance erupted shortly after occupation, when Territorial Governor Bent was scalped by a mob of Indians and Mexicanos. Too little is known about the precise nature and constituency of this uprising, except that it seems to have involved both extremes of the local social scale. It may have been partially instigated by certain elite[40] but nevertheless took its heaviest toll at the Pueblo, where resisters and others fleeing the American army were howitzered in the church. Simmons believably suggests that the revolt was motivated less by patriotism than by long-standing local frustrations and land conflicts.[41]

The Territorial Period

During the six territorial decades that followed annexation, the land situation in northern New Mexico became a whirlwind of ownership transfers, shifting boundaries, and large-scale speculation. The overall trend in ownership went from multiple communally and individually held lands to ever larger tracts concentrated in the hands of a few outside entrepreneurs. A significant proportion of these larger tracts eventually ended up under federal control. At least eighty percent of the grant land claimed by Hispano subsistence farmers in New Mexico was lost by the early 1900s, when the process of federal land adjudication was finally complete.[42] Knowlton has described the various means by which this dispossession took place, including, to name but a few, forfeiture through back taxes, credit foreclosure, lawyers' fees, outright purchase, swindle, appropriation of *ejido* (common land) into the public domain, and the arcane nature of the land claims process itself.[43] Of 650,890 acres claimed for at least twenty-six land grants in Taos County, the Court of Private Land Claims rejected 406,914.[44] Ultimately only fourteen grants in the county were confirmed by Congress and patented, beginning with the two Pueblo leagues (Taos and Picuris) and the entrepreneurial Sangre de Cristo, which lies partly in Colorado.[45] Many individually claimed nongrant holdings were also lost in one way or another, along with the entire public domain, the county's backbone mountain wilderness, containing the watersheds of every village and town. Appropriation of community common lands was probably the single most devastating blow dealt the native agro-pastoral subsistence economy.[46] The only lands nonwealthy Hispanos managed to hold onto in any significant proportion were, for the most part, individual, privately owned irrigated parcels in and around the villages, in addition to some pasture and dry grazing tracts.

But the full economic repercussions of expropriation were not felt until late in the territorial period, after the ranching, timber, mining, and railraod booms which exploited the Maxwell and other nearby wilderness areas had begun to die down, and ceased providing employment. Taos maintained its reputation as the granary of New Mexico into the early 1900s. It supplied fruit and grain to Elizabethtown and other mining camps during the 1860s and 1870s, and participated in the overall increase in agricultural production that occurred in the region between 1890 and 1910, when new lands rejected by the Court of Private Land Claims became open to new settlement. A U.S. Geological Survey report from 1904–1905 tellingly conveys the tenor of this period in the following recommendation for Taos's rich timber resources:

> All of the timber can be removed by means of logging railroads built up the main streams which offer no serious engineering difficulties, or by moveable sawmills, with wagon roads constructed to haul the lumber out. This latter method is probably the more economical when the low rate of wages paid the Mexicans is taken into consideration.[47]

Gold and copper mines boomed briefly and sporadically in the upper Rio Hondo watershed at Amizette in 1893, renamed Twining in 1903. Mining enjoyed a more sustained and productive development outside the Taos valley, particularly on the Maxwell, where in addition to gold and copper, large reserves of bituminous coal were extracted.[48] Cattle ranching also centered on the Maxwell, so that Taos, which contained a higher proportion of sheep, remained just beyond the western fringe of the Colfax-San Miguel cattle ranching boom and concomitant social disruption.[49] Prior to statehood a number of outside entrepreneurs had grandiose schemes for the exploitation of Taos. These included Arthur Manby, the ill-fated Englishman who dreamed of transforming the lower Rio Hondo watershed and Antonio Martinez grant into an international health spa,[50] and Gusdorf and Laughlin, who planned large orchard projects for tracts within the Gijosa and La Serna grants, requiring elaborate water reclamation projects that never came to pass. Nor did the railroad which was to have linked Taos with St. Louis and California.[51]

Just around the time of statehood, Taos seems to have gone from a valley of golden promise to an economically stagnant backwater, awaiting touristic discovery. It seems likely that by 1910 Taos had become an established exporter of labor. The trend in agricultural employment and production has been downward ever since, and Taos became known, among other things, for its high unemployment rate. When the booms dried up and the ejido was gone, workers had to leave to make a living. At first, people were mostly seasonal migrants. Men followed the sheep camps or families followed the crops. Gradually employment became more urban, and people left for years and decades instead of months (although sheepherders were also sometimes gone for years). This meant that a significant proportion of every native generation left, for good or for many years. Little solid, longitudinal data on out-migration appear to exist for Taos.[52] Even today, many who have settled elsewhere as adults maintain family ties and come home for fiestas and funerals, and stubbornly hold onto some tiny piece of property in hope of one day returning.

In 1906, two years after the Court of Private Land Claims closed, Theodore Roosevelt proclaimed the public domain in Taos County national forest, later named for Kit Carson. This consolidated nearly half the county land mass, including the mountain wilderness containing every village watershed, under federal control and Forest Service supervision. The act curtailed all traditional Indian and Hispano uses of the wilderness. It laid the groundwork for restrictions that would be enforced with disastrous results in the 1930s on grazing, woodcutting, and other small-scale extractions rural Hispanos depended upon. It also inaugurated sixty-four years of litigation between Taos Pueblo and the Forest Service over Blue Lake, the traditional or "sacred" mountain use area containing the Pueblo-town watershed. The federal government thus became the single largest landowner and source of revenue within the county, as well as a major cause of its insufficient tax base.

This situation of federal ubiquity was underscored by the determination in 1913 that the Pueblo Indians were wards of the federal government. Prior to that, the legal status of Pueblo Indians and their lands had been ambiguous, to say the least, under all three governments—and indeed they remain so today, as Hall's essay in this volume so vividly demonstrates. Only a very simplified version of one aspect of this complex issue as it unfolded in the modern period can be offered here, with particular reference to what it meant or came to mean at a practical, local level in Taos.

During the territorial period, non-Indian settlers were favored by local courts in land-water disputes with the Pueblos, who fared similarly at the federal level, where the Indians were regarded more or less as full citizens whose land was alienable. This approach had been encouraged by an 1877 Supreme Court decision (*United States v. Joseph*) which decreed that Pueblo peoples owned complete and therefore alienable title to their lands.[53] But however confusing its legal status, de facto settler encroachment on the Pueblo league, for example in the upper and middle Rio Lucero watershed, or by downtown Taos itself, persisted as it always had. The 1913 *Sandoval* decision decreed, however, that the Pueblos be accorded trust status as tribal Indians, their lands to be administered as federal reservations. This provided the legal basis for the reclamation of alienated and encroached-upon lands. Long and bitter court battles followed or in many cases simply continued, between the Pueblo and non-Indian claimants, and most of the latter were Hispanos.

In 1922 the Bursum Bill was introduced to Congress, which proposed confirmation of all pre-1902 non-Indian titles and placement of land-water adjudication under state jurisdiction.[54] The bill was defeated with the help of a powerful Anglo lobby organized in part by artists and intellectuals who had settled around Taos and Santa Fe, including Stella Atwood, Mabel Dodge, and John Collier.[55] In 1924 the Pueblo Lands Act, also authored by Bursum as a kind of compromise, was approved. It called for immediate investigation and final settlement of all non-Indian titles to Pueblo lands and promised monetary compensation for land lost to settlers who could meet a highly restricted set of requirements. Most Taos claims were adjudicated in the 1920s and 1930s. Among the first to be considered was the town itself, including the plaza, which not surprisingly the court found irrecoverable. An oversight in the original settlement gave the Pueblo a lingering claim over all town streets and alleys. At one point in the process, which ran concurrently with the ongoing Blue Lake issue, the Pueblo was evidently misled into thinking it could exchange compensation for the town land for Blue Lake (the two were separate cases involving different branches of the federal government). Eventually Hispanos were ejected from the Tenorio tract, where in Arroyo Seco families had settled on the north side of the Rio Lucero, and also from lands in El Prado and Ranchitos. Needless to say, this caused deep resentment among many Hispanos, who saw the Indians as benefiting unjustly at Hispano expense.

Settlement of Indian claims continues into the 1980s. Among those made in the 1970s, a decade inaugurated by the landmark Blue Lake victory, were recompense for the streets of Taos, return of Bear Lake or "Tract C" in the mountains, and ejection of a Hispano family from their house in El Prado. Blue Lake was resolved when President Nixon signed the bill H.R. 471, giving Taos Pueblo trust title to the lake and surrounding area. Its enormous symbolic import notwithstanding, the decision in some sense represents the administrative transfer of some 48,000 acres, containing the town watershed, from one arm of the federal octopus (Department of Agriculture) to another (Department of the Interior). As Bodine has shown, the Blue Lake case evolved under a complex and somewhat unusual set of socioeconomic and cultural circumstances. In a word, it was shaped by the course of tourism development, centered originally around the emergence of the Taos-Santa Fe art colony.

The social and economic history of Taos in the twentieth century is the history of tourism development and of the struggle of Indians and Hispanos to preserve their overlapping land bases with the political context of this essentially government-based, outsider-controlled economy. The form of capitalism that took root after the territorial period extractive booms expired would market local resources symbolically as well as literally. Indeed, it would come to rely on as literal a preservation as possible of material and cultural resources in their ostensibly "natural," "traditional," or "unspoiled" states. Such a claim necessarily constituted an elaborate if largely unconscious fiction, one that went nicely in hand with the land and Indian management agendas of the federal government, working as always in cooperation with wealthy private enterprise. This arrangement of interests and powers, themselves driven and shaped by world economic change, is at the root of Taos's and northern New Mexico's overall condition of underdevelopment. Taos since statehood has been known locally for its lack of employment opportunities. Yet to those born elsewhere, as a tourist attraction it seems far removed from the everyday struggle to survive. The unhappy marriage of these disparate views is an integral part of Taos's contemporary social reality.

Taos has undergone two tourism booms in this century. The first occurred roughly between the two world wars and centered on the marketing of Indian ethnicity, a Latin ambience, the natural environment, and art. To use V. Smith's typology, it was a blend of ethnic, cultural, and environmental tourism. The second boom began in the

1960s and continues into the early 1980s, and is essentially recreational-environmental. Between these booms were two decades of population decline and gradual modernization, punctuated by World War II and the Korean War. Each of these periods will be discussed below. This background is given in some detail in order to contextualize, and thereby make comprehensible, the Hispano ethnopolitical mobilization that emerged after 1970 and focused on issues of land and water.

The Art Colony

Tourism's earliest beginnings in New Mexico date from the latter nineteenth century, when a few health seekers, artists, and other railroad travelers began coming through the Southwest. But its real emergence in Taos coincided with the growth of the art colony, which began in earnest after Mabel Dodge arrived in 1917. Until World War I, farming and sheepherding were still important in Taos but in decline. Local commerce was firmly controlled by a number of mostly nonnative merchants with businesses in town. Santa Fe was already well on its way to becoming a health resort, and had attracted a nucleus of writers and artists much taken with the region's scenic combination of frontier wilderness and cultural exotica. A few artists had already settled in Taos, including Blumenschein and Phillips, whose broken wagon wheel incident in 1898 would become the art colony's origin myth.[56] They had been promoting the Taos Indians through their paintings for years (with the help of Fred Harvey),[57] but it was really Dodge who inaugurated the campaign to make Taos famous. She was a restless heiress from Buffalo, New York, who during World War I transferred her salon from Greenwich Village to the outskirts of Taos Pueblo. During the next two decades she invited a stream of distinguished artists and literati to Taos for the purpose of inspiring them to proclaim or interpret it, especially the Pueblo, in their works.

The development of the Taos-Santa Fe art colony is a much celebrated, still too little analyzed, psychocultural phenomenon that probably could only have occurred in a colonized region. Works by Bodine,[58] Grimes,[59] Briggs,[60] and Weigle and Fiore[61] have laid the foundation for a deeper, more comprehensive analysis that must one day be written about the relation between tourism, the art colony, and ethnic relations in New Mexico. The peculiar blend of romantic indianism and bohemian individualism that Taos and Santa Fe became famous for represents a pronounced theme in American cultural history, and perhaps bears comparison—as well as contrast—with the indianism (*indigenismo*) that emerged among Mexican artists and intellectuals during roughly the same period.[62]

The Anglo bohemian cult of indianism and creative individualism that developed in the Southwest needs to be seen in relation to the economic and social order it accompanied and mystified. The art colony took root more or less concurrently with the establishment of federal ownership of most of the county. It came to depend upon and actively lobby in favor of the policies of "preservation" and "conservation"—or de facto segregation and underdevelopment—that comprised federal programs of land and Indian management. Bodine refers to Dodge and her associates as ethnicity seekers and "cultural plunderers," while Simmons applies the softer term, "yearners," to the peculiar breed of artists, intellectuals, scholars, and dropouts who were drawn to Taos and Santa Fe, where they "in varying degrees identified with Pueblo life and affected styles of Indian dress."[63] They also spearheaded causes such as those against the Religious Crimes Code or Bursum Bill, or in favor of Pueblo ownership of Blue Lake. This enclave of culturally disaffected spiritual refugees from urban, industrial America played an important role in the development of southwestern ethnic symbolism. Members of an alien, superordinate and colonizing society, they lived like expatriates and appropriated indigenous symbols as their own in a manner that relied on and yet belied a social system of stringent ethnic-racial stratification and segregation. As Brody[64] and Briggs have shown, some of them "discovered" or "revived" and promoted Indian and Hispanic folk arts, and in the process transformed them as well. They moreover incorporated symbols from these traditions into their own works. Much of their artistic and intellectual production took its inspiration from Indian ceremonialism and from what they imagined to be the relationship between Indian culture and the natural environment. Apart from this and literary gossip about each other, their principal subject matter tended to be introspective, with the individual ego cast large against the mythic, solitary landscape.[65]

The most salient characteristic of the art produced by Taos and Santa Fe artists and writers is its almost total lack of reference to or description of the immediate social reality within which it was created. This is odd given that the art is otherwise so "regional." Rather than an arid, difficult environment governed by a pervasive system of stratified ethnic or race relations, New Mexico became an enchanted landscape populated by mystical tribes of noble savages. Insofar as Hispanos or Mexicans were included in this universe, they tended to be cast as an afflicted, somehow blameworthy source of social irritation or danger, a kind of folk who were really a class. Their culture was valued only for the quaint, "relaxed," Latin peasant ambience it lent the place, but not for any perceived intrinsic quality or beauty. As Bodine noted, only the so-called *penitente* and *santo* traditions seemed to attract the somewhat morbid fascination of these "ethnicity seekers." While the Spanish myth helped to promote the idea of New Mexico's uniqueness, the region's Hispanos were nevertheless subject to the long heritage of Anglo-American hispanophobia, anti-Mexican sentiment, and anti-Catholicism most newcomers brought with them.[66] If to the "yearner" sensibility the Indian was innocent and wise, the Hispano was ignorant but not innocent and, although poignant at times, generally troublesome. The Hispanos were seen as having subjugated the Indians and then been deservedly subjugated themselves. They partook of the corruption but not the enlightenment of European civilization, while their perceived backwardness had none of the primordial spirituality imputed to Indians. It is therefore no mere coincidence that while an Anglo lobby stepped forth to advocate the Indian land cause, none did so for the Hispano. The lineaments of this moral dichotomy between the Indian and the Mexican or "Spanish American" in the bohemian imagination were well in evidence by the end of the pre-World War II tourism boom. It would take two wars and as many decades of slow pressure to assimilate to put the finishing touches on what in 1968 Bodine would call Taos's tri-ethnic trap.

The First Tourism Boom

The twenties seem to have been a decade during which the art colony and tourism together took root as the town's economic mainstay. Workers continued to migrate out while newcomers straggled in, and the overall population continued to grow. The area got electricity in the 1920s, and by the early 1930s the Taos-Santa Fe highway was fully paved.

Tourism and the arts became fully entrenched and institutionalized in the 1930s. It was a decade when important changes took place and the modern character of the town emerged. The business-art community was fused into a civic entity when the town incorporated in 1934 and began to promote itself as a tourist attraction. This was done, for example, by inventing the "traditional" summer fiestas, replete with a well-orchestrated "historical" parade, still observed today. The figure of Kit Carson, "America's Forgotten Hero," was revived and promoted.[67] Somewhat prophetically, a group of artists and professionals formed a ski club, to promote awareness of the sport's potential in New Mexico. A hospital and a library were donated to the town by Mabel Dodge (by then Luhan) and Lucy Case Harwood respectively, and businessmen organized a volunteer fire department after a series of disastrous fires on the plaza. A few Anglos participated in local Hispano-dominated electoral politics. The first of Taos's two Anglo mayors, a well-known dentist and businessman, was elected in 1938; the second, a well-known doctor, served two terms, in 1944–1948.

A now familiar theme in Taos's interethnic politics had emerged by the 1930s, of conflict between native "progressives" who wanted modernization, and mostly upper-middle-class newcomers who wanted to preserve and enhance Taos's quaint, rustic character. Such a dispute surfaced around 1938, for example, when an artist-conservationist contingent favored gas lamps to illuminate the plaza area, while a progressive politico contingent wanted electricity. The former prevailed, temporarily.[68]

Locals who remember will jokingly comment that the Depression was not so bad in Taos, which was already long accustomed to poverty. The county population increased by twenty-eight percent during the 1930s, so far the largest increment in this century.[69] Some of this was natural growth in addition to a steady trickle of Anglo immigrants, but a significant proportion was comprised of natives who had migrated out for work and now returned. Possibly spurred by the United States movement to deport or "repatriate" Mexican nationals, people came home to get by on a combination of farming and welfare. Federal dependency and control gained significant ground in Taos during the 1930s. Hispanos continued to lose property through back taxes, while new restrictions curtailed livestock grazing in the mountains. For the first time, large amounts of federal revenue began to flow into the county, in the form of Works Progress Administration (WPA) and welfare programs. The New Deal inaugurated the federal subsidy of local politics and underwrote a wholesale transition from Republican to Democratic party domination. Sanchez's classic study *Forgotten People* captured Taos during this period, and described its still recognizable class structure:

> The social structure of Taos County embraces all levels. Wealthy, highly educated families have found in Taos an appealing environment and have established homes there. The artist group, and the writers, make up a body of people whose interest, training, and experience place them in a very favorable position. Some of the business and professional people, together with a few federal employees, join with the above groups in forming the upper stratum of Taos society. The middle social class embraces most of the school teachers, the clerks, the small shopkeepers, some of the public employees, and similar average income groups. At the lower end of the social scale are found the small farmers and laborers who constitute the bulk of the population of the county.
>
> The significance of this fairly evident demarcation of classes is appreciated when it is realized that the New Mexican of Taos County, the taoseño, constitutes over 90 per cent of the total population of the county (estimated at 14,229 for 1938) and that, as a rule, he is found in the lower social stratum, though a few are in the professions and in business. He elects the public officials. He controls the public affairs in the county and wields the political power of the county in state affairs. The leadership for this political influence of the taoseño has too often come from those of his own group who haven't the background of experience or of training or the inclination to use this influence in behalf of the people.[70]

Sanchez's study and the Carnegie-funded Taos Project it heralded took place just prior to World War II. Throughout the 1920s and 1930s the Indian land claims process continued, attended by a devoted Anglo lobby. No such lobby fought the slow process of Hispano dispossession. An important but unremarked (by the literati) land case which occurred in the immediate prewar period involved the threatened dispossession of some 250 Hispano families who had settled along the Rio Costilla on the Sangre de Cristo grant, and failed to pay back taxes. "Montana Wheat King" Thomas Campbell arranged to purchase the land from the state tax commission for the amount due and announced plans to start a large commercial sugar beet farm there. Senator Dennis Chavez loudly championed the settlers' cause and ultimately they were saved from ejection by an arrangement to repurchase their land from the government, a resolution that gave birth to the still-existent protective Rio Costilla Livestock Association.[71]

World War II and the Fifties

World War II promptly ended the town's tourism boom and flattened local morale for its duration. Taos was affected by the war early on, when the entire New Mexico National Guard minus one thousand men was drafted to defend Corregidor in the Philippines, a military disaster culminating in the Bataan Death March, and followed by nearly four years in Japanese prison camps. A substantial number of families in all three ethnic groups spent the war not knowing what had happened to these men. This experience plus the war effort in general served to pull together diverse segments of the local social structure, submerging but never dissolving the boundaries which divided them.[72] Women perforce filled more roles outside the household, and assumed additional responsibilities within it. But the greatest impact of the war was felt when the men came home, transformed, and a campaign was launched to further civilize Taos, to "clean it up" and bring it technologically and hygienically into the mid-twentieth century. Conflict emerged at the Pueblo, between conservative or traditionalist factions and progressives, often veterans, some of whom had returned with foreign wives, and who now balked at tribal proscriptions on their personal behavior or plans to modernize their homes. On such issues the bohemian element staunchly sided with the conservatives, apparently without ever doubting its own right to a public opinion.[73]

Modernization of the town was organized primarily by Anglo doctors and other professionals and businessmen who vigorously attacked Taos's high infant mortality rate and low sanitation standards. In the process Taos came to be locally identified as an unclean place, a theme that persists and crops up periodically in the newspaper.[74] A window on at least one segment of the upwardly mobile Hispano milieu is revealed in the Spanish-page editorials of the Taos newspaper during the late forties, in which rueful, often self-accusatory advice is offered. La Raza was exhorted, for example, not to indulge in the basically lower-class kinds of behavior it was stereotyped for, such as slovenliness or welfare abuse, and urged to be fastidious, reliable, and hard-working in order to advance, or not to sell one's land for so little.[75] During the late 1940s and the 1950s the town converted gradually from hand-dug wells and outhouses to indoor plumbing, and hard plaster began to replace adobe on many buildings, while new construction was increasingly of cinderblock. Many natives left to find work and commercial growth was very slow. Businessmen constantly fretted over the sluggish economy and Taos's public image. As elsewhere, the fifties in Taos were pervaded with McCarthyism, the disconcerting emergence of a rebellious adolescent subculture, and a muted pressure to assimilate into mainstream middle America, whatever that was.

In the late fifties the plaza was paved, with most town streets to follow within another decade. There were seven art galleries and two real-estate agents in the town. Overall employment in the county had decreased during the decade from an estimated 3,869 to 2,835 jobs. The most dramatic decrease was in agriculture, which had declined from 1,572 jobs in 1950 to 414 in 1960. Some employment gains were made in the services, public administration, trade, and commerce.[76] Anglo in-migration would soon pick up, and a handful of newcomers was beginning to sustain year-round businesses that did not depend largely upon native patronage. A ski resort was established in the upper Rio Hondo watershed in 1956, at the old site of Twining. It would grow steadily during the next decade.

The Sixties: The Real Estate Boom Begins

By 1960 Taos was on the threshold of rapid change. Between 1961 and 1963 five large subdivisions were made by out-of-state development corporations, covering 90 percent or 45,267 of all subdivided plats in the county. They were all located in the most arid and sparsely populated northern and western parts of the county. The largest tract, located *en la otra banda* or across the gorge, had been purchased for several thousand dollars from a single Hispano owner, who had used it for grazing. It was subdivided into over twenty thousand lots and then sold as prime residential estates to unsuspecting buyers at the World's Fair. The magnitude of the fraud came to light gradually, as thousands of disillusioned absentee landowners defaulted on their taxes. The tax rolls expanded threefold, which soon required additional personnel in the county assessor's office. Their volume and confusion continue to multiply as lots are auctioned off or transferred. In many cases the establishment of clear title is impossible, and the pattern of ownership of these lands is now so fragmented that reassembly for any single purpose, such as grazing, is seen as virtually impossible.[77]

The twenty-year population decline since World War II began to reverse itself in the 1960s, even though a steady stream of native youth continued to leave for employment, education, and before long, another war. Late in the decade Taos was hit by what is generally remembered as the Great Hippie Invasion. Over a period of about four summers, between 1968 and 1971, thousands of young, itinerant, middle-class urban (or suburban) Anglos began to arrive in Taos, in search of the same romantic utopia their bohemian predecessors had sought over a generation earlier. But unlike most tourists who had previously moved to Taos, many hippies came with dreams of going "back to the land" and living as farmers. For several years they were able to buy up parcels of irrigated land rather cheaply from Hispanos, who needed the cash and had little inkling of the transformation about to occur. After a winter or two of rustic hardship, many newcomers sold their land at a profit and moved on. Ownership turnover then escalated along with land price, and within another decade the average price of an irrigated acre had increased by as much as forty times. This meant that very few Hispanos, at least thirty percent of whom have subpoverty-level incomes,[78] could afford to buy land, and an increasing number could no longer afford to hold onto it. In concert with the subdivision flurry, this initiated Taos's contemporary real-estate boom, which by the mid-1970s was fueled primarily by the ski industry.

It is noteworthy that Hispano group violence against Anglos erupted for perhaps the first time in more than a century during the hippie period. The hippies exhibited a combination of behaviors that amused some Indians, antagonized many Hispanos, and alienated an influential segment of the Anglo population, mostly the businessmen. This rendered them vulnerable in an unprecedented manner, and some of them were openly attacked by groups of Chicano youth. The hippies were accused of being dirty, lazy, and immoral, but probably what most infuriated Hispanos about them, apart from their public displays, occasional petty thievery and land purchase, was their collection of welfare and food stamps. E. Smith attributes the demise of the hippie communes which had mushroomed around Taos to the violence, and suggests that the "flower children" who remained were forced to rationalize their preparation for self-defense.[79]

Most of the hippies who stayed in Taos gradually settled into somewhat more conventionally middle-class—or in some cases upper-middle-class or "hipoisie"—lifestyles for which they found ample margin. An important trend inaugurated during the hippie era was Anglo competition on the local unskilled labor market. Prior to around 1969, few Anglos received welfare or competed with Hispanos for the limited manual labor and service jobs in Taos. This changed with the influx of semi-transient, often college-educated youth, who today compete favorably with Hispanos in the tourism-related service and construction job markets. It has been a contributing factor in the intensification of anti-Anglo sentiment among at least some segments of the Hispano population.

The violence against hippies erupted at the same time that a new Chicano militance was emerging in the cities and universities, and it also followed the widely publicized activity of Reies Tijerina and the Alianza. Taos was not particularly known as a stronghold of Alianza membership, but Tijerina did have support there. He made it his business to visit the Pueblos, land grant villages, and hippie communes in the area, possibly operating on the assumption that anyone at odds with the "establishment" was a potential ally. The Tierra Amarilla courthouse raid took place near the beginning of the hippie period, which also happened to be the height of the Vietnam War, as well as of black and other national minority mobilizations. The intrusion of national upheaval into the local scene created conditions under which, for perhaps the first time, Taos's interethnic dynamics were openly described as racist. Taos no longer seemed isolated from the rest of America.

By the end of the sixties, the face of old Taos was changing fast. The construction industry was expanding along with the number of realtors, and many new businesses, including national franchises, had been established. Spurred by the political unease the Alianza had engendered, a new flood of federal "war on poverty" funds was flowing into the county to underwrite an increase in public employment. The ski industry, enthusiastically embraced by local businessmen as the solution to Taos's dilemma of a seasonal, feast-or-famine economic cycle, was beginning to flourish. The old Our Lady of Guadalupe church next to the plaza had burned early in the decade and been replaced by a modern, "supermarket-type" building nearby. The long-standing social influence of the parish priest and Loretto nuns in town was fading. Most of the town streets were being paved, and neon advertizing was in vogue. The county courthouse, the nerve center of local politics, was transferred from the plaza to a modern building on south Santa Fe road, a move that signaled a shift of business concentration away from a nuclear to a more dispersed or "strip" pattern. Town officials were beginning to talk about city planning and zoning. Mabel Dodge Luhan was dead, and movie star Dennis Hopper and a coterie of counterculture groupies were living in her house.

Eclipsed during the forties along with many other local issues, the Blue Lake controversy resurfaced during the fifties, gained momentum during the sixties and, as already mentioned, was finally resolved in 1970. Bodine's chronicle shows how the case was kept alive over decades by a handful of powerful Pueblo personalities who were committed to the cause, but who also used it to manipulate circumstances for their own political purposes.[80] His account reveals that the religious freedom argument became increasingly explicit through time, no doubt because it worked. This is not to say that the lake, or for that matter other locales in the Taos basin, did not have aboriginal religious significance. Rather, it points to the fact that Blue Lake came to be explicitly identified with the Taos tribe's religious freedom and continuation as a people under a particular set of legal, political, and economic circumstances. The course of the case was certainly influenced by the presence of a good many "yearners," and correspondingly, by the astute use made by prominent Pueblo individuals of their Anglo admirers' willingness to help. Not all Anglos sided with the Indians of course, and needless to say many Hispanos found the issue particularly galling in light of their own land situation, which included ejections within recent memory from Indian lands. Nevertheless, some older Hispanos did support the Pueblo and even testified in its behalf, a sympathy enhanced among the younger generation by a growing awareness that Chicanos have a common cause with other minorities. The symbolic import of the Blue Lake victory was intensified by the general social and political climate of the times, and it reinforced the already established connection in local perception not only between land, water, and physical survival, but also between land and cultural survival. This connection was dramatized for Hispanos by the Alianza, a development which itself is comprehensible only within its larger historical and sociological contexts.

Luxury Tourism and the Emergence of Protest

Events in Taos during the seventies served to deepen the sense of connection among at least some Hispanos between their continued occupation of and control over their lands, ditches, and villages, and their persistence as the people they know themselves to be, or to put it another way, as culturally and ethnically distinct from Anglos. The decade brought increased growth and development, but also an intensified—or at any rate more articulated—sense of resistance, most explicitly in the form of public protest. At the same time, cleavages were expressed between the expanding middle class of urbanized Hispano businessmen, and poorer, more rural farmers and ranchers who live in the villages and still use the ditches.

Two major protests stand out in the 1970s: the one against Indian Camp Dam, lasting from 1971 to 1976, and the other against Taos Ski Valley, a protest that emerged in 1974 and has continued into the early 1980s. Both of these cases, as well as a proliferation of similar or related ones during the early 1980s, began as disputes over water.

Indian Camp Dam. Described by both Reynolds and Nichols, the Indian Camp Dam issue involved the proposed construction of a large dam and reservoir above Talpa and Ranchos on the Rio Grande del Rancho, southeast of Taos.[81] The project allegedly was intended to boost irrigation agriculture through the formation of a conservancy district, but local opposition understood it as a government-assisted ploy to promote tourism at the expense of Hispano farmers by taxing them for what in fact would become a recreational lake. Opposition leaders included older acequia, land grant (La Serna), and community water system officers from the Ranchos-Cañon-Los Cordovas areas, some of whom had originally favored the project. In what appears to have been a first-time Hispano-Anglo alliance against big developers and "progress," these otherwise socially and politically conservative native protesters were supported by an emergent element of mostly ex-hippie environmentalists. Nichols's popular fictional account of the "Milagro Beanfield War" based on this issue both publicizes and satirizes the Hispano land plight in Taos.[82] The case dragged on for five years, but achieved at least temporary resolution when the conservancy district was annulled on a technicality.[83] The struggle against the conservancy district and dam gave birth to a still active alliance of acequias within the general *tres rios* (Rio Chiquito, Rio Grande del Rancho, Rio Fernando) area. This organization has since supported the cause of Rio Hondo acequias against developers, and has become an important participant in a larger protective organization, Acequias del Norte, which unites ditch associations from several northern counties, and which itself grew out of a water struggle near Española in the 1970s. Along with the ski valley issue that began to take shape concurrently, the Indian Camp Dam controversy marked the beginning of a new kind of protest activity in Taos. A post-1960 influence is discernible in its often ethnically mixed constituency and public, increasingly direct, style of activism.

The Ski Valley Issue. Organized protest against the ski valley emerged in 1974 when, after six years of expansion and sewage pollution of the Rio Hondo, ski valley developers sought improved access through national forest to private land where a 4,500 "pillow" resort, named Kachina Village, was planned. Taos Ski Valley is located not far below the source of the Rio Hondo, which supports Valdez nine miles downstream, Arroyo Hondo two to three miles below that, Cañoncito between them, and the western upland settlement of Des Montes. At least nineteen households on the river use its waters for domestic purposes, including drinking and cooking.[84] Roughly ninety percent of the ski area, that is, its trails and lifts, is located in Carson National Forest, on land leased from the Forest Service. Downstream residents, including Hispano farmers, ditch officers and their families, Chicano activists, and Anglo environmentalists, protested vociferously enough *en masse* at a still well-remembered public hearing to dissuade the Forest Service from improving access, at least until a bigger and better sewage treatment plant could be built. It was during the Kachina Village controversy that the image of the Rio Hondo flowing in the veins of its native downstream users was invoked and used to great effect.

During the next six years a variable, ethnically mixed committee of protesters persisted in a largely unsuccessful legalistic strategy to block formation of a Twining sanitation district, and to compel the appropriate state and federal agencies to enforce their own sanitation standards. By 1981, the Forest Service and ski valley had worked out a thirty-year master growth plan,. while the Environmental Protection Agency (EPA) and the ski valley completed designs for a new, $1.5 million sewage treatment plant.

In 1982 the EPA approved the new plant without requiring a graduated hook-up policy linked to performance, and the plant was built, using private funds, in the late fall. To the downstream protesters, the failure to require a hook-up policy meant, in effect, that while the Twining district would forego federal funding, it could continue to expand to the new plant's full capacity without first demonstrating it could meet and maintain clean-water standards. After years of litigation and participation on government-sponsored citizen's advisory committees dealing with the ski valley, the protesters reached a new peak in their level of frustration. For fourteen consecutive years of violations, neither state nor federal agencies had enforced their own standards. Agency collusion with developers seemed beyond doubt.

On the day before Easter and the last weekend of the 1981–1982 ski season, about three hundred downstream residents and their supporters held an unprecedented mass demonstration at the ski valley. It was conducted as a mock funeral for the river, complete with coffin, hearse, and motorcade, in addition to religious banners and the parish priest's solicited blessing. The roughly 150-vehicle caravan departed from Arroyo Seco and wended its way slowly up Hondo Canyon, honking in unison when it reached the ski area. A second demonstration was held not long after the new plant was completed, this time the day after Christmas, at the height of the 1982–1983 season. This somewhat smaller and less elaborate but equally vocal demonstration was held despite the Forest Service's allegedly illegal refusal to grant a permit. On both occasions demonstrators picketed and leafleted skiers, and were extensively photographed by Forest Service, ski valley, and law enforcement personnel, in addition to being covered by the media. Pairs of protesters continued to leaflet skiers on weekends for the remainder of the season, while the new plant polluted heavily.

In the autumn of 1983, repeatedly postponed state and federal hearings were finally held on the matter of past violations, and the Twining Water and Sanitation District was fined $4,500 by the State District Court, payable to the Environmental Improvement Division (EID). It agreed to a $30,000 settlement out of federal court, where it might face a possible maximum fine of $1,000 per day. Out of the settlement amount, $5,000 went to the downstream acequias for "improvements," while the remainder went to the EPA.[85] It remains to be seen whether the new plant will continue to pollute, and if so, what downstream response will be.[86]

In addition to the ski valley protest against pollution, in 1982 a coalition of downstream ditch associations opposed large transfers (one for about seventeen acre-feet) of priority water rights from Arroyo Hondo to the ski valley, that were to be used for commercial purposes, including snow making. Such transfers are routinely approved by the state engineer, whose de facto policy is to consider each application in isolation, thereby ignoring their obvious cumulative impact. This impact threatens the viability and integrity of the ditch system by removing water as well as labor, and it also renders farmland forever fallow and useless for anything except residential development. This is because once the surface water rights are removed from a piece of land, it can no longer be irrigated, and the Taos area is generally too dry to allow for dryland farming. The only water such a piece of land can thereafter have legal access to must come from an underground well, and may be used for residential purposes only. Since a given ditch system must be maintained by the collective labor of its users of *parciantes,* each time a parcel loses its water rights, a proportional amount of labor and ditch fees is also lost to the system as a whole, thereby increasing the burden of maintenance upon the remaining parciantes. Each member is a link in the chain of community water use and control, and each time a member and his quota of water and labor are lost, the overall chain is weakened. This deleterious impact is maximized for those lowest on the ditch. The members of a ditch system may protest a proposed transfer, but the burden of proof of potential damage from water loss rests upon them. In other words, the applicant for the transfer is not required to prove that the transfer will not be deleterious. Moreover, the costs of filing a protest and any ensuing litigation must somehow be borne by the water users themselves.[87]

The ski valley demonstrations were part of an overall escalation of protest activity that took place in 1982, focused primarily in the Hondo watershed, but also apparent in milder form throughout much of the municipal district, where public meetings were held in almost every community to discuss the merits and dangers of rural zoning as a possible way to forestall if not prevent the steady advance of luxury housing development and its likely consumption of all remaining farmland and water.

The dozens of community meetings held in the Taos area during 1982–1983 tended to reveal that zoning was by no means an appealing or popular idea among the majority of rural Hispanos, but the one point most people could agree on was that no one wanted a condominium next door or upstream. Along with the ski valley issue, the rural zoning debate served first as a backdrop to, but then itself gained momentum from, what came to be known as the Valdez "condo war." This involved unified action by the village of Valdez against a large luxury condominium planned for the upper Valdez valley. The condo war showed how far villagers were willing to go in order to stop such a development in their midst. The case epitomizes the struggle rural Taoseños are engaged in to maintain their fragile hold on traditional uses and ownership of land and water, and it illustrates the conspiracy of structures that militates against them.

But before proceeding to the condo war and related rural zoning movement, some additional background will be given in order to elucidate more fully the conditions under which local Hispano resistance to outside encroachment has intensified.

Modern Taos

The 1970s brought a significant and locally obvious augmentation of Anglo presence and control, not simply in the economic sphere, but in most areas of public life. A corresponding self-protectiveness emerged among Hispanos with respect to those domains of their own traditional predominance, such as, for example, local politics and government, including the school system. At the same time, a handful of wealthy, upwardly mobile Hispano businessmen enhanced their niche as elite brokers within the expanding economy, and moved into higher levels of finance, such as banking.[88]

All sectors of the local economy grew during the 1970s except for agriculture, which declined from 6.4 percent to 5.4 percent of all jobs.[89] Growth was stimulated by expansion of the molybdenum mine in Questa, and by the ski industry which, in the 1979–1980 season, claimed to generate an estimated income of $11,532,000.[90] Most of the jobs generated by tourism are in trade, services, and construction, which together make up roughly 55 percent of all jobs within the county.[91] For the most part, tourism-related jobs tend to be low-paying, seasonal, and without benefits, upward mobility, or security. The best jobs to be had from the standpoint of these factors are at the "Moly" mine, the county's single largest private employer, which accounts for 11.5 percent of all jobs.[92] The other major sector is public employment or government, which includes the school system and comprises 24 percent of all jobs.[93]

Yet despite economic growth, the county still ranks in the state's bottom five in terms of unemployment, averaging 14.2 percent for the period 1970–1981.[94] The official unemployment rate in 1983 averaged 17 percent,[95] and was reported at around 20 percent early in the 1985 summer season.[96] In 1980, the average income *per capita* was $6,128, while 20 percent of all personal income came from transfer payments or some form of federal assistance.[97] Although a large proportion of Hispanos is employed in the private sector, a comparatively small, though nevertheless growing, segment occupies positions of ownership or power within it. By contrast, in the nonfederal part of the public sector, Hispanos predominate in virtually all hired positions controlled by the electorate, which they dominate by sheer numerical majority. Whereas the trend in upper and lower levels of the private sector has been toward greater integration (by virtue of expanding in-migration on the one hand, and limited upward mobility on the other), the opposite seems true in local politics and government, where in 1984 an Anglo (not to mention Indian) mayor or county commissioner seemed well beyond the realm of possiblity, and the ubiquitous Anglo school administrator of a generation ago had been replaced by a Chicano bureaucrat.[98]

It is both ironic and significant that Anglos will not infrequently complain of discriminatory treatment in the schools, or claim they cannot get a fair trial in a dispute with a Hispano.[99] While racism as an issue has surfaced as such during the past two decades, there is nevertheless a strong taboo against discussing it openly in public or ethnically mixed company, although thinly veiled allusions and pointed insinuations are often made. The long-manifest, privately acknowledged, yet almost never explicitly articulated ethnographic truth about Taos is its de facto segregation, which obtains virtually everywhere outside the everyday world of business, such that membership in one group effectively precludes full participation in the key sociocultural events of the other two. Taos in this respect is a little like the classical shamanistic cosmos of three superimposed, mutually invisible layers or worlds, where the denizens of each live mirroring but only accidentally interpenetrating lives. Exclusion of each group from intimate knowledge of or involvement in the lives of the other two is a dominant feature of Taos as an inclusive social system. For example, an event can take place which has tragic or scandalous significance among one of the ethnic groups, reverberating quickly throughout its informational and social networks, while most people in either of the other two groups barely take note. For the most part, members of each group celebrate their religious holidays, weddings, funerals, and Saturday nights in the company of their co-ethnics, class and other sociocultural subdivisions notwithstanding. Friendship is predominantly intraethnic. Yet mutual awareness among the groups is differential by virtue of differential power. Because Anglos control the media and theirs is the dominant language, events of significance to their elites receive the greatest publicity and are thus widely known. Their interpretation usually becomes the "official version." At the same time, as Spicer notes, members of a dominant group tend to be less aware of ethnic boundaries than those who are subordinated. The latter are constantly reminded of their constrained universe, while the former must seldom confront their own part in perpetuating it. This segregated, unequal reality is contradicted by the more pleasant, tourism-promotional public-relations image of Taos as a slightly zany marvel of "tri-cultural harmony" or "colorful historical pageantry." Recent demographic shifts, however, seem to have thrown Hispano-Anglo boundaries into higher relief.

Between 1970 and 1980, Anglo in-migration increased to such an extent that long-standing ethnic proportions went from 86 percent Hispano, 7 percent Anglo, and 7 percent Indian to 67 percent, 27 percent, and 7 percent, respectively, possibly the largest Anglo increment this century.[100] Moreover, by 1980 Anglos owned at least half the land in eight of the fourteen major settlement areas inside the municipal district, although they outnumbered Hispanos in only four of them, including the town, Las Colonias, San Cristobal, and Twining.[101] Las Colonias and Arroyo Seco both became predominantly Anglo-owned in the 1960s.[102] Along with Des Montes, they are located along the road to the ski valley, and together these three settlements have borne the main impact of the ski industry's secondary or associated luxury residential development. Twining, which includes the privately owned portion of Hondo Canyon above Valdez, has been mostly Anglo owned and populated since its beginnings as a mining camp in the last century.[103] By 1980, more than half the land in Twining and Las Colonias, which along with the town are the main foci of condominium development, was owned by nonnatives who live elsewhere for most of the year. All told, only 38 percent of the 1,444,480 acres of land in Taos County is privately owned.[104]

The real estate and construction boom that began in the 1960s grew during the 1970s from a number of comparatively small-scale enterprises to a multimillion dollar, increasingly luxury-oriented industry. By 1983 the real estate market supported at least eighty realtors, most of whom had lived in Taos for less than ten years. One hundred and thirty-five were reported for the county in 1985, as the boom seemed to be tapering off.[105] Their advertising in the local newspaper went from a few items in 1960 to nearly four pages in 1984. An acre of irrigated land in the Hondo watershed which sold for perhaps $600 in 1960 might sell in 1984 for as much as $22,000, while the water rights alone might bring anything from $3,000 to $6,000 per acre-foot. Most advertised adobe houses near town were going for $100,000 or more.[106]

Each of the communities around Taos has experienced and responded to the population and construction booms differently, according to its own internal composition, particular geographic locale, and relation to the town on the one hand, and to its neighbors in the same or adjacent watersheds on the other. An account of each individual village situation cannot be provided here, although each deserves its own telling. Only the broadest outline can be given.

Those communities nearest Taos are faced with whether to be absorbed by the town's relentless spread, or to resist assimilation and defend their individual autonomy, identities, and traditional boundaries. None has chosen the former alternative, and of the two inside the town's three-mile-wide extra-territorial zone, El Prado and Cañon, each has pursued a very different course in meeting the municipal mandate either to zone itself or be zoned by the town.[107] A key issue for these communities as well as for Ranchos and its neighbors is whether to maintain or construct its own independent water and sewage system, or to hook up to the town's, and thereby be incorporated into the city. The ability of these communities to maintain their autonomy is undermined by the construction of large housing or other tourism-related developments, whose promoters are eager to hook up to the town's system and other services, and whose prospective clientele has little interest in the preservation of traditional village boundaries or resource use patterns.

The town itself does not have enough water rights to accommodate more than the next twenty years of growth at most and has, for the time being, addressed its most immediate needs by purchasing 400 acre-feet of San Juan-Chama diversion water rights.[108] By law this water must be pumped from outside the Taos basin, from one or more wells, or from the Rio Grande itself. In order to qualify for federal funds to enable it to buy, locate, and pump the water into town, and also pay for its new, expanded sewage system, Taos must demonstrate and guarantee a certain level of growth. It has done this primarily by contracting with two nonlocal (but instate) housing developers who, in concert with municipal planners, have worked out designs for large housing projects to be located southeast of the town. Although these projects include graduated price ranges for their units, it is clear that not even the cheapest of these units will be affordable by most natives, except for perhaps a few young professionals or management-level employees and those of comparable strata. This is true for the vast majority of the housing being built or planned for Taos. Despite a pressing shortage of middle-to-low-cost housing, and except for single family dwellings and one or two low-cost housing projects, the new construction is being built for and by newcomers, often as second homes.

The town first zoned itself in the 1960s, although a skeletal set of regulations, never enforced, had been drawn up at the time of incorporation in 1934. During the 1970s the town came up with a more sophisticated code and additional personnel to administer it. County government has authority over subdivisions and, after the 1960s fiasco, enacted regulations for dealing with them. The county commission also has the power to zone the county, but has not done so. It therefore lacks jurisdiction over nonsubdivision construction outside the city limits and buffer zone. Such construction is approved in Santa Fe without consultation with any local body, although once approved, plans must be filed with the county clerk.

In the late 1970s public pressure induced the county commission to contract for a comprehensive planning study as prerequisite to drafting county-wide zoning regulations. The study was completed by a Santa Fe consultancy firm, and a zoning code was prepared, based largely on the one adopted by Santa Fe. A petition against the code was then widely circulated, causing the commission to kill the plan just before the election, which all three incumbents lost anyway. The new commission was loathe to take up such a despised cause, and the matter of county zoning was dropped. In the meantime ever bigger and fancier developments continued to mushroom in the vicinity of every settlement as well as in formerly unsettled areas such as the west mesa.

Once the issue of county zoning was officially dead, it began to crop up in the communities, invariably in response to some proposed and therefore imminent project that promised to consume a substantial portion of an already over-allocated and jealously guarded water supply.

Rural zoning tends to have several types of proponent in Taos: Anglo environmentalists of various stripes; mostly younger, urbanized Hispanos or Chicanos, who have lived away and returned; and a few of the older ditch and land grant officers and their families, who have been actively involved in defending the ditches since at least Indian Camp Dam. In some instances, coalitions of either the first two or all three of these categories would organize a meeting in a given community to discuss the possibility of zoning. Invariably most newcomers would favor the idea, some locals (often those with larger landholdings) would oppose it vehemently, and the usually silent majority would listen skeptically.[109] The spur to debate and in some cases to action always involved a proposed multiple-unit housing development that would consume water, discharge sewage, and serve outsiders.

This then, was the general setting in which the Valdez condo war erupted, and within which the struggle continues to unfold. This struggle involves the effort of rural and urbanizing Hispanos to preserve their community resource domains. In the autumn of 1981, and for the twenty or more months following, by far the most frequently and hotly debated public issue in town and the surrounding communities concerned the protection of increasingly scarce land and water against the onslaught of in-migration and luxury housing development.

III. *The Valdez Condo War*

Valdez

Valdez is located about twelve miles north of Don Fernando, at the mouth of Hondo or Twining canyon, nine miles below the ski valley and roughly four miles east of the church of Nuestra Señora de Dolores in upper Arroyo Hondo (see Map 13). Known originally as San Antonio, Valdez evidently acquired its present name after a postmistress in 1894.[110] It was first settled as the upper placita of Arroyo Hondo community grant in 1815, becoming a separate extension of the grant in 1823. Today the legal remnant of the grant consists of the thirty-seven-member San Antonio corporation, renamed in 1984 La Merced de Arroyo Hondo Arriba, which has pieced together and now collectively owns about 2,400 acres of nonirrigated hillside land above the Valdez valley.

Valdez is clearly bounded. It is set deep in a narrow, irrigated valley that extends for about three miles along the Rio Hondo, between Twining and the pinch of bluffs at Cañoncito, below which the Arroyo Hondo valley opens out. Valdez contains approximately 150 people living in about 50 households dispersed along the valley, with some concentration near the centrally located placita. Roughly eighty percent of the population is Hispanic, and some residents are evidently descended from original grantees. Today the placita consists of the church of San Antonio, the old schoolhouse (now a community center), a post office, and a cantina, all located in or around the original square still outlined by old houses. The valley floor is banded by strips of irrigated land, dotted with adobe houses and trailers, and divided lengthwise by the tree-lined river. Seen from above, along the rim one must descend in order to enter Valdez, the valley has a picturesque, miniature-looking beauty.

To outsiders, Valdez has a self-contained remoteness defined geographically and accentuated by its proximity to the predominantly Anglo areas of Twining and Des Montes.[111] In Taos, Valdez is known for its rural Hispanic character, its ditch that appears to run uphill (as well as one that runs right through the cantina) and its old reputation for *brujos* (witches). To neighbors it is known for its church, abundant fruit, cantina, and kin, and rights with respect to the river: upstream from (but now third priority to) Arroyo Hondo, and below the "uphill" acequia to Des Montes.[112]

Although nearest to the Swiss-style Anglo-European resort community at Taos Ski Valley, Valdez has remained the native settlement least developed by the tourism-related real estate boom that has overtaken the Hondo watershed since 1970. The deep little valley offers some prime agricultural land, but it has been less attractive than Des Montes, Arroyo Seco, or Arroyo Hondo to realtors promoting isolation, vast altiplano vistas, and luxury housing. To this sensibility Valdez has been more to be looked at than lived in, although resort and subdivision activity has nevertheless begun to eat at its peripheries. By local account, the men and some families in Valdez have long followed a pattern of seasonal out-migration for work, in sheep camps or harvesting crops. During the 1940s, 1950s, and early 1960s, Valdez's population declined, but since then the village has begun to repopulate and grow, largely with the families of young adult natives who had been working and living elsewhere. This has revitalized community life in the placita.

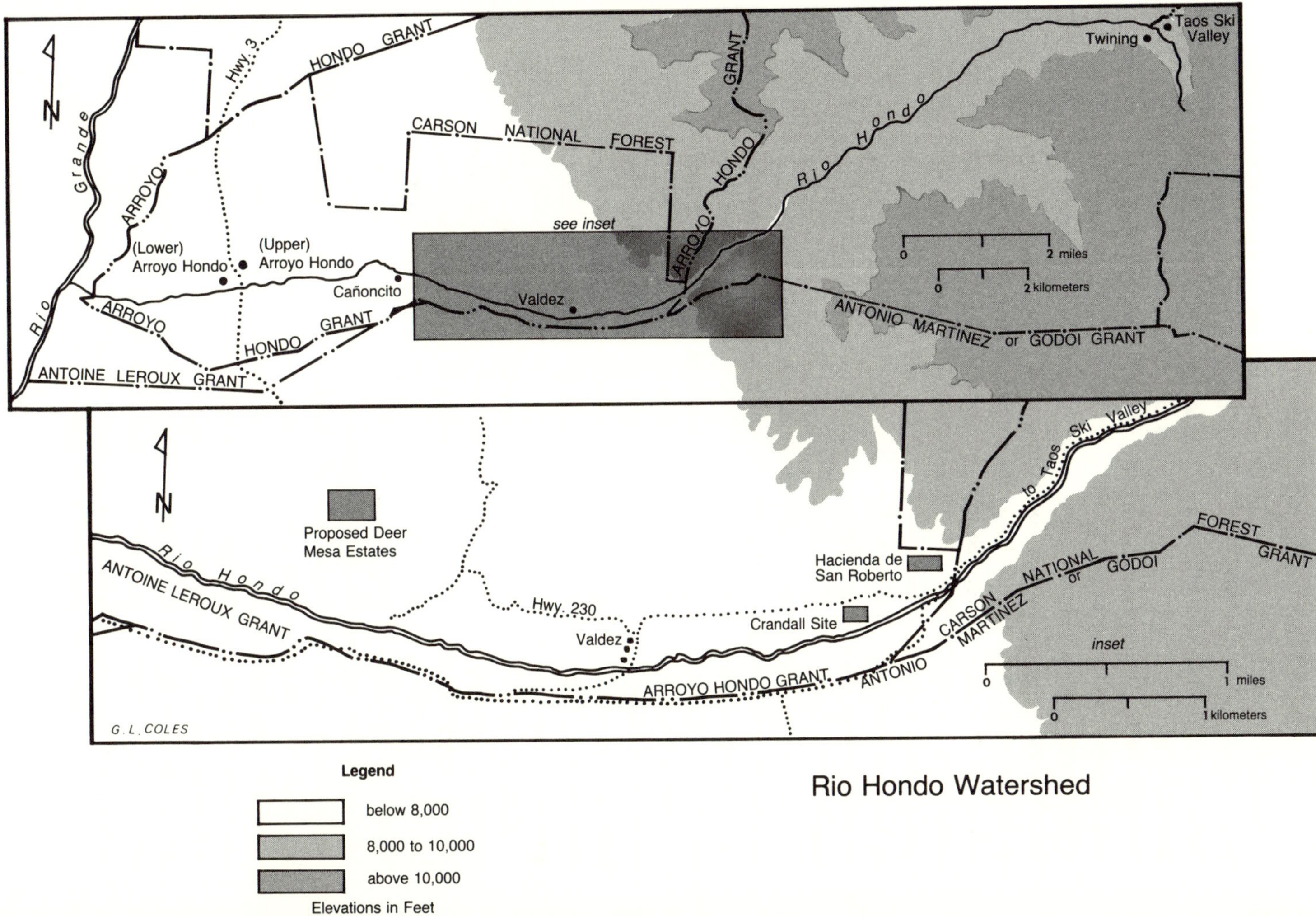

MAP 13. Rio Hondo watershed

Today a number of Valdez men work at the mine some twenty miles away in Questa, some have jobs or businesses in town, others work at the ski valley, and a substantial proportion receive some form of federal assistance.

Anglos—including farmers, retirees, wealthy seasonal residents, hippies, and semi-tourist transients—live in or near Valdez, but none own property right on the placita. Except for the few farmer-ranchers who use the ditch system, Anglos participate little or not at all in the fundamental life of the community, which centers upon the ties of kinship and *compradrazgo* (fictive kinship) that interweave local parish, ditch, and community water organizations. Local Hispanic families participate to varying degrees and at various levels in the area's tourism-welfare-government economy, but for the most part their social interaction is with one another and takes place within the larger context of extended multicommunity ties and organizations. In Valdez, as in other villages around Taos, Spanish remains the primary language in all but intermarried or intensely upwardly mobile Hispano households, or those in which language loss has occurred through protracted out-migration.

Like other Taos area villages, Valdez both changes constantly and remains "traditional." It appears that the ability of local residents to maintain, revive, or actively defend traditional practices and resources depends in part on a certain degree of economic stability, education, and/or land tenure. The past few decades have shown that, while an overall trend toward acculturation may be taking place, the attenuation of certain forms and practices may not be permanent. Cultural revivals and innovations seem to occur right alongside apparent culture loss. Revivals are not infrequently religious in nature. Probably the most striking recent example of this is the cultural renaissance revolving around the San Francisco de Asisi parish centered in Ranchos. During the past decade, the parish has helped to initiate an annual pilgrimage for vocations to Chimayo from Amalia, undertaken the restoration of the famous church's adobe exterior by community labor, and contracted for the restoration of its two *reredos* or altar screens, one of which was rededicated in 1982 to Los Hermanos de Nuestro Padre Jesus Nazareno, or the so-called *penitente* brotherhood. Like Arroyo Hondo, Valdez sold its morada, which now sits vacant and crumbling by the roadside, owned by a nonresident outsider. The local Hermanos are still active, however, and use their various parish chapels and the Arroyo Seco morada during Lent and Holy Week and other occasions. In 1983, shortly after the condo war about to be described, Valdez revived its San Antonio mass, procession, and fiesta, which had not been conducted for at least twenty-five years. Arroyo Hondo parishioners in 1984 contracted for the 150-year anniversary reproduction of their church's reredo, the original of which is in a Colorado museum, while most of its santos and the morada are owned by a wealthy Anglo. The slow quadrupling of San Antonio Corporation acreage during the past fifty years is another indication that village residents seek not only to retain but to recover traditional boundaries.[113]

Although Valdez has borne the most direct brunt of ski valley pollution of the Rio Hondo, with the exception of one Anglo farmer married to a local Hispana, no one from there has been particularly active in the drawn-out legalistic battle to make Taos Ski Valley-Twining clean up the river. The core constituency has come mostly from Arroyo Hondo. This may be partly because Hondo is larger and more heterogeneous, and also because few people from there work at the ski valley, whereas a number from Valdez do, as maids and maintenance men. Nevertheless, the ski valley issue was the immediate context within which people in Valdez finally did protest. Protest in Valdez first emerged in the autumn of 1981, when the community succeeded in getting a sewage discharge permit denied for the Hacienda de San Roberto, a condominium then under construction just above the head of the valley. Valdez protesters persuaded the EID to deny the application to discharge sewage into the Rio Hondo by submitting nineteen affidavits which attested that nearly as many households in Valdez and Cañoncito depended on the river for all domestic uses. The construction involved the expansion of a small restaurant and lodge into a large condominium by the Sikhs, a religious-entrepreneurial sect made up of out-of-state Anglo converts and based in Española. Just after the permit was denied, the half-completed condominium went into the receivership of seven banks, all but one out-of-state.

The protest against the Hacienda was initiated by the Valdez Mutual Domestic Water Users Association (MDWUA), the organization of the users of the community well that serves about thirty households in the area of the placita. The president and secretary of the MDWUA wrote a letter to the EID requesting a public hearing on the Hacienda's sewage discharge application after a legal notice had appeared in a nonlocal newspaper—the EID having failed to publish such notice in the Taos paper. After meeting with some community organizers whose prior contact with Valdez had come through ski valley protests and a rally in support of a Hispano family involved in a Rio Arriba County land grant case, the MDWUA officers decided to organize a public hearing.[114] Leaflets were circulated door-to-door in the Hondo and Valdez valleys, and a well-attended prehearing community meeting was held at the church in Valdez. The affidavits on water use were collected during this period. House-to-house contact, community strategy meetings, and careful preparation for public meetings and confrontations were to become characteristics of protest in Valdez. The community organizers later became residents of Valdez and went on to play a key facilitative role in the condo war and in the related effort to zone the valley. While the role of the organizers was critical to the success of both condominium protests in Valdez, it became obvious that the movement derived its power and legitimacy from its broad-based Hispano constituency. The precipitating factors for the protest, discussed in the previous section, were clear-cut and exerted a cumulative impact brought to bear on Valdez, the Hondo watershed, and the greater Taos area during 1982.[115]

The "Condo War"

In January 1982 a representative of the State Engineer's Office began knocking on doors in the upper Valdez valley about a mile above the placita, to ask how deep people's wells were. Residents then learned that in late November and early December, concurrently with the Hacienda protest and permit denial, Peter Crandall had applied to transfer 4.6 acre-feet of water from the San Antonio ditch to underground use in order to supply a well for a multiple-unit condominium.[116] Since no one objected to the transfer during the three-week legal notice publication period or for ten days thereafter, the request was routinely approved. The small-print legal notice in *The Taos News* mentioned tract number, the surveyor's coordinates, and the San Antonio ditch, but not the name of Valdez, and no one in the valley noticed it.

Homeowners adjacent to Crandall's nine-acre strip were quickly alarmed by the prospect of a large condominium whose well would be at least fifty feet deeper than their own wells and whose sewage would have to go into either the river or the ground-water. Their other concerns were the effect of development on traffic along the narrow winding road in the valley where children and livestock frequently play or meander, and the overall social impact so many new, wealthy, urban Anglo residents would have on the community. From the beginning, people in Valdez expressed the fear that the condo inevitably would result in the destruction of their valley and way of life. Opposition to the project was expressed as a struggle for cultural survival and community self-determination. At a community meeting held in the schoolhouse to discuss the idea of zoning in the Hondo watershed, the people of Valdez decided to send a letter of protest to the state engineer and did so on 28 January, along with a petition bearing sixty signatures. Their protest was denied some weeks later because it was "untimely." No physical tests were conducted, but the state engineer was satisfied that significant well "draw-down" would not occur.

After their protest was denied, people in Valdez joined others in the Hondo watershed in petitioning the county commission for a symbolic moratorium on major development in their area, while they undertook to zone themselves. In this, they followed the example of Llano Quemado where, faced with a proposed apartment complex that threatened an apparently dropping water table tapped by shallow, hand-dug wells, residents had successfully petitioned the new commission for a moratorium in early January. Both moratoria were said to be strictly symbolic because the county commission claimed it had no power to enforce them. The commissioners nevertheless imposed a six-month limit on the Hondo watershed moratorium, granted at a public hearing. The single dissenting voice at the hearing was that of Crandall himself, a young developer from a prominent Anglo family owning one of Taos's car dealerships. He claimed, among other things, that the sewage discharge from his condominium would be "drinking water pure."

More than a dozen public meetings on zoning were held in the Hondo watershed during the winter and spring of 1982. The immediate threat posed by Crandall's condominium moved people in Valdez to undertake the necessary steps to form a Special Zoning District (SZD), which for reasons of size and agreement they did in cooperation with Arroyo Seco and San Cristobal.[117] The widespread debate about rural zoning took its text from a rather ambiguous and scanty state statute (3-21-26 N.M.S.A. 1978), which states that residents from within an unzoned area containing a minimum of 150 households may delineate and form an independent SZD if they present a petition to the county clerk bearing the signatures of at least 51 percent of the registered voters resident within the proposed district. Once the zoning petition and zoning plat have been filed with the clerk, the county commission must set a date within sixty days for the election of a five-person zoning commission to draw up the code.

Spurred by the approach of construction season, people in Valdez managed on 4 May to vote on a broad plan and to elect a zoning commission candidate committed to that plan. The essence of their zoning plan was a code to protect customary patterns of settlement and land use and to curtail condominium and other tourism-related luxury residential and commercial development. Described as "zoning for poor people," it would place no restrictions on trailers, junk cars, livestock, and other rural and agricultural uses, including the traditional division of land among heirs. Because of its small size, Valdez was compelled to zone as part of a larger district, one that eventually came to be known as Los Tres Valles. From spring until fall, people from Valdez, Arroyo Hondo, and San Cristobal repeatedly petitioned the county commission to hasten or at least facilitate the zoning process, which in fact the commission made every effort to undermine, despite considerable public pressure and media coverage.[118]

In May, Crandall filed his condominium declaration with the county clerk, and some weeks later people in Valdez learned from it that he planned 39 units, rather than his publicly announced figure of 24 units, with options to build up to 99 over a 15-year period. On 12 July they held a meeting at the *escuelita* (schoolhouse) to discuss what they would do to stop construction, which seemed likely to begin any day. This meeting inaugurated the active phase of the protest. About fifty people attended, including adults of all ages, teenagers, and children; most were Hispanic. Some people from Arroyo Hondo and San Cristobal were also there. A majority of the tactics that would unfold during the next month were decided on at this meeting. By then people had consulted a legal services lawyer, who finally told them he was too overburdened to take the case, and realized they had at best tentative legal grounds for stopping construction. Only the sewage discharge permit, which Crandall had not yet applied for, would provide an obvious opportunity to file a legal protest, through either the EID or the EPA. A copy of a unit floor plan was passed around. It showed for each unit two fireplaces, an open shower area, a spa, and outlets for washers. Each unit was priced at $250,000. People agreed to pursue legalistic avenues as long as the effort did not incur lawyer's fees, but they also decided to apply public pressure against Crandall, as their only direct recourse.

Six basic actions were decided on at the 12 July meeting. People agreed to paint anti-condo signs and put them up around the valley; to send another letter to the state engineer and to the newspaper, pointing out that the condo was significantly larger than was stated publicly or on the water transfer application; and to give other objections to the project. They planned a float for the annual Taos fiesta "historical-hysterical parade" on 25 July, and a separate march through Taos to Gilson Motor Company, the lucrative family business established by Crandall's grandfather in the 1940s. They also decided to ask the county commission to enforce the moratorium. And people agreed to make a banner from a sheet on which community members would sign their name and age beside a stain of their own blood. The banner would be carried on a march to present to Crandall, who worked as a salesman at Gilson's, with the statement: "The blood of Valdez is on your hands." During the next three weeks, people wandered in and out of the escuelita to have their fingers pricked for signature on the banner. Customers at the cantina would be invited over to make their contribution. Interestingly, the men tended to be more squeamish about this operation than women and children. The latter were especially enthusiastic.

On the weekend after the meeting, about twenty-five adults and children met at the schoolhouse with boards and paint to make over forty signs which they then placed along the road into and through the valley. The signs read, for example:

> "Pete Crandall: Give Up and Get Out"
> "Pete Crandall's Condos Not Welcome in Valdez"
> "Peter Crandall's Condos Are An Insult to the Community of Valdez"
> "The Community is United so Don't be Misguided"
> "Nuestro Pueblo No Se Vende" ["Our village is not for sale"]
> "Rich People are Greedy"
> "Condos Kill Raza."

And, Burma-shave fashion, "You'll Be Hated—On the Hondo—If You Buy—A Crandall Condo." Two very large signs with dripping red handprints or hearts read, "Pete Crandall: the Blood of Valdez is on Your Hands." The district attorney (D.A.) later requested the last ones be taken down for fear they "might incite to violence." The signs were featured by newspapers and television, and quickly became the talk of Taos.

The following weekend Valdez had entries in both the children's and historical parades for the Taos fiestas. In the first about ten younger Valdez children marched, wearing donated anti-condo T-shirts and carrying a sign that read, "Save Our Valley, No Condos." The entry received an honorable mention. In the other, the Valdez float featured a young Dracula hovering over an elaborately fenced-in condominium with death-heads at the windows and dollar-sign grillwork, plastered with play money, and juxtaposed on a flatbed to children and small animals seated on bales of hay, wearing their T-shirts beneath a sign that read, "The Future of Valdez." They chanted "No Condos en Valdez!" at the tops of their lungs.

The next day, people from Valdez and some neighbors asked the county commission to enforce their moratorium. The commission demurred and postponed the matter. Late the following night, the signs disappeared during a violent thunderstorm and were seen in Crandall's brother's van, before they were dropped the 650 feet or so from the Rio Grande gorge bridge. Within twenty-four hours they were amply replaced by a somewhat less varied edition of signs, featuring a number of death-head images and one sign, placed before the bridge near the placita, that read:

> Commandments Against Condos:
>
> Thou shall not build condos
> Thou shall not pollute our water
> Thou shall not disrespect our way of life
> Thou shall not pollute our land
> Thou shall not covet our land and water
> Thou shall not steal what belongs to our children
> Thous shall not kill our valley.

On 31 July, blessed by the parish priest, approximately eighty-five people from Valdez and other communities held a protest march from Kachina Lodge north of the plaza to Gilson Motor Company, about two miles to the south. The procession was headed by the dramatically stained "Blood of Valdez" banner, and a life-size wooden puppet with movable joints and lower jaw, that was modeled after miniature Mexican skeletons and lifted and munched a dripping red heart labeled "Valdez." People chanted and carried signs. The plan was to present Crandall with the banner. But Gilson's was closed for the occasion, and on their showcase windows were handscrawled signs which read: "To Whom it May Concern: Gilson Motor Co. has Nothing to do with Pete Crandall Building Condos in Valdez. Pete Crandall Does Not Work Here Anymore." Despite Crandall's father's disavowal of any connection with the project, Gilson's was targeted not only because Crandall worked there (having taken leave to work on his project), but also because the motor company and condominium corporation boards of directors consisted entirely of Gilson-Crandall family members, with Peter and one brother sitting on both.

Crandall's personal response to all this attention was strong. He had appeared at the cantina shortly before the meeting on 12 July, demanding to know who had written the flyer announcing the meeting, and threatening that his lawyer would attend. He harangued the Anglo owner of the photocopy store where the flyer (as well as his condominium documents) had been reproduced, and threatened her with a businessmen's boycott. He intimidated the Hispano owners of a neighborhood grocery in Des Montes near where he grew up, because they had consented to display a poster for the meeting. Two domestic employees of Crandall's parents, people from Valdez who had participated in the protest, were quietly "let go." During August Crandall avoided, then sought out, the press. He released a brief "fact sheet" on the project. He addressed the local realtor's association about it. He claimed he received telephone threats. He called a secret television press conference, which the totem-bearing protesters got wind of beforehand and partly co-opted.

The next county commission meeting was packed. Valdez's young Chicano lawyer, working pro bono, asked the commission to enact emergency interim zoning to avert a confrontation and possible violence. The D.A. was there and testified that this was "the number one issue in the county," and confirmed that both he and the sheriff knew the situation to be "explosive." He nevertheless counseled, along with the county attorney, against an emergency ordinance, for fear of incurring a "million dollar lawsuit." Crandall's paternal aunt, holding a sign, stood and announced her support for Valdez, amid applause. The volatile crowd was appeased by the promise of an afternoon meeting at which county representatives, protesters, and their lawyer supposedly would work out an agreement whereby Valdez, Arroyo Hondo, and San Cristobal would compose an interim ordinance that the county commission would pass the following week, but would not enforce, so as to avoid suit. The SZD, once formed, would then file to enjoin Crandall from building. During the next week, zoners worked frantically to complete this process and held a meeting at which people from the three communities approved an expanded version of the 4 May plan already adopted by Valdez.

A day or so prior to the next scheduled commission meeting, Reies López Tijerina telephoned Valdez to express support and ask if he and some friends might attend. Zoners consented if he would not speak. This meeting, also packed beyond seating capacity with placard-bearing protesters and other interested parties, was one of those memorable occasions when all the conflicts and contradictions that seethe in Taos seem telescoped and epitomized. Crandall, dressed as usual in a three-piece suit, addressed the commission and attempted to persuade the largely hostile crowd of his native, "pre-D. H. Lawrence" pedigree, freedom from "prejudice," and beneficent intentions toward "any citizen willing to work" for his job-generating project, which would also establish a "Southwestern Institute for Human Relations," whereby he and other philosophically inclined individuals would conduct dialogue with the community. He was questioned and heckled, and finally fled the room, visibly on the verge of tears, while his mother, grandmother, brother, and brother-in-law sat frozen among the crowd. An elderly Taos Indian seated with the family, for years for employee, rose to say: "This is *our* land. The people are talking about land. *We're* the owners—what the hell are they complaining about that!" Heated speeches followed, all ignoring the attempt to raise the Hispano vs. Indian issue, and culminated in a bitter, explosive exchange between Hispana protesters and a local realtor, who had commented that surely Crandall's condos would look a lot better than the "indiscriminate shacks and trailers" scattered around the valley. Deputies were called in to restore order. The county attorney now claimed the commission had no authority to enact the interim ordinance, and they once again defused the situation by setting up another meeting, for which their attorney proposed to contact all landowners within the proposed district by registered mail. He proposed this course of action on the basis of a statute pertaining to proposed changes in established zoning regulations, but entirely unrelated to the statute for creating SZDs. The next public hearing on the proposed interim ordinance was set for 10 September, allowing for three weeks of legal publication.

Tijerina's appearance at the commission meeting heightened media attention and sent shock waves through the business and real-estate community in Taos. Outside contractors recalled recent heavy equipment vandalism in Questa and wondered just how safe the situation in Taos might be. Repeating the local truism that "only Anglos protest," town businessmen were quick to claim the protest was the work of "hippies and a few outside agitators." The perception that any ethnically mixed protest is instigated and dominated by Anglos is common and reinforced by the marked proclivity of Anglo men to monopolize public speaking, as well as by a subtle media bias. Anglo reporters have a tendency to contact Anglo members of a mixed protest. There are no Hispanic reporters on the Taos paper, and in fact all the print and television media people with whom the protesters had an opportunity to speak were Anglo.

The actual constituency of the protest is noteworthy. It included Anglos but was predominantly Hispanic, and involved farmers, miners, and service workers of both sexes and representing a broad spectrum of ages. It involved several interethnic (Anglo-Hispana) couples, including the community organizers who had joined the Hacienda protest some eight months earlier, and an enthusiastic contingent of children. This author was also an active supporter.[119] The Valdez group contained ditch, domestic water system, and land grant officers, the Democratic and Republican precinct chairmen, the postmistress, the cantina owners, and all of the church *mayordomos* (annual caretakers), as well as a range of other lifelong and recent residents, including the two Anglo subsistence farmers in the valley. Women assumed key interhousehold organizing roles. Only one prominent extended family dissented, which generated some tension. The grassroots, mixed-yet-native nature of the protest gave it legitimacy and power. Valdez's cause drew sympathy while Crandall seemed to repel people from his own. The intense level of protest activity was sustained for a period of about three months, because a number of people devoted their primary efforts to the unceasing effort to block construction. Bumper-stickers were donated, and eventually donations and fundraising activities produced some thousands of dollars of support money.

By mid-August the SZD had filed its petition and plat, so the commission was required to schedule an election, which it did belatedly and under pressure from the state attorney general who was consulted by protesters. During the following weeks, Crandall announced several starting dates, and told local realtors and television reporters that all units were presold. The turning point came when he lost his funding. A local bank had agreed to lend him $1.5 million for the first five units, but rescinded under the pressure of letters from other clients. Then his subsequent source of funding, Oklahoma-based Penn Square, collapsed. His contractors quit, and rumor had it his engineer quit, and numerous workers declined employment on the project for fear of violence. Shots were fired near Crandall's land. The electrician for the project claimed his house was shot at. Rumors were rampant about Crandall's agitated state, disintegrating domestic situation, and indiscreet public behavior.

On 18 August Valdez called for a boycott of Gilson Motor Company, and set up an eight-hour-per-day, two-person-two-hour shift picket which, after an initial attempt to thwart it by the town mayor and police chief, was maintained for sixty days, until 19 October, when protesters declared a cautious victory. At the end of August a construction trailer, double fence, locked gate, and security lights went up on the site. An all-Hispano security guard was established, increasing tension. Valdez held a well-attended benefit dance at a popular lounge in town. Two days later heavy equipment began moving earth on the land.

County commissioners failed to appear for their own public hearing on 10 September, for which presumably thousands of registered notices had been mailed out at county expense. Therewith their so-called interim ordinance which, unlike the draft zoners had given them, neither named nor described "condominium" as a prohibited use, finally died. A delegation to the attorney general in Santa Fe put pressure on the county commission to schedule an election, and one was finally held in November, when the community slate of candidates was elected, unopposed.

In late September, Valdez held a rally on land across the Rio Hondo from Crandall's site, where construction had still not begun. Some three hundred people attended and heard music and the speeches of a number of local and regionally active notables in the rural and urban Chicano movement, including Tijerina. Their recurrent themes were the connection between land, water, and cultural survival, and an appreciation of Valdez as symbolic of rural Hispano struggle against wealthy outside developers, who more than Anglos per se were seen as the "enemy." Especially reviled were the native *vendido* and *lambe,* or "sellout" and "bootlicker." The following poem was performed by Cleofes

Vigil, widely acknowledged poet laureate of *La Tierra Santa de la Sangre de Cristo.* Its text is reproduced in full and broadly translated because it expresses, in traditional form and with eloquence and passion, a mythopoetic, native version of the expropriation of La Raza in Taos:

Valles del Condado de Taos
[Valleys of Taos County]

1

Valle del Condado de Taos
donde fui nacido y criado
ya se hacabo tu hermosura
que mis ojos la miraron
Cuando tenias armonia
Vecinos amigos y hermanos

Taos County valley
where I was born and raised
your beauty is gone
which my eyes beheld
when you had harmony
neighbors friends and brothers

2

Por tu pureza retenida
de tu agua viento y campo
Con sagazida de alavia
an venido millionarios
Penetrandole al celebro
al nativo ser humano

For your retained pureness
of your water air and land
millionaires have come
with shrewd flattery
penetrating to the brain
of the native human being

3

Estrangeros avanzados
Con su grande dios dinero
que nomas te la enseñan
te arrodias ante ellos
y te hechan un lazo
apretado hasta el hueso

Strangers advanced
With their great god money
which they merely show
you kneel before them
and they put a lasso around you
tightened to the bone

4

OH hello ther mi señor
Con aquella gran ansia
desea usted mi terreno
deme lo que a usted le nasca
que yo ahorita me muero
y usted necesita mi casa

Oh hello there my lord,
with that great anxiety
do you desire my land?
give me what you please
I will soon die
and you need my house

5

Ya les damos la historia
los que estos valles nos davan
sin mas que un cavador
y una hoz en la mano
un arado de palo
y un tirito de cavallos.

And we gave them the history that
these valleys had given us
with only a hoe
and a sickle in hand
a wooden plow
and a team of horses.

6

Montaña Sangre de Cristo
Con laderas y valles amplios
Cuando llego el D. H. Lawrence
ya le llamavan Kit Carson
donde empeso la mentira
la avarizia y el engaño.

Sangre de Cristo mountain
With slopes and wide valleys
When D. H. Lawrence arrived
They already called it Kit Carson
where the lie began
the greed and deception

7

Sigio la gran epidemia
de langostas desolando
la armonia que habia
pronto la destrozaron
con alavia de You are my Friend
al infierno nos mandaron.

The great plague followed
of locusts desolating
the harmony that had once been
they destroyed it quickly
with flattery of You are my Friend
they sent us to hell

8

A nativos adiestraron
a lambes muy competentes
a estos los an usado
Pa que chingan a su gente
Piojos resucitados
Vendidos y dementes.

They trained natives
to be very competent bootlickers
they have used them
to screw their own people
sold-out and demented
resuscitated (fattened) lice.

9

Llego el fraule con papeles
al nativo de estos valles
esto es la ley my Friend
Ya tu palabra no vale
si no saves alfabeto
una eques X es vastante.

The paper fraud came
to the native of these valleys
this is the law my friend
your word doesn't matter now
if you don't know the alphabet
an "X" is enough.

10

Pues una vez que ya firmo
ya todo es derecho
donde el dicho se aserto
de que no hay cosa mas triste
que un esclavo satisfecho

Once you have signed
everything is legal
as the saying goes
there's nothing sadder
than a satisfied slave.

11

Antes de esta epidemia
Nuestros valles heran paraizo
donde habia bendeciones
Y amor para el ser humano
buenos dias le de Dios
como esta usted mi hermano.

Before this plague
our valleys were paradise
where there were blessings
and love for the human being
may God grant you a good day
how are you my brother.

12

Este muy grande progreso
del estrangero tirano
Por amor a su dios dinero
todos estamos destraidos
al verdadero creador
ya lo hemos olvidado

This great progress
of the foreign tyrant
for love of his money god
we are all distracted
we have forgotten
the true creator

13

Doz muy fuertes palabras
escritas en dicionario
democracia y Cristiandad
las usan para escudo
Mas y mas calamidad
heridas de filo agudo.

Two very strong words
written in the dictionary
democracy and Christianity
they use as a shield
more and more calamity
wounds from a sharp edge.

14

Con una voz consonante
es mi deseo decir
de que todo lo que aqui escrito
lo verifica Cleofes Vigil
Con mi esperencia que tengo
No me pueden desmentir
que solo mi Dios save
que sera el Porvenir.

With one resonant voice
It is my desire to say
that Cleofes Vigil verifies
everything written here
With the experience I have
no one can contradict me
only God knows what the
future will be.[120]

The picket continued and Crandall did not begin construction. His checks were said to be bouncing all over town, and his employees went unpaid. The security guard disappeared, followed by the trailer and security lights, some of which had been shot out. Crandall appeared in town with an Anglo body guard, on one occasion to harass an Anglo shopkeeper whose wife was picketing. He let go his project manager and then vacated his rented office in town. Twice he requested and then failed to show up for meetings with a few community representatives. On 19 October Valdez called a press conference in front of Gilson's to announce a cautious victory and an end of the picket but not of the boycott, until Crandall would publicly withdraw.

A few weeks later Crandall published an article, rather than a letter, in *The Taos News,* in which he announced he was leaving town for a while, that he was not bitter and "would never say quit," and cautioned against trying "to preserve Taos in amber." In late November his lawyer requested a meeting with people in Valdez, to discuss the possibility of alternative construction acceptable to the community. He acknowledged that multifamily units for seasonal occupants would not be built. He was told that perhaps one house per two acres might be acceptable. He indicated Crandall would not build the condos, and that his client simply wanted to recover his investment. On 14 February 1983, the attorney requested another meeting, and this time offered a plan for twelve condominiums. He revealed that in addition to over two dozen units, this "compromise plan" deleted the swimming pool and activity center, neither of which had been mentioned in the original condo declaration.[121] His proposal was politely rejected as insulting. On 21 April, *The Taos News* reported that Centinel Bank of Taos had initiated foreclosure proceedings for a mortgage on the land, for which Crandall and his corporation owed a total of $83,140. A "For Sale" sign was posted on the land. In late 1983 Crandall, no longer living in Taos, filed for bankruptcy. By the summer of 1985 he was back in Taos, again working at Gilson's. The bank held an auction for the land in June, but there were no bidders. However, by the end of August it had been sold to a private party, whose plans remain to be seen.

The Valdez condo war captured local and regional attention in the north, and became a popular cause among Chicano groups in Albuquerque and other urban areas. The character and outcome of the issue had a broader, albeit not universal, appeal however. It inspired hope in native peoples' ability to resist constant encroachment and displacement and stimulated interest in rural zoning. In all, during its peak period in the summer and early autumn of 1982, the controversy had been the focus of at least eight highly charged county officials' meetings, and the subject of over thirty newspaper articles, twenty-six published letters and editorials, numerous instances of television coverage, and three nonlocal radio programs. It was later named "story of the year" by *The Taos News*. The intense phase of protest activity ended with Crandall's retreat in the late autumn, although neither the sentiment of resistance nor the developmental assault it was a response to subsided.

Just as Crandall's project had surfaced immediately upon the Hacienda's demise, so did the latter revive right after Crandall's defeat, along with several other proposed projects, like the hydra which sprouts two heads for each one severed. The Hacienda reopened in the late fall with intentions to resume construction for its expansion, under the receivership of six out-of-state and one local (Centinel) bank, and under the management of the other major car dealer in Taos. The new holding corporation, named Carson, Inc., was able to obtain a septic tank and leach field sewage permit from the EID without having to publish a legal notice, and had eighteen rental units open during the 1983 and 1984 ski seasons. Not only did EID officials neglect to notify Valdez residents of the application as they had been repeatedly asked and had promised to do, but they also failed to initiate action when, during the winter of 1983, the Hacienda exceeded its 1,800 gallons-per-day discharge limit.[122] Carson, Inc. became the object of a letter campaign, and during 1983 Hacienda management met with and even attempted to buy off Valdez representatives with the offer of a cash donation to the community center.[123] Finally, in the spring of 1984, the Hacienda worked out an arrangement with the EID and Valdez whereby the condominium and its sewage treatment capacity would not expand beyond its already existing eighteen units. Also in late 1982, a wealthy Englishman with a seasonal home in Valdez planned a $40 million, 200-home "model community," named Cindercone, to be located between Valdez and Arroyo Hondo, replete with "recreational facilities and complexes for visual and performing arts, and a model farm." After several meetings with selected but decidedly recalcitrant representatives from Valdez and Hondo, this developer evidently reconsidered the wisdom of his plan and dropped it, at least for the time being. Both the Hacienda and Cindercone were the targets of another anti-condo sign campaign in the early summer of 1983, and once again Valdez children marched in the Taos fiesta parade.

During the winter and early spring of 1983, the Tres Valles Zoning

Commission composed and held a series of public meetings to discuss the new code. After due publication of legal notice, the code was officially approved and adopted by the Tres Valles Zoning Commission in June, at a public hearing held in Arroyo Hondo. Present at the hearing were the lawyer and project manager for Deer Mesa Estates, a New York-based corporation with plans to develop a ninety-one-acre subdivision in the lower Valdez valley. They objected to passage of the code, and were instructed to submit their project plans to the zoning commission for consideration. They subsequently refused to do this, preferring instead to deal exclusively with the county commission, which attempted to accommodate them. However, the commission finally was persuaded that its own treatment of the subdivision would be legally subject to Tres Valles regulations. Deer Mesa then filed suit in district court against Tres Valles on several grounds, including the claim that the SZD act is unconstitutional. This interpretation was upheld by District Judge Frank Allen, Jr., who ruled the statute unconstitutional on 9 July 1984. Tres Valles appealed the decision, and the appeal was lost in late 1985. Meanwhile, the Hacienda again went up for sale. And during the summer of 1985, the project manager for Deer Mesa left that endeavor to assume an administrative position with the EID.

Summary and Conclusions

The ability of rural zoning or, for that matter, any other tactic to help protect traditional patterns of Hispano land tenure, will be further challenged during the next months and years, along with the survival of Hispano land tenure itself. Since the middle of the last century, Hispanos in northern New Mexico and southern Colorado have faced massive and more or less continuous expropriation and displacement from their farmlands surrounding land grant villages, towns, and their offshoot settlements. Economic need has forced them from the land and out of the villages into migrant labor, towns, or cities, and into local dependency on a fragile combination of federal subsidy, outside extractive industry, and tourism. Today the forces and conditions that conspire against the ability of rural and semi-rural Hispanos to hold onto their remaining land and water around Taos appear to be multiplying and gaining momentum.

My central argument here is that this ongoing process of expropriation and its recent acceleration have, in concert with various local, regional, and macrosocial factors, intensified rural Hispano resistance to further usurpation and displacement, and stimulated the crystallization of land as a symbol of Hispano cultural survival. The articulators of this self-conscious land symbolism come mostly from living generations of Hispano-Chicano activists, artists, writers, and others, including, to name but three, Rudolfo Anaya, Cleofes Vigil, and, of course, Tijerina himself. This increasingly explicit symbolization represents not only a strategy of ethnic boundary maintenance but also a manifestation of the oppositional process. The latter concept would seem to presuppose the former, and their difference would seem to be more a matter of degree than character. What distinguishes a persistent identity system in Spicer's sense from simple ethnic identity is the oppositional process, and the self-consciousness it engenders over time.[124]

This is not to suggest, however, that the land is of only recent symbolic importance to Hispanos or that it has not long held a different meaning for them than for Anglos or, for that matter, Indians. On the contrary. The psychohistorical wellsprings of contemporary Hispano-Chicano land symbolism lie in an earlier legal, social, and cultural system of land tenure quite different from the Anglo-American system that displaced it, and in the collective trauma of massive land loss. The differences and conflicts between these two systems have been documented by various land grant scholars, including those in this volume. As Van Ness puts it:

> At the outset, the Spanish American and Anglo American forms of land tenure were in striking contrast in terms of the ways in which land units and exploitative rights to land and its resources were technically defined, distributed, and recorded in the two societies and of the economic ends to which exploitation was directed.[125]

Economic considerations serving the maximization of marketability determined the Anglo-American method of land measurement, description, recording, possession, and transfer. In the Spanish American system of land use and occupancy, however, sociopolitical and other contextual factors customarily outweighed purely commercial or profit-motivated considerations. In New Mexico, it was a system in which the use value of land, for the subsistence of the resident population, was primary, rather than its exchange value for nonresident speculators. While land could be held privately and sold, "sales were normally circumscribed by local considerations."[126] As Knowlton reports:

> The village with its attached land and water rights was thought of as a single indivisible community. It was regarded as a crime against the moral order of the universe for any political authority to separate the village from its traditional land and water rights. A village community so separated was like a man who had lost an arm and a leg. The villages who have lost land or water, as most have done, regard themselves as having suffered serious moral wrongs. Even though a hundred years may have passed since a village lost its land, the village inhabitants still know the location of every acre that has been lost. The present owners and users of the land are defined as usurpers who do not have the right to use the land that once belonged to the village. There is an aching sense of injustice that will never end until the village is totally abandoned or until the land is restored to the village.[127]

Some version of this abiding resentment against Anglos smoulders deep within many if not most Hispanos in the communities around Taos, an often suppressed sentiment understandably widespread among Chicanos in general. One of the striking facts about this sense of resentment in Taos is its virtual absence from public discourse or record, which simultaneously reflects, promotes, and denies the status quo of Anglo domination. The invisible or submerged aspect of this otherwise ubiquitous ethos is further reinforced publicly by differential boundary awareness among groups or strata.

But despite the intrinsic elusiveness to outsiders of a subordinated group's ethos of resentment and resistance, the latter necessarily assumes a variety of direct, although perhaps more often symbolic, expressions. Social scientists have devised numerous techniques for measuring and, often unwittingly, influencing minority responses to conditions of oppression. A once favorite approach, today much criticized, and exemplified by Kluckhohn and Strodbeck's famous Five Cultures project, has been the "measurement" of values and attitudes as indices—and even explanations—of acculturation.[128] Following in this tradition, Eastman, et al. tested, among a sample of respondents from seven northern New Mexico counties including Taos, the hypothesis that: "Spanish-Americans are more traditional in their attitudes toward land ownership and usage than are Anglo-Americans."[129] Their summary of their findings reads as follows:

> Land attitudes are strongly influenced by years of education and to a lesser extent by socioeconomic status. Residence and birthplace have an effect, because rural birth and residence seem to cause a reverse acculturation. Land ownership (past or present) also influences land

> attitudes. Equally important as the related variables are the several characteristics not related to land attitudes. There is no generation gap in attitudes toward land; young people have essentially the same scores as do their elders in both ethnic groups. Spanish-Americans may be acculturating, but not in their attitudes toward land. Similarly, geographical mobility—living outside the Southwest—and exposure to the mass media have little influence on land attitudes. Thus, effects associated with age are not bridging the difference between ethnic groups, nor is geographic mobility, nor exposure to the larger culture via the mass media. This leaves education as the most viable vehicle for changing land attitudes.[130]

Apart from its implicit cultural determinist framework and assimilationist bias, this approach presupposes a primordialist view of ethnic identity, or one that assumes ethnic distinctions result from geographic and social isolation and diminish in response to contact and modernization. Such a perspective fails to account for the study's actual findings, including the positive or uneven correlation between "traditional" land attitudes and several conventional measures of acculturation. Eastman's findings and other contemporary ethnic phenomena better fit Barth's more reactive view of ethnicity, which holds that ethnic distinctions are creatures and reflections of structural and institutional arrangements, and of differential patterns of use of and competition for limited resources. This view accounts for, or is at least consistent with, widely observed phenomena of ethnic resurgence, under both developing and advanced conditions of economic and political modernization.[131]

That Indians, Hispanos, and Anglos have differentially occupied, utilized, competed for, and possessed land and water around Taos constitutes the area's most overriding historical circumstance. Differential conquest, subordination, expropriation, impoverishment, and social displacement have been the hallmark of the psychohistorical experience of Indians in Taos since 1540, and of Hispanos since 1847. This experience in each case constituted a process of what I will call *minoritization.* Each case has evolved differently under different political and economic conditions, but they share several features, not simply as ethnic minorities, but also as what Spicer calls "persistent identity systems."[132]

To start with, both Indians and Hispanos have existed under two or more systems of state organization, and both groups have resisted, in different ways and at different as well as overlapping periods, pressures for economic, political, and cultural assimilation into the dominant society.[133] Within this context each has developed "well-defined symbols of identity differentiating it from other groups or the larger society."[134] Finally, each of these sets of identity symbols is "necessarily characterized by some combination of land and language elements."[135]

The case for Taos and other Pueblos as persistent peoples in Spicer's sense is obvious and easily made. Resistance to encroachment and incorporation, passive and overt, has characterized their dealings with outsiders since around 1600. The case for Hispanos in Taos and elsewhere in northern New Mexico and southern Colorado is more complex. They are, for one thing, a more "recent" people, who like other mestizos, occupy the intermediate and perhaps somewhat paradoxical position of being distinctly bounded and yet historically constituted by virtue of boundary permeability. Furthermore, the political, economic, and social incorporation of Hispanos and other Mexican Americans into the United States has been different from that of Indians, given their role as the major source of cheap labor throughout the American Southwest. Finally, less is known about the social history, cultural systems, internal community dynamics, and psychohistorical experience of Hispano and other Mexican American populations than about most southwestern Indian peoples. A great deal of ethnohistorical, ethnographic, and other social research is needed in order to illuminate the nature and dynamics of local and regional variation on the one hand, and of general socioeconomic and cultural features on the other.

It is proposed that Hispanos in Taos and northern New Mexico, like Chicanos elsewhere in the Southwest, are in the process of evolving into a self-identified, persistent people. This process has been underway for nearly four hundred years in Taos and has been tied to the preservation of a combination of land, language, and contiguous, originally kin-based village residence—that is, a core component of their traditional niche. During the late eighteenth century, Hispanos began to occupy and defend farming and grazing lands centered primarily on the lower Rio Pueblo, Rancho del Rio Grande, and lower Rio Lucero watersheds. During the course of the nineteenth century, they spread to and consolidated landownership and village boundaries within the Arroyo Seco, upper Rio Lucero, Arroyo Hondo, and San Cristobal watersheds (as well as elsewhere in the county), and then, after Americanization, suffered the loss of a large proportion of the lands they had occupied and used for generations. In this century, land has become a symbol of ethnic persistence to landless and urban Hispanos as well as to rural Hispanos who still own land. The motor of land symbolization has been its loss. A growing historical self-awareness has accompanied or followed this progressive loss, in spite of widespread institutional effort to educate against such awareness. The earlier development of ethnic land symbolization among the Taos Indians was fostered in part by a cultural climate of bohemian, selective ethnophilia, companion to a growing tourism economy. Thus the notion of a mystical connection between territory and native population was already present or "in the air" when during the modern period other influences and conditions began to precipitate the emergence of an explicit land symbolism among Hispanos. These included, on the one hand, national and regional impacts of Chicano and other ethnic group—but especially the Alianza—mobilization; and on the other, increasing demographic pressure—intensified by accelerating Anglo in-migration—upon limited local land, water, and other economic resources.

The prognosis for Hispano land tenure in Taos and its relationship to ethnic boundary maintenance is not clear. It seems to be widely assumed that rural Hispanos, like Indians, are doomed to disappear as such, but it can also be observed that ethnic boundaries have persisted and changed for four hundred years, and today show no signs of dissolving. They are sustained by the very structures of stratification, without, however, being reducible to them. Certainly one possible scenario for the future involves the complete and final expropriation of virtually all nonwealthy Hispanos within another generation. The territorial basis for Hispano ethnic differentiation would then yield to an entirely, albeit already well-entrenched, socioeconomic one. A predictable concomitant of this outcome would be continued reduction in the Hispanic proportion of the expanding population, followed by a corresponding integration and Anglo takeover of local electoral politics. Although this chain of events may or may not be inevitable, the continued increase in Anglo in-migration and takeover of local resources seems certain. The University of New Mexico Bureau of Business and Economic Research predicts a thirty-four percent population growth for Taos County in the 1980s and eighteen percent for the 1990s.[136] The response of Hispanos to these and other pressures will depend in part on local and regional economic conditions, including, for example, the commercial viability of the Moly mine, whether or not the local economy can diversify or continues to become ever more dependent upon tourism, and the impact on the Southwest in general of such factors as energy development, and Sun Belt as well as Latin American immigration.

Tourism traditionally has fostered the marketing of ethnicity as a commodity, but it otherwise affords a weak and uncertain material basis upon which to maintain a firm foothold against the onslaught of the luxury real-estate development it now spawns. While the early, ethnic-cultural phase of tourism development in Taos encouraged the preservation of Indian ethnicity along with a specific land base, the contemporary, luxury recreational type of tourism seems inimical to the preservation of a rural Hispano land base. In some sense, the Blue Lake case represents the symbolic consecration of the town watershed to the economic and cultural requirements of ethnic-cultural tourism. By contrast the ski valley-condominium issue represents the literal consecration of the Hondo watershed to the economic and material needs of luxury recreational tourism. The strategies Indians and Hispanos have pursued in trying to maintain their fragile holds over these and other "homeland" areas, including the ways in which each group has recruited Anglo support, reflect the particular opportunities and constraints imposed by their respective political and economic situations as conquered and dependent yet differentially incorporated peoples.

Those Hispanos least likely to initiate, actively participate in, or publicly support protest against tourism development are those whose entire livelihoods depend directly upon tourism. Those most likely to publicly condemn such protest are the well-off and upwardly mobile who are prospering or who hope to, from the boom. The remaining majority is by no means homogeneous with respect to source and level of income, landholdings, urban-rural orientation, ethnopolitical orientation, language use, age, or education. Diverse elements within this broad spectrum are variously subject to and critical of the economic, political, and social pressures brought to bear by local and regional power structures against ethnopolitical dissidents. While the pressure to assimilate has continued unabated for many decades, it is only comparatively recently that local Hispanos have had a broader ethos of *Chicanismo* from which to draw a renewed and expanded sense of historical identity and collective resistance to oppression. It is perhaps ironic that this influence is partly a creature of urbanization.

But while urbanization and even out-migration can be consistent with the maintenance and politicization of ethnicity, the ability of local

Hispanos to hold onto their remaining land base would seem to depend upon the creation of a solid, diversified, largely locally controlled economy. Only thus can they survive without literally losing ground, and be able to keep what they still own, and at the same time gain access to the benefits of American middle-class life, including steady, adequate employment with a possibility for advancement; adequate housing, nutrition, medical care, and post-secondary education; and a voice as well as a role in the future of their communities.

For most of this century, an official and pervasive assimilationist bias has held that the acquisition of such benefits is incompatible with the retention of a non-Anglo-Saxon ethnic or cultural identity. And indeed, the interlocking mechanisms of race, class, and ethnic stratification have made this largely the case. Upward mobility has been equated with assimilation, and ethnicity, in this case Mexicanness, with poverty, ignorance, and an intrinsic inability to advance. More recently, however, Chicano and other minority activists have explicitly challenged the justice and wisdom of such a view, while the widespread phenomena of ethnic resurgence and mobilization have caused social scientists to reconsider its accuracy. If New Mexico's and the Southwest's tourism industry has promoted the idea of cultural pluralism and flourished because of its existence, it has also gone hand-in-hand with a deeply entrenched, deeply mystified, system of structural inequality. One of the great challenges which today faces both modern and developing nations is whether and how ethnic and cultural pluralism can be reconciled with genuine social, economic, and political equality and self-determination. Neither the theoretical nor practical dimensions of such an arrangement are established or agreed upon. But whatever the difficulties inherent in such a goal, or the probability of its realization, one thing seems certain: the further expropriation and displacement of territorial native peoples does not represent a step in that direction.

Recommendations for Further Research

I will conclude with a brief series of recommendations for ethnohistorical, ethnographic, and other social research that needs to be done in Taos as in other parts of northern New Mexico and southern Colorado. These recommendations are meant to be suggestive and provocative rather than detailed and exhaustive. The research they would involve holds potential substantive, theoretical, and practical value. Although they are couched specifically in terms of research on the Taos area, they are applicable and may be generalized to other community and/or multicommunity areas in the region.

The land grant history of Taos has yet to be comprehensively investigated and written, particularly in relationship to the settlement sequence and history of each village. Each village or community should be focused upon both as an individual—or individuating—entity, and as part of an inclusive multicommunity system. This would apply, in the case of Taos County, to the Questa-Amalia-Costilla and Peñasco-Picuris-Vadito multicommunity areas as well as to the Don Fernando municipal district. The history of each community should be investigated through a combination of archival, documentary, oral-historical, and archaeological methods.[136]

Each settlement's ethnohistoric past should be linked to its ethnographic present. Ideally, ethnographic research would involve ongoing team efforts in which natives would assume active planning and investigatory roles. Given that no single individual in a multiethnic, stratified community such as Taos can have universal access to all of the diverse and frequently embattled segments of local society, the ideal research team would be mixed with respect to ethnicity, age, class background, sex, and origin. This would be particularly important where the focus of inquiry included or had bearing upon interethnic relations.

Two considerations should enter into the design and execution of ethnographic research, particularly when the focus is upon a minority group.[137] First, certainly one—though not the only—criterion of ethnographic accuracy should be whether or not it produces a description in which the natives under study can find more than a fleeting trace of self-recognition. The early ethnographic literature on Mexican Americans has become notorious for its lack of fit between how Mexicanos see themselves and their communities and how they have been described by (mostly Anglo) anthropologists.[138] With few exceptions, it seems to be the case that anthropologists have failed to capture an *emic* or native account of day-to-day Mexicano, Hispano, or Chicano social reality. In this respect, it lags behind the ethnographic literature on Black Americans.[139] The second consideration relates to the first, and has implications for ethnohistorical research as well. It concerns the need to investigate, illuminate, and interpret Hispano behavior not only in terms of the concept of ethnic boundary maintenance but also of resistance, or what Spicer calls the oppositional process. Apart from its organized and overt manifestations, Hispano resistance has assumed myriad covert, oblique, passive, ambiguous, repressed and convoluted, often highly symbolic, forms in northern New Mexico. It has also fluctuated through time. Yet it has not usually been identified as such in the literature. If ethnographic, the research in this case shows an oversight with methodological (including linguistic) causes and dimensions.[140] In general, however, such oversight is perhaps structurally endemic to the dominant perspective in a colonial situation, wherein the invisibility of actual minority resistance may be coupled with an exaggerated if subliminal fear of its sudden or gratuitous outbreak. But however complex the sources of silence or blindness on the matter of how social inequality has shaped face-to-face ethnic interaction in New Mexico, it can become overcome primarily through making this effect itself an explicit focus of study. In short, the proposition that resistance has been a persistent theme or undercurrent in Hispano life since 1847 may help to render much historical and behavioral data into a more coherent picture than has often been perceived.[141]

There are several kinds of problems that historical research and reconstruction could help to illuminate. For all the romance that has been perpetrated about the "unique cultural blend" that developed in Nuevo Mexico, little in fact is known about the everyday nature and character of village or multicommunity life, or about the quality, structure, and extent of face-to-face interethnic relations. While the archival and documentary sources may not justify a descriptively "thick" account of many behavioral and cultural aspects of social history, they may well support a more detailed picture than we have at present of the eighteenth- and nineteenth-century political and household economies in the Taos area. On the one hand, a developing commercial center like Taos should be looked at in terms of the special assets offered by its internal diversity. This diversity was based on a variety of microniches within several watersheds draining into the Taos basin. The ethnic and social composition of village households, and the economic and kinship relations among them, need to be mapped out wherever possible. Similarly, the economic, social, and kinship ties and exchanges between communities, as well as across ethnic boundaries, need to be reconstructed through time to whatever extent made possible by a variety of coordinated research strategies. On the other hand, the dynamics and transformations in Taos must be examined and ultimately explained in terms of their regional and international or global macro-social contexts. This is particularly necessary with respect to local labor history, which must also be documented and analyzed through time, including the major role out-migration has played for at least the whole of this century. Another important line of inquiry is the evolution and composition of Taos's class structure, which, despite the celebrated "leveling effect" of frontier conditions, we may safely assume was fully operative by the time of the Spanish reconquest, and which for reasons in need of investigation, appears to have accommodated a swift American economic takeover during the Mexican period.[142]

A great deal of research is needed on the twentieth century and especially contemporary Taos, including further documentation and analysis of the economic, political, and cultural development of tourism. At least two questions should help to guide research on tourism: (1) Does or has tourism progressively promote(d) the underdevelopment or nondevelopment of alternative economies (and if so, in what specific ways)? and (2) What further effect, beyond that already discussed in these pages, does the marketing of ethnicity and culture have on specific interethnic and intraethnic politics, and on peoples' awareness of and perception of their own or another's ethnicity?

Finally, in a more applied yet theoretically important vein, two further lines of inquiry are suggested. The history and causes or correlates of pressing social problems, such as today's apparently epidemic incidence of alcoholism across classes among all three ethnic groups, need to be investigated and analyzed comparatively, in order to inform public policy with respect to their treatment. And last but not least: viable and acceptable long-range economic alternatives to Taos's present trajectory need to be discovered.

Notes

1. In keeping with the prevailing trend in the contemporary ethnographic and ethnohistorical literature on the region, the term Hispano will be applied specifically to the subgroup of Mexicanos or subsequently Mexican Americans who settled in the Upper Rio Grande and adjacent regions of northern New Mexico and southern Colorado. The inclusive terms Mexicano (of emic import), Mexican American (etic), and Chicano are also used, the latter in reference to mostly younger, urbanized, and ethnically politicized Mexican Americans. My use of the term homeland derives in part from Spicer's

concept of persistent identity systems (see note 3), and from Nostrand's controversial homeland thesis on Hispanos in New Mexico. Richard Nostrand, "The Hispano Homeland in 1900," *Annals of the Association of American Geographers,* 70, no. 3 (1980): 382–96; see J. M. Blaut and A. Rios-Bustamante, "Commentary on Nostrand's 'Hispanos' and Their 'Homeland,'" and M. Simmons, Fray A. Chavez, D. W. Meinig, and T. Hall, "Rejoinders," in *AAAG,* 74, no. 1 (1984): 157–71. I argue here that the emic or native notion of a homeland, like the evolution of a given population's self-identity as a people, is something that takes place over time and under certain conditions. It is a product of history, of ongoing social interaction and change. My position with respect to the specific issues raised by the heated Hispano homeland debate is developed in the paper, "The Hispano Homeland Debate," presented at a panel discussion of the controversy held during the Western Social Science Association Meeting in April 1985, in Fort Worth. Also see note 18.

2. See Clark Knowlton, "Causes of Land Loss Among the Spanish Americans of Northern New Mexico," in Gilberto Lopez y Rivas, ed., *The Chicanos* (New York: Monthly Review Press, 1973), 111–21; Malcolm Ebright, *The Tierra Amarilla Grant: A History of Chicanery* (Santa Fe: The Center for Land Grant Studies, 1980); John and Christine Van Ness, eds., *Spanish and Mexican Land Grants in New Mexico and Colorado* (Manhattan, Kansas: Sunflower University Press, 1980).

3. Edward Spicer, "Persistent Cultural Systems," *Science,* 174 (1971): 795–800, esp. 797. For a more detailed discussion of the merits and weaknesses of Spicer's model with reference to Hispanos, see S. Rodriguez, "Hispanos in Taos: A Persistent Identity System?" (Paper presented at the annual meeting of the American Society for Ethnohistory, New Orleans, November 1984).

4. Spicer, op. cit. Also see George P. Castille and Gilbert Kushner, eds., *Persistent Peoples* (Tucson: University of Arizona Press, 1981).

5. For various approaches to the proletarianization of Mexicanos after 1847 see, for example, Tomas Almaguer, *Interpreting Chicano History: The 'World System' Approach to Nineteenth Century California* (Berkeley: Institute for the Study of Social Change, Working Papers Series no. 101, 1977); Mario Barrera, *Race and Class in the Southwest* (Notre Dame: University of Notre Dame Press, 1979); Juan Gomez-Quiñones, *Development of the Mexican Working Class North of the Rio Bravo* (Los Angeles: Popular Series No. 2, Chicano Studies Research Center Publications, University of California, Los Angeles, 1982).

6. Fredrik Barth, "Introduction," in *Ethnic Groups and Boundaries* (Boston: Little, Brown and Company, 1969), 19–21.

7. Spicer, "Plural Society in the Southwest," in E. Spicer and R. Thompson, eds., *Plural Society in the Southwest* (Albuquerque: University of New Mexico Press, 1972), 54–55.

8. Michael Hannan, "The Dynamics of Ethnic Boundaries in Modern States," in John Meyer and M. Hannan, eds., *National Development and the World System: Educational, Economic, and Political Change, 1950–1970* (Chicago: University of Chicago Press, 1979), 260.

9. Thomas Hall, "Lessons of Long-Term Change for Comparative and

Historical Study of Ethnicity," *Current Perspectives in Social Theory* 5 (1984): 126.

10. Myra Ellen Jenkins, "Taos Pueblo and Its Neighbors, 1540–1847," *New Mexico Historical Review* 41 (April 1966): 85–114.

11. Spicer, op. cit., 1972.

12. See, for example, Pierre van den Berghe, "Ethnic Pluralism in Industrial Societies: A Special Case?" *Ethnicity* 3 (1976): 242–55.

13. See Hall, this volume, for an in-depth account of the confusing status of Pueblo Indian landownership.

14. John Bodine, "A Tri-Ethnic Trap: The Spanish Americans in Taos," in June Helm, ed., *Spanish-Speaking People in the United States* (Proceedings of the 1968 American Ethnological Society): 145–53. Also see Etsuko Kuroda, "Ethnicity and Ethnic Culture in Crisis: The Struggle for Existence of the Spanish Americans in Taos, New Mexico" (Osaka: The National Museum of Ethnology, 1981).

15. This combines categories of Valene Smith's typology of tourism. See "Introduction" in V. Smith, ed., *Hosts and Guests* (Philadelphia: University of Pennsylvania Press, 1977), 1–13.

16. J. Bodine, "Attitudes and Institutions of Taos, New Mexico: Variables for Value System Expression" (Ph.D. diss., Tulane University, 1967).

17. For sources on Tijerina and the Alianza see: Patricia Bell Blawis, *Tijerina and the Land Grants: Mexican Americans in Struggle for Their Heritage* (New York: International Publishers, 1971). Richard Gardner, *Grito! Reies Tijerina and the New Mexico Land Grant War of 1967* (New York: Bobbs-Merrill Co. Inc., 1970). Michael Jenkins, *Tijerina* (Albuquerque: Paisano Press, 1968). Frances Leon Swadesh, "The Alianza Movement: Catalyst for Social Change in New Mexico," in Helms, ed., op. cit. (see note 14): 162–77. Reies López Tijerina, *Mi Lucha Por La Tierra* (Mexico, D.F.: Fondo de Cultura Economica, 1978).

18. The argument put forth in this paper independently parallels the thesis of John R. Chavez's recent book based on his disseration, *The Lost Land* (Albuquerque: University of New Mexico Press, 1984). Chavez argues historically for Chicanos in general and the Southwest as a whole what this paper argues for Taos and the Rio Arriba ethnographically: that a collective mythos of a lost or stolen homeland, known as "Aztlan," has developed among Chicanos as a people.

19. Dean MacCannell, "Reconstructed Ethnicity: Tourism and Cultural Identity in Third World Communities," in *Annals of Tourism Research* 11 (1984): 376–77.

20. Ibid., 383–85.

21. Ibid.; 388. Also see MacCannell, *The Tourist* (New York: Schocken Books, 1976).

22. J. Bodine, "Taos Pueblo," in Alfonso Ortiz, ed., *Handbook of North American Indians* vol. 9, *Southwest* (Washington, D.C.: Smithsonian Institution, 1979), 257–58.

23. Myra Ellen Jenkins and John Baxter, "Land History of the Pueblo of Taos, 1598–1900" (unpublished manuscript, n.d.), 20–21.

24. See Elsie Clews Parsons, *Taos Pueblo* (New York: Johnson Reprint Corp., 1970; orig. 1936). Bodine, "Taos Pueblo," in Ortiz, ed., *Handbook* esp. 257, 263.

25. See Jenkins and Baxter, "Land History," 22–25. Also Joe Sando, "The Pueblo Revolt," in A. Ortiz, ed., *Handbook,* 194–97.

26. Jenkins and Baxter, "Land History," 31–32.

27. This essay makes no attempt to provide a complete account of the tangled and contradictory land grant history of Taos County. Such a work remains to be written. The reader is referred to Jenkins and Baxter, op. cit., and M. E. Jenkins, "Taos Pueblo and Its Neighbors, 1540–1847," op. cit., and J. J. Bowden, "Private Land Claims in the Southwest," Southern Methodist University (1969, L.L.M. thesis), 885–1031. These are my principal sources on Taos grants. Bowden lists a total of thirty-one grants for Taos, nine of which are only partly inside the county, twenty-three entirely within its boundaries. Victor Westphall lists twenty-six, not including the Pueblo league, in *Mercedes Reales* (Albuquerque, University of New Mexico Press, 1983), Appendix I, 276–77. Ultimately only fourteen were confirmed by Congress and patented. Also see Rowena Martinez, "Land Grants in the Taos Valley" (Taos: Taos County Historical Society Pub. no. 2, n.d.).

28. Jenkins and Baxter, op. cit., 33.

29. Oakah Jones, *Los Paisanos* (Norman: University of Oklahoma Press, 1979), 140–49, 164.

30. See Ramon Gutierrez, "Report on the Taos Valley Population" (6 October 1982), Defendant's Exhibit II, prepared for the La Serna land grant trial, or Kristen Selph vs. Lt. James Alger, et al., January 1983, for a breakdown of the 1796 census report. It lists the placitas by their patron saints' names, including Nuestra Señora de Dolores, which could be either Cañon or El Prado, since until recently NSD was patroness of both. The third largest placita listed is Santa Getrudis; there seems to be no other record and no memory of a chapel or placita in her name in the Taos valley. I suspect it refers to Los Cordovas, whose patron is and has long been San Isidro, but further investigation is needed to determine its identity.

31. Jenkins and Baxter, "Land History," 43. The town, today known simply as Taos, has also been called San Fernando and Fernandez de Taos. Don Fernando was evidently the original name.

32. Richard N. Ellis, "Taos Pueblo," unpublished manuscript on Taos Pueblo legal history of land and water disputes from 1848–1924, n.d.: Part II: 1–3.

33. Gutierrez, "Report," 6.

34. The exact settlement sequence of the Taos area villages has not been definitively determined, and so this account, while broadly accurate, is nevertheless somewhat speculative.

35. David Snow, "Rural Hispanic Community Organization in Northern

New Mexico," Paul Kutsche, ed., *The Survival of Spanish American Villages* (Colorado Springs: Colorado College, 1979), 15: 45–62.

36. John Van Ness, "Hispanic Village Organization in Northern New Mexico: Corporate Community Structure in Historical Comparative Perspective," in Kutsche, ed., *The Survival,* 21–44; also "Hispanos in Northern New Mexico: the Development of Corporate Community and Multicommunity" (Ph.D. diss., University of Pennsylvania, 1979). Ruben Reina, "Town, Community and Multicommunity," *Estudios de Cultura Maya* 5 (1965): 361–90. Francisco Aguilera, *Santa Eulalia's People* (St. Paul: West Publishing Co., 1978).

37. Ramon Gutierrez, "Marriage, Sex, and the Family: Social Change in Colonial New Mexico, 1690–1846" (Ph.D. diss., University of Wisconsin-Madison, 1981).

38. Westphall, *Mercedes Reales,* 65.

39. See David Weber, *The Taos Trappers* (Norman: University of Oklahoma Press, 1970, 1971); also Janet Lecompte, "A Babel-Tongued Multitude on the Upper Arkansas," in Kutsche, ed., *The Survival,* 63–78.

40. See, for example, Nancie Gonzalez, *The Spanish Americans of Northern New Mexico* (Albuquerque: University of New Mexico Press, 1967), 117–18, for speculation as to the constituency of the revolt. Like Twitchell, Gonzalez assumes Padre Martinez to have been an instigator, a view refuted by Fray Angelico Chavez in *But Time and Chance* (Santa Fe: Sunstone Press, 1981), 81–86.

41. Marc Simmons, "History of the Pueblos Since 1821," in A. Ortiz, ed., *Handbook,* 208–9.

42. Roxanne Dunbar Ortiz, *The Roots of Resistance* (Los Angeles: Chicano Studies Research Center and American Indian Studies Center, University of California, Los Angeles, 1980), 93.

43. Knowlton, "Causes of Land Loss Among the Spanish Americans of Northern New Mexico," op. cit.

44. White, Koch, Kelly, and McCarthy, *Land Title Study* (Santa Fe: State Planning Office, 1971): Appendix I: 246–47. They list thirty-two grants for Taos County.

45. Rowena Martinez, op. cit. She lists fourteen grants, including the Ojo Caliente and Sebastian Martin, both of which lie mostly in Rio Arriba County.

46. See, for example, C. Knowlton, "Changing Spanish-American Villages of Northern New Mexico," *The Journal of Mexican American Studies* I, no. 1 (Fall 1970): 36. Olen Leonard, *The Role of the Land Grant* (Albuquerque: Calvin Horn, 1976, orig., 1940), esp. Chap. V.

47. Theodore Rixon, "Report on an Examination of the Taos Forest Reserve, Territory of New Mexico" (U.S. Geological Survey Report, 1905), 13.

48. M. E. Jenkins, "Development Potential of the Taos Pueblo Area in 1906," unpublished manuscript (1983), 7–9.

49. See, for example, Robert Rosenbaum, *Mexicano Resistance in the Southwest* (Austin: University of Texas Press, 1981).

50. See Frank Waters, *To Possess the Land* (Chicago: The Swallow Press, 1973).

51. A railroad did get as far as Taos Junction, roughly ten miles south of town in the gorge, whence it proceeded westward to Tres Piedras. Known as "The Chili Line," this railroad was discontinued in 1941, and never approximated the entrepreneurial potential envisioned in territorial days.

52. Charles Loomis provides some data on wartime out-migration from northern New Mexican villages including some in Taos County, in "Wartime Migration from the Rural Spanish Speaking Villages of New Mexico," *Rural Sociology* 7, no. 4 (1941): 384–95.

53. Simmons, "History of the Pueblos Since 1821," in A. Ortiz, ed., *Handbook,* 214–15.

54. Ibid., 215.

55. Ibid.

56. See, for example, Claire Morrill, *A Taos Mosaic* (Albuquerque: University of New Mexico Press, 1973): 94–97.

57. See Keith Bryant, Jr., "The Atchison, Topeka and Santa Fe Railway and the Development of the Taos and Santa Fe Art Colonies," *The Western Historical Quarterly* 9, no. 4 (October 1978): 437–53.

58. See notes 14, 16.

59. Ronald Grimes, *Symbol and Conquest* (Ithaca: Cornell University Press, 1976).

60. Charles Briggs, *The Wood Carvers of Cordova, New Mexico* (Knoxville: University of Tennessee Press, 1980).

61. Marta Weigle and Kyle Fiore, *Santa Fe and Taos, The Writer's Era* (Santa Fe: Ancient City Press, 1982).

62. The differences between North American and Mexican indianism are as noteworthy as their similarities. Both contained bohemian elements and emerged at broadly comparable stages in national and capitalist development. In the case of modern Mexican indiansim, glorification of the (usually Precolumbian) Indian was and is promoted by an urban mestizo intelligentsia to endorse, paradoxically, a program of forced assimilation, which historically constitutes the very basis of Mexican national identity. In the U.S. Southwest indianism was originally promoted by artists and literati from a conquering society. Like their Mexican contemporaries, they sought and believed they were discovering or forging an authentically American, rather than Eurocentric or Euro-imitative psychocultural identity. In both cases indianism is used to promote tourism. For discussions of Mexican indianism see George Collier, *The Fields of Tztozil* (Stanford: Stanford University Press, 1975), Chap. 9; Judith Friedlander, *Being Indian in Hueyapan* (New York: St. Martin's Press, 1975). For insight into the artistic and bohemian society of mostly pre-World War II Mexican indianism, see Hayden Herrera, *Frida: A Biography of Frida Kahlo* (New York: Harper and Row, 1983).

63. Bodine (1967): 131. Simmons, op. cit., 218–20.

64. J. J. Brody, "The Creative Consumer: Survival, Revival and Invention

in Southwest Indian Arts," in Nelson Graburn, ed., *Ethnic and Tourist Arts* (Berkeley: University of California Press, 1976), 70–84.

65. For examples of the Taos-Santa Fe ethos of bohemian "creative individualism," see above all, Mabel Dodge Luhan's memoirs on Taos: *Lorenzo in Taos* (1932), *Winter in Taos* (1935), *Edge of the Taos Desert: Escape to Reality* (1937). Also see "Taos and Individualism," *New Mexico Quarterly* 21, no. 2 (Summer 1951). For a masterpiece of documentation of the literary circles, see Weigle and Fiore, eds., *Santa Fe and Taos.*

66. See, for example: Raymund Paredes, "The Mexican Image in American Travel Literature 1831–1869," *New Mexico Historical Review* 51 (January 1977): 5–29; "The Origins of Anti-Mexican Sentiment in the United States," *New Scholar* 6 (1977): 139–65. David Weber, "'Scarce More than Apes': Historical Review of Anglo-American Stereotypes of Mexicans," in D. Weber, ed., *New Spain's Far Northern Frontier* (Albuquerque: University of New Mexico Press, 1979), pp. 293–307. Arnoldo De Leon, *They Called Them Greasers* (Austin: University of Texas Press, 1983).

67. Blanche Grant, who edited his autobiography and painted a well-known portrait of him, was an ardent proponent of Kit Carson, and instrumental in producing the special fiesta "Kit Carson Edition" of the *Taos Review* (18 July 1940). See B. Grant, ed., *Kit Carson's Own Story of His Life* (1926).

68. See, for example, the *Taos Review* (8 December 1938).

69. *New Mexico Statistical Abstract* (Albuquerque: Bureau of Business and Economic Research, University of New Mexico, 1979–80 edition), 97.

70. George Sanchez, *Forgotten People* (Albuquerque: Calvin Horn, 1940, 1967), 55.

71. See the *Taos Review,* 1940 (11 January, 9 May, 30 May, 1 August, 31 September). The *Taoseño* (throughout 1940–41, esp. 3 April, 17 April, 31 July, 11 September, 6 October 1941; 30 April 1942). During this same period Hispanos in Ranchitos and El Prado were fighting their eventual ejection from Indian claims. In the 1980's the Rio Costilla Livestock Association became involved in the development of a ski resort on some of the grant lands. In fact the settlers of Costilla Cañon had fought ejectment since shortly after they arrived there around the turn of the century, after having been "kicked off" the Maxwell on the other side of the mountains (personal communication, Marianne Stoller).

72. Two examples: the middle class Anglos who were drafted from Taos became officers in the division sent to Bataan; the Indian women's Red Cross contributions were organized separately.

73. Bodine (1967): 274–308.

74. See, for example, "Taos Campaigns Against Filth," concerning outhouses, *Taos Review* (14 March 1940); or as recently as *The Taos News,* April 1984 issues, concerning the streets.

75. See, for example, Spanish Page editorials by Felix Valdez, in *El Taoseño-Taos Review* (14 March 1940; 12 February, 18 February 1942; 13 May, 12 August 1943; 27 June 1946; 7 August 1947).

76. W. F. Turney and Associates, "Taos County Comprehensive Area-

Wide Plan for Water and Sewer" (Santa Fe: New Mexico Planning Office, November 1966), 55.

77. Mimbres and Associates, "Taos County Comprehensive Planning Program" (December 1978), Working Paper no. 1, "The Land," 45.

78. The figures on the percentage of the population subsisting at a sub-poverty level vary from source to source, and even in different reports from the same source. For example, the Bureau of Business and Economic Research (BBER) reports the figure for 1979 at 24.1 percent (*NM Statistical Abstract 1984*), whereas in a more recent update, it is reported at 27.5. According to U.S. Bureau of the Census data for 1970, 35.8 percent of families in Taos were below the poverty level *Census of Population: 1970, General Social and Economic Characteristics, Final Report PC(I)-33, New Mexico,* Table 124 and Appendix B, 13, 29, 30.

79. Estelle Smith, "Cultural Variability in the Structuring of Violence," Thomas Williams, ed., *Psychological Anthropology* (The Hague: Mouton Pubs., 1975): 342–48.

80. Bodine (1967): 185–273.

81. See C. L. Reynolds, "Decision-Making and Cultural Change: the Status of Spanish American Small Farms in Northern New Mexico" (Ph.D. diss., Southern Methodist University, 1975); Reynolds, "Economic Decision-Making: the Influence of Traditional Hispanic Land Use Attitudes on Acceptance of Innovation," *The Social Science Journal* 13, no. 3 (October 1976): 21–34. John Nichols, *If Mountains Die* (New York: Alfred Knopf, 1979), 121–29.

82. J. Nichols, *The Milagro Beanfield War* (New York: Holt, Rinehart and Winston, 1974).

83. Nichols (1979), 129.

84. In 1981 nineteen affidavits were collected which attested to this; see text, 68.

85. *The Taos News* (24 November, 29 December 1983).

86. EID studies for the first full year of operation for the new plant showed some of the worst conditions on record with respect to aquatic biota in the reaches of the river above and below the plant. Studies for 1985, however, indicated that for the first time the pollution problem was under control while biota also showed improvement. See S. Rodriguez, "The Impact of the Ski Industry on the Rio Hondo Watershed," *Annals of Tourism Research,* forthcoming.

87. The filing fee for a protest against a water rights transfer application is $250. Lawyers' and filing fees are usually paid for with funds ditch officers manage to collect from water users. Other sources include occasional fund-raising activities such as bake sales or benefit dances, private donations, and some legal services assistance.

88. Since around 1970 Hispanos have progressed from being officers in Anglo-owned banks (a post-World War II development) to becoming owners of new banks.

89. John Temple and Lynn Wombold, *Population Employment and Income*

for Counties in New Mexico: Historical Data: 1970–1980 and Projections: 1980–2000 (Albuquerque: Bureau of Business and Economic Research, University of New Mexico, January 1983): 213–15, Table 6–3.3: 217. The number of non-agricultural jobs (i.e., manufacturing, construction, trade, services, government, etc., went from 3,519 in 1970 to 6,501 in 1981; see Table 6–3.2: 216.

90. *Environmental Impact Statement for the Proposed Taos Ski Valley Master Development Plan* (U.S. Dept. Agriculture, Forest Service, April 1981), 57.

91. Temple and Wombold (1983), Table 6–3.2: 216; Table 6–3.4: 218.

92. Ibid.

93. Ibid.

94. Ibid.

95. As reported monthly over local radio station KKIT during 1983.

96. In August 1985, Taos reported the third highest unemployment rate in the state. By the end of the year it was second, due to layoffs at the Moly mine, which is due to shut down in early 1986, an economic disaster for the county which promises to drive the unemployment rate to 27 percent to 32 percent. *The Taos News* (8 August 1985; 1 February 1986).

97. Temple and Wombold (1983): Table 6–3.6: 220; Table 6–3.5: 219.

98. In 1985 an Anglo attorney, well-known for service to the Hispanic poor, was elected to the school board.

99. Blanche Grant claims this in *When Old Trails Were New* (Glorietta, NM: The Rio Grande Press, Inc., 1934, 1983), Chap. 29, esp. p. 153. A more recent example is the Martindale case in the late 1970s, when an Oklahoma man shot and killed an unarmed Chicano youth and later successfully requested a change of venue on the grounds that as an Anglo he could not get a fair trial in Taos. In the public schools, some Anglo children, their parents, as well as teachers who fail to receive tenure, complain of "race" or ethnic discrimination by "the Spanish."

100. The 1970 census reported the Spanish language or surnamed population of the county to be 15,109 or 86.3 percent. *New Mexico Statistical Abstract* (Albuquerque: University of New Mexico, 1979–80), 106. According to *The Taos News* (19 March 1981), the 1980 census reckoned Hispanics at 66 percent, with one out of every four residents an Anglo, nearly twice what it had been in 1970. Final BBER 1980 Census figures report Hispanics at 69 percent (13,442), including over 2,000 Mexicans, presumably nationals (Summer Tape I, 1980 NM Census). Reasonably consistent and accurate longitudinal data on ethnic proportions in Taos are hard to come by. Sanchez, op. cit.: 30, reports that in 1938 the Hispanic proportion was 93 percent or 14,229. All this suggests that not only is the Hispanic proportion declining, but its absolute number as well, despite the highest fertility rate (14.35 percent) among all three groups; see *Selected Health Statistics, New Mexico 1979* (Santa Fe: Health & Environment Department), 34.

101. Twining is counted in the tax rolls as part of the Valdez district, but the two are geographically and socially distinct, Valdez proper still being

predominantly Hispano owned and populated. The Hispano-Anglo proportion in San Cristobal is roughly equivalent.

102. "Predominantly" means more than 50 percent Anglo owned. Based on review of 1931–1980 tax rolls.

103. "Anglo" is employed here in its common folk usage, which subsumes a variety of non-Anglo Saxon, non-Hispanic, western European ethnic and national groups.

104. Total federal (50.8 percent), state (6.7 percent), and Indian (4.3 percent) lands come to 61.8 percent of the acreage in Taos County. See Mimbres & Assoc. (1978): Paper no. 1: 31. Also Jerry Williams and Paul McAllister, eds., *New Mexico in Maps* (Albuquerque: University of New Mexico Press, 1979), 116.

105. *The Taos News* (26 September 1985).

106. *The Taos News* (16 August 1985). The average price of a house at this time was $108,000.

107. El Prado adopted a plan with a commercial strip along the highway, whereas farmers, ditch and water officers, and others in Cañon resisted considerable pressure to do the same, and came up instead with a more conservative rural-agricultural plan, closer in spirit to the one developed later by the Tres Valles Special Zoning District.

108. In autumn 1985 the town arranged to buy—or actually to lease—another 2,000 acre-feet of San Juan-Chama water rights from the Bureau of Reclamation, part of the 4,520 acre-feet which had been allocated to the now defunct Indian Camp Dam project. See *The Taos News* (19 September 1985; 26 February 1985). This should help to meet projected demands to the turn of the century. Presumably the lease of San Juan-Chama water will temporarily forestall the need for the city ultimately to condemn all surface water rights in the Taos basin and appropriate them for municipal use, in order to accommodate further growth.

109. This account is based upon 21 months of ethnographic fieldwork in Taos between August 1981 and June 1983, during which time I attended scores of rural zoning meetings in communities around Taos.

110. Simon Tejada, "Historia de Valdez" (WPA Writers' Project Files, State Records Center and Archives, Santa Fe, 25 August 1939), 7.

111. Twining is predominantly "Anglo" owned and populated, more than half by seasonal residents, whereas more than half the land in Des Montes is still Hispano owned, but the greater number of residents is Anglo.

112. By local account, Valdez originally had second priority to Arroyo Hondo, but lost it to Des Montes through some "mishap" during recent adjudication.

113. It is perhaps coincidental but deserving of investigtion that the Ranchos revival followed upon the defeat of Indian Camp Dam. Revival of the fiesta of San Antonio in Valdez took place the spring after the condo war, and involved, significantly, a procession to and blessing of the river. Recent Chicano innovations include Cinco de Mayo festivities, celebrated for the first

time in 1983, replete with a lowrider parade, Danza Azteca, and Corky Gonzales as keynote speaker.

114. These organizers were unaffiliated and independent.

115. It was during the Hacienda protest that I became, more or less fortuitously, resident in Valdez, and involved in the events that unfolded there.

116. This is a pseudonym. All participants on either side of the issue described in this account will remain anonymous.

117. La Lama, a small settlement to the north of San Cristobal, is also included within the Tres Valles district, although its residents were not actively involved in the protest.

118. The complete story of the county commission's remarkable behavior during the condo war cannot be told here, and would in any case be more appropriately part of a discussion of how local government and county politics function in Taos. In recent years both the county commission and school board have been the foci of intense controversies between local factions, interests, and personalities.

119. I assisted in fund-raising efforts, contacted potential supporters, provided public but not easily available information to community members, and donated labor as needed. My decision to do this seemed morally compelled and flowed, on the one hand, from my perception and understanding of the situation as a bi-ethnic native and citizen of Taos, and on the other, from my perception and understanding of the situation as an anthropologist. I believe my actions to be consistent with the 1971 AAA (American Anthropological Association) Statement on Ethics, particularly what I take to be the meaning of Sections 1 and 2d. The methodological and theoretical implications of my involvement will be taken up elsewhere.

120. I gratefully acknowledge Mr. Vigil's permission to include his poem, and also wish to thank both him and Mrs. Vigil for their guidance and help in making the translation. The orthography and Spanish of the poem are New Mexican and Mr. Vigil's.

121. Crandall had filed his condo declaration on 17 May, just forty-eight hours before the new state Condominium Act, containing stricter disclosure requirements, went into effect.

122. By keeping the gallon per day (gpd) limit below 2,000, the Hacienda circumvented the need to publish their permit application, which the EID routinely approved. In principle, one violation was sufficient to revoke the permit, which of course did not, and probably never does, happen. Publicity of these facts after the violation eventually resulted in the arrangement whereby a representative from Valdez, in addition to someone from EID, would monitor Hacienda meter readings.

123. This was done through the caretaker, sent to surrepticiously monitor Valdez zoning meetings at the *escuelita*.

124. Anya Peterson Royce, *Ethnic Identity* (Bloomington: Indiana University Press, 1982), 43–50.

125. John Van Ness, "Spanish American vs. Anglo American Land Tenure

and the Study of Economic Change in New Mexico," *Social Science Journal* 13, no. 3 (October 1976): 46.

126. Ibid., 47–48.

127. Knowlton, "Changing Spanish-American Villages of Northern New Mexico," *Journal of Mexican American Studies* I, no. 1 (Fall 1970): 33.

128. See Florence Kluckhohn and Fred Strodbeck, *Variations in Value Orientations* (Evanston: Row & Peterson, 1961). Evon Vogt and Ethel Albert, eds., *People of Rimrock: A Study of Values in Five Cultures* (New York: Atheneum, 1970). For Chicano critiques of this approach see Octavio Romano, "The Anthropology and Sociology of Mexican Americans," *El Grito* 2, no. 1 (1968): 13–26; and "Social Science, Objectivity, and the Chicanos," *El Grito* 4, no. 1 (Fall 1970): 4–16. Nick Vaca, "The Mexican American in the Social Sciences, 1912–1970," esp. Part II: 1936–1970, *El Grito* 4, no. 1 (Fall 1970): 17–51; and "The Comparative Study of Values in Five Cultures Project and the Theory of Value," *Aztlan* 12, no. 1 (Spring 1981): 89–120.

129. Clyde Eastman, Garrey Carruthers, and James Liefer, *Evaluation of Attitudes Toward Land in North Central New Mexico* 1 (Las Cruces: New Mexico State University Agricultural Experiment Station Bulletin 577, May 1971): 10–11. They employ Knowlton's characterization of Hispano land attitudes found in "Conflicting Attitudes Toward Land Use and Land Ownership in New Mexico," *Proceedings of the Southwestern Sociological Association* 18 (1967): 60–68.

130. Eastman, et al. Ibid.: 1. Eastman follows a similar approach in *Assessing Cultural Change in North Central New Mexico* (Las Cruces: NMSU Agricultural Experiment Station Bulletin 592, January 1972).

131. For a primordialist view of how ethnic or tribal ties impede nation building see Karl Deutsch's "Introduction," in K. Deutsch and W. J. Flotz, eds., *Nation Building* (New York: Atherton Press, 1963). For contrasting views see Edward Shils, "Primordial, Personal, Sacred, and Civil Ties," *British Journal of Sociology* 8 (1957): 130–45, or Clifford Geertz, "The Integrative Revolution: Primoridal Sentiments and Civil Politics in New States," in Geertz, ed., *Old Societies and New States* (Glencoe, Ill.: Free Press, 1963). For more recent discussions incorporating Barth's reactive view of ethnicity as well as world systems theory, see Michael Hannan, "The Dynamics of Ethnic Boundaries in Modern States," in John Meyer and M. Hannan, eds., op. cit. (1970). For an overview of non-Marxist perspectives of ethnicity see Anya Peterson Royce, op. cit. (1982).

132. Spicer suggests that the possession of state power tends to dissipate a persistent identity system, although under "certain rather special conditions" it might reinforce such a system (1971): 797. I suggest that the decisive factor or event in the creation or evolution of Chicano identity has been the psychohistorical experience of the loss of state power and ethnopolitical dominance, which entailed expropriation and ethnic subordination. It is in relation to Spicer's feature of seldom or only temporarily holding state power that the proposed designation of Hispanos as a persistent people is most problematic. This is essentially the problem of how class and ethnicity have, do, and will

interact in New Mexico. More research is needed on the nature and character of the ethnic boundary system during colonial periods. The most promising macrotheoretical framework for diachronic analysis of this problem would probably be Wallerstein's approach. See Immanual Wallerstein, *The Modern World System: Capitalist Agriculture and the Origins of the European World-Economy in the Sixteenth Century* (New York: Academic Press, 1974); *The Capitalist World Economy* (New York: Cambridge University Press, 1979).

133. Spicer (1971), 797. Royce (1982), 44.

134. Royce (1982), 44.

135. Spicer (1971), 798.

136. For a proposed approach along these lines, see P. Kutsche, J. Van Ness, and A. Smith, "A Unified Approach to the Anthropology of Hispanic Northern New Mexico," *Historical Archaeology* 10 (1976): 1–16.

137. It should be clear that "minority" refers to relative power and is therefore a political and not a demographic concept.

138. See Romano, Vaca (note 128), and Americao Paredes, "On Ethnographic Work Among Minority Groups, A Folklorist's Perspective," *New Scholar* 6 (1977): 1–32.

139. See, for example, John Gwaltney, *Drylongso* (New York: Vintage, 1981); Carol Stack, *All Our Kin* (New York: Harper & Row, 1974); Bettylou Valentine, *Hustling and Other Hard Work* (New York: The Free Press, 1978).

140. See Paredes (1977).

141. My use of the term "resistance" here is broader than Rosenbaum's. He distinguishes several kinds of Mexicano response to Anglo conquest and domination, namely withdrawal, accommodation, assimilation, and resistance, by which he specifically means violent resistance. He sees accommodation-assimilation as largely a response by the elite and upwardly mobile, with which I agree, but suggest that these tactics in particular are often ambivalently and ambiguously felt and expressed, and can contain and mask elements of indirect resistance. Perhaps Spicer's oppositional process would appropriately cover what seems a continuum of variously expressed group responses and individual strategies. See Rosenbaum (1981), 14–15.

142. See note 37.

Contributors

CHARLES L. BRIGGS, trained as an anthropologist at the University of Chicago, is co-author of *Hispano Folklife of New Mexico: The Loren W. Brown Federal Writers Project Manuscripts* and author of *The Woodcarvers of Cordova, New Mexico.* He currently teaches in the Department of Anthropology at Vassar College.

MALCOLM EBRIGHT is a lawyer who is president and co-founder of The Center for Land Grant Studies in Santa Fe, New Mexico. He is co-author of the Land Title Study, which deals with title problems on land grants, and author of *The Tierra Amarilla Grant: A History of Chicanery.* He has also written numerous article on land and water and has served as an expert witness in several court cases recently concerning land grants. He lives near Guadalupita, New Mexico.

G. EMLEN HALL is an attorney, historian, and writer. He teaches at the University of New Mexico Law School and is the author of *Four Leagues of Pecos: A Legal History of the Pecos Grant, 1800–1933,* the second volume in this series. He has also written numerous articles concerning land and water in New Mexico.

ROBERT W. LARSON is a professor of history at the University of Northern Colorado. He is the author of *New Mexico's Quest for Statehood, 1846–1912, New Mexico Populism: A Study of Radical Protest in a Western Territory, Populism in the Mountain West,* and numerous articles devoted to the territorial period in New Mexico.

SYLVIA RODRÍGUEZ took her Ph.D. in anthropology-psychology at Stanford University. A native of Taos, New Mexico, she teaches anthropology at the University of California at Los Angeles. She is currently completing a major study of the interethnic dynamics in the Taos region.

ROBERT J. ROSENBAUM received his Ph.D. in history from the University of Texas, Austin. He is the author of *Mexicano Resistance in the Southwest: The Sacred Right of Self-Preservation.* He lives in Austin, Texas, where he is a research and writing specialist for the office of the Texas Attorney General.

JOHN R. VAN NESS took his Ph.D. in cultural anthropology at the University of Pennsylvania. He is co-editor of *Spanish and Mexican Land Grants in New Mexico and Colorado* and co-author of *Cañones: Values, Crisis and Survival in a Northern New Mexico Village.* He is currently Vice President and Adjunct Professor of Anthropology at Ursinus College, in Pennsylvania.

Index